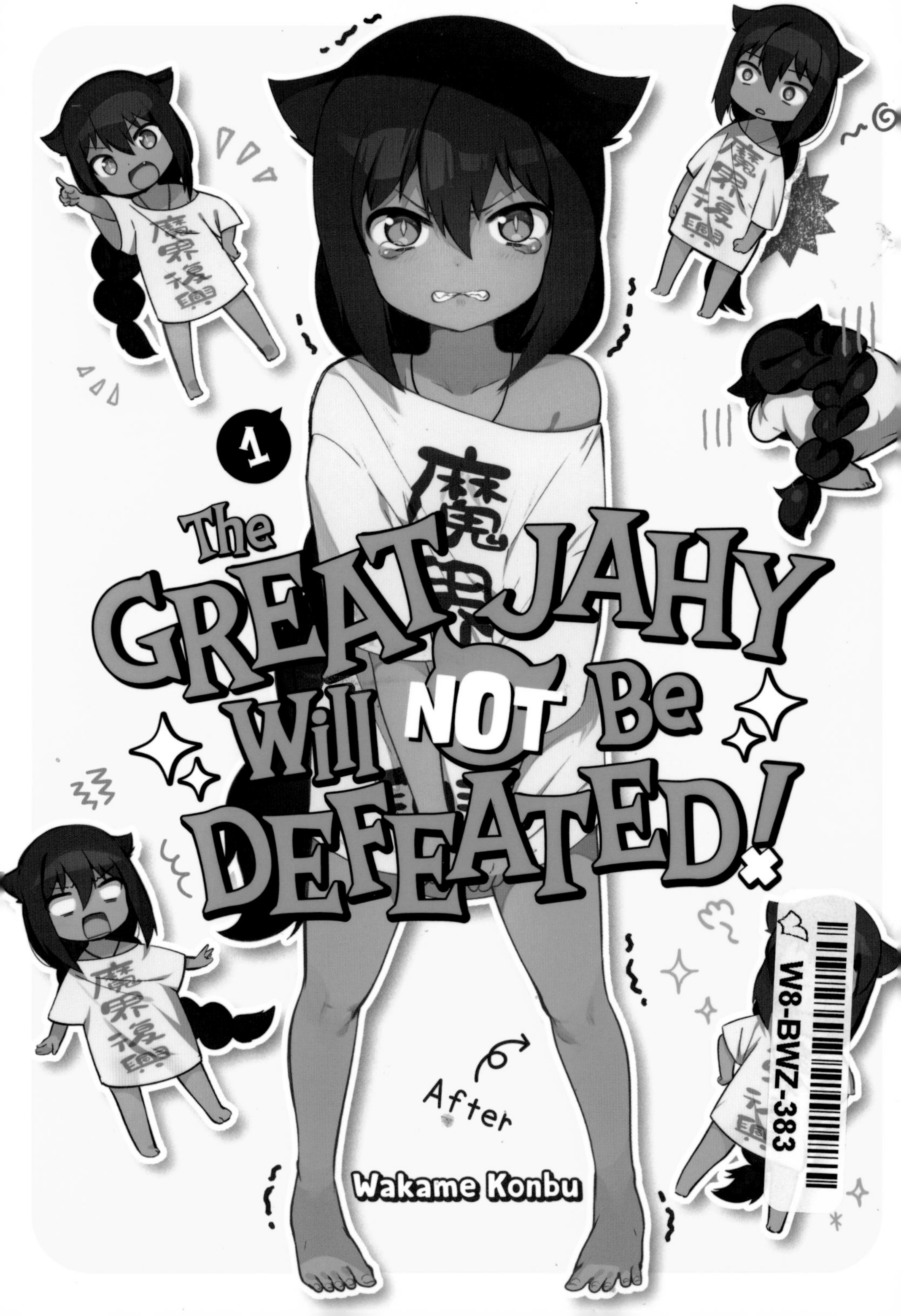
1
The GREAT JAHY Will NOT Be DEFEATED!
魔界復興
After
Wakame Konbu

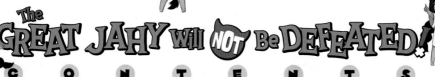

The GREAT JAHY Will NOT Be DEFEATED!

CONTENTS

RESTORATION PLAN

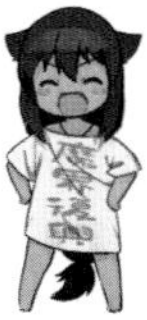
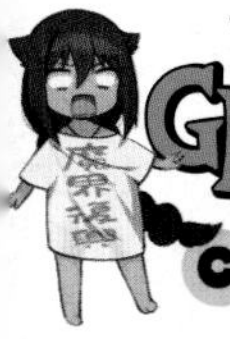
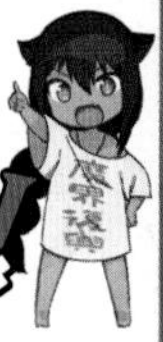
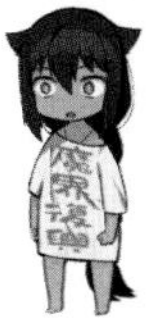
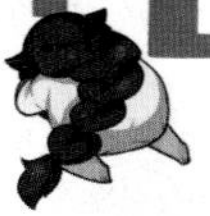
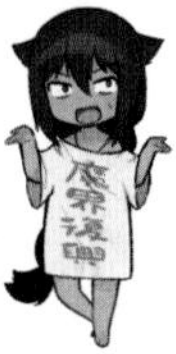

The GREAT JAHY Will NOT Be DEFEATED!

1

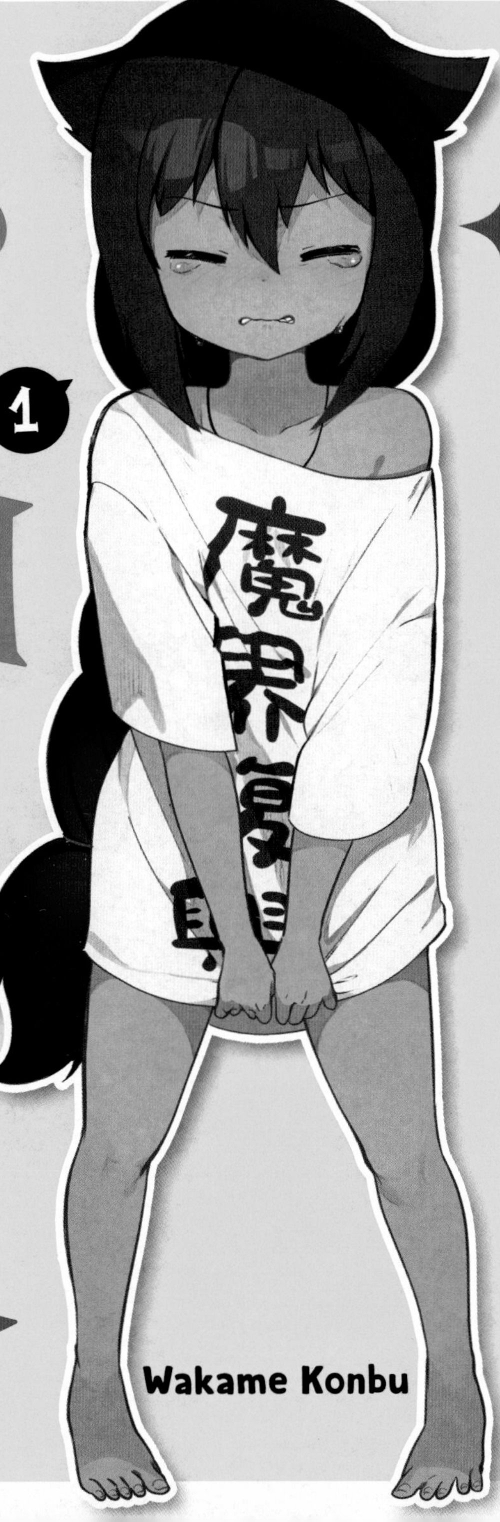

Wakame Konbu

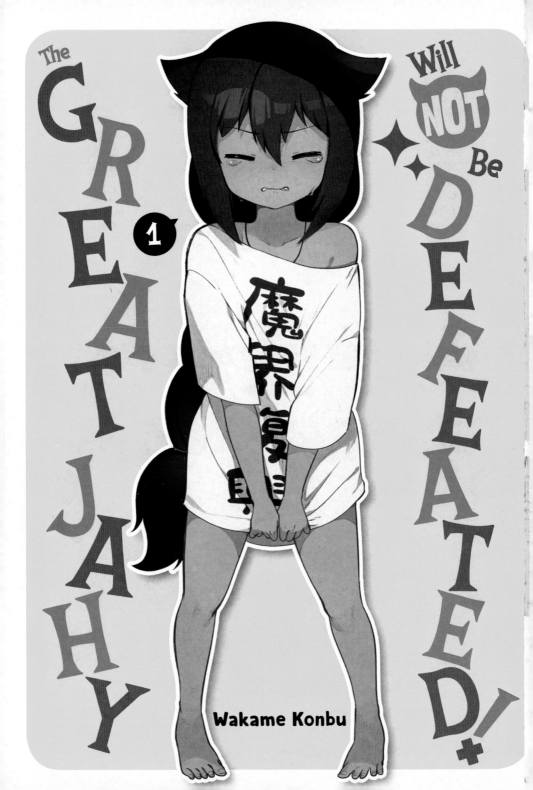

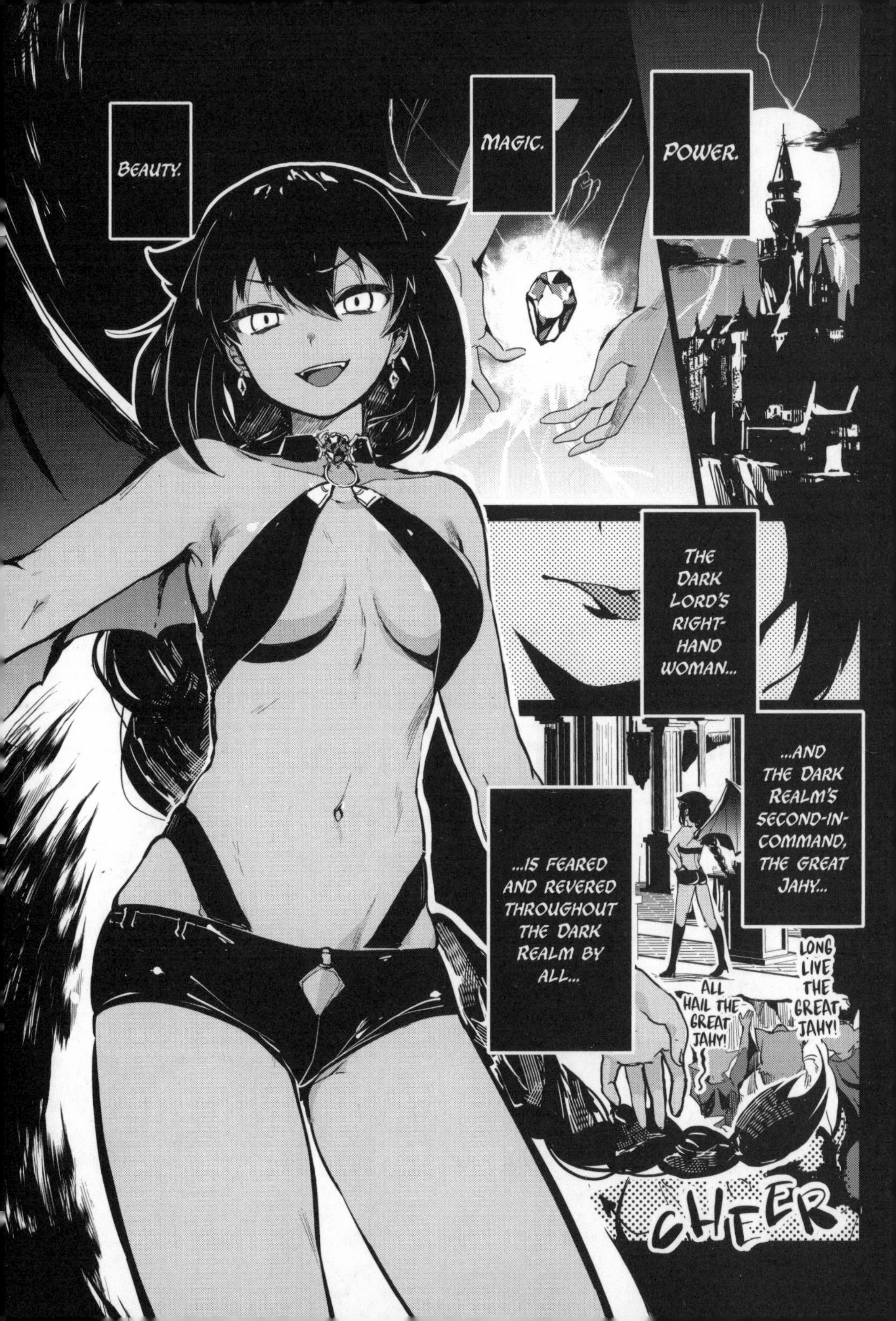
POWER.
MAGIC.
BEAUTY.
THE DARK LORD'S RIGHT-HAND WOMAN...
...AND THE DARK REALM'S SECOND-IN-COMMAND, THE GREAT JAHY...
...IS FEARED AND REVERED THROUGHOUT THE DARK REALM BY ALL...
LONG LIVE THE GREAT JAHY!
ALL HAIL THE GREAT JAHY!
CHEER

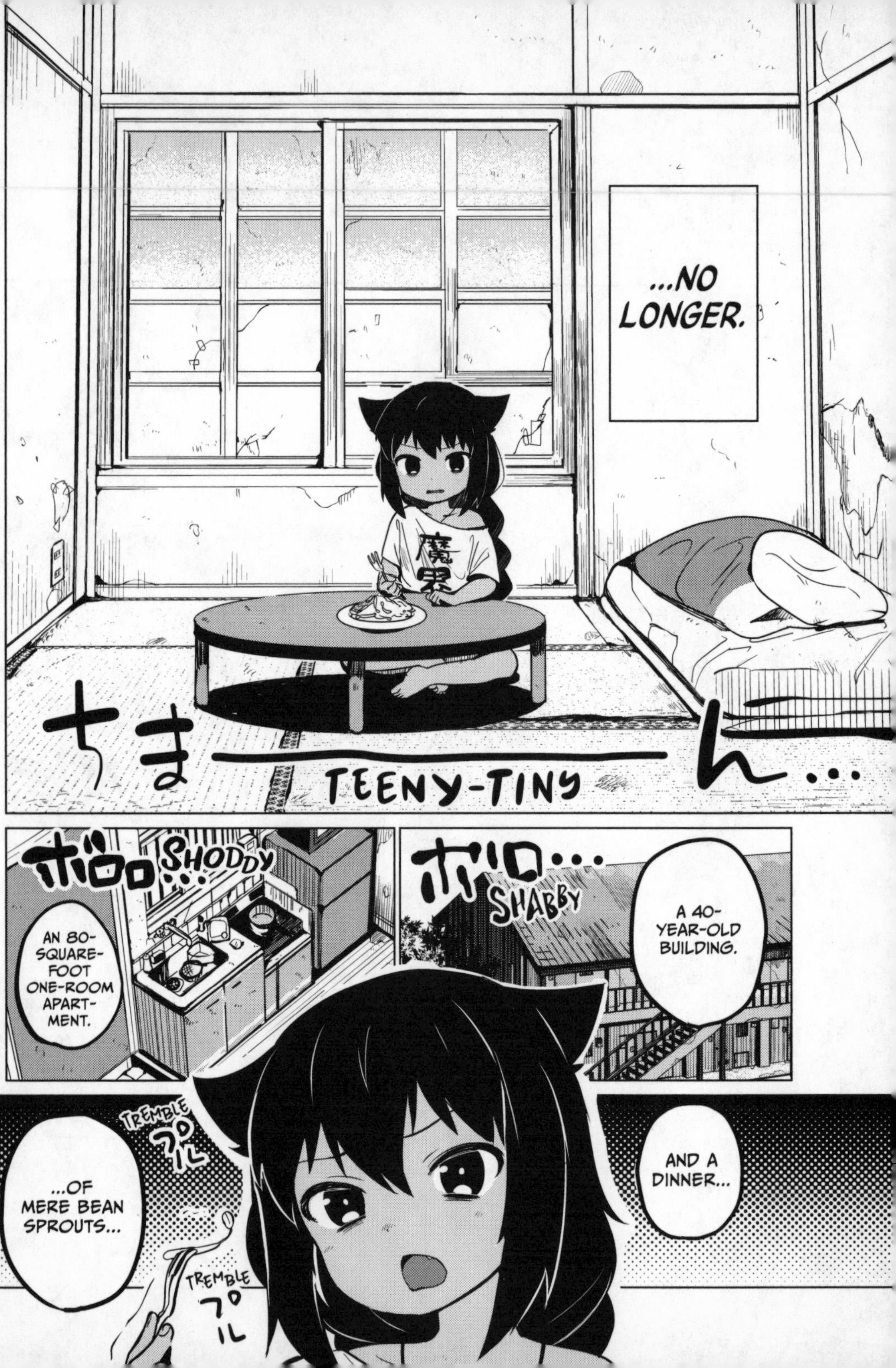
...NO LONGER.
ちま――ん…
TEENY-TINY
ボロ…
SHABBY
A 40-YEAR-OLD BUILDING.
ボロ
SHODDY
AN 80-SQUARE-FOOT ONE-ROOM APARTMENT.
AND A DINNER...
TREMBLE
プル
...OF MERE BEAN SPROUTS...
TREMBLE
プル

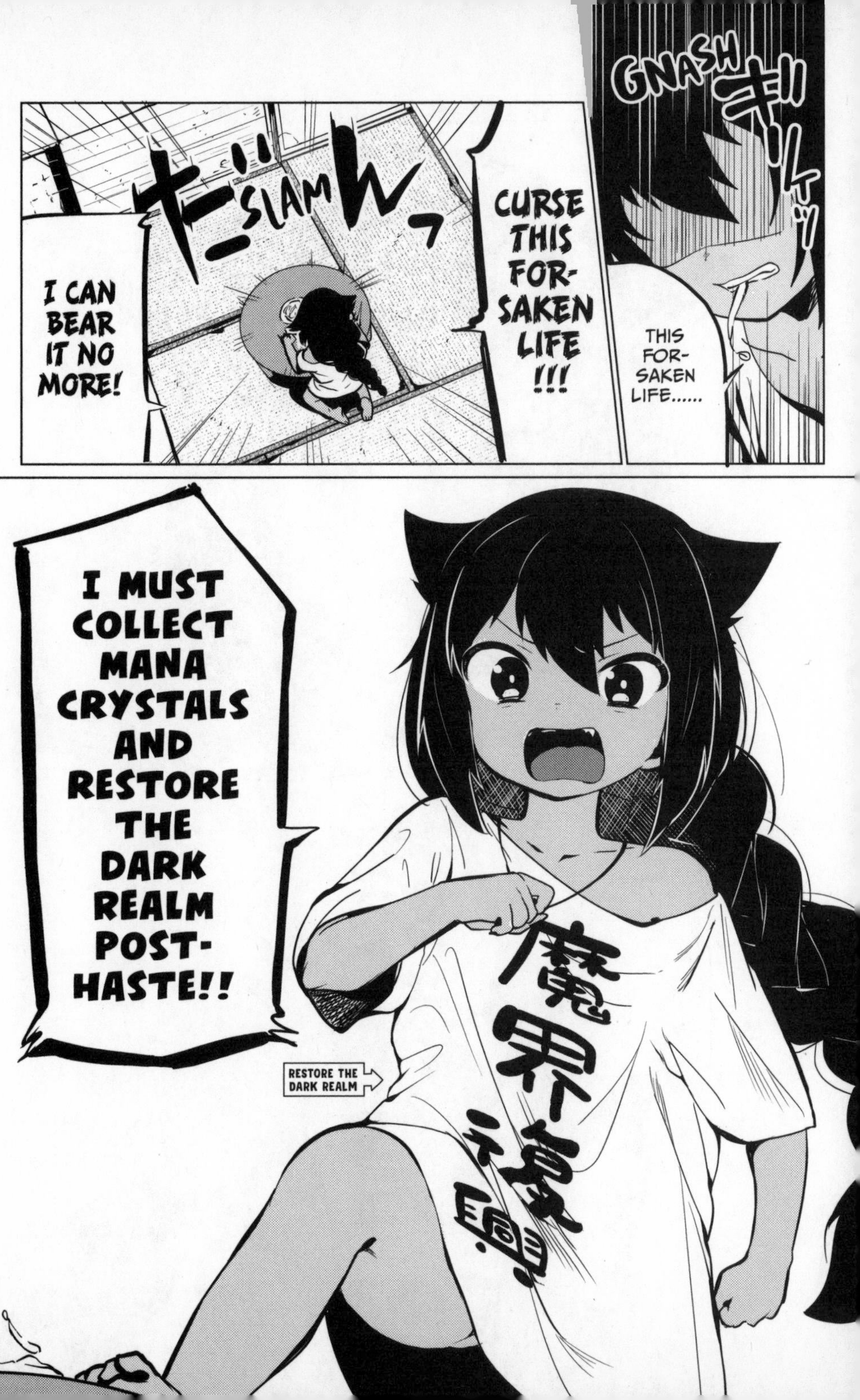
GNASH
THIS FORSAKEN LIFE......
SLAM
CURSE THIS FORSAKEN LIFE!!!
I CAN BEAR IT NO MORE!
I MUST COLLECT MANA CRYSTALS AND RESTORE THE DARK REALM POSTHASTE!!
魔界復興
RESTORE THE DARK REALM

RESTORATION PLAN No. Ø.1

The Great Jahy & the Smile

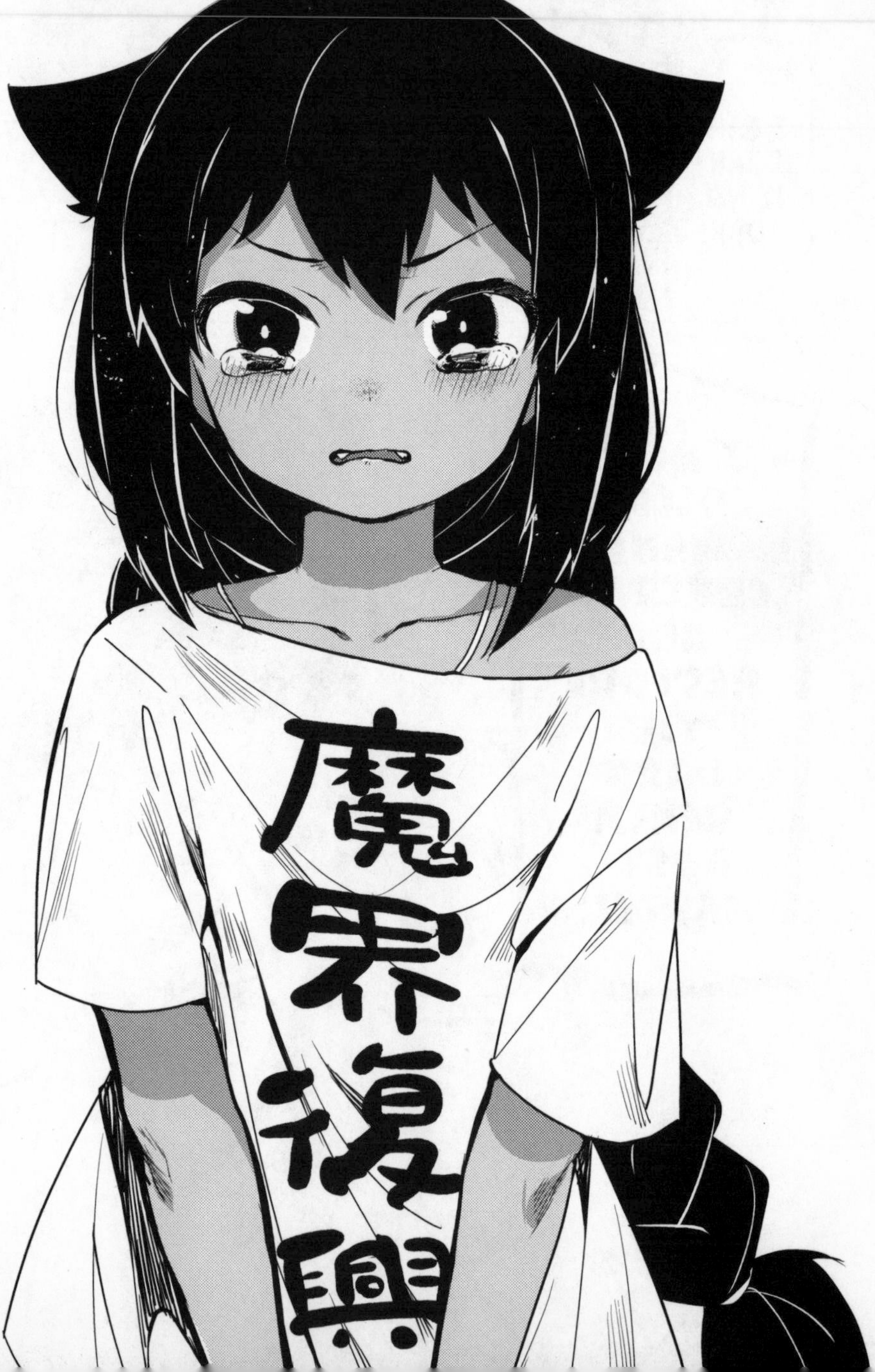
魔界復興

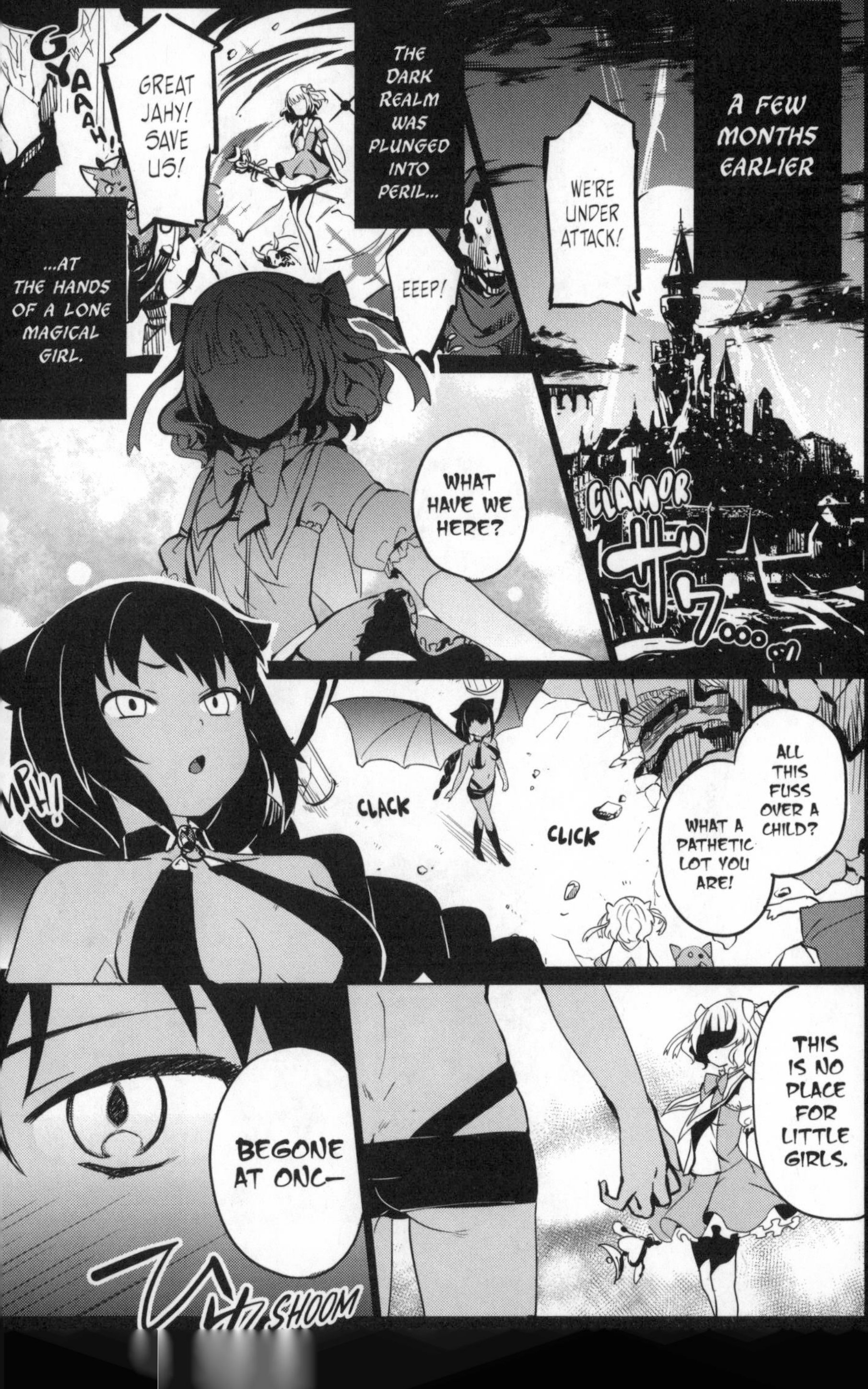

A FEW MONTHS EARLIER
WE'RE UNDER ATTACK!
CLAMOR
THE DARK REALM WAS PLUNGED INTO PERIL...
EEEP!
GREAT JAHY! SAVE US!
GYAAAH!
...AT THE HANDS OF A LONE MAGICAL GIRL.
WHAT HAVE WE HERE?
ALL THIS FUSS OVER A CHILD?
WHAT A PATHETIC LOT YOU ARE!
CLICK
CLACK
MPH!
THIS IS NO PLACE FOR LITTLE GIRLS.
BEGONE AT ONC—
SHOOM

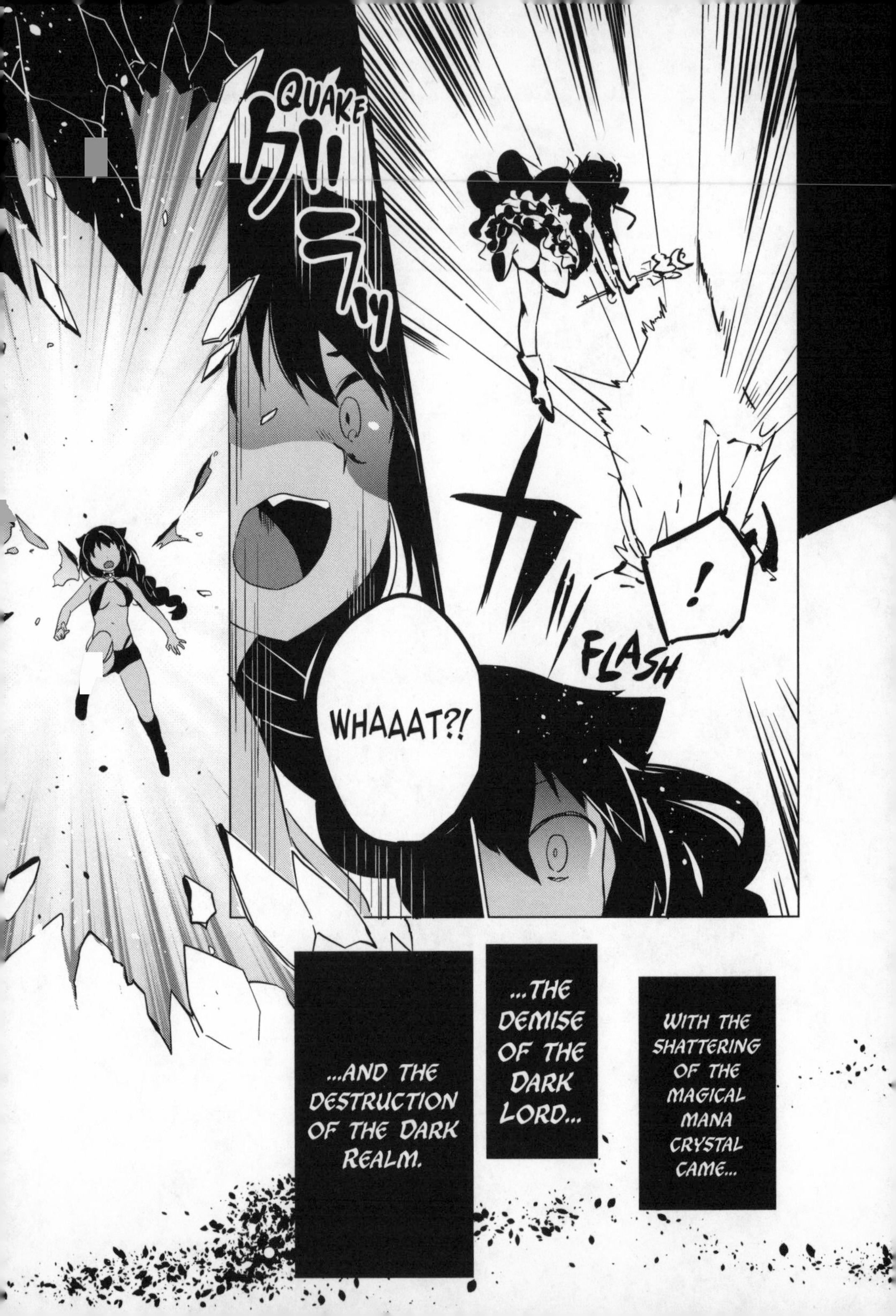
!
FLASH
QUAKE
WHAAAT?!
WITH THE SHATTERING OF THE MAGICAL MANA CRYSTAL CAME...
...THE DEMISE OF THE DARK LORD...
...AND THE DESTRUCTION OF THE DARK REALM.

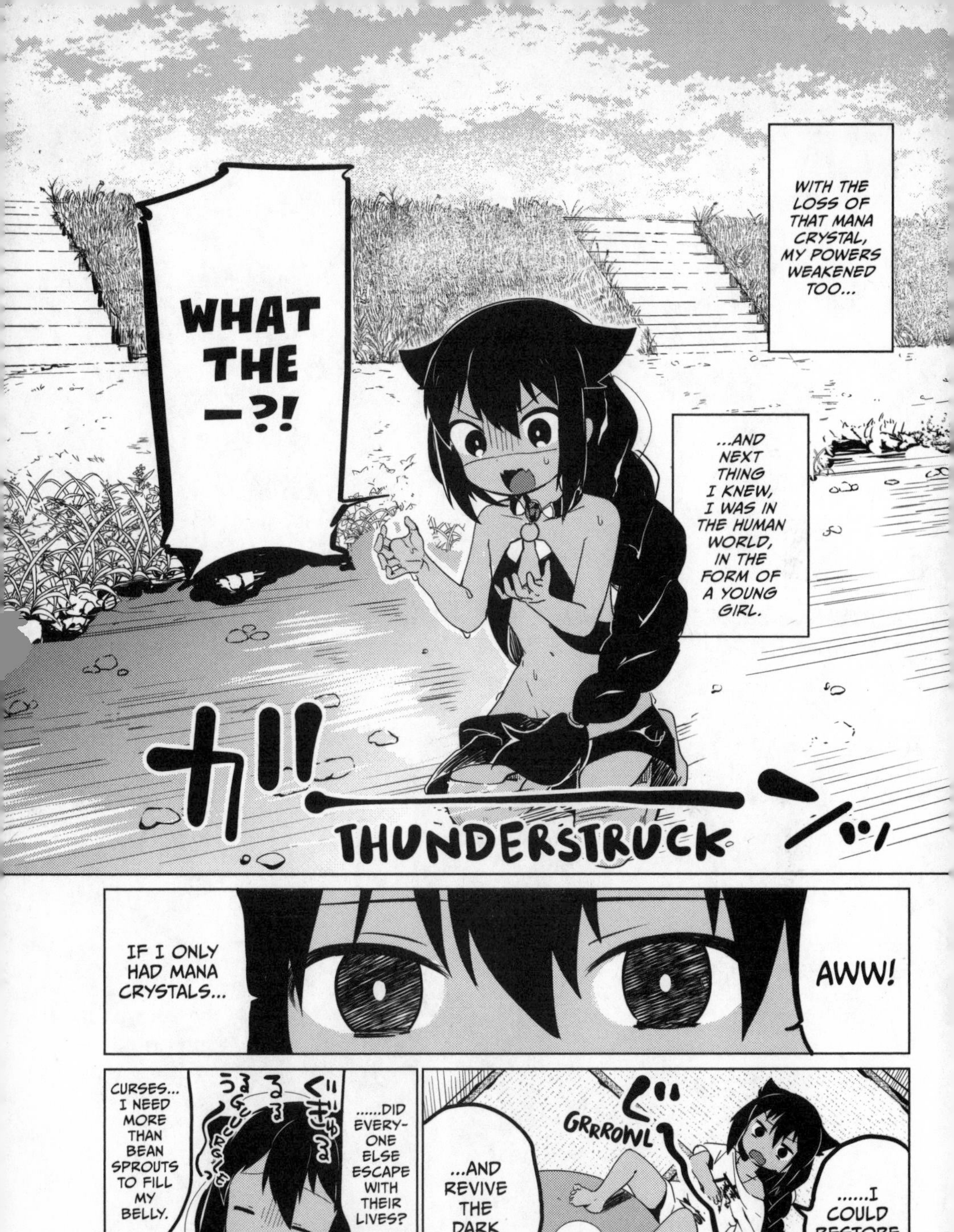

WITH THE LOSS OF THAT MANA CRYSTAL, MY POWERS WEAKENED TOO...
...AND NEXT THING I KNEW, I WAS IN THE HUMAN WORLD, IN THE FORM OF A YOUNG GIRL.
WHAT THE—?!
THUNDERSTRUCK
AWW!
IF I ONLY HAD MANA CRYSTALS...
......I COULD RESTORE THE DARK REALM...
GRRROWL
...AND REVIVE THE DARK LORD TOO.
......DID EVERYONE ELSE ESCAPE WITH THEIR LIVES?
CURSES... I NEED MORE THAN BEAN SPROUTS TO FILL MY BELLY.

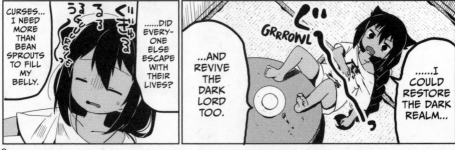

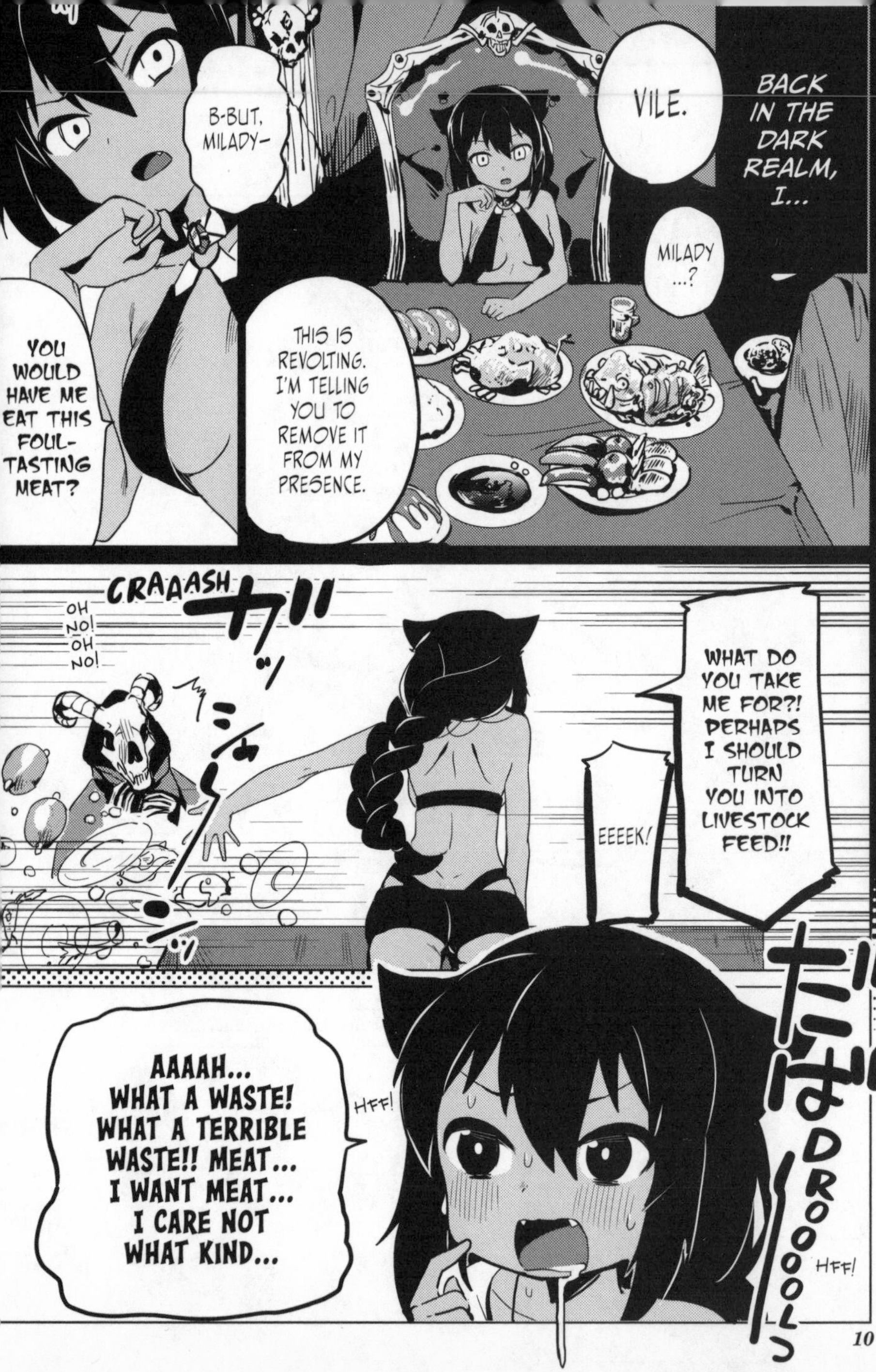
BACK IN THE DARK REALM, I...
VILE.
MILADY ...?
THIS IS REVOLTING. I'M TELLING YOU TO REMOVE IT FROM MY PRESENCE.
B-BUT, MILADY—
YOU WOULD HAVE ME EAT THIS FOUL-TASTING MEAT?
WHAT DO YOU TAKE ME FOR?! PERHAPS I SHOULD TURN YOU INTO LIVESTOCK FEED!!
EEEEK!
CRAAASH
OH NO! OH NO!
DROOOOOL
AAAAH... WHAT A WASTE! WHAT A TERRIBLE WASTE!! MEAT... I WANT MEAT... I CARE NOT WHAT KIND...
HFF!
HFF!

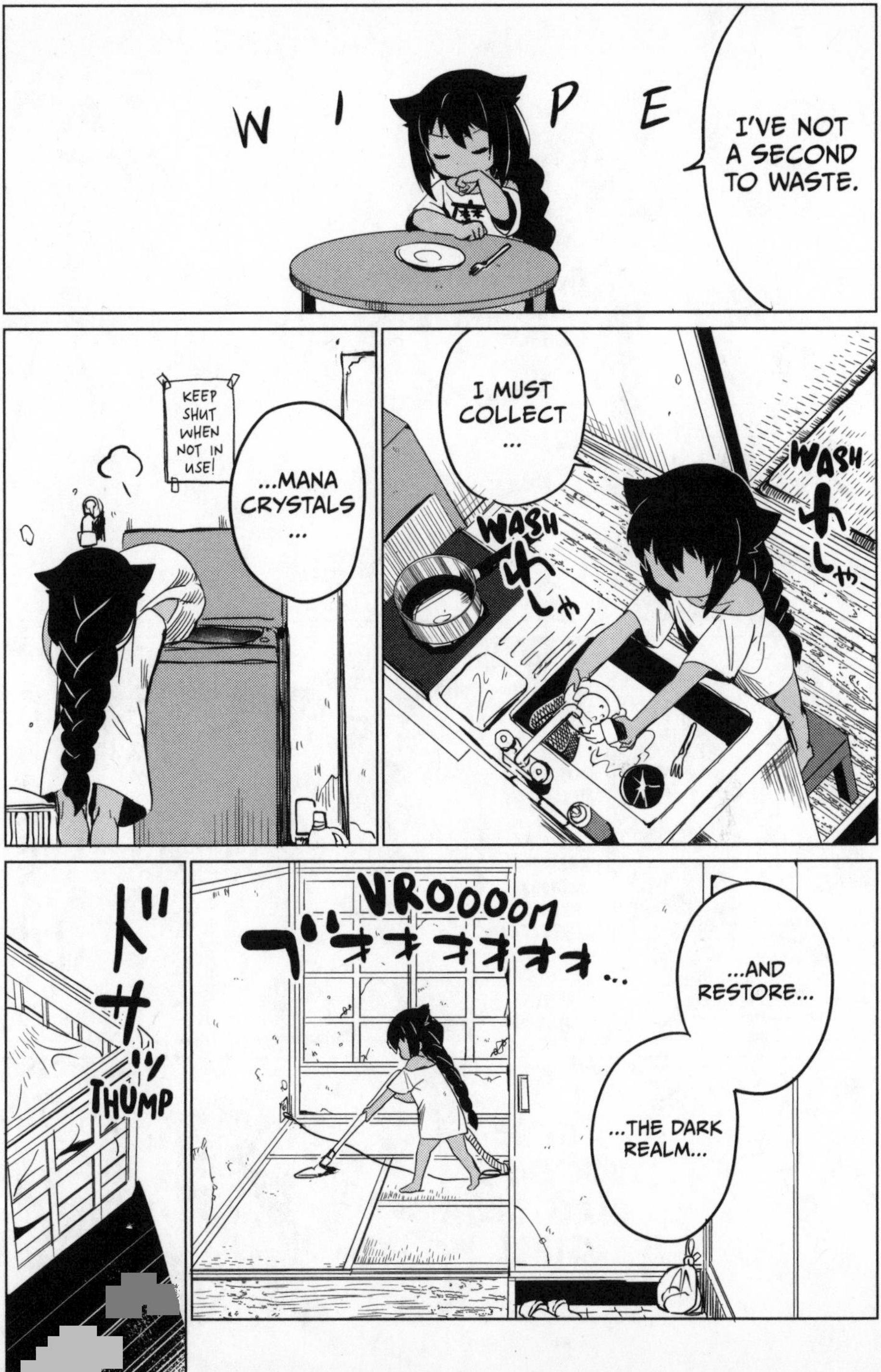
I'VE NOT A SECOND TO WASTE.
W I P E
I MUST COLLECT ...
WASH わしゃ
WASH わしゃ
KEEP SHUT WHEN NOT IN USE!
...MANA CRYSTALS ...
...AND RESTORE...
...THE DARK REALM...
VROOOOM ブォォォォォォ…
ドサッ THUMP

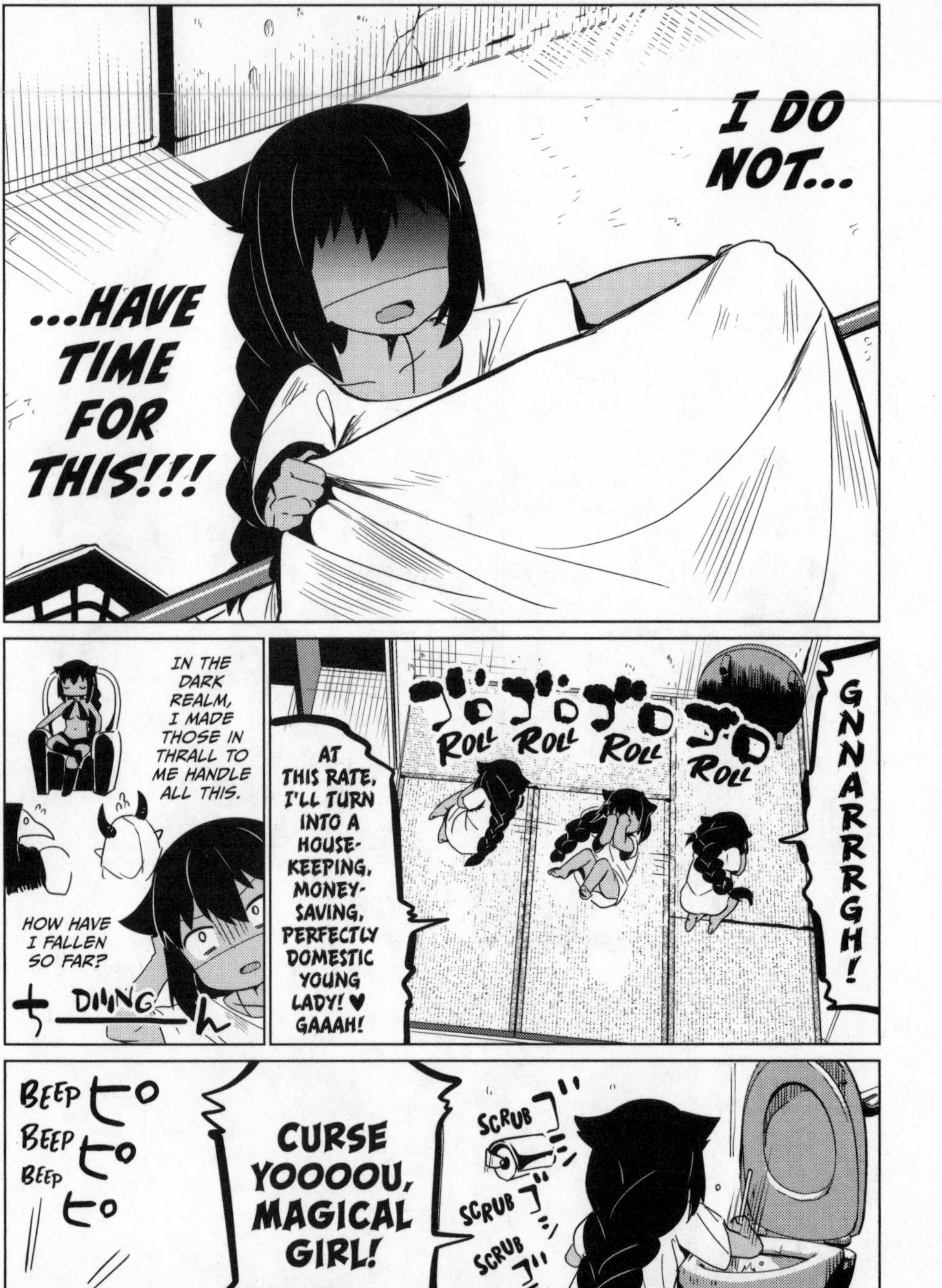
I DO NOT...
...HAVE TIME FOR THIS!!!
GNNARRRGH!
ROLL ROLL ROLL ROLL
AT THIS RATE, I'LL TURN INTO A HOUSE-KEEPING, MONEY-SAVING, PERFECTLY DOMESTIC YOUNG LADY! ♥ GAAAH!
IN THE DARK REALM, I MADE THOSE IN THRALL TO ME HANDLE ALL THIS.
HOW HAVE I FALLEN SO FAR?
DIIING
SCRUB
SCRUB
SCRUB
CURSE YOOOOU, MAGICAL GIRL!
BEEP
BEEP
BEEP

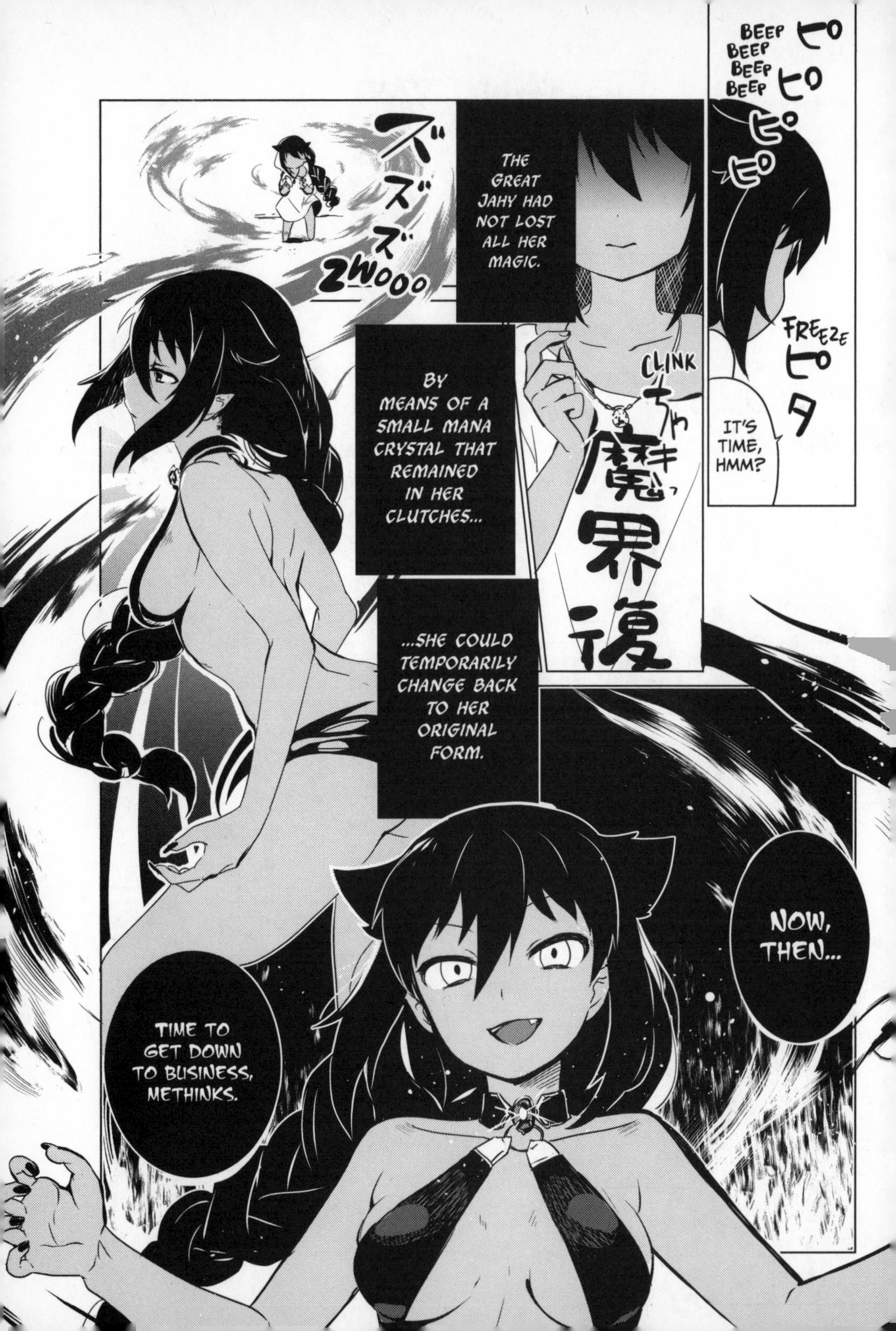
BEEP BEEP BEEP BEEP
ピピピピ
FREEZE
ピタ
IT'S TIME, HMM?
THE GREAT JAHY HAD NOT LOST ALL HER MAGIC.
CLINK
ちゃキッ
魔界復
ズズズ
ZWOOO
BY MEANS OF A SMALL MANA CRYSTAL THAT REMAINED IN HER CLUTCHES...
...SHE COULD TEMPORARILY CHANGE BACK TO HER ORIGINAL FORM.
NOW, THEN...
TIME TO GET DOWN TO BUSINESS, METHINKS.

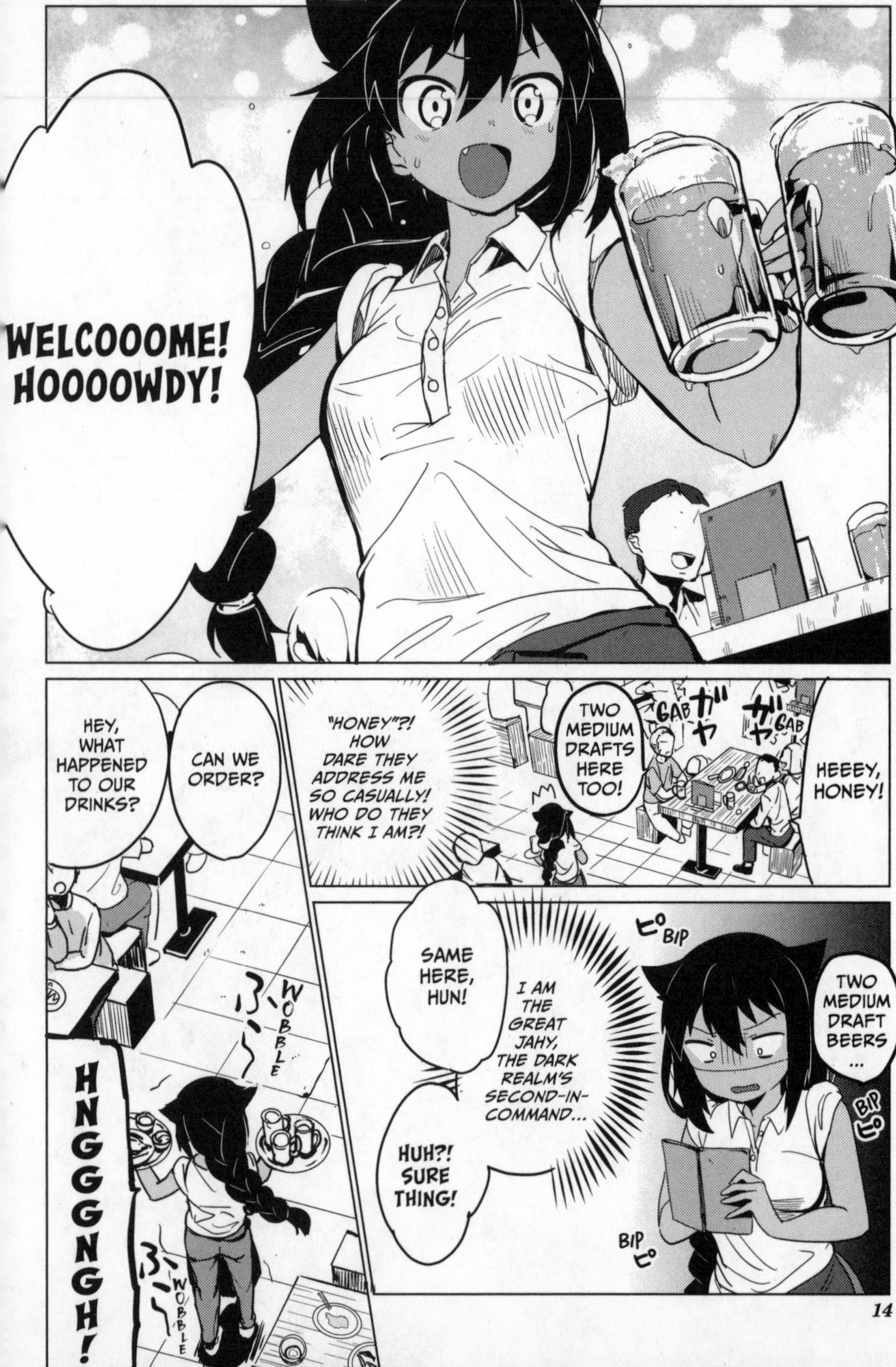
WELCOOOME! HOOOOWDY!
HEEEY, HONEY!
TWO MEDIUM DRAFTS HERE TOO!
GAB
GAB
"HONEY"?! HOW DARE THEY ADDRESS ME SO CASUALLY! WHO DO THEY THINK I AM?!
BIP
TWO MEDIUM DRAFT BEERS...
BIP
I AM THE GREAT JAHY, THE DARK REALM'S SECOND-IN-COMMAND...
SAME HERE, HUN!
HUH?! SURE THING!
BIP
CAN WE ORDER?
HEY, WHAT HAPPENED TO OUR DRINKS?
WOBBLE
HNGGGNGH!
WOBBLE

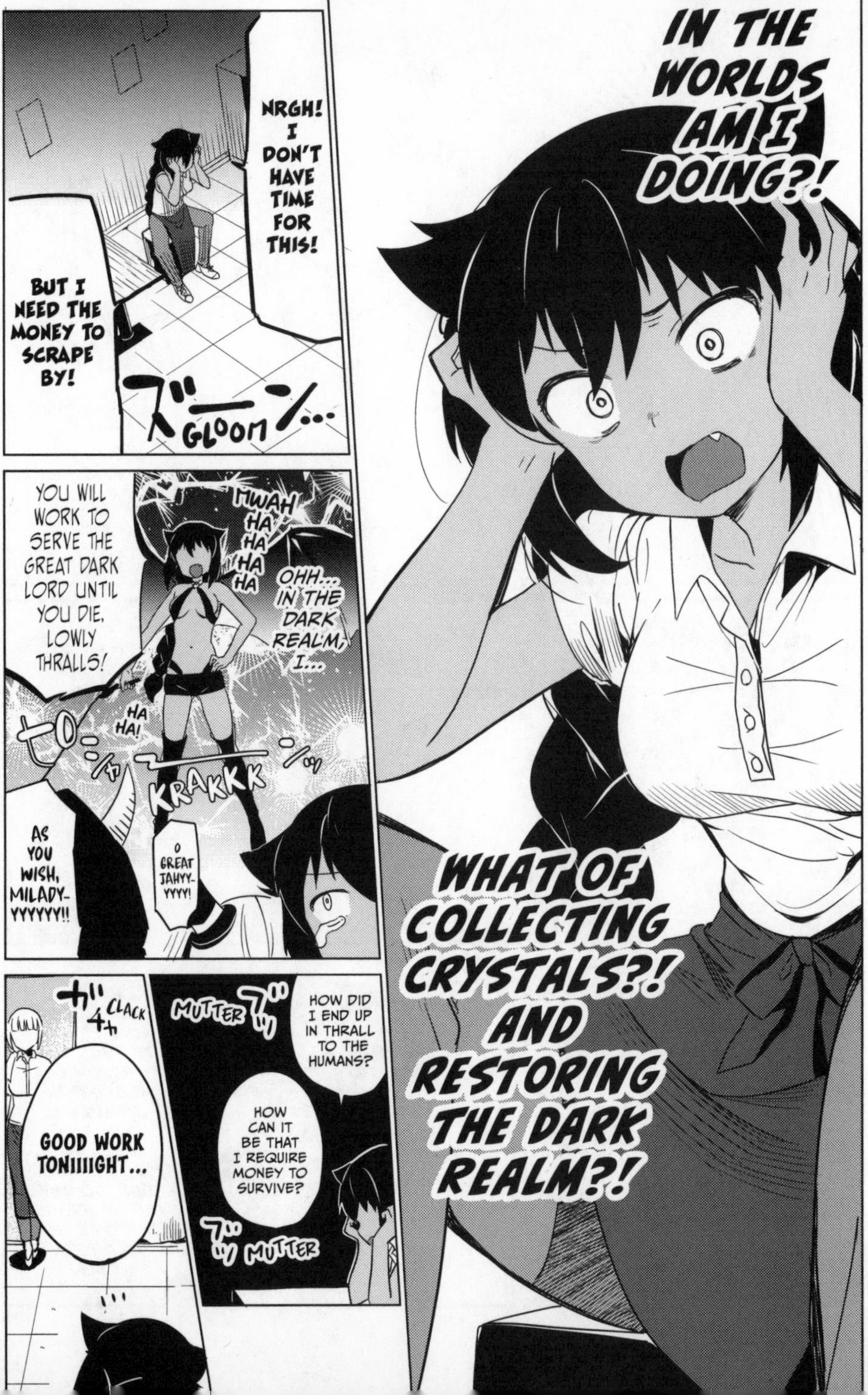
WHAT IN THE WORLDS AM I DOING?!
WHAT OF COLLECTING CRYSTALS?! AND RESTORING THE DARK REALM?!
NRGH! I DON'T HAVE TIME FOR THIS!
BUT I NEED THE MONEY TO SCRAPE BY!
GLOOM
MWAH HA HA HA HA HA
OHH... IN THE DARK REALM, I...
YOU WILL WORK TO SERVE THE GREAT DARK LORD UNTIL YOU DIE, LOWLY THRALLS!
HA HA!
KRAKKK
O GREAT JAHYY-YYYY!
AS YOU WISH, MILADY-YYYYYY!!
MUTTER
HOW DID I END UP IN THRALL TO THE HUMANS?
HOW CAN IT BE THAT I REQUIRE MONEY TO SURVIVE?
MUTTER
CLACK
GOOD WORK TONIIIIGHT...

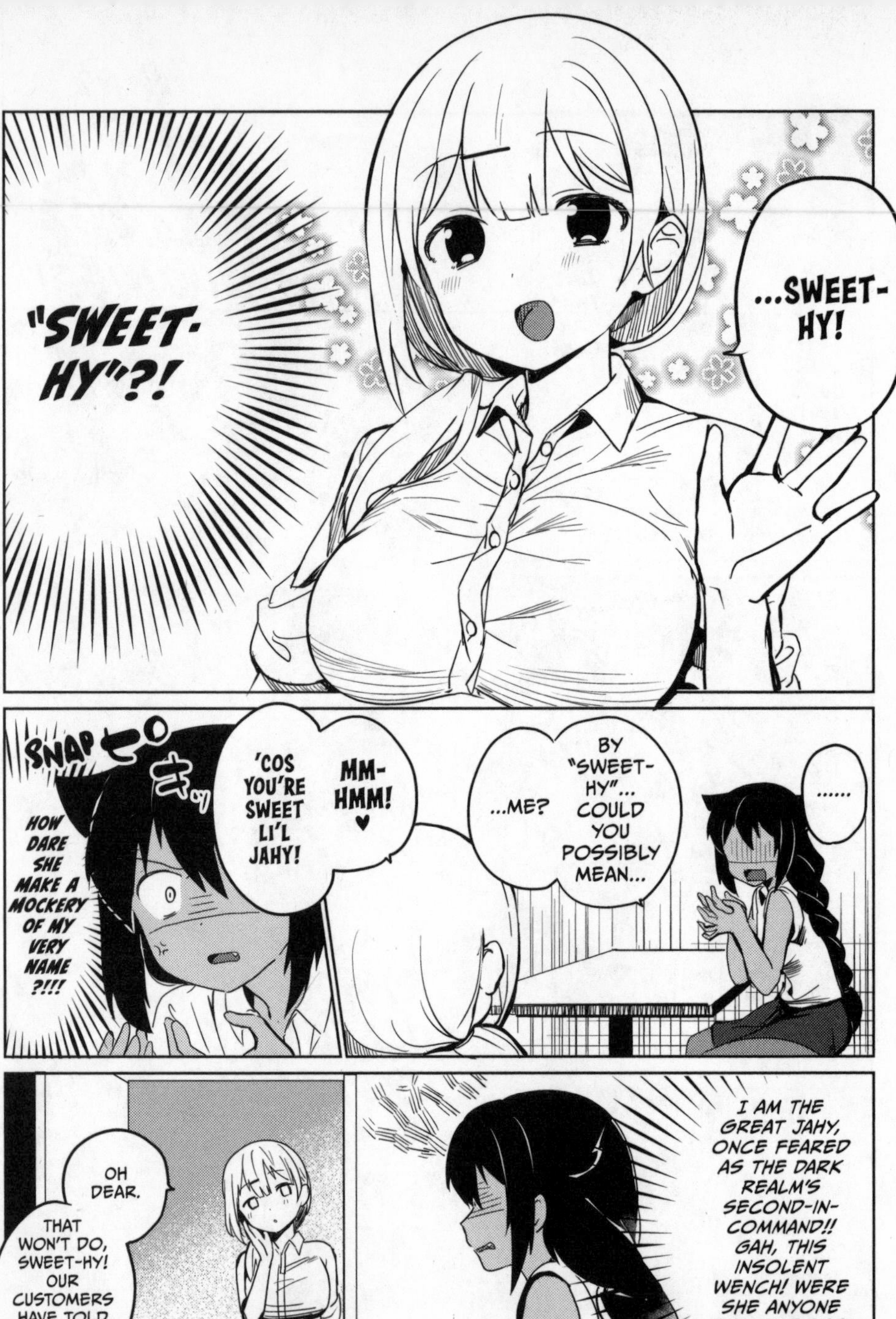
...SWEET-HY!
"SWEET-HY"?!
......
BY "SWEET-HY"... COULD YOU POSSIBLY MEAN...
...ME?
MM-HMM! ♥
'COS YOU'RE SWEET LI'L JAHY!
SNAP ピキッ
HOW DARE SHE MAKE A MOCKERY OF MY VERY NAME?!!!
I AM THE GREAT JAHY, ONCE FEARED AS THE DARK REALM'S SECOND-IN-COMMAND!! GAH, THIS INSOLENT WENCH! WERE SHE ANYONE BUT MY BOSS, I'D TEAR HER LIMB FROM LIMB!
OH DEAR.
THAT WON'T DO, SWEET-HY! OUR CUSTOMERS HAVE TOLD YOU TOO, RIGHT?

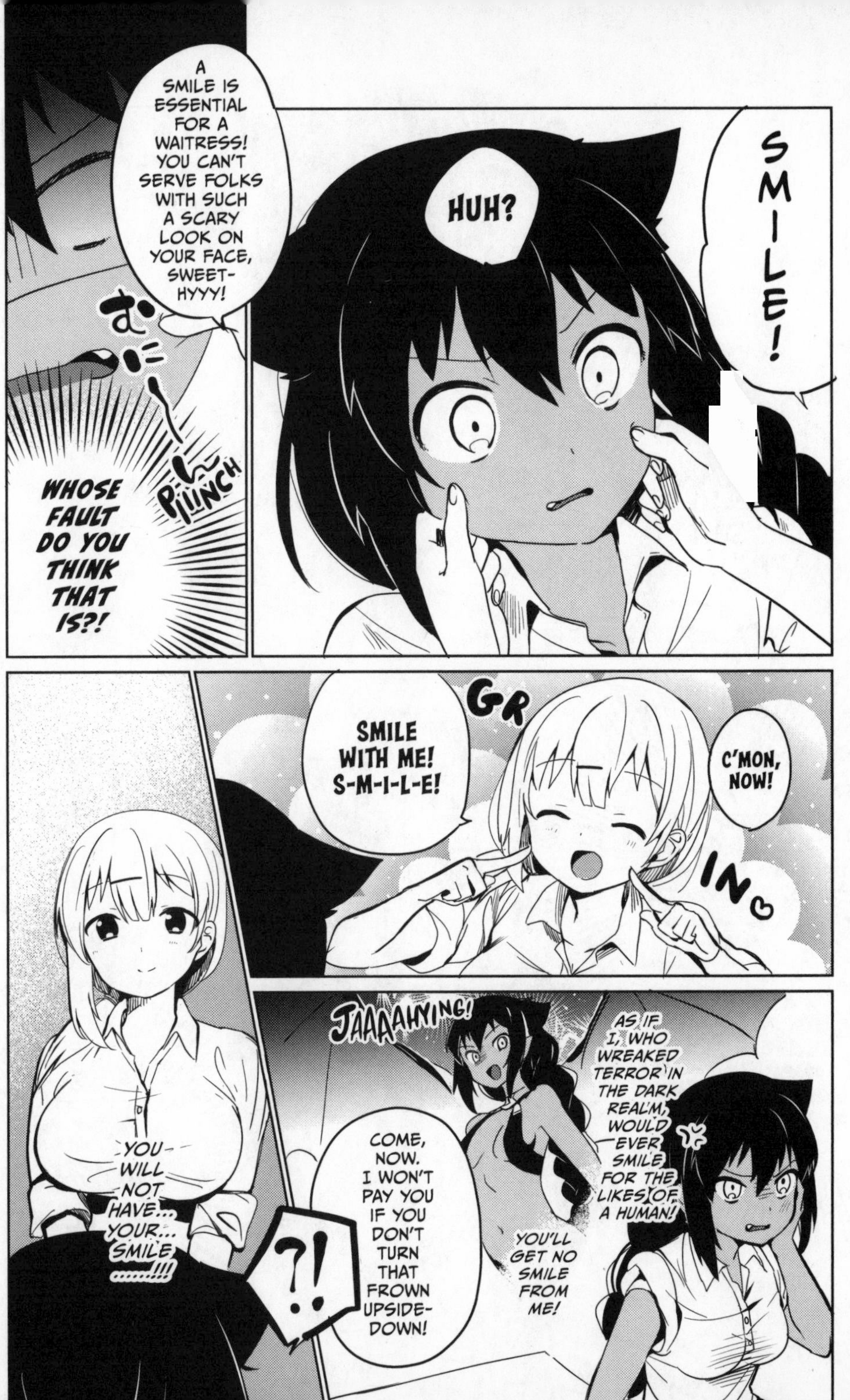
SMILE!
HUH?
A SMILE IS ESSENTIAL FOR A WAITRESS! YOU CAN'T SERVE FOLKS WITH SUCH A SCARY LOOK ON YOUR FACE, SWEET-HYYY!
PIIINCH
WHOSE FAULT DO YOU THINK THAT IS?!
C'MON, NOW!
GR
IN
SMILE WITH ME! S-M-I-L-E!
JAAAAHYING!
AS IF I, WHO WREAKED TERROR IN THE DARK REALM, WOULD EVER SMILE FOR THE LIKES OF A HUMAN!
COME, NOW. I WON'T PAY YOU IF YOU DON'T TURN THAT FROWN UPSIDE-DOWN!
YOU'LL GET NO SMILE FROM ME!
?!
YOU WILL NOT HAVE... YOUR... SMILE ......!!!

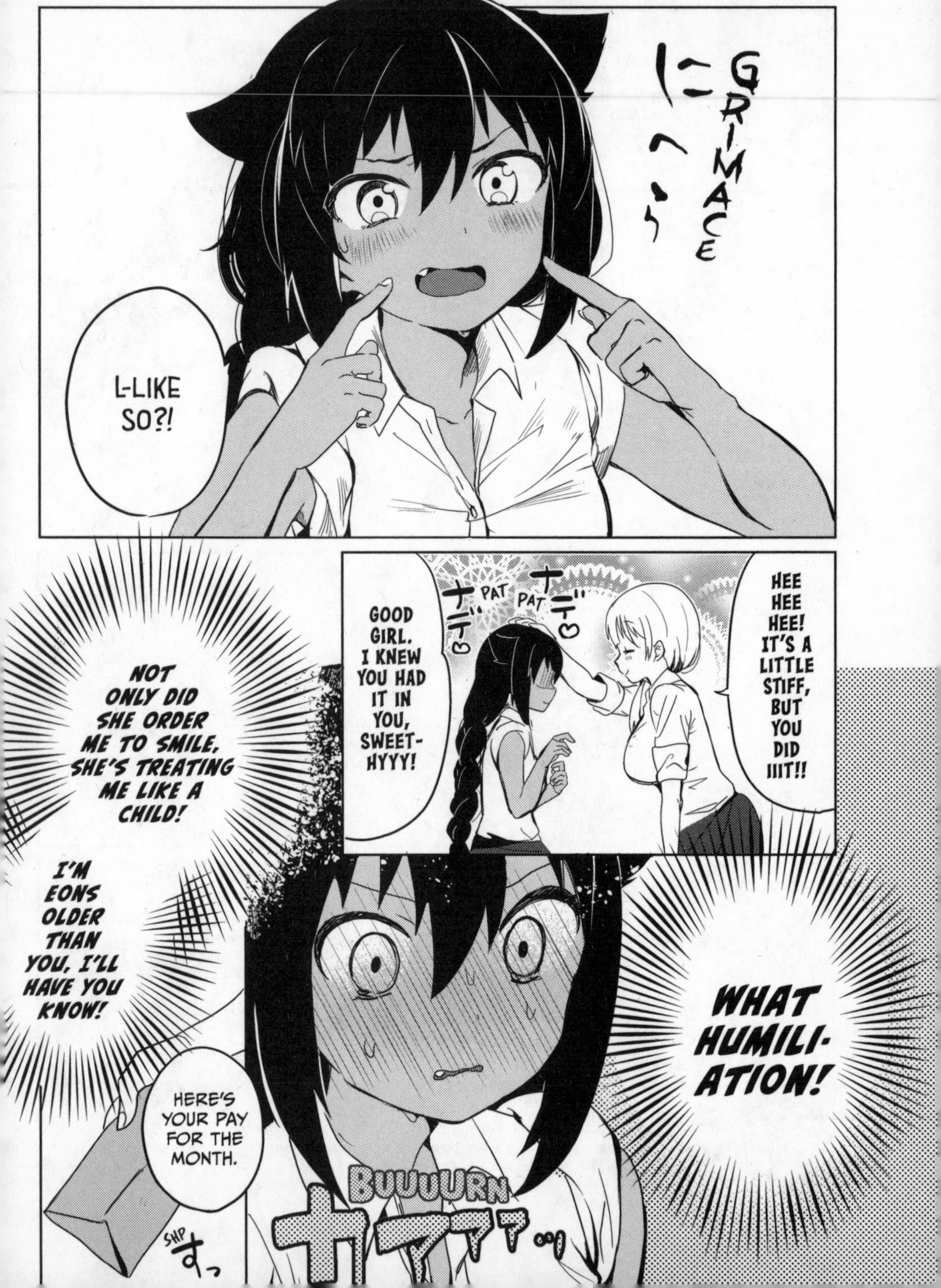
GRIMACE
L-LIKE SO?!
HEE HEE HEE! IT'S A LITTLE STIFF, BUT YOU DID IIIT!!
PAT PAT
GOOD GIRL. I KNEW YOU HAD IT IN YOU, SWEET-HYYY!
NOT ONLY DID SHE ORDER ME TO SMILE, SHE'S TREATING ME LIKE A CHILD!
WHAT HUMILI-ATION!
I'M EONS OLDER THAN YOU, I'LL HAVE YOU KNOW!
HERE'S YOUR PAY FOR THE MONTH.
BUUUURN
SHP

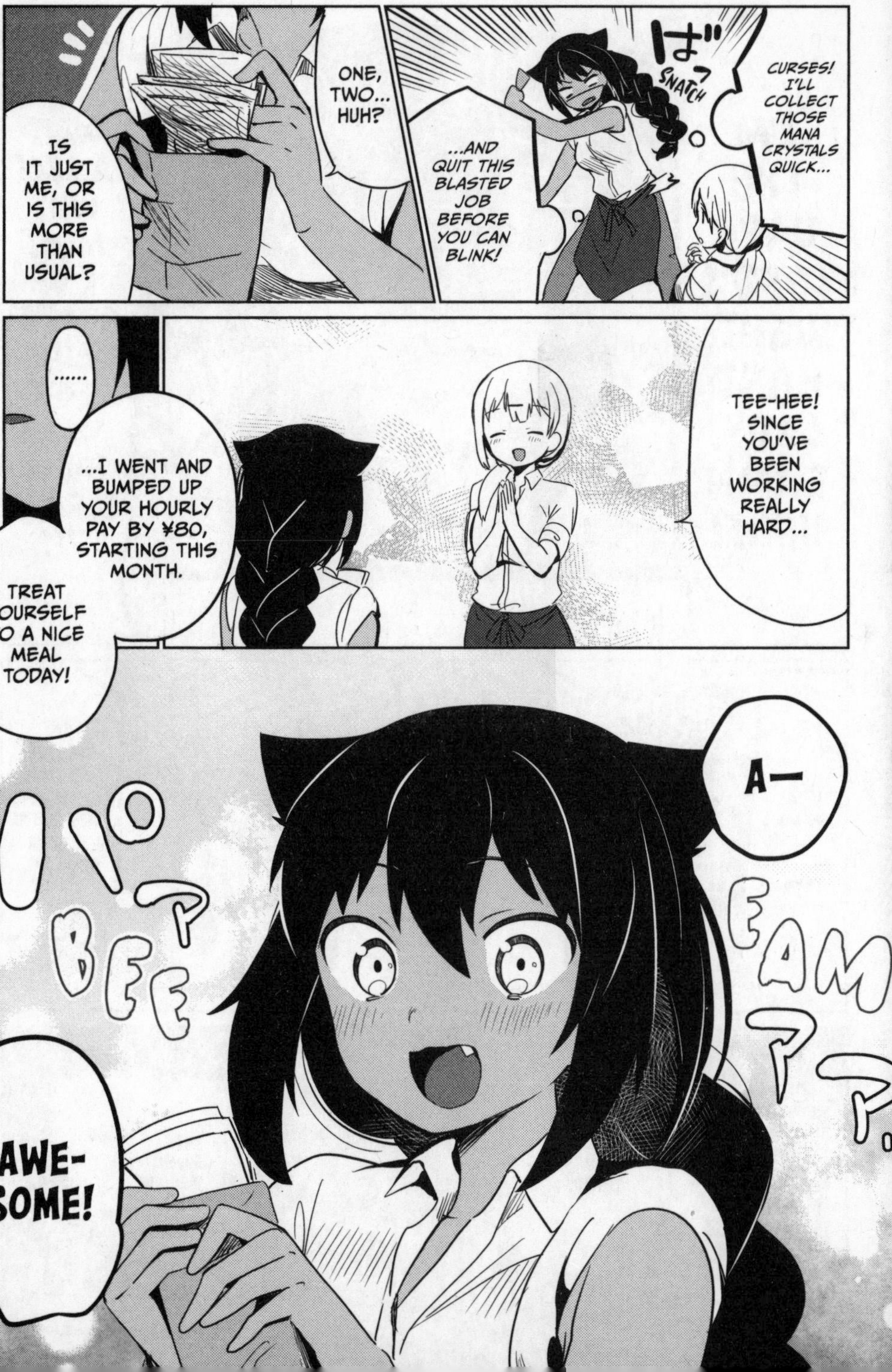
ばっ
SNATCH
CURSES! I'LL COLLECT THOSE MANA CRYSTALS QUICK...
...AND QUIT THIS BLASTED JOB BEFORE YOU CAN BLINK!
ONE, TWO... HUH?
IS IT JUST ME, OR IS THIS MORE THAN USUAL?
TEE-HEE! SINCE YOU'VE BEEN WORKING REALLY HARD...
...I WENT AND BUMPED UP YOUR HOURLY PAY BY ¥80, STARTING THIS MONTH.
TREAT YOURSELF TO A NICE MEAL TODAY!
......
A—
パア BEE
EAM アア.
AWE-SOME!

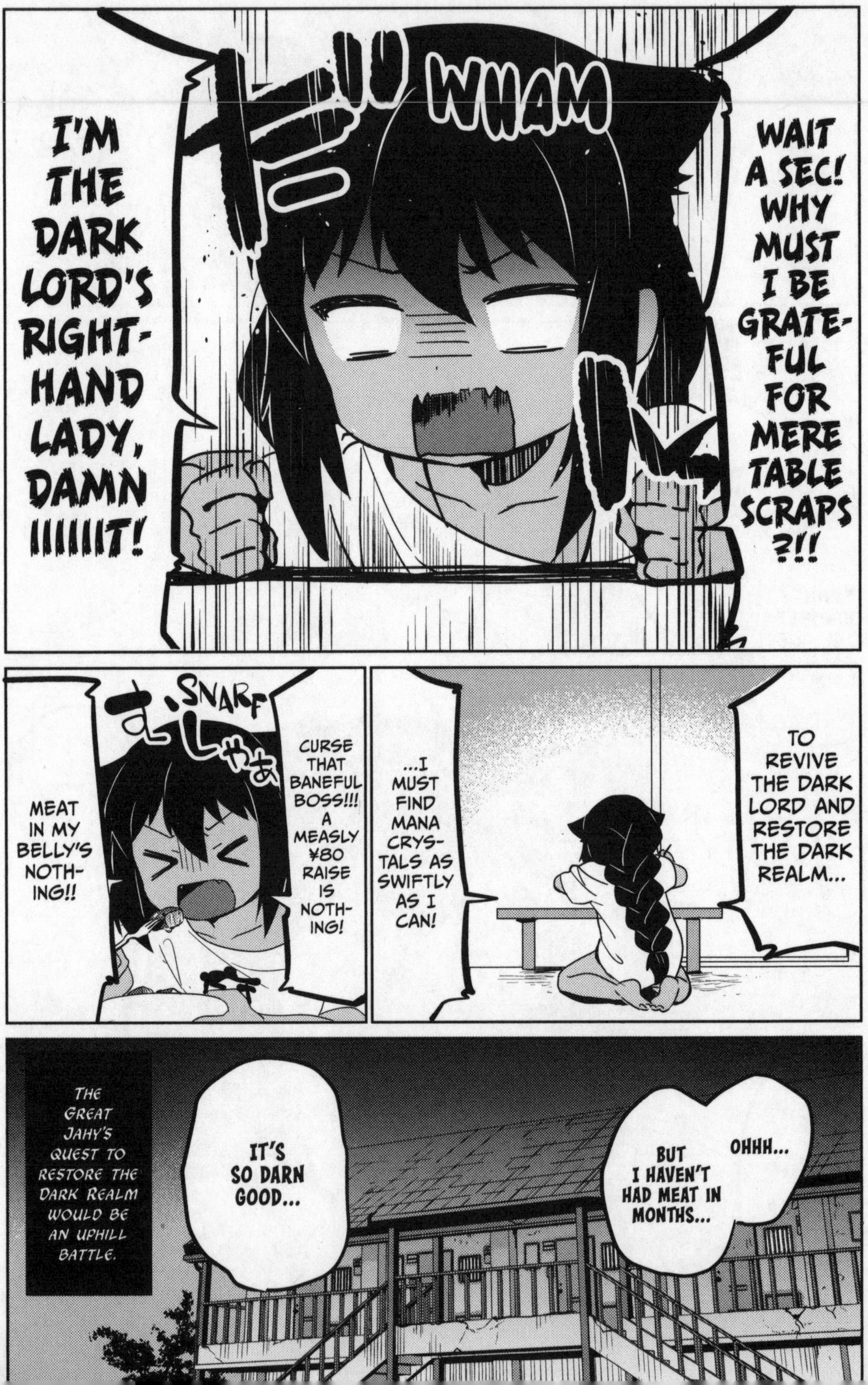
WAIT A SEC! WHY MUST I BE GRATE-FUL FOR MERE TABLE SCRAPS?!!
WHAM
I'M THE DARK LORD'S RIGHT-HAND LADY, DAMN IIIIIIIT!
TO REVIVE THE DARK LORD AND RESTORE THE DARK REALM...
...I MUST FIND MANA CRYS-TALS AS SWIFTLY AS I CAN!
SNARF
CURSE THAT BANEFUL BOSS!!! A MEASLY ¥80 RAISE IS NOTH-ING!
MEAT IN MY BELLY'S NOTH-ING!!
OHHH...
BUT I HAVEN'T HAD MEAT IN MONTHS...
IT'S SO DARN GOOD...
THE GREAT JAHY'S QUEST TO RESTORE THE DARK REALM WOULD BE AN UPHILL BATTLE.

MEAT...
SHOOOO
GOOD...

MMPH.

The GREAT JAHY Will NOT Be DEFEATED!

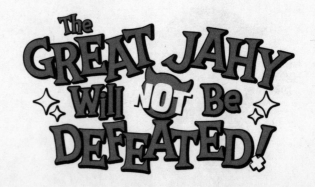

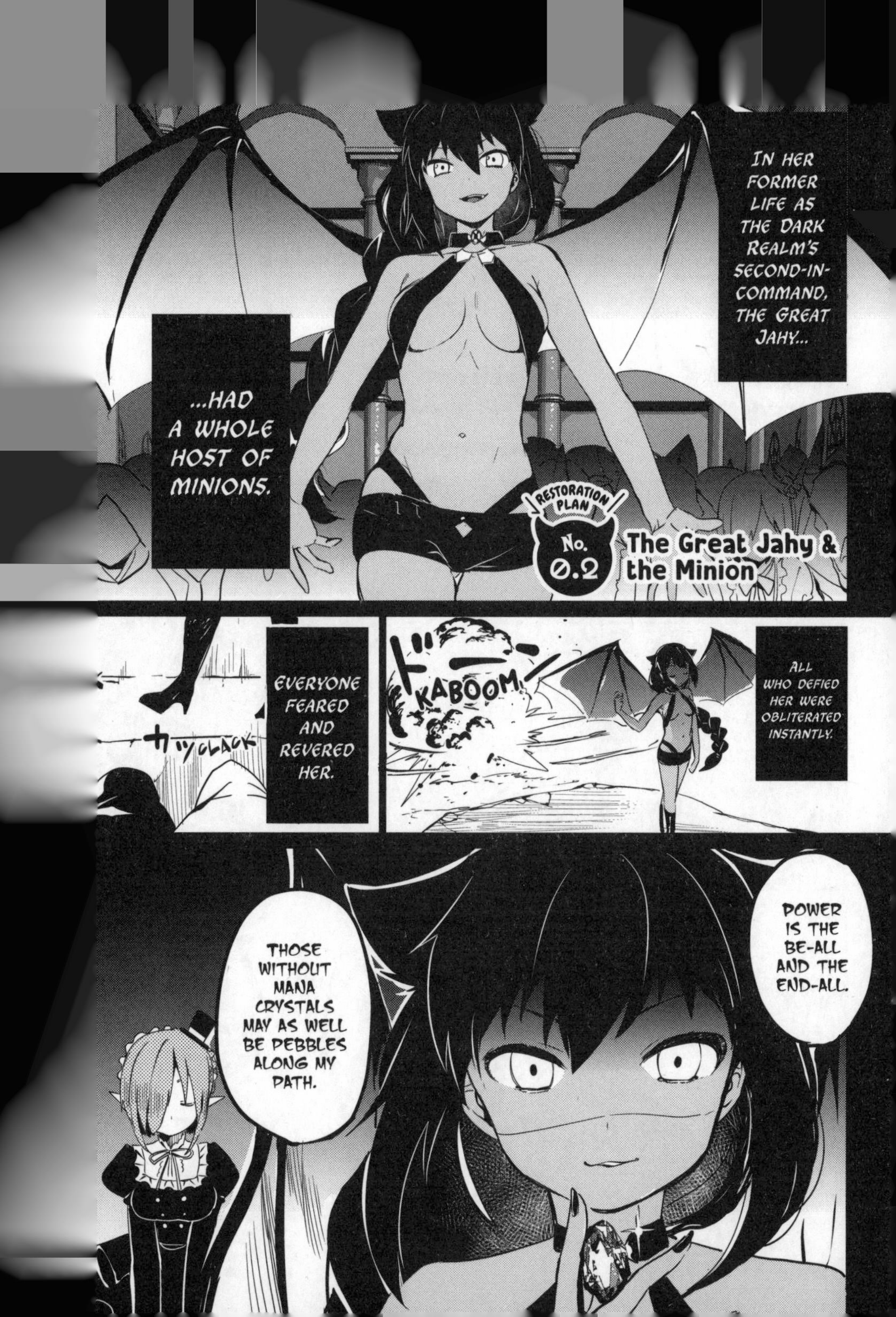
IN HER FORMER LIFE AS THE DARK REALM'S SECOND-IN-COMMAND, THE GREAT JAHY...
...HAD A WHOLE HOST OF MINIONS.
RESTORATION PLAN No. 0.2
The Great Jahy & the Minion
ALL WHO DEFIED HER WERE OBLITERATED INSTANTLY.
KABOOM
EVERYONE FEARED AND REVERED HER.
CLACK
POWER IS THE BE-ALL AND THE END-ALL.
THOSE WITHOUT MANA CRYSTALS MAY AS WELL BE PEBBLES ALONG MY PATH.

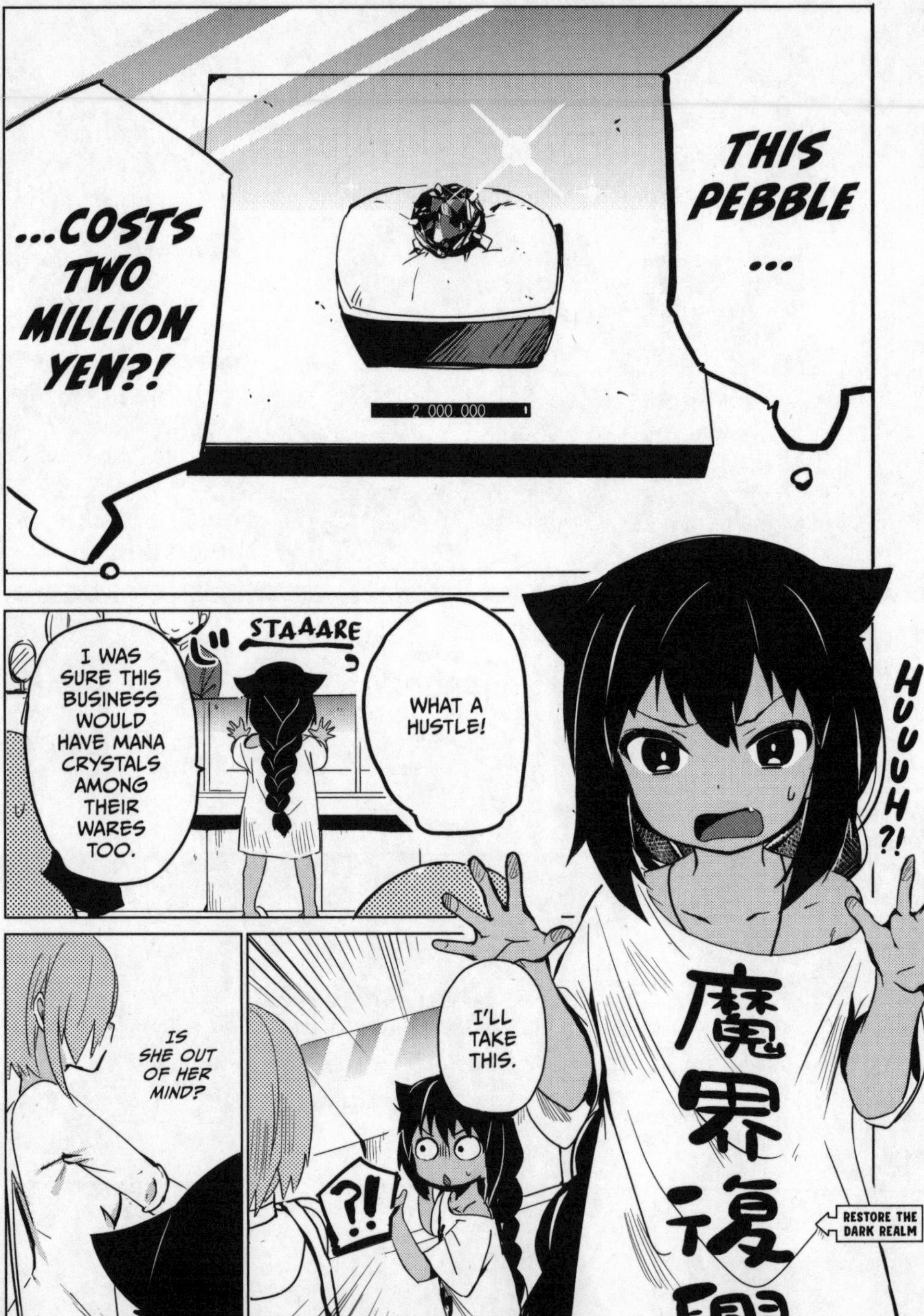
THIS PEBBLE ...
...COSTS TWO MILLION YEN?!
2,000,000
WHAT A HUSTLE!
STAAARE
I WAS SURE THIS BUSINESS WOULD HAVE MANA CRYSTALS AMONG THEIR WARES TOO.
I'LL TAKE THIS.
?!
IS SHE OUT OF HER MIND?
HUUUH?!
魔界復興
RESTORE THE DARK REALM

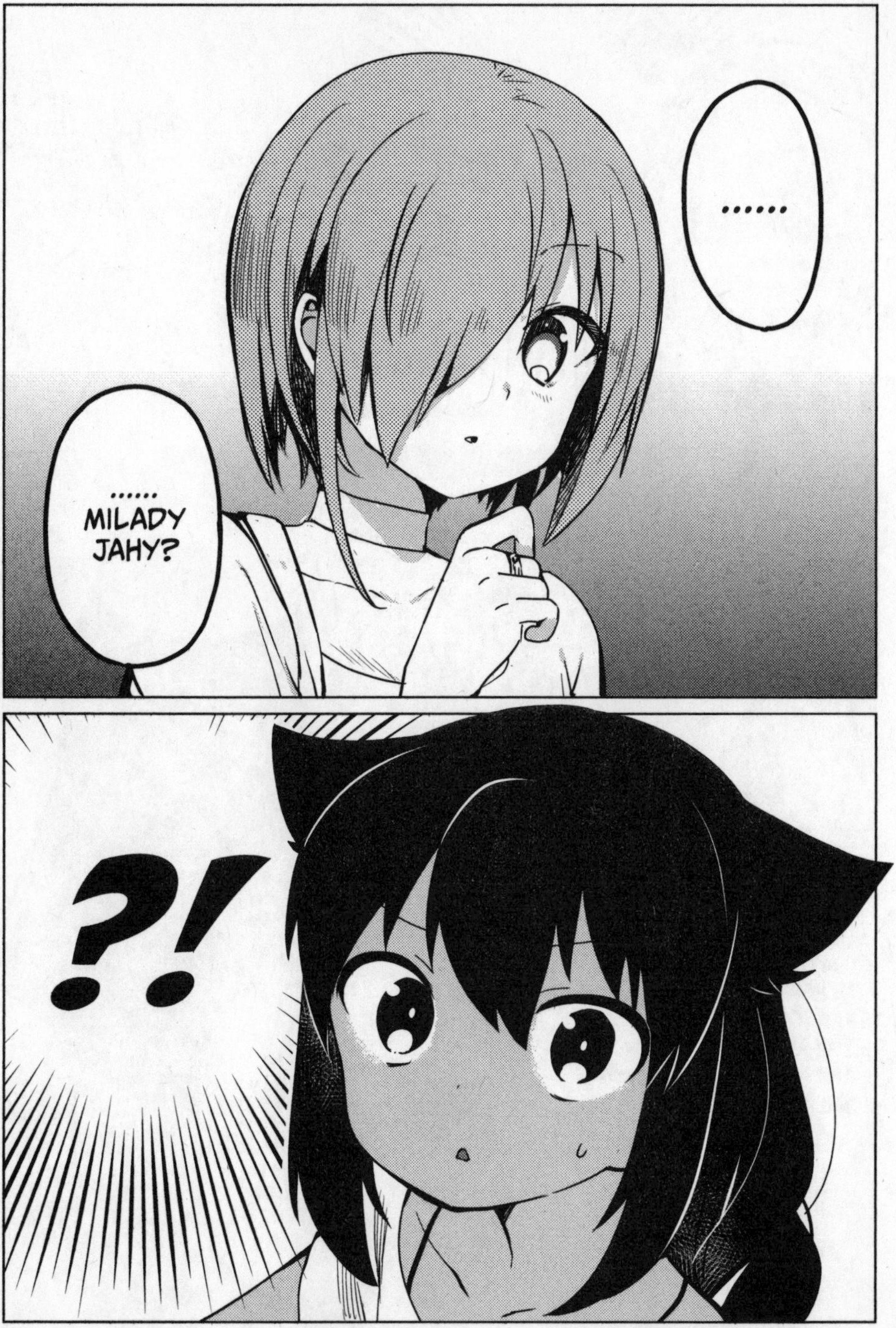
......
...... MILADY JAHY?
?!

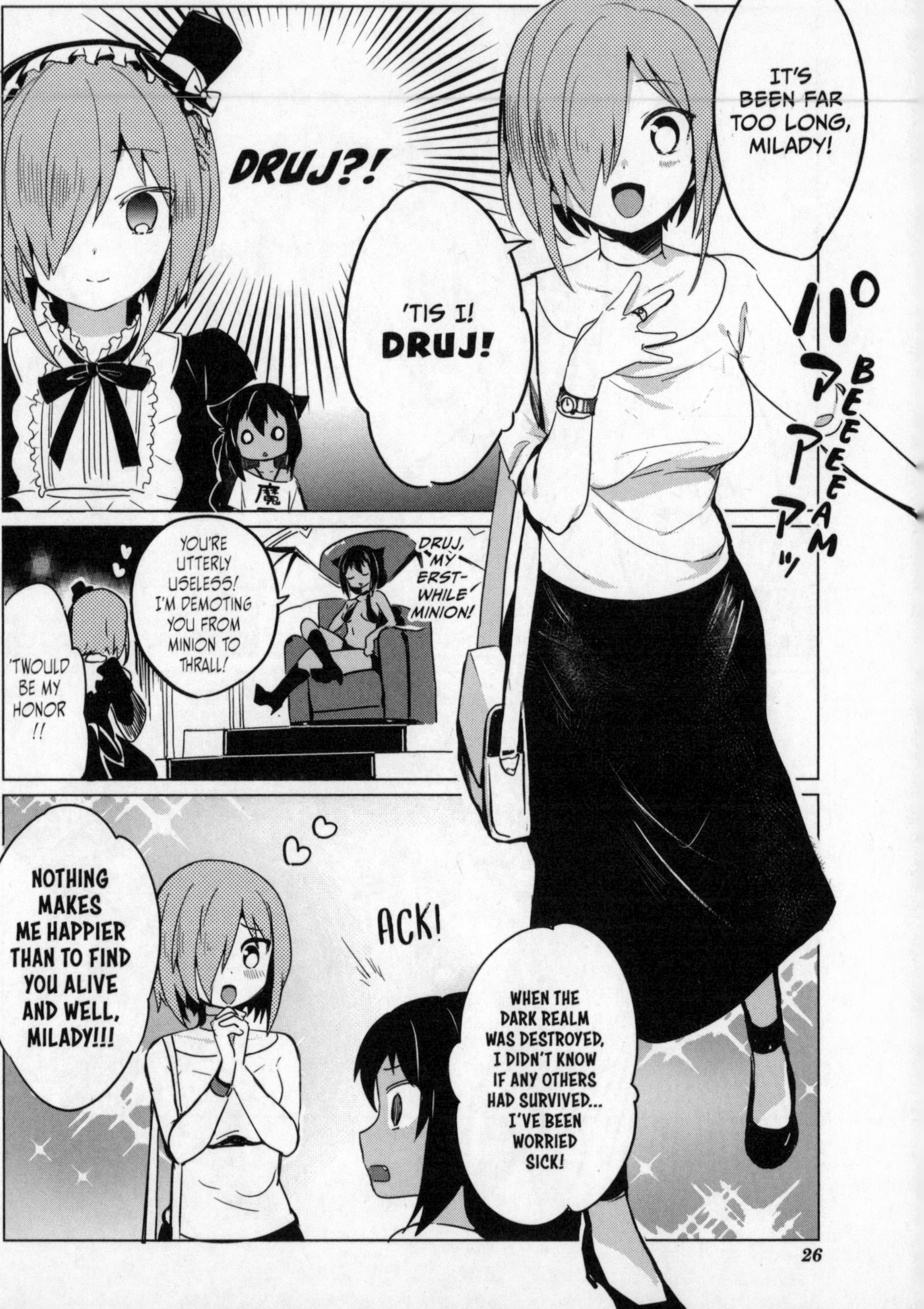
IT'S BEEN FAR TOO LONG, MILADY!
'TIS I! DRUJ!
パァーアーアッ
BEEEEEEAM
DRUJ?!
DRUJ, MY ERST-WHILE MINION!
YOU'RE UTTERLY USELESS! I'M DEMOTING YOU FROM MINION TO THRALL!
'TWOULD BE MY HONOR!!
WHEN THE DARK REALM WAS DESTROYED, I DIDN'T KNOW IF ANY OTHERS HAD SURVIVED... I'VE BEEN WORRIED SICK!
ACK!
NOTHING MAKES ME HAPPIER THAN TO FIND YOU ALIVE AND WELL, MILADY!!!

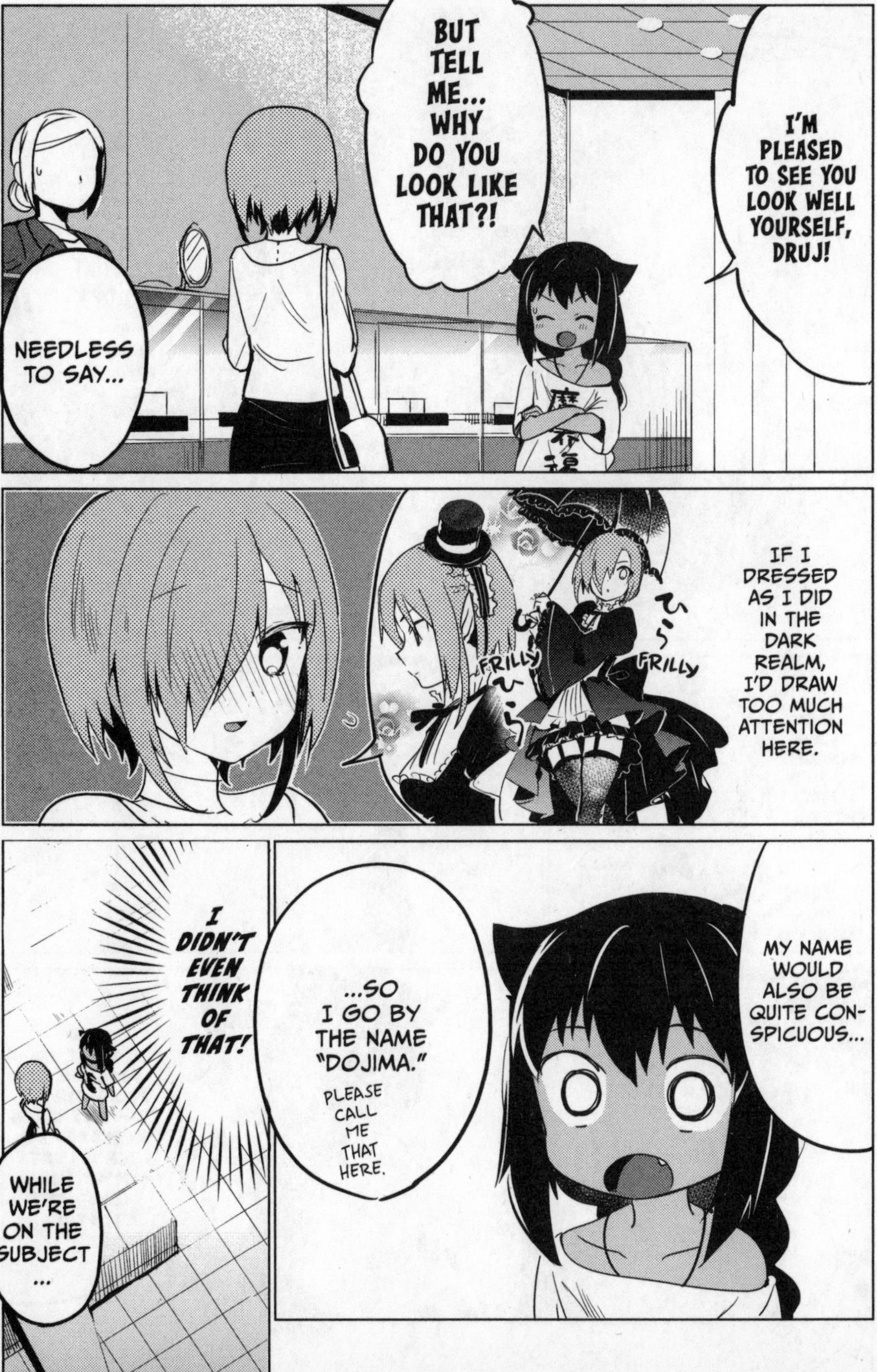
I'M PLEASED TO SEE YOU LOOK WELL YOURSELF, DRUJ!
BUT TELL ME... WHY DO YOU LOOK LIKE THAT?!
NEEDLESS TO SAY...
IF I DRESSED AS I DID IN THE DARK REALM, I'D DRAW TOO MUCH ATTENTION HERE.
ひら FRILLY
ひら FRILLY
MY NAME WOULD ALSO BE QUITE CON-SPICUOUS...
...SO I GO BY THE NAME "DOJIMA."
PLEASE CALL ME THAT HERE.
I DIDN'T EVEN THINK OF THAT!
WHILE WE'RE ON THE SUBJECT ...

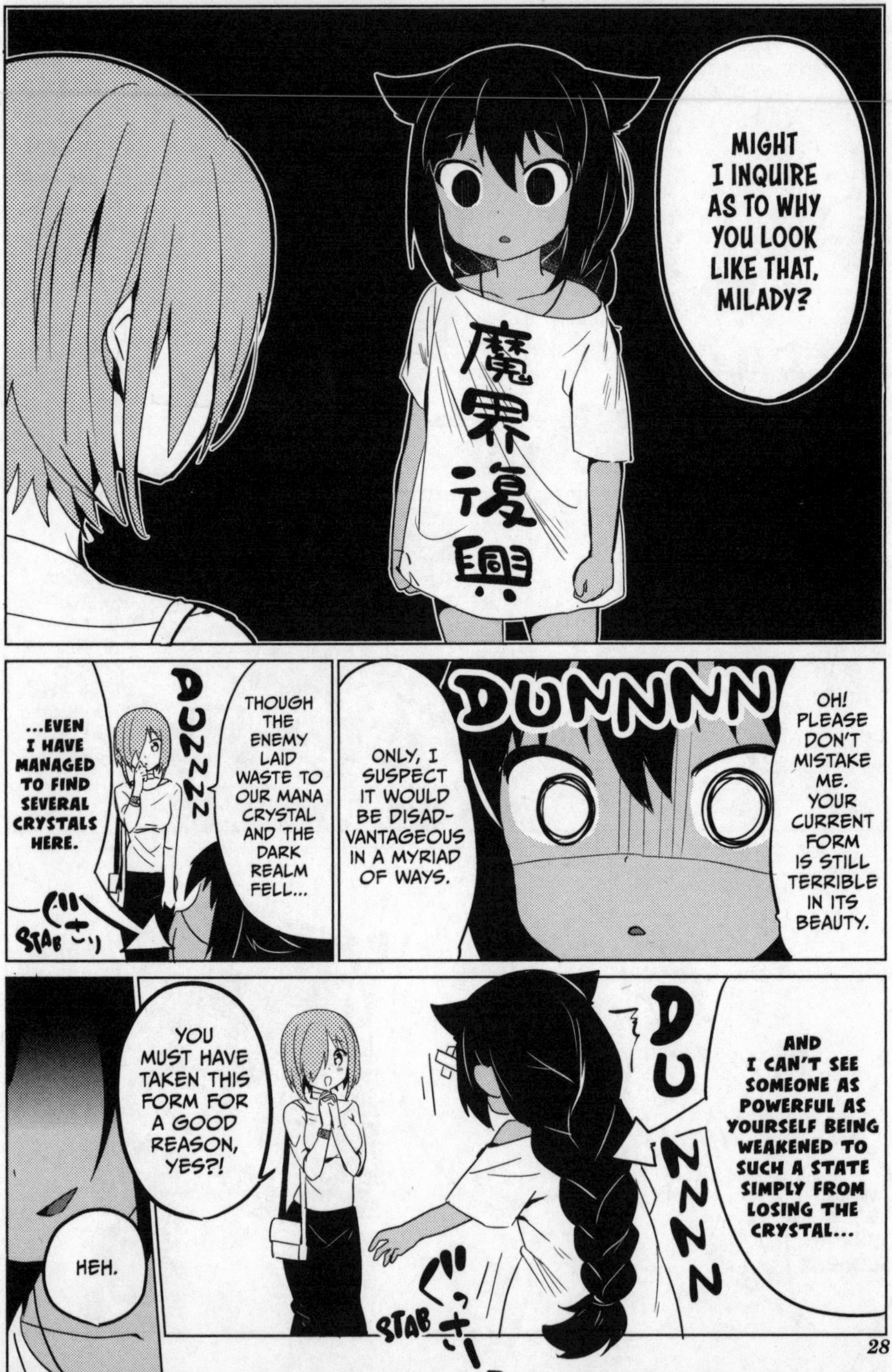
MIGHT I INQUIRE AS TO WHY YOU LOOK LIKE THAT, MILADY?
魔界復興
DUNNNN
OH! PLEASE DON'T MISTAKE ME. YOUR CURRENT FORM IS STILL TERRIBLE IN ITS BEAUTY.
ONLY, I SUSPECT IT WOULD BE DISAD-VANTAGEOUS IN A MYRIAD OF WAYS.
THOUGH THE ENEMY LAID WASTE TO OUR MANA CRYSTAL AND THE DARK REALM FELL...
DUNNNN
...EVEN I HAVE MANAGED TO FIND SEVERAL CRYSTALS HERE.
STAB
AND I CAN'T SEE SOMEONE AS POWERFUL AS YOURSELF BEING WEAKENED TO SUCH A STATE SIMPLY FROM LOSING THE CRYSTAL...
DUNNNN
YOU MUST HAVE TAKEN THIS FORM FOR A GOOD REASON, YES?!
STAB
HEH.

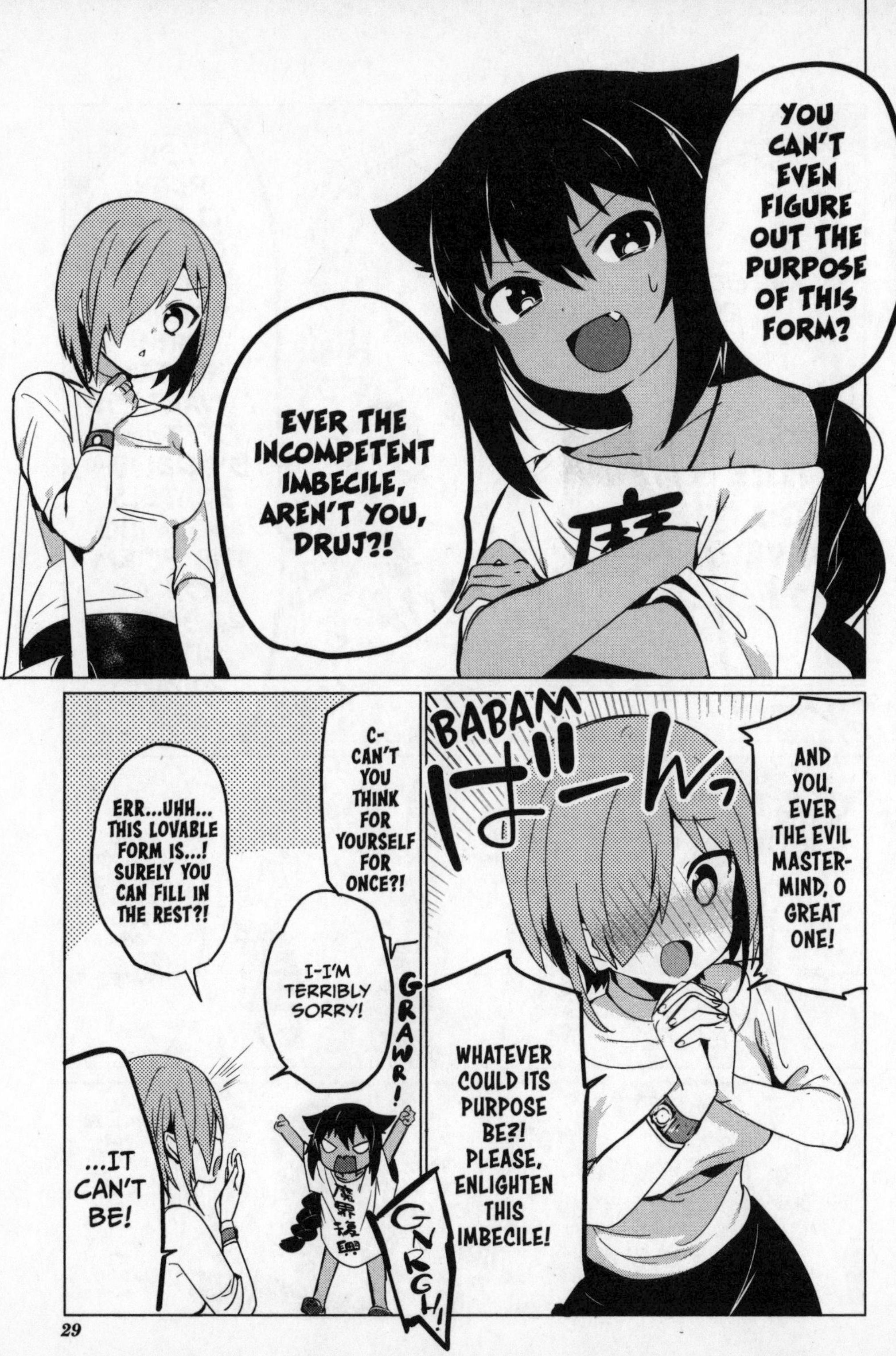

YOU CAN'T EVEN FIGURE OUT THE PURPOSE OF THIS FORM?
EVER THE INCOMPETENT IMBECILE, AREN'T YOU, DRUJ?!
BABAM
ばーんっ
AND YOU, EVER THE EVIL MASTER-MIND, O GREAT ONE!
WHATEVER COULD ITS PURPOSE BE?! PLEASE, ENLIGHTEN THIS IMBECILE!
C-CAN'T YOU THINK FOR YOURSELF FOR ONCE?!
ERR...UHH... THIS LOVABLE FORM IS...! SURELY YOU CAN FILL IN THE REST?!
I-I'M TERRIBLY SORRY!
GRAWR!
GNRGH!
...IT CAN'T BE!

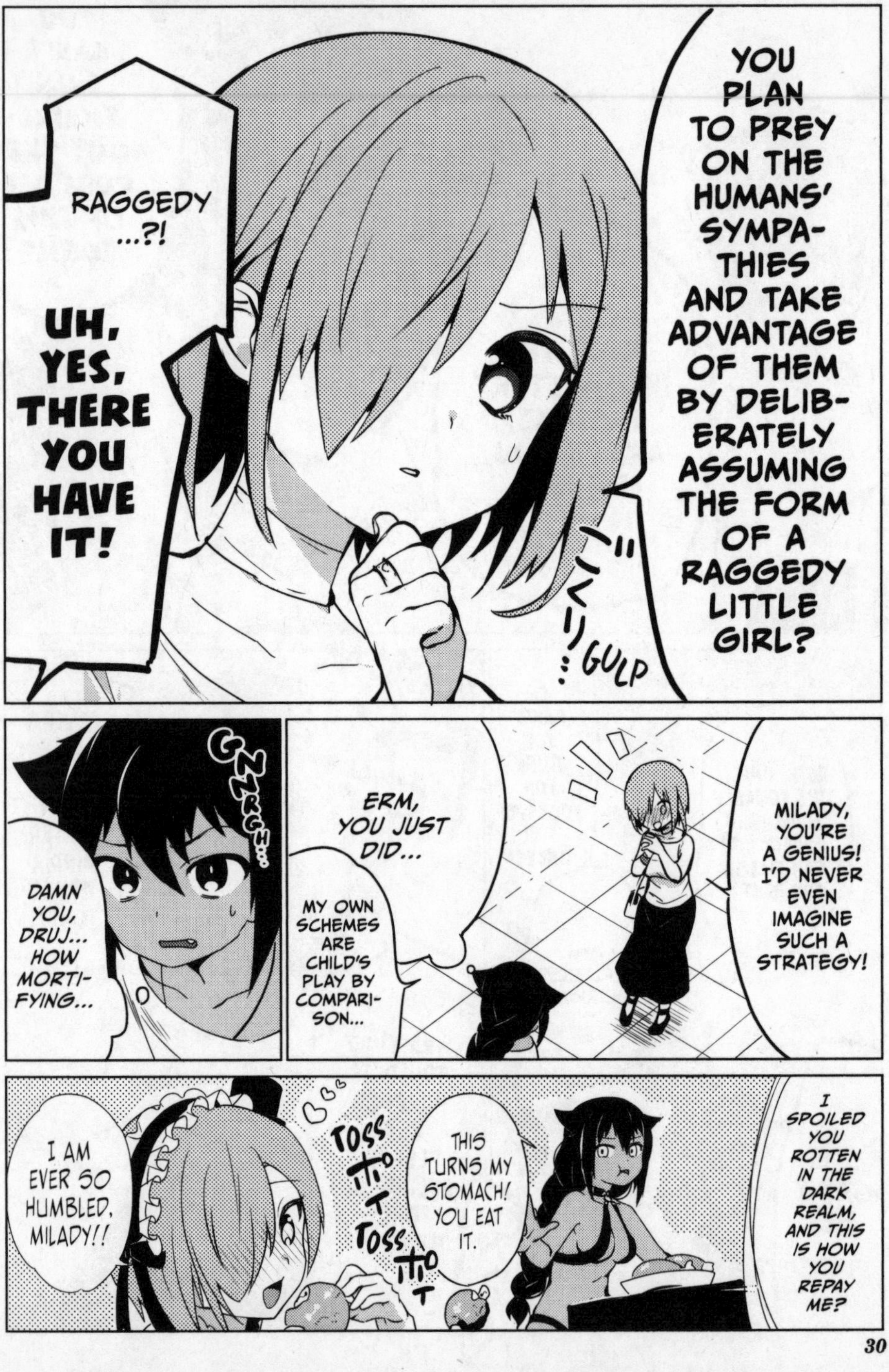
YOU PLAN TO PREY ON THE HUMANS' SYMPATHIES AND TAKE ADVANTAGE OF THEM BY DELIBERATELY ASSUMING THE FORM OF A RAGGEDY LITTLE GIRL?
RAGGEDY ...?!
GULP
UH, YES, THERE YOU HAVE IT!
MILADY, YOU'RE A GENIUS! I'D NEVER EVEN IMAGINE SUCH A STRATEGY!
ERM, YOU JUST DID...
MY OWN SCHEMES ARE CHILD'S PLAY BY COMPARISON...
GNRGH...
DAMN YOU, DRUJ... HOW MORTIFYING...
I SPOILED YOU ROTTEN IN THE DARK REALM, AND THIS IS HOW YOU REPAY ME?
THIS TURNS MY STOMACH! YOU EAT IT.
TOSS
TOSS
I AM EVER SO HUMBLED, MILADY!!

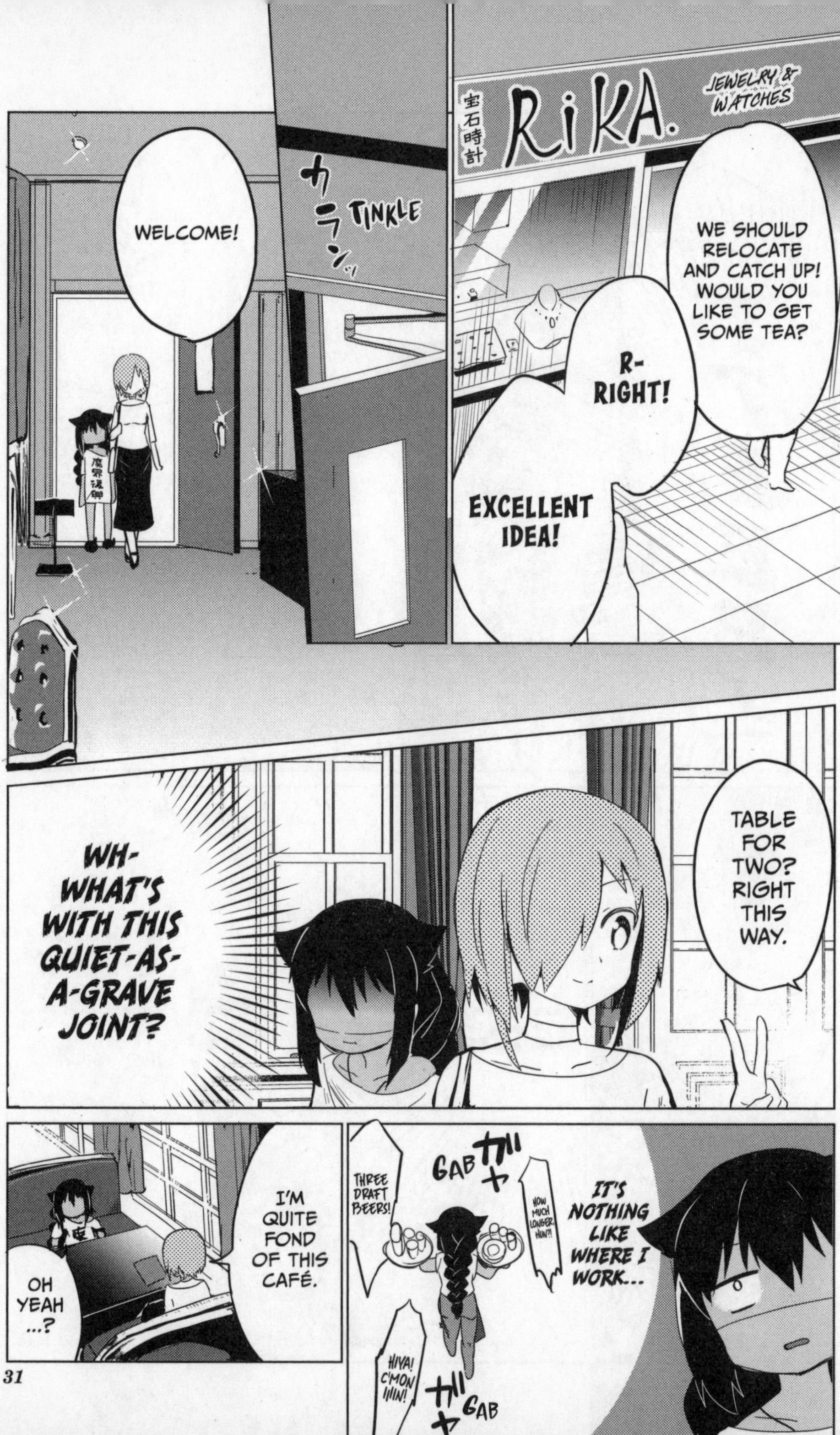

宝石時計
RiKA.
JEWELRY & WATCHES
WE SHOULD RELOCATE AND CATCH UP! WOULD YOU LIKE TO GET SOME TEA?
R-RIGHT!
EXCELLENT IDEA!
カラン
TINKLE
WELCOME!
TABLE FOR TWO? RIGHT THIS WAY.
WH-WHAT'S WITH THIS QUIET-AS-A-GRAVE JOINT?
IT'S NOTHING LIKE WHERE I WORK...
GAB
THREE DRAFT BEERS!
HOW MUCH LONGER HUN?!
HIYA! C'MON IIIIN!
GAB
I'M QUITE FOND OF THIS CAFÉ.
OH YEAH ...?

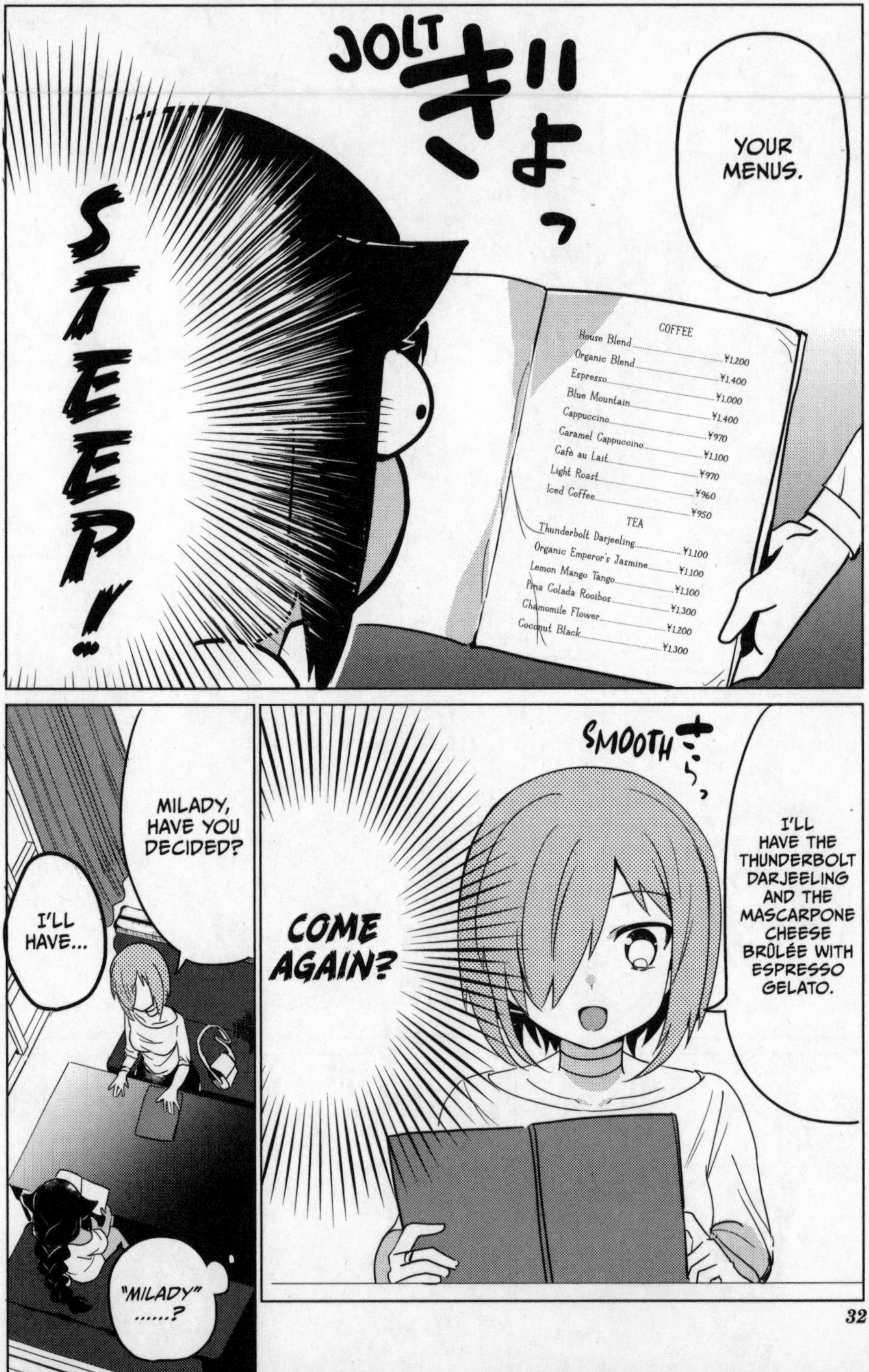
YOUR MENUS.
JOLT
ぎょっ
COFFEE
House Blend
Organic Blend ¥1,200
Espresso ¥1,400
Blue Mountain ¥1,000
Cappuccino ¥1,400
Caramel Cappuccino ¥970
Café au Lait ¥1,100
Light Roast ¥970
Iced Coffee ¥960
¥950
TEA
Thunderbolt Darjeeling ¥1,100
Organic Emperor's Jasmine ¥1,100
Lemon Mango Tango ¥1,100
Pina Colada Rooibos ¥1,300
Chamomile Flower ¥1,200
Coconut Black ¥1,300
STEEP!!
SMOOTH
さらっ
I'LL HAVE THE THUNDERBOLT DARJEELING AND THE MASCARPONE CHEESE BRÛLÉE WITH ESPRESSO GELATO.
COME AGAIN?
MILADY, HAVE YOU DECIDED?
I'LL HAVE...
"MILADY" ......?

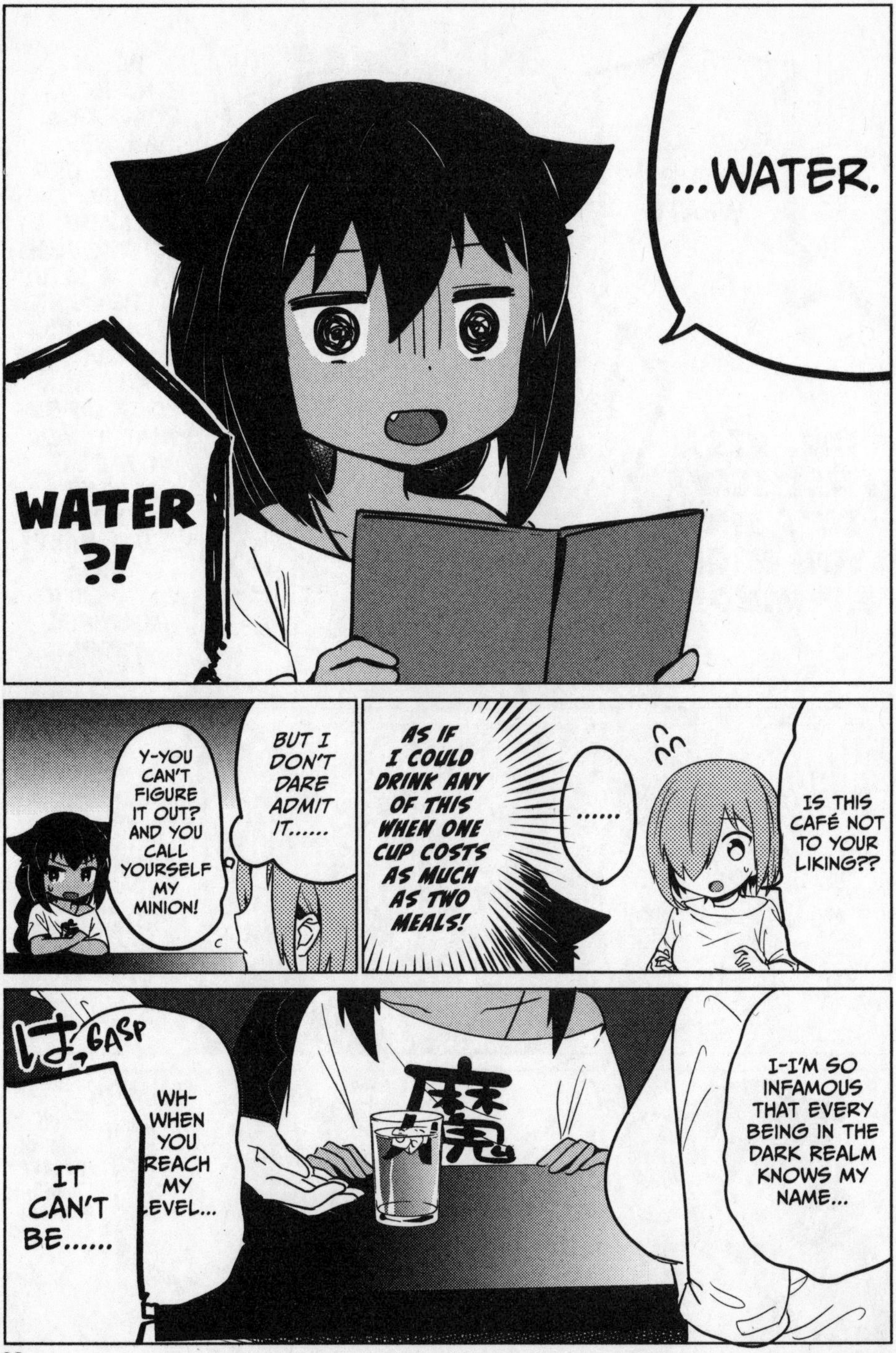
...WATER.
WATER ?!
IS THIS CAFÉ NOT TO YOUR LIKING??
......
AS IF I COULD DRINK ANY OF THIS WHEN ONE CUP COSTS AS MUCH AS TWO MEALS!
BUT I DON'T DARE ADMIT IT......
Y-YOU CAN'T FIGURE IT OUT? AND YOU CALL YOURSELF MY MINION!
I-I'M SO INFAMOUS THAT EVERY BEING IN THE DARK REALM KNOWS MY NAME...
魔
WH-WHEN YOU REACH MY LEVEL...
はっ GASP
IT CAN'T BE......

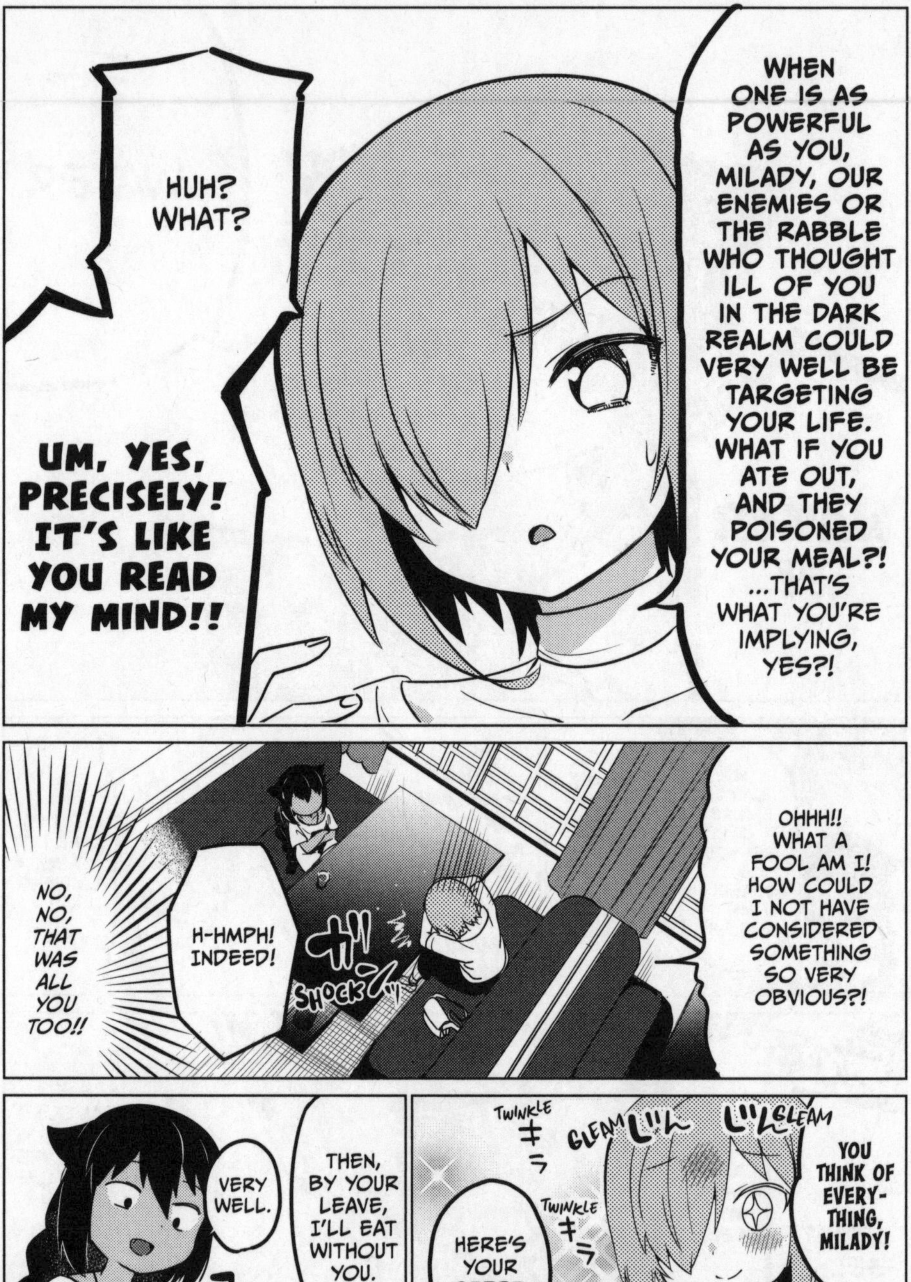
WHEN ONE IS AS POWERFUL AS YOU, MILADY, OUR ENEMIES OR THE RABBLE WHO THOUGHT ILL OF YOU IN THE DARK REALM COULD VERY WELL BE TARGETING YOUR LIFE. WHAT IF YOU ATE OUT, AND THEY POISONED YOUR MEAL?! ...THAT'S WHAT YOU'RE IMPLYING, YES?!
HUH? WHAT?
UM, YES, PRECISELY! IT'S LIKE YOU READ MY MIND!!
OHHH!! WHAT A FOOL AM I! HOW COULD I NOT HAVE CONSIDERED SOMETHING SO VERY OBVIOUS?!
SHOCK
H-HMPH! INDEED!
NO, NO, THAT WAS ALL YOU TOO!!
TWINKLE
GLEAM
GLEAM
TWINKLE
YOU THINK OF EVERY-THING, MILADY!
HERE'S YOUR ORDER.
THEN, BY YOUR LEAVE, I'LL EAT WITHOUT YOU.
VERY WELL.
CLINK

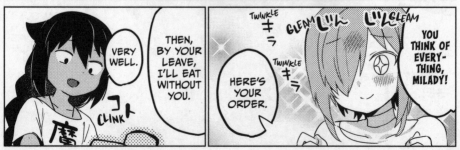

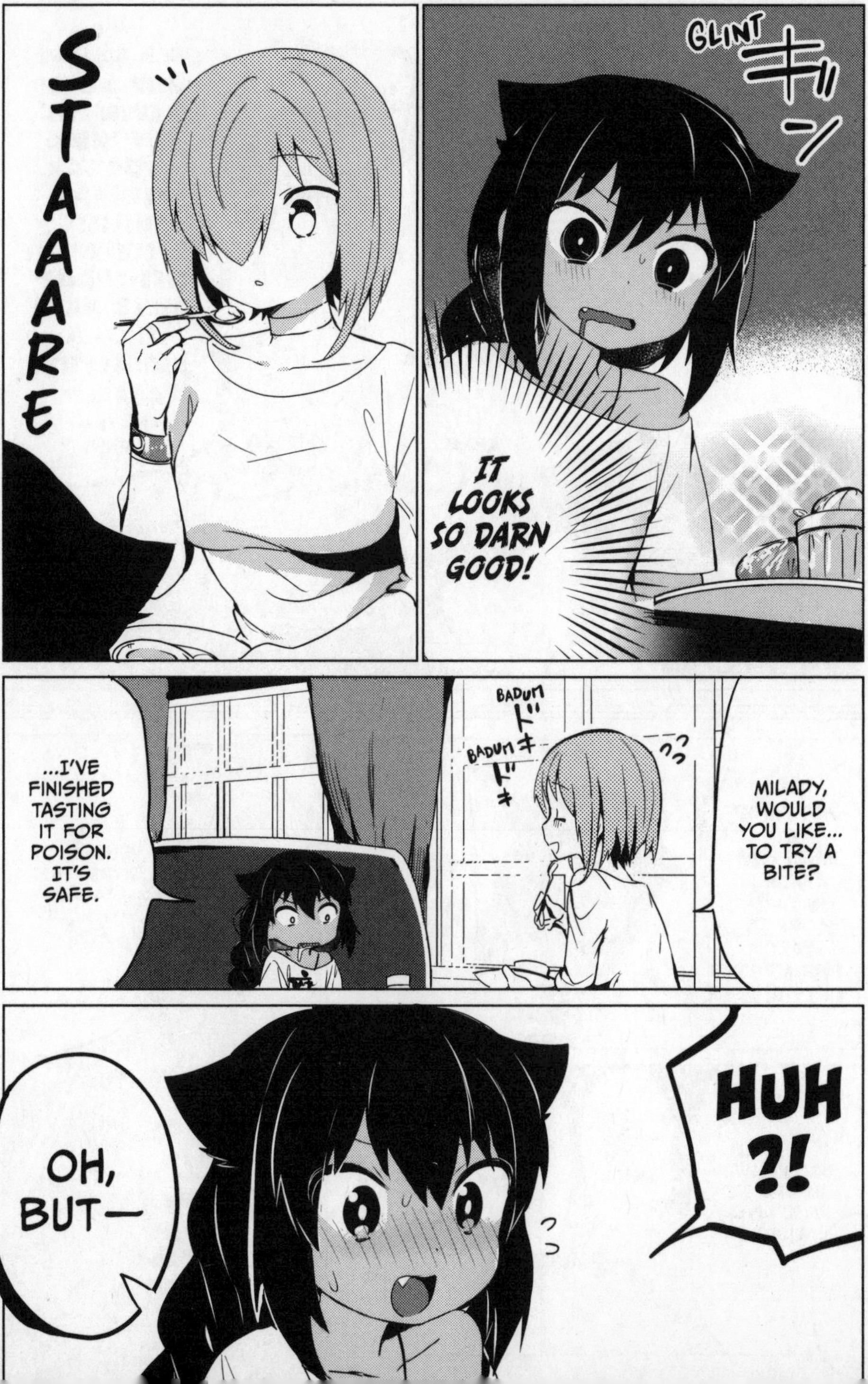
GLINT
ギン
IT LOOKS SO DARN GOOD!
STAAARE
MILADY, WOULD YOU LIKE... TO TRY A BITE?
BADUM ドキ
BADUM ドキ
...I'VE FINISHED TASTING IT FOR POISON. IT'S SAFE.
HUH ?!
OH, BUT—

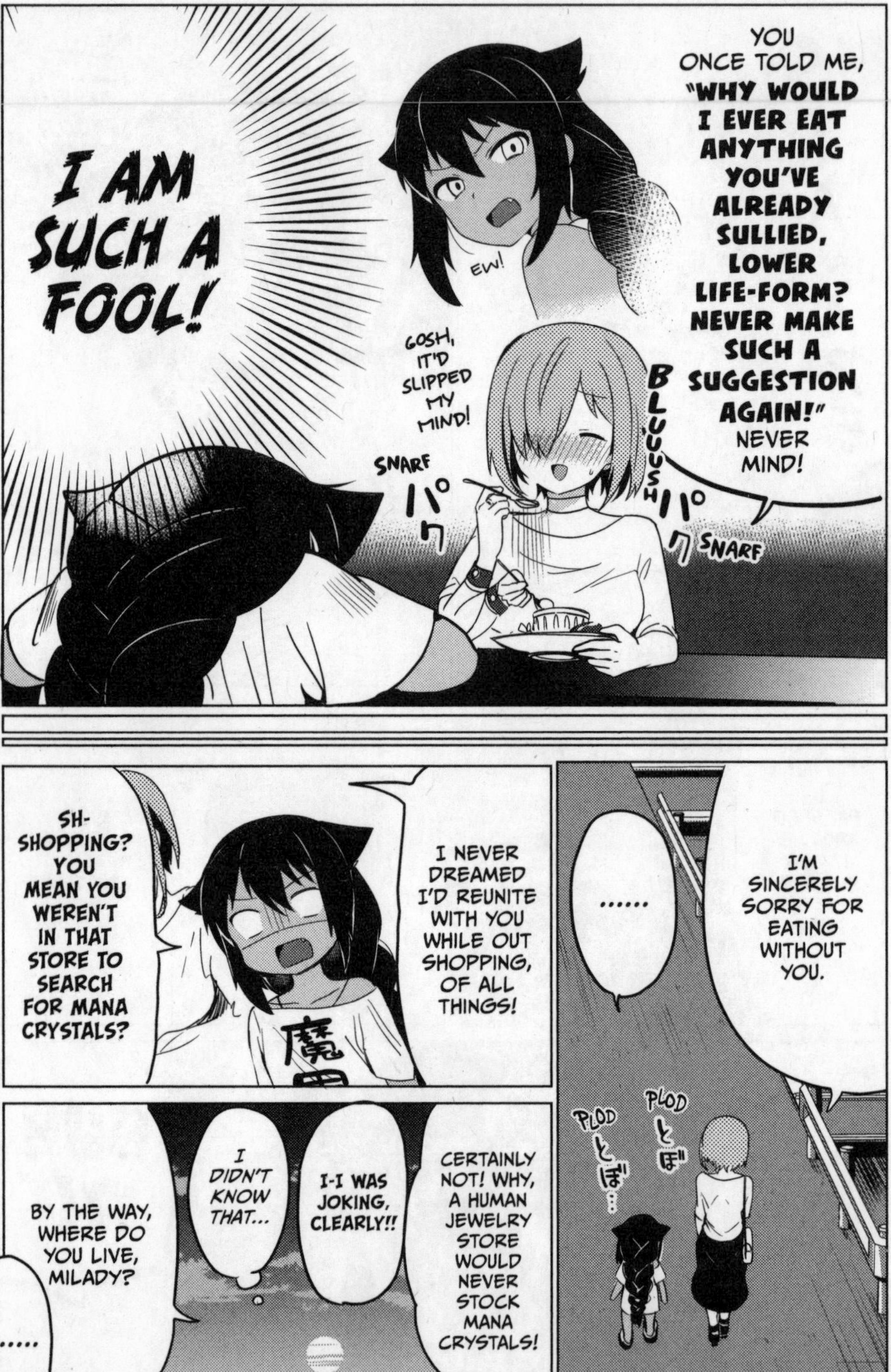
YOU ONCE TOLD ME, "WHY WOULD I EVER EAT ANYTHING YOU'VE ALREADY SULLIED, LOWER LIFE-FORM? NEVER MAKE SUCH A SUGGESTION AGAIN!"
EW!
I AM SUCH A FOOL!
NEVER MIND!
BLUUUSH
GOSH, IT'D SLIPPED MY MIND!
SNARF
パク
SNARF
パク
I'M SINCERELY SORRY FOR EATING WITHOUT YOU.
......
PLOD とぼ
PLOD とぼ…
I NEVER DREAMED I'D REUNITE WITH YOU WHILE OUT SHOPPING, OF ALL THINGS!
SH-SHOPPING? YOU MEAN YOU WEREN'T IN THAT STORE TO SEARCH FOR MANA CRYSTALS?
CERTAINLY NOT! WHY, A HUMAN JEWELRY STORE WOULD NEVER STOCK MANA CRYSTALS!
I-I WAS JOKING, CLEARLY!!
I DIDN'T KNOW THAT...
BY THE WAY, WHERE DO YOU LIVE, MILADY?
......

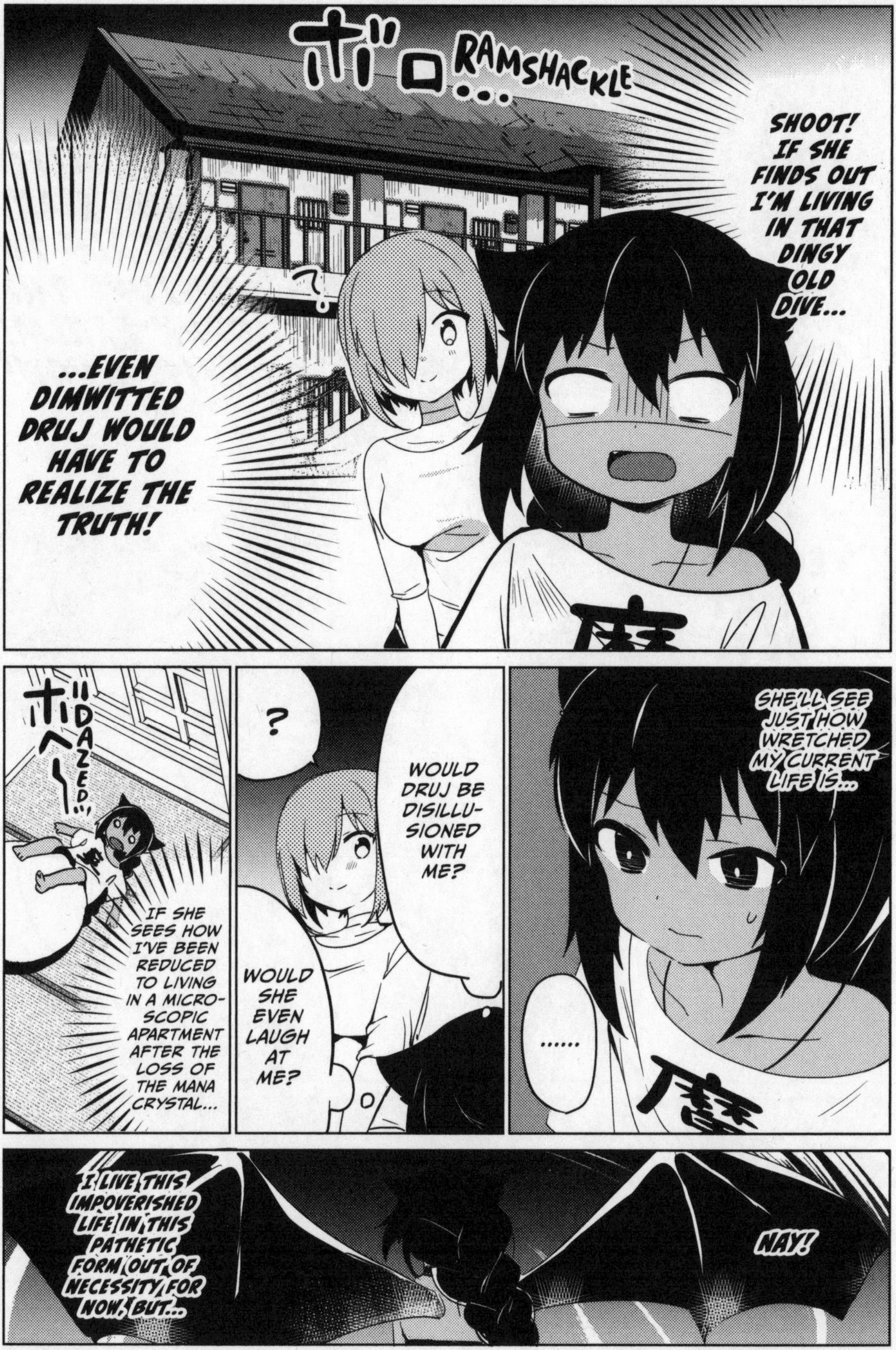
ボロ RAMSHACKLE...
SHOOT! IF SHE FINDS OUT I'M LIVING IN THAT DINGY OLD DIVE...
...EVEN DIMWITTED DRUJ WOULD HAVE TO REALIZE THE TRUTH!
SHE'LL SEE JUST HOW WRETCHED MY CURRENT LIFE IS...
......
?
WOULD DRUJ BE DISILLU-SIONED WITH ME?
WOULD SHE EVEN LAUGH AT ME?
DAZED...
IF SHE SEES HOW I'VE BEEN REDUCED TO LIVING IN A MICRO-SCOPIC APARTMENT AFTER THE LOSS OF THE MANA CRYSTAL...
NAY!
I LIVE THIS IMPOVERISHED LIFE IN THIS PATHETIC FORM OUT OF NECESSITY FOR NOW, BUT...

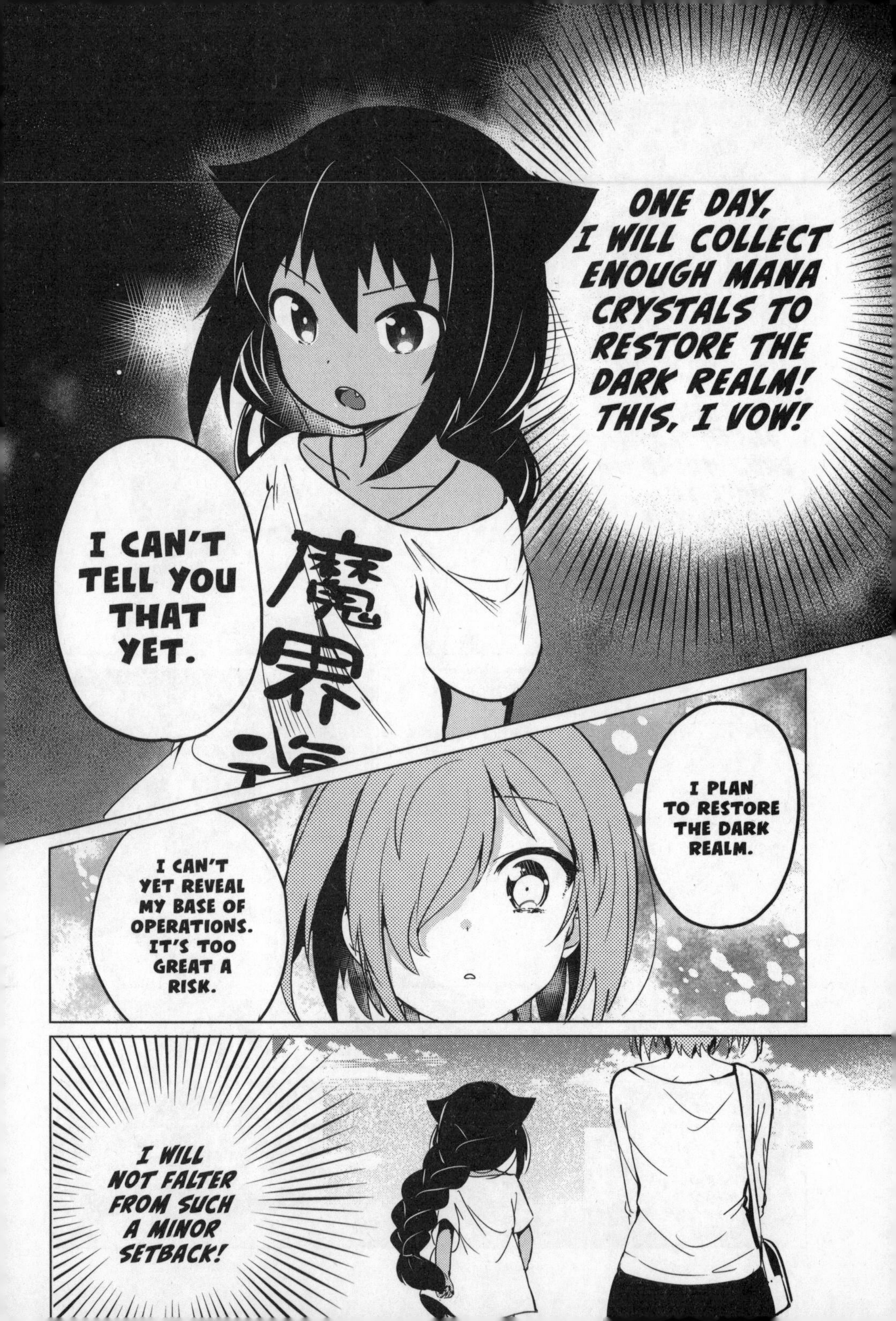
ONE DAY, I WILL COLLECT ENOUGH MANA CRYSTALS TO RESTORE THE DARK REALM! THIS, I VOW!
I CAN'T TELL YOU THAT YET.
魔界
I PLAN TO RESTORE THE DARK REALM.
I CAN'T YET REVEAL MY BASE OF OPERATIONS. IT'S TOO GREAT A RISK.
I WILL NOT FALTER FROM SUCH A MINOR SETBACK!

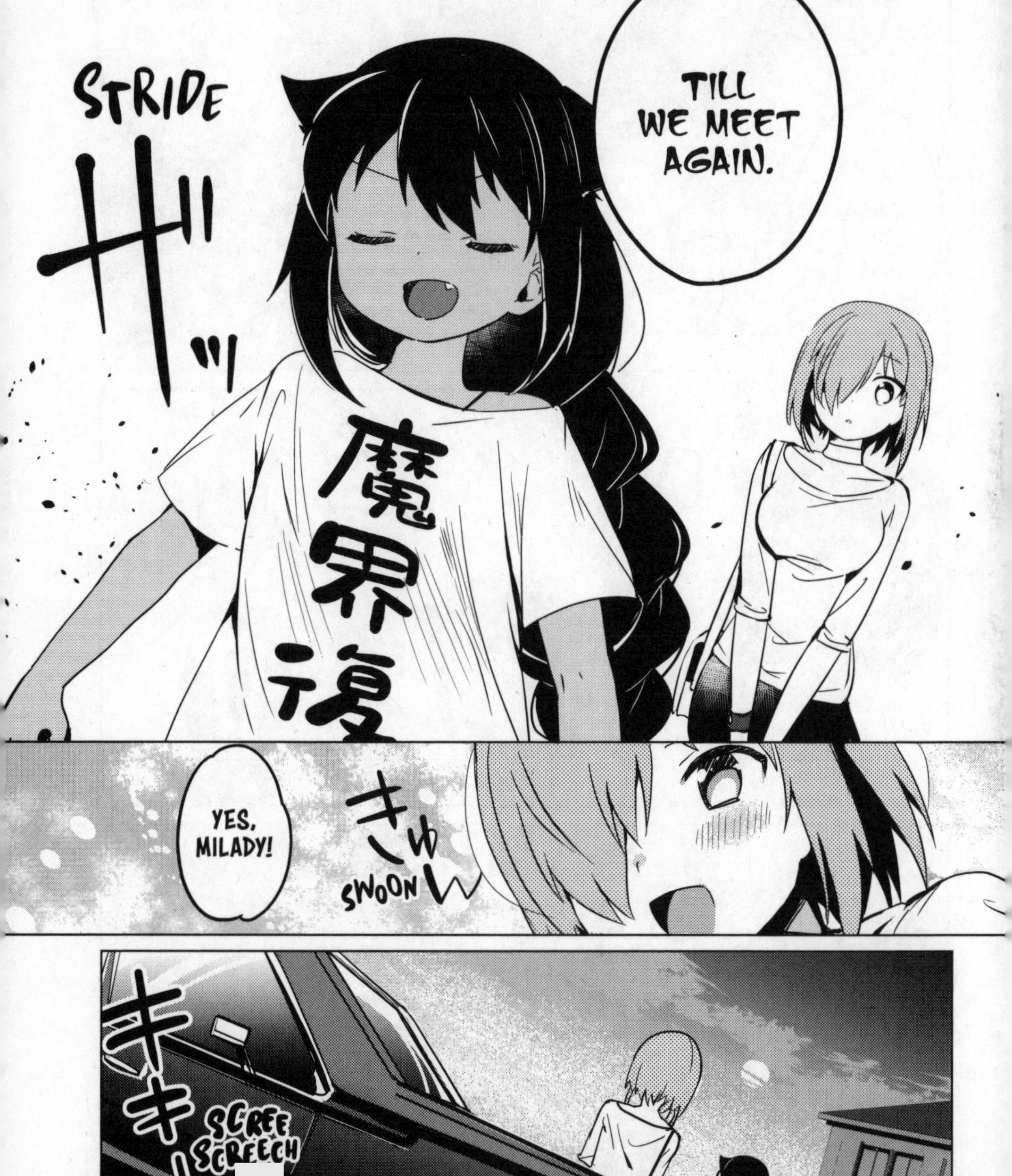

TILL WE MEET AGAIN.
STRIDE
ザッ
魔界復
きゅん
SWOON
YES, MILADY!
キキー
SCREE SCREECH

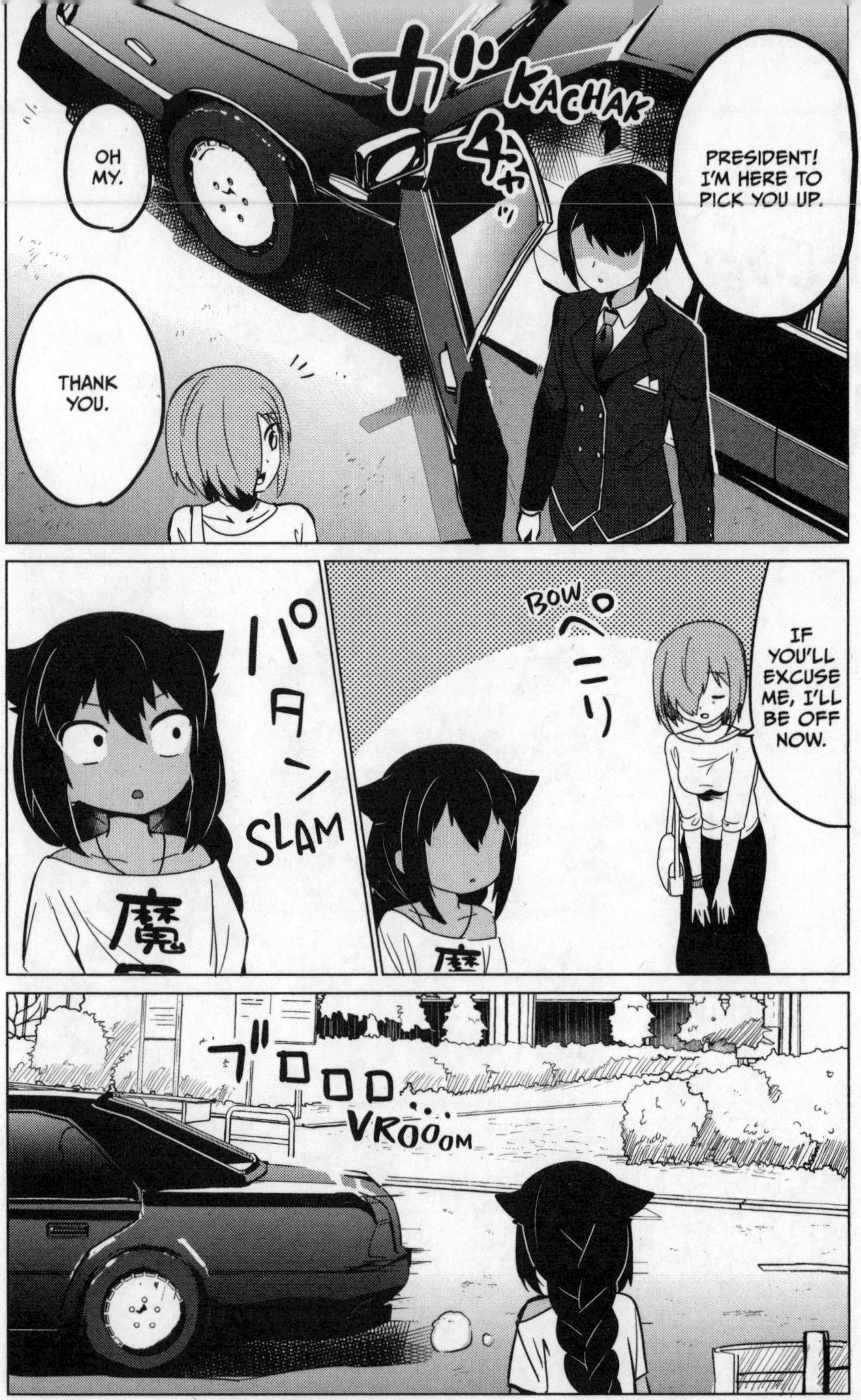
PRESIDENT! I'M HERE TO PICK YOU UP.
カチャッ
KACHAK
OH MY.
THANK YOU.
IF YOU'LL EXCUSE ME, I'LL BE OFF NOW.
ペこり
BOW
パタン
SLAM
ブロロロ...
VROOOM

LEFT IN THE DUST...

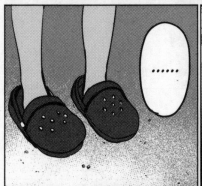

......

CAAAW! CAAAW!

......

CLENCH

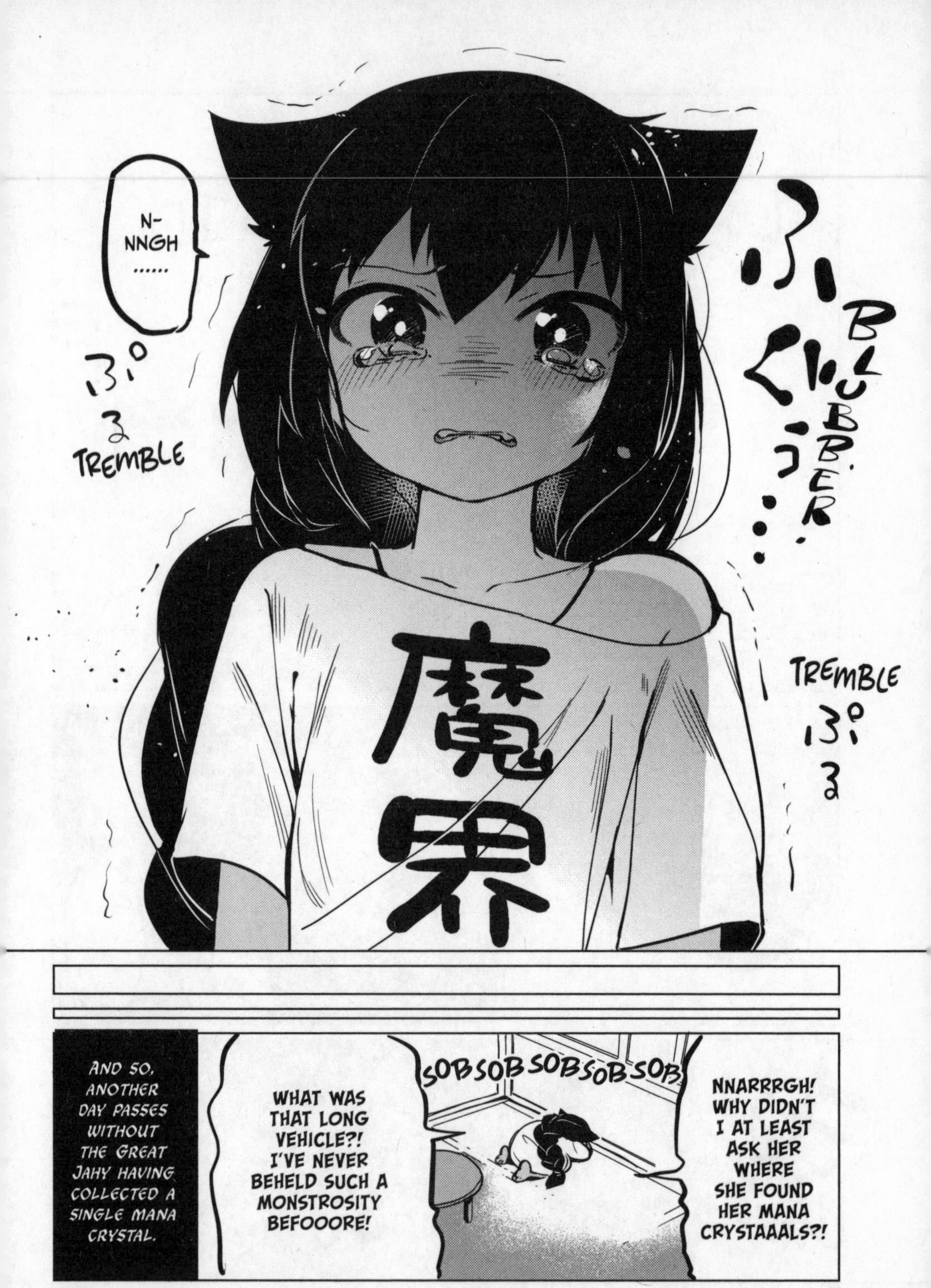

ふくっ...
BLUBBER
N-NNGH......
TREMBLE
ぷる
ぷる
TREMBLE
NNARRRGH! WHY DIDN'T I AT LEAST ASK HER WHERE SHE FOUND HER MANA CRYSTAAALS?!
SOB SOB SOB SOB SOB
WHAT WAS THAT LONG VEHICLE?! I'VE NEVER BEHELD SUCH A MONSTROSITY BEFOOORE!
AND SO, ANOTHER DAY PASSES WITHOUT THE GREAT JAHY HAVING COLLECTED A SINGLE MANA CRYSTAL.

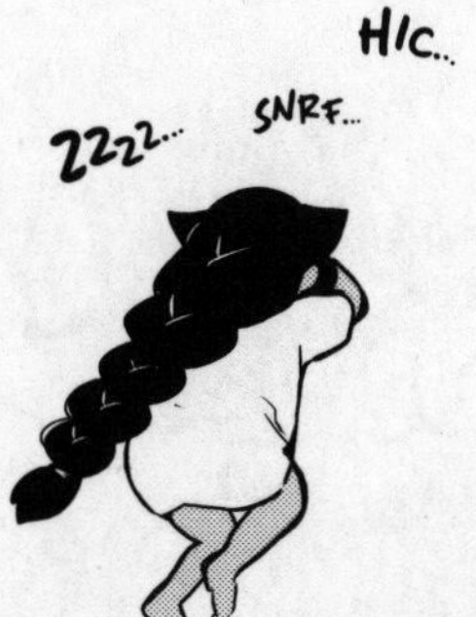
HIC...
SNRF...
ZZZZ...

The GREAT JAHY Will NOT Be DEFEATED!

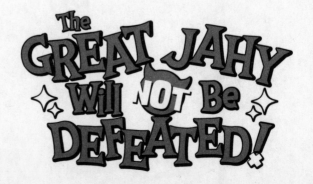

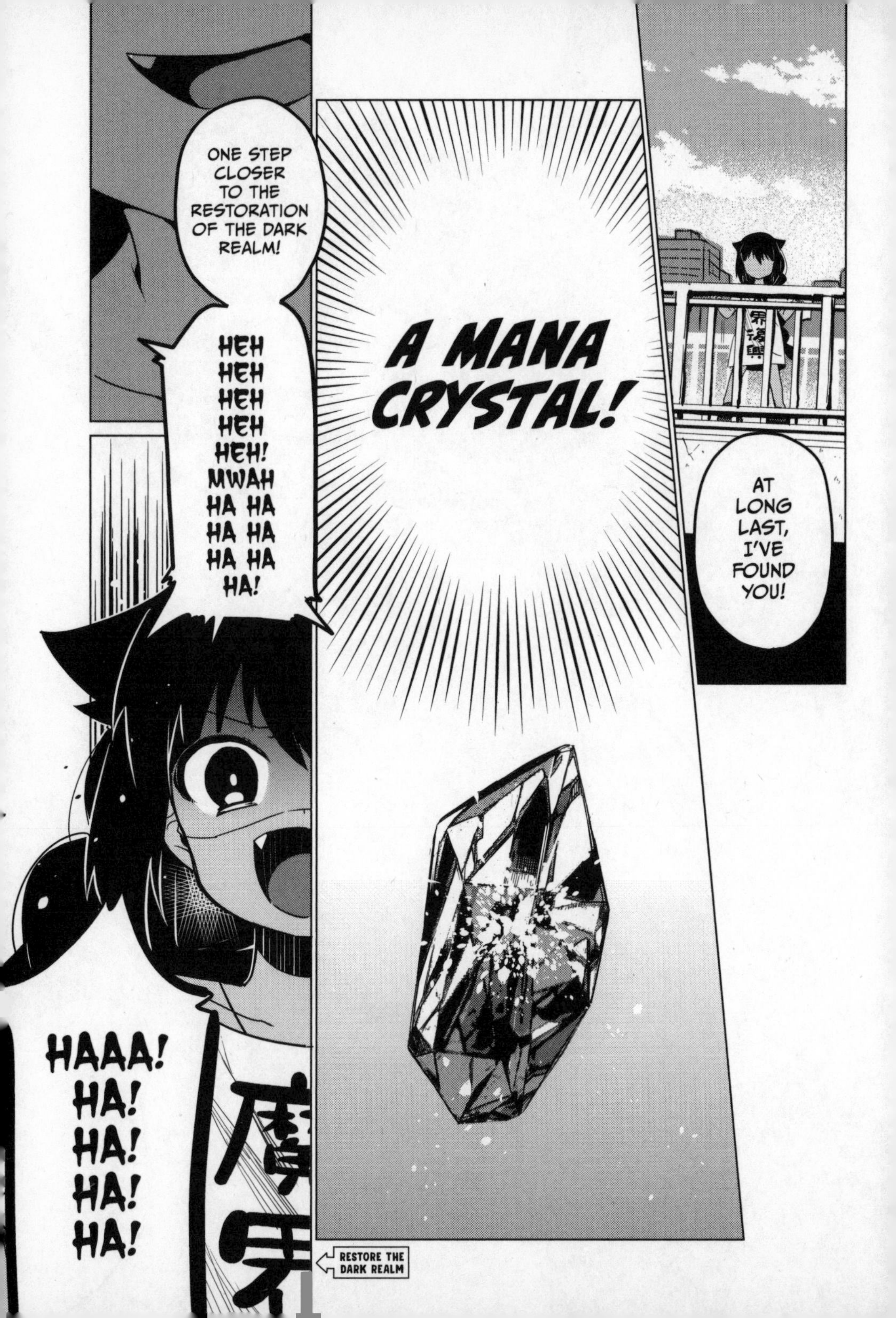
AT LONG LAST, I'VE FOUND YOU!
A MANA CRYSTAL!
ONE STEP CLOSER TO THE RESTORATION OF THE DARK REALM!
HEH HEH HEH HEH HEH! MWAH HA HA HA HA HA HA HA!
HAAA! HA! HA! HA! HA!
RESTORE THE DARK REALM

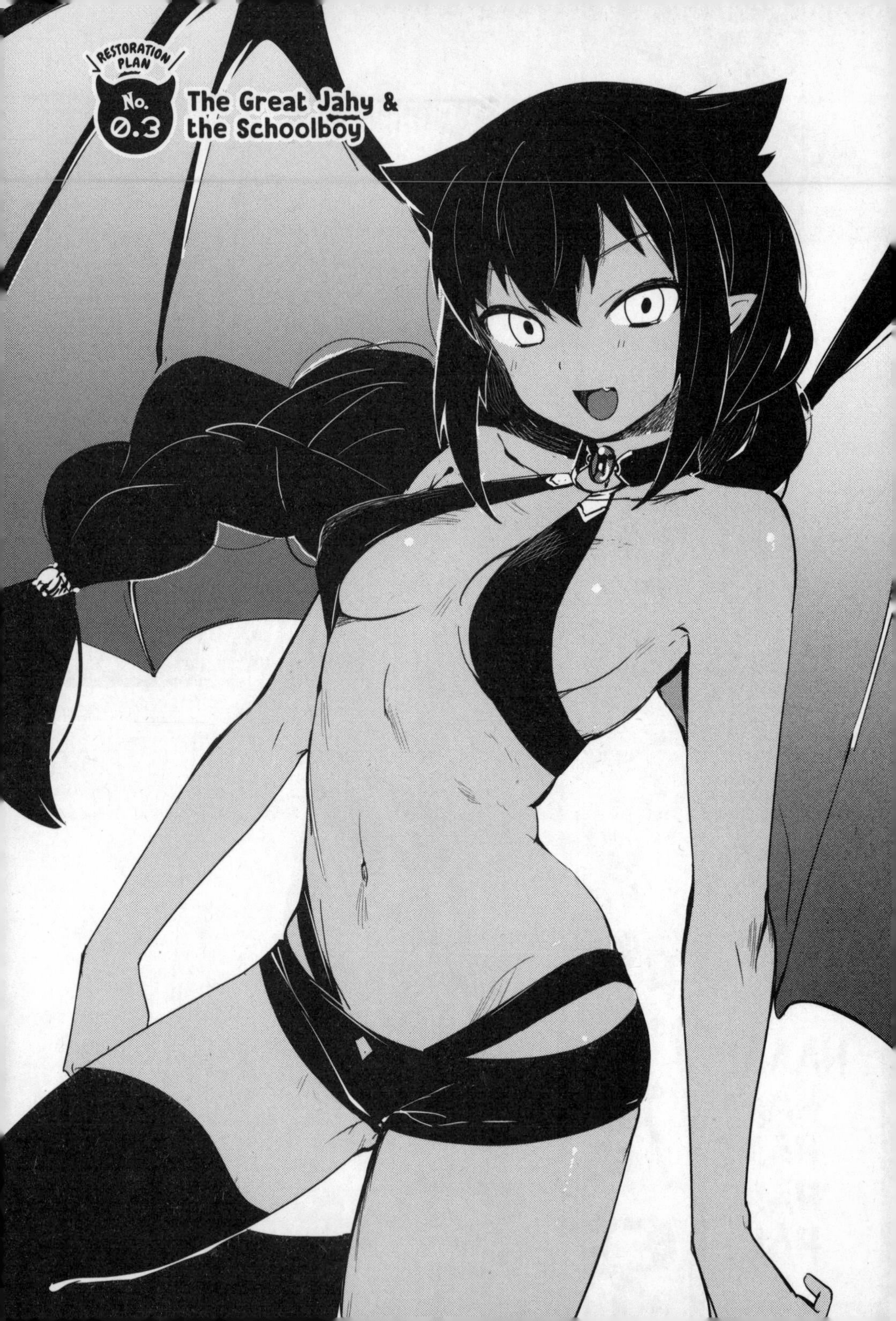
RESTORATION PLAN
No. 0.3
The Great Jahy & the Schoolboy

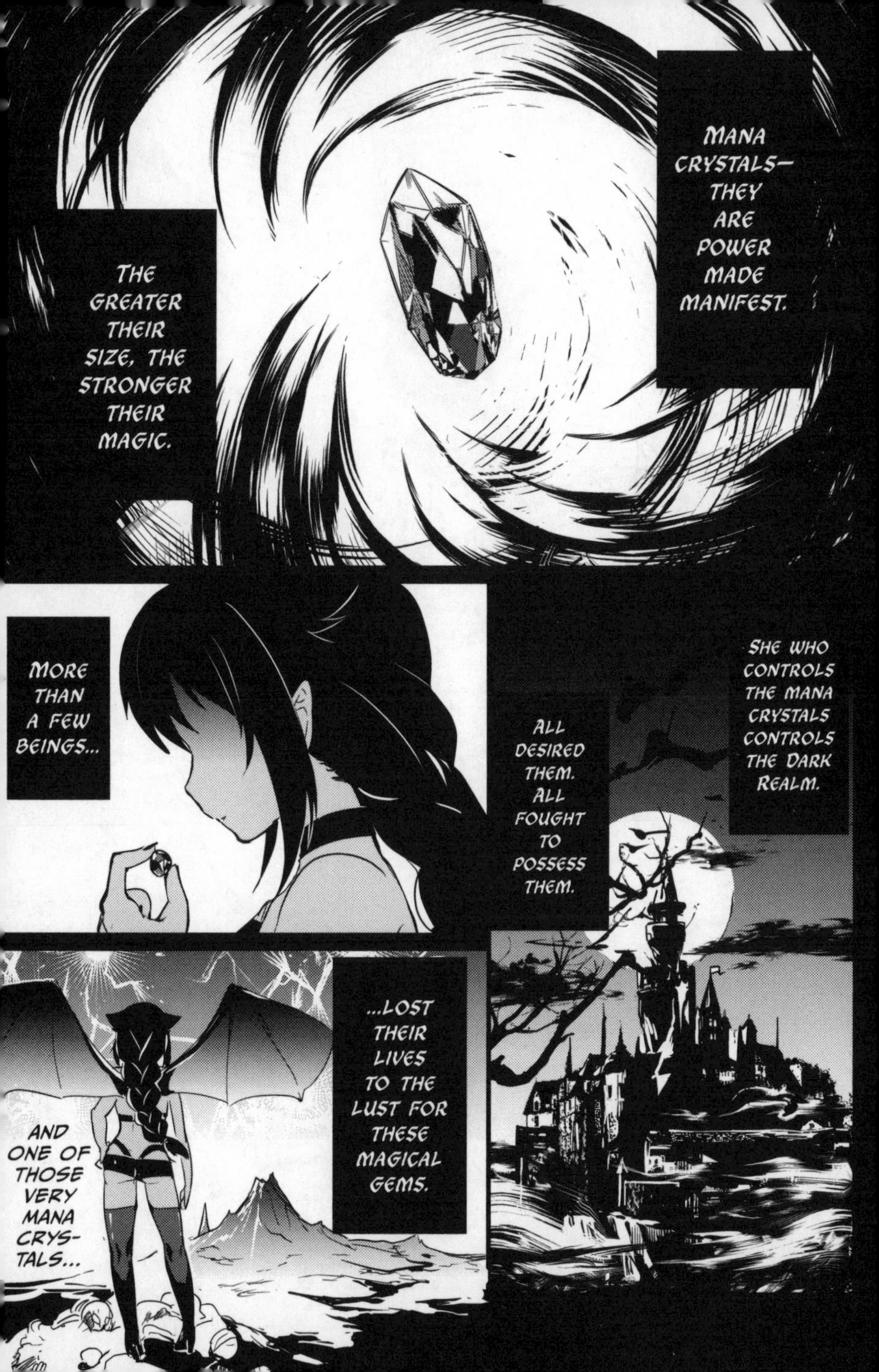
MANA CRYSTALS—THEY ARE POWER MADE MANIFEST.
THE GREATER THEIR SIZE, THE STRONGER THEIR MAGIC.
SHE WHO CONTROLS THE MANA CRYSTALS CONTROLS THE DARK REALM.
ALL DESIRED THEM. ALL FOUGHT TO POSSESS THEM.
MORE THAN A FEW BEINGS...
...LOST THEIR LIVES TO THE LUST FOR THESE MAGICAL GEMS.
AND ONE OF THOSE VERY MANA CRYS-TALS...

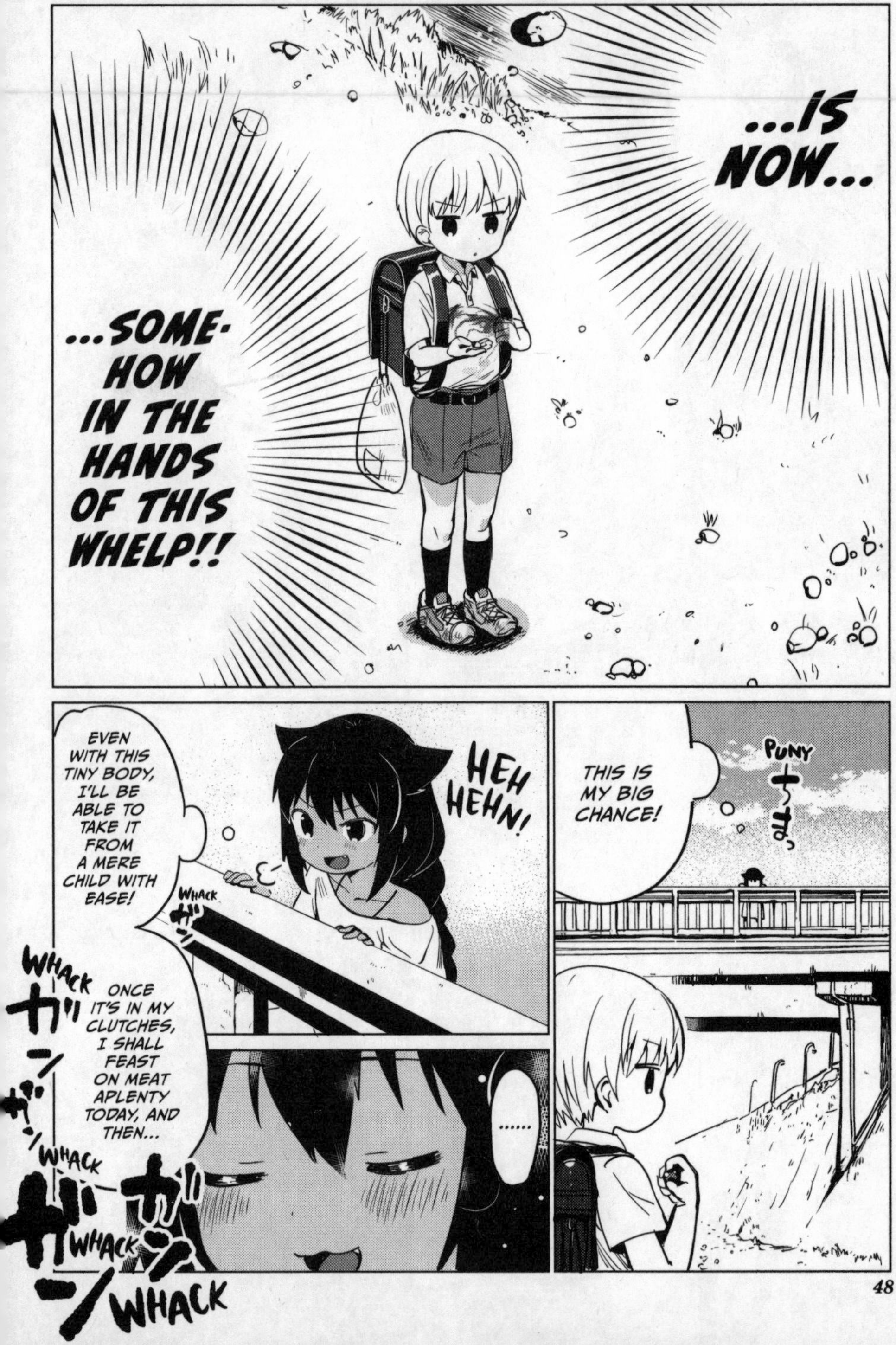
...IS NOW...
...SOME-HOW IN THE HANDS OF THIS WHELP!!
PUNY
THIS IS MY BIG CHANCE!
EVEN WITH THIS TINY BODY, I'LL BE ABLE TO TAKE IT FROM A MERE CHILD WITH EASE!
HEH HEHN!
WHACK
ONCE IT'S IN MY CLUTCHES, I SHALL FEAST ON MEAT APLENTY TODAY, AND THEN...
......
WHACK
WHACK
WHACK
WHACK

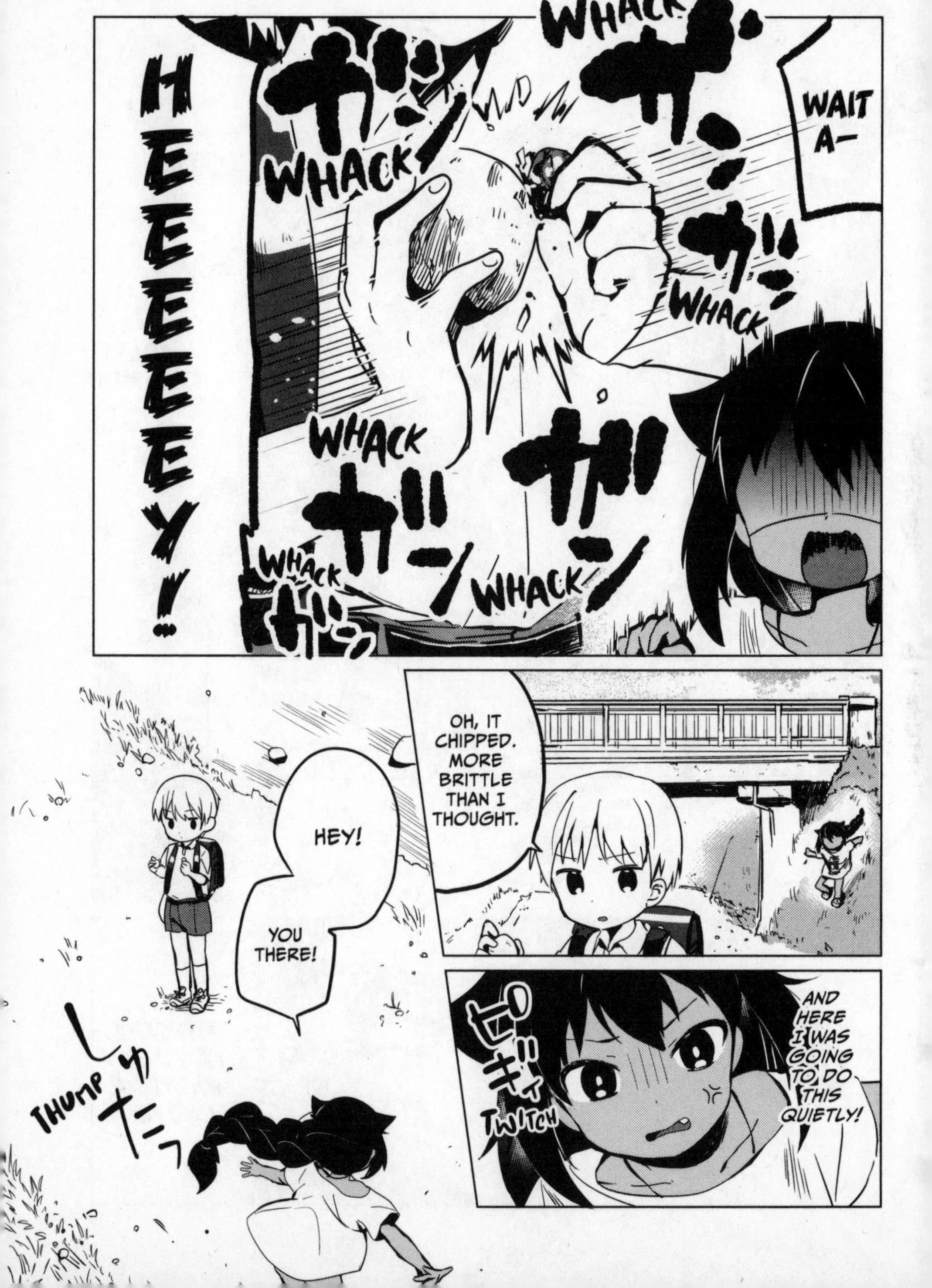
WAIT A—
WHACK
WHACK
WHACK
WHACK
WHACK
WHACK
HEEEEEEEY!!
OH, IT CHIPPED. MORE BRITTLE THAN I THOUGHT.
TWITCH
AND HERE I WAS GOING TO DO THIS QUIETLY!
HEY!
YOU THERE!
THUMP

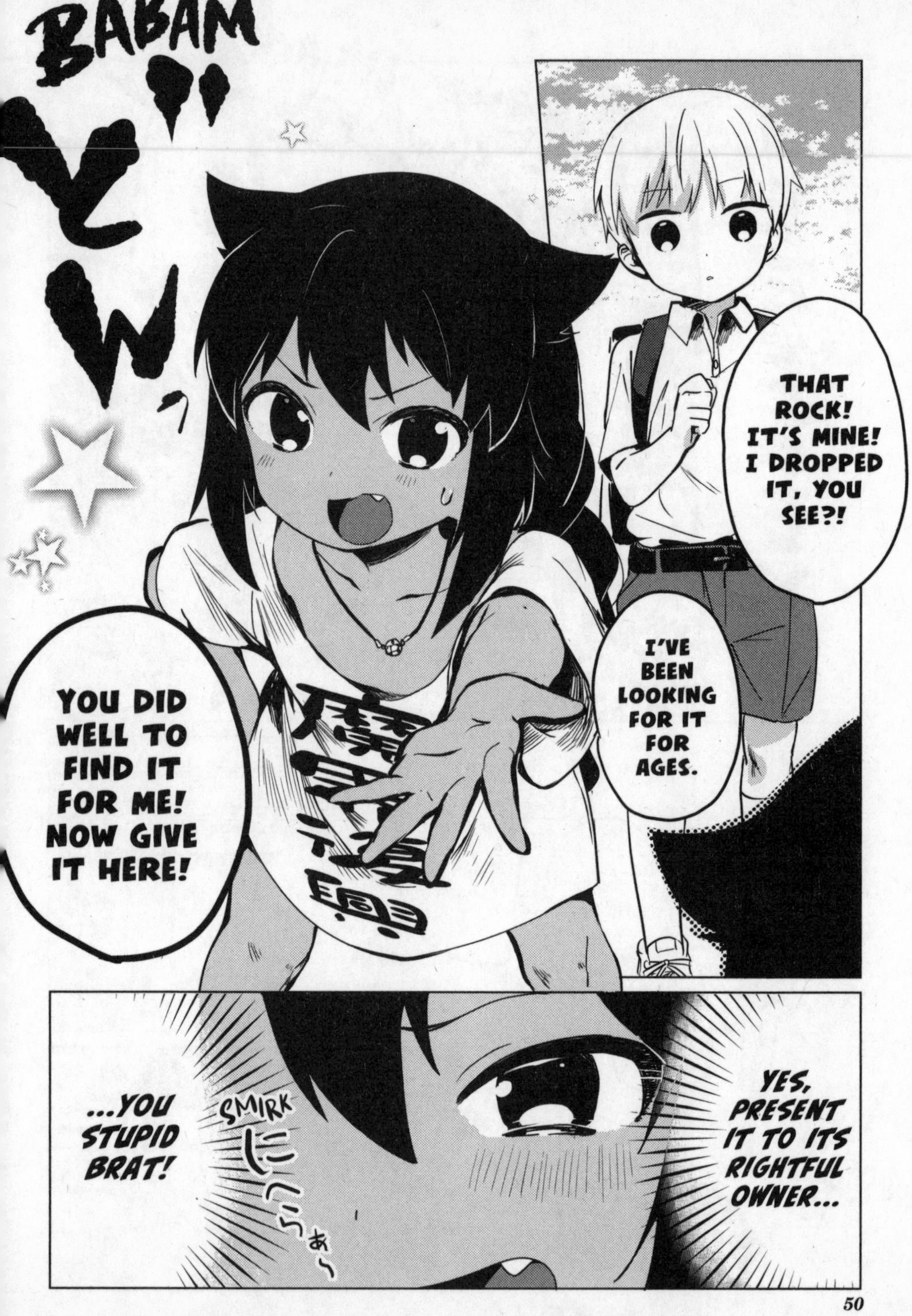
BABAM
THAT ROCK! IT'S MINE! I DROPPED IT, YOU SEE?!
I'VE BEEN LOOKING FOR IT FOR AGES.
YOU DID WELL TO FIND IT FOR ME! NOW GIVE IT HERE!
YES, PRESENT IT TO ITS RIGHTFUL OWNER...
SMIRK
...YOU STUPID BRAT!

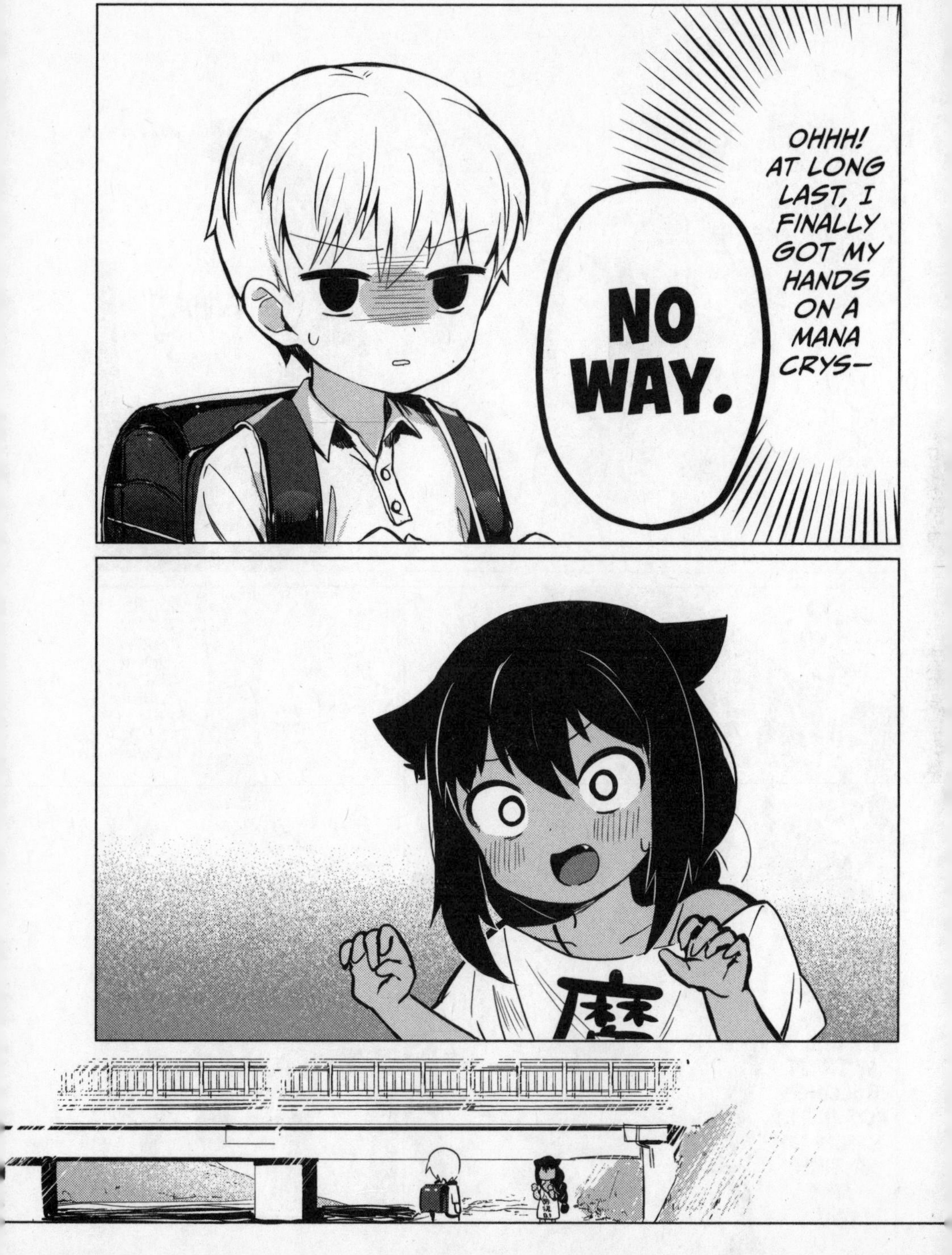
OHHH! AT LONG LAST, I FINALLY GOT MY HANDS ON A MANA CRYS—
NO WAY.

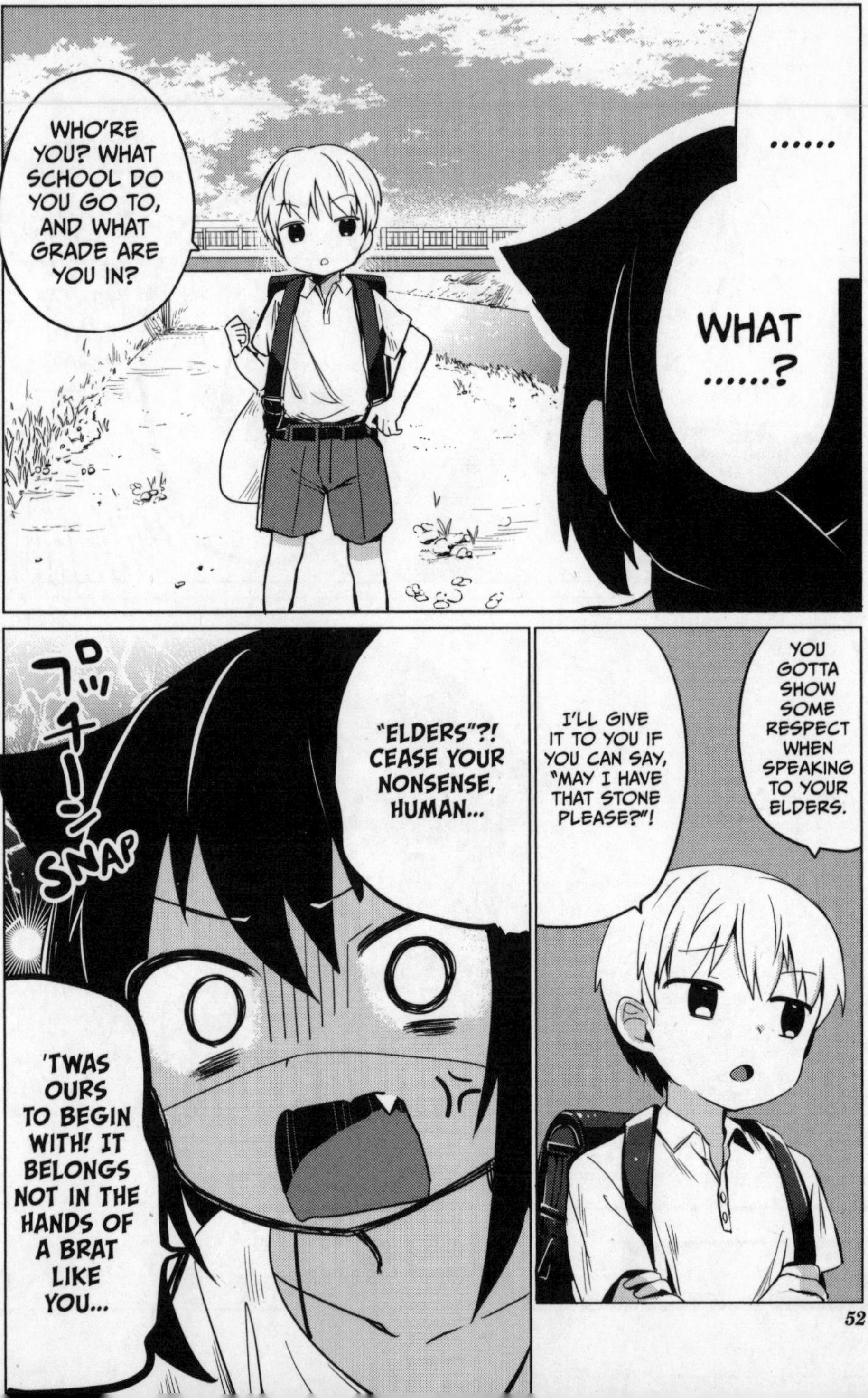
......
WHAT ......?
WHO'RE YOU? WHAT SCHOOL DO YOU GO TO, AND WHAT GRADE ARE YOU IN?
YOU GOTTA SHOW SOME RESPECT WHEN SPEAKING TO YOUR ELDERS.
I'LL GIVE IT TO YOU IF YOU CAN SAY, "MAY I HAVE THAT STONE PLEASE?"!
"ELDERS"?! CEASE YOUR NONSENSE, HUMAN...
SNAP
'TWAS OURS TO BEGIN WITH! IT BELONGS NOT IN THE HANDS OF A BRAT LIKE YOU...

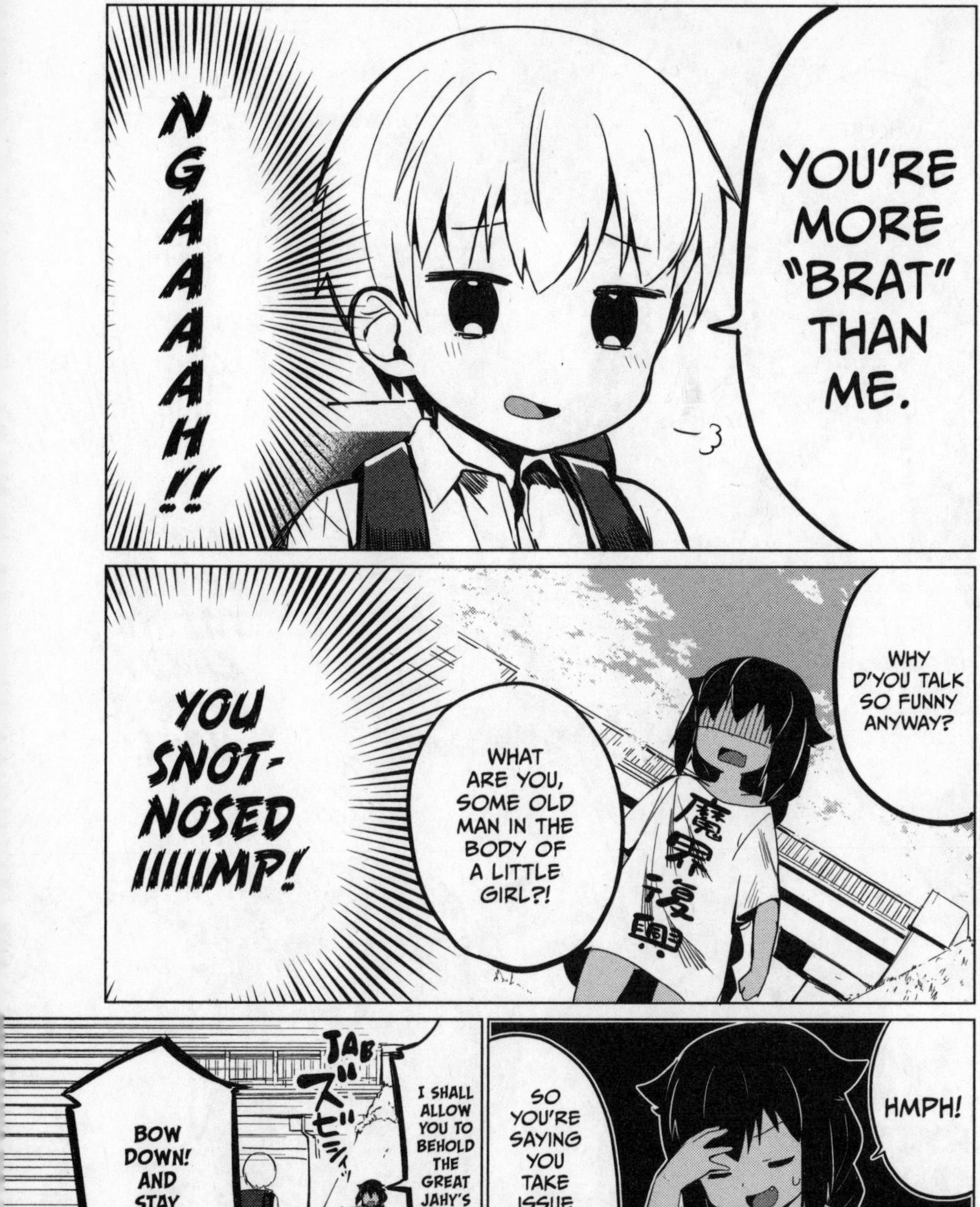
YOU'RE MORE "BRAT" THAN ME.
NGAAAAAH!!
WHY D'YOU TALK SO FUNNY ANYWAY?
WHAT ARE YOU, SOME OLD MAN IN THE BODY OF A LITTLE GIRL?!
YOU SNOT-NOSED IIIIIMP!
魔界復興
HMPH!
SO YOU'RE SAYING YOU TAKE ISSUE WITH MY FORM, HMM?
I SHALL ALLOW YOU TO BEHOLD THE GREAT JAHY'S TRUE FORM!
JAB
ズビシッ
BOW DOWN! AND STAY RIGHT THERE!

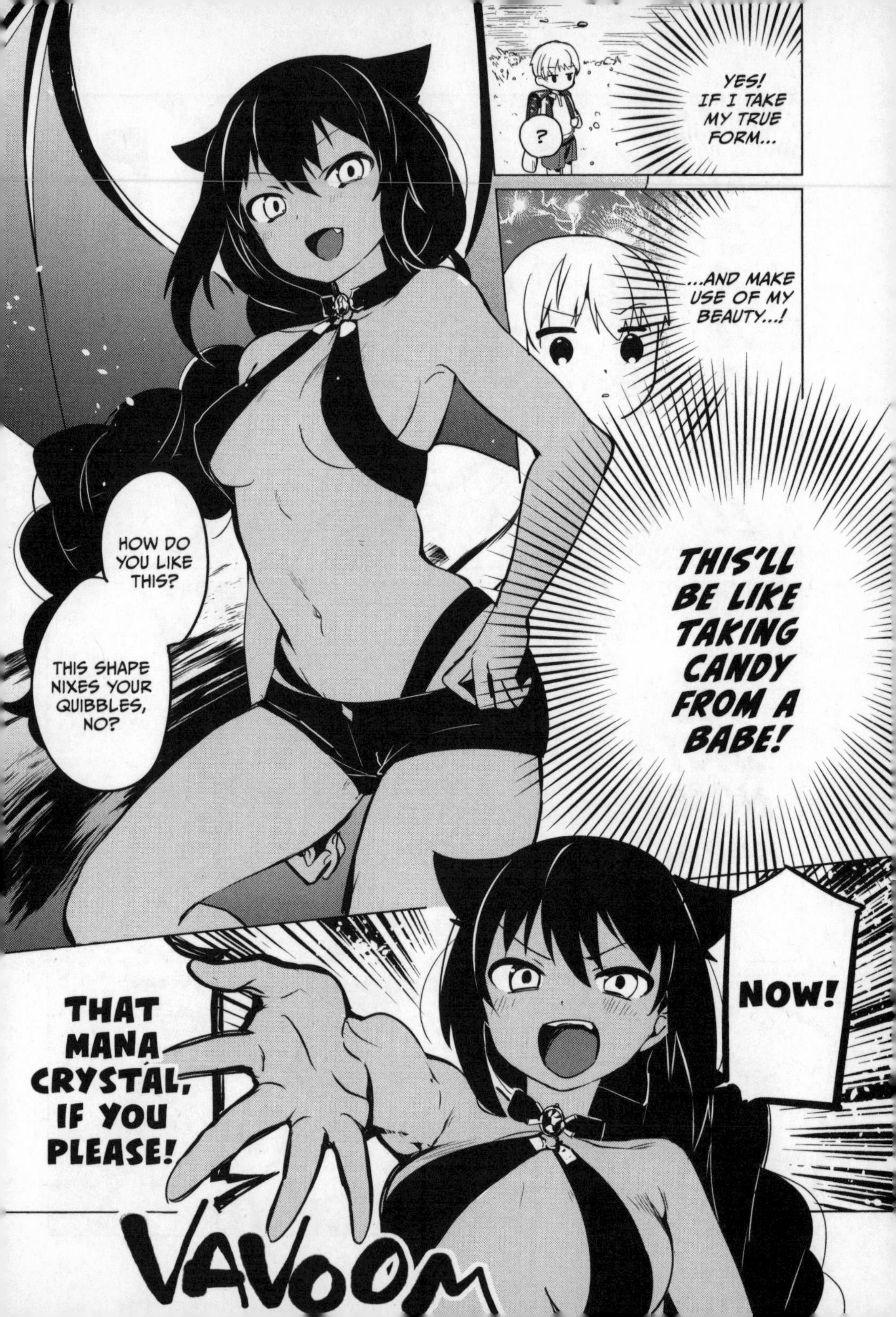
YES! IF I TAKE MY TRUE FORM...
?
...AND MAKE USE OF MY BEAUTY...!
THIS'LL BE LIKE TAKING CANDY FROM A BABE!
HOW DO YOU LIKE THIS?
THIS SHAPE NIXES YOUR QUIBBLES, NO?
NOW!
THAT MANA CRYSTAL, IF YOU PLEASE!
VAVOOM

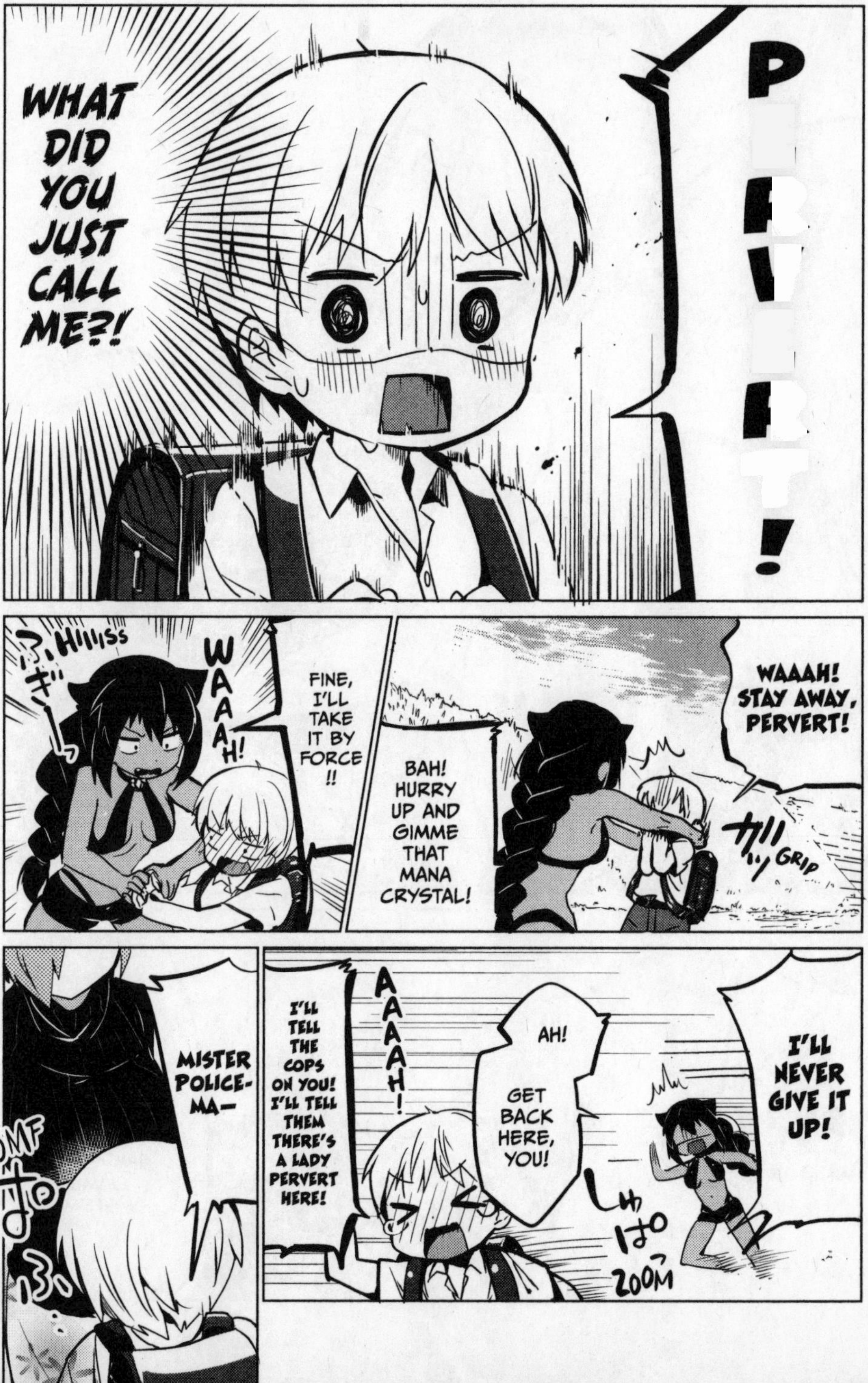
WHAT DID YOU JUST CALL ME?!
WAAAH! STAY AWAY, PERVERT!
ガリッ GRIP
BAH! HURRY UP AND GIMME THAT MANA CRYSTAL!
FINE, I'LL TAKE IT BY FORCE !!
WAAAAH!
ふぎーっ HIIISS
I'LL NEVER GIVE IT UP!
AH!
GET BACK HERE, YOU!
しゅぱっ ZOOM
AAAAH!
I'LL TELL THE COPS ON YOU! I'LL TELL THEM THERE'S A LADY PERVERT HERE!
MISTER POLICE-MA—
ぽふ POOMF

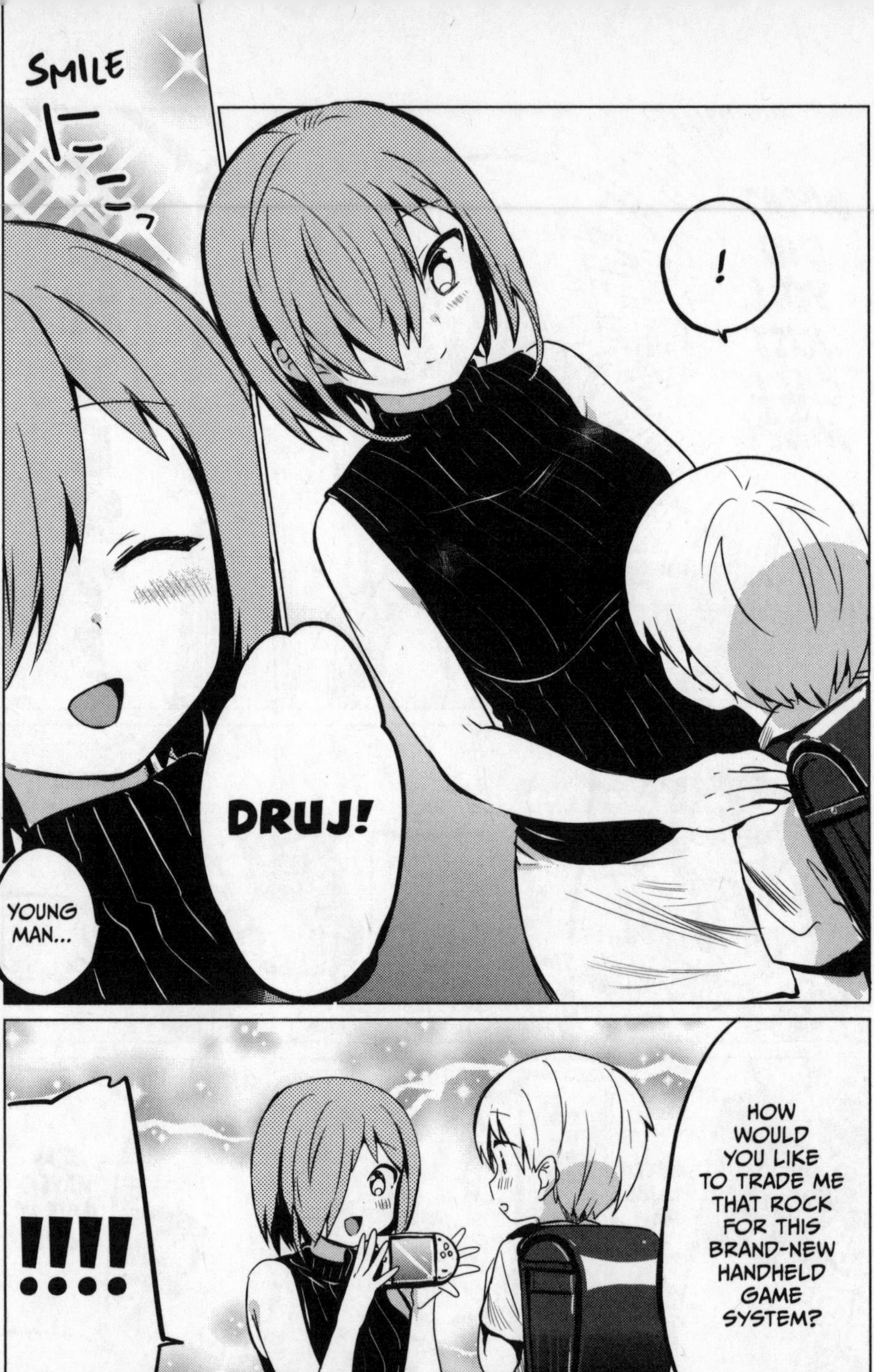
!
SMILE
DRUJ!
YOUNG MAN...
HOW WOULD YOU LIKE TO TRADE ME THAT ROCK FOR THIS BRAND-NEW HANDHELD GAME SYSTEM?
!!!!

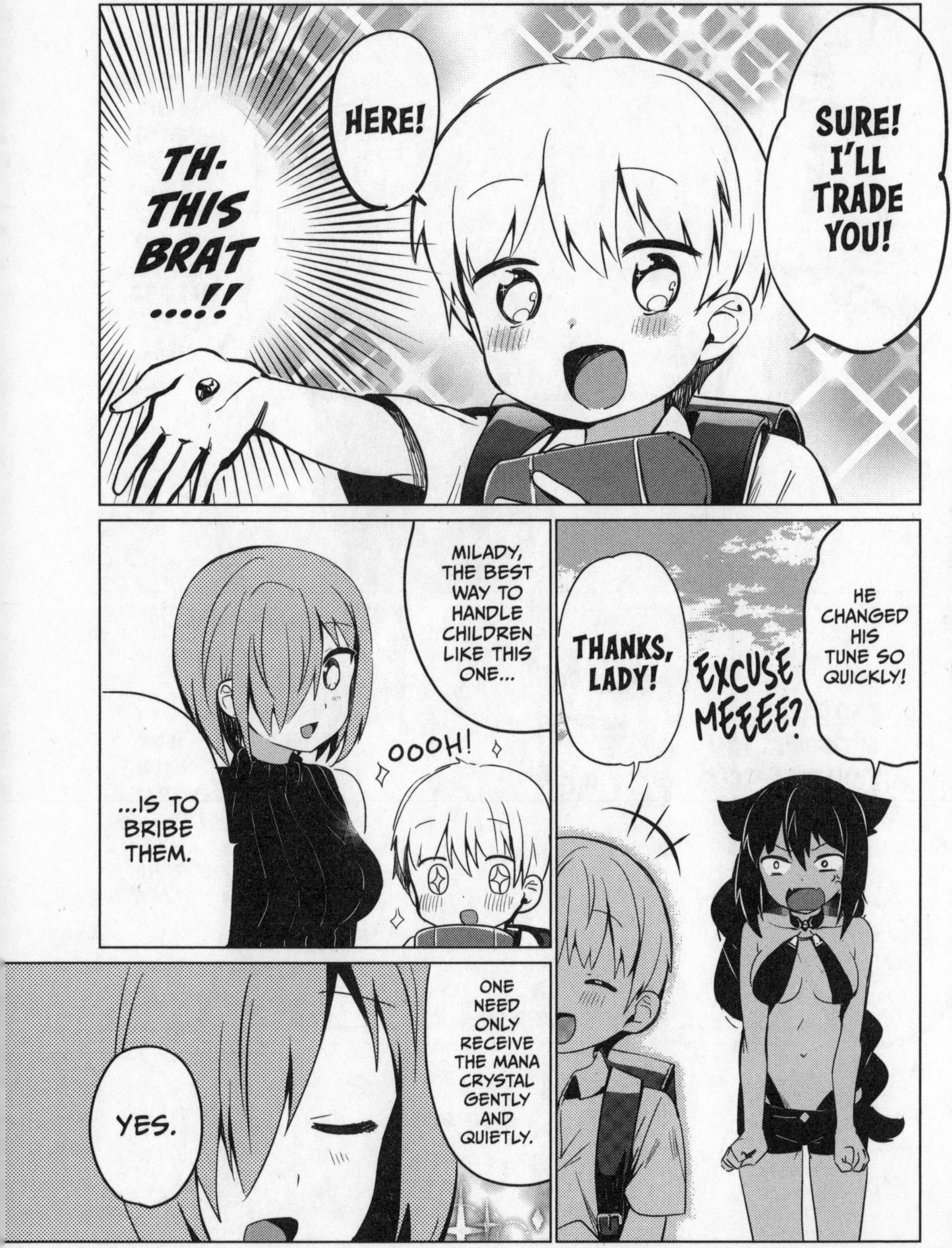
SURE! I'LL TRADE YOU!
HERE!
TH-THIS BRAT ...!!
HE CHANGED HIS TUNE SO QUICKLY!
EXCUSE MEEEE?
THANKS, LADY!
MILADY, THE BEST WAY TO HANDLE CHILDREN LIKE THIS ONE...
OOOH!
...IS TO BRIBE THEM.
ONE NEED ONLY RECEIVE THE MANA CRYSTAL GENTLY AND QUIETLY.
YES.

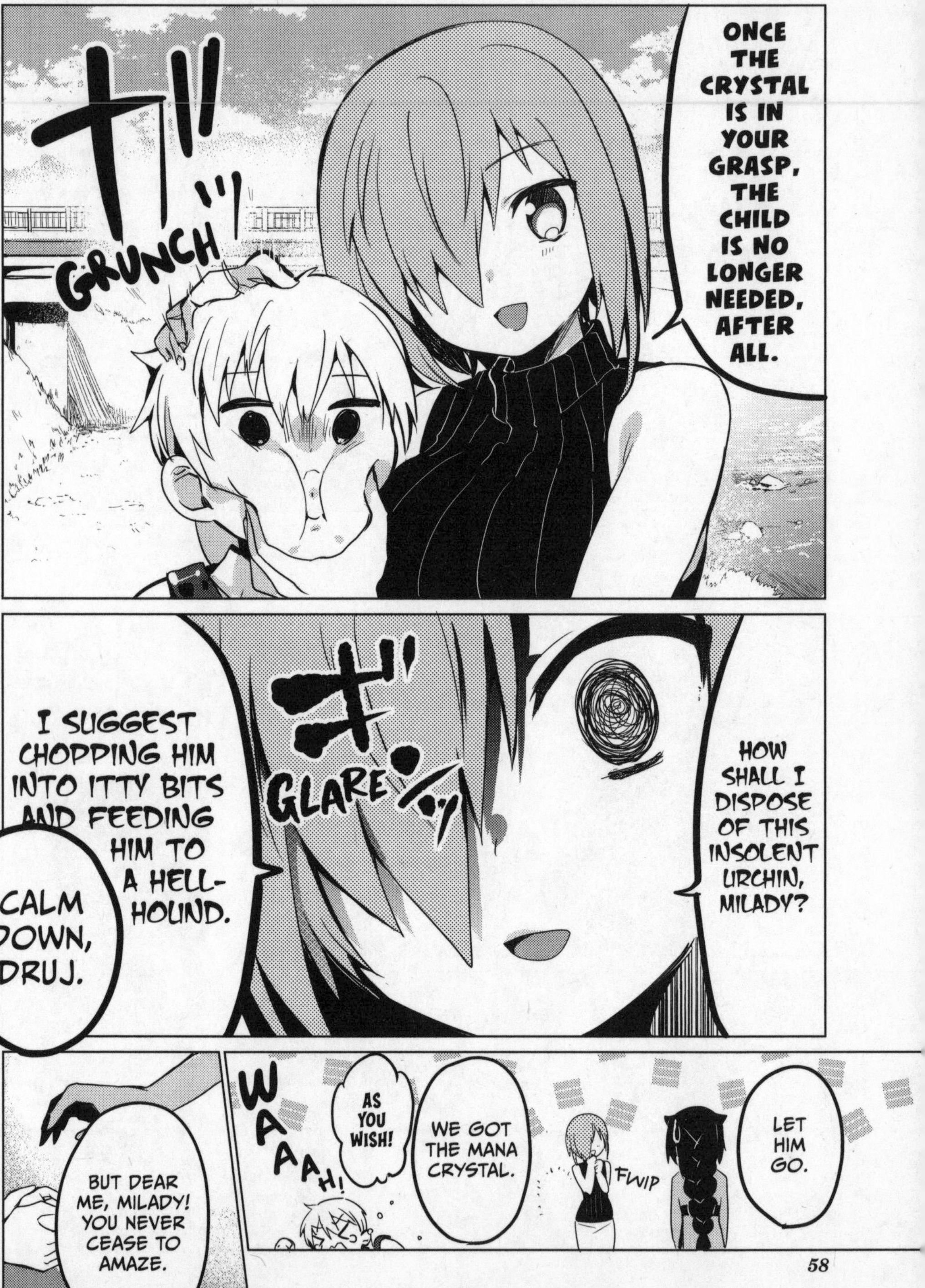
ONCE THE CRYSTAL IS IN YOUR GRASP, THE CHILD IS NO LONGER NEEDED, AFTER ALL.
GRUNCH
HOW SHALL I DISPOSE OF THIS INSOLENT URCHIN, MILADY?
GLARE
I SUGGEST CHOPPING HIM INTO ITTY BITS AND FEEDING HIM TO A HELL-HOUND.
CALM DOWN, DRUJ.
LET HIM GO.
FWIP
WE GOT THE MANA CRYSTAL.
AS YOU WISH!
WAAAAH!
BUT DEAR ME, MILADY! YOU NEVER CEASE TO AMAZE.

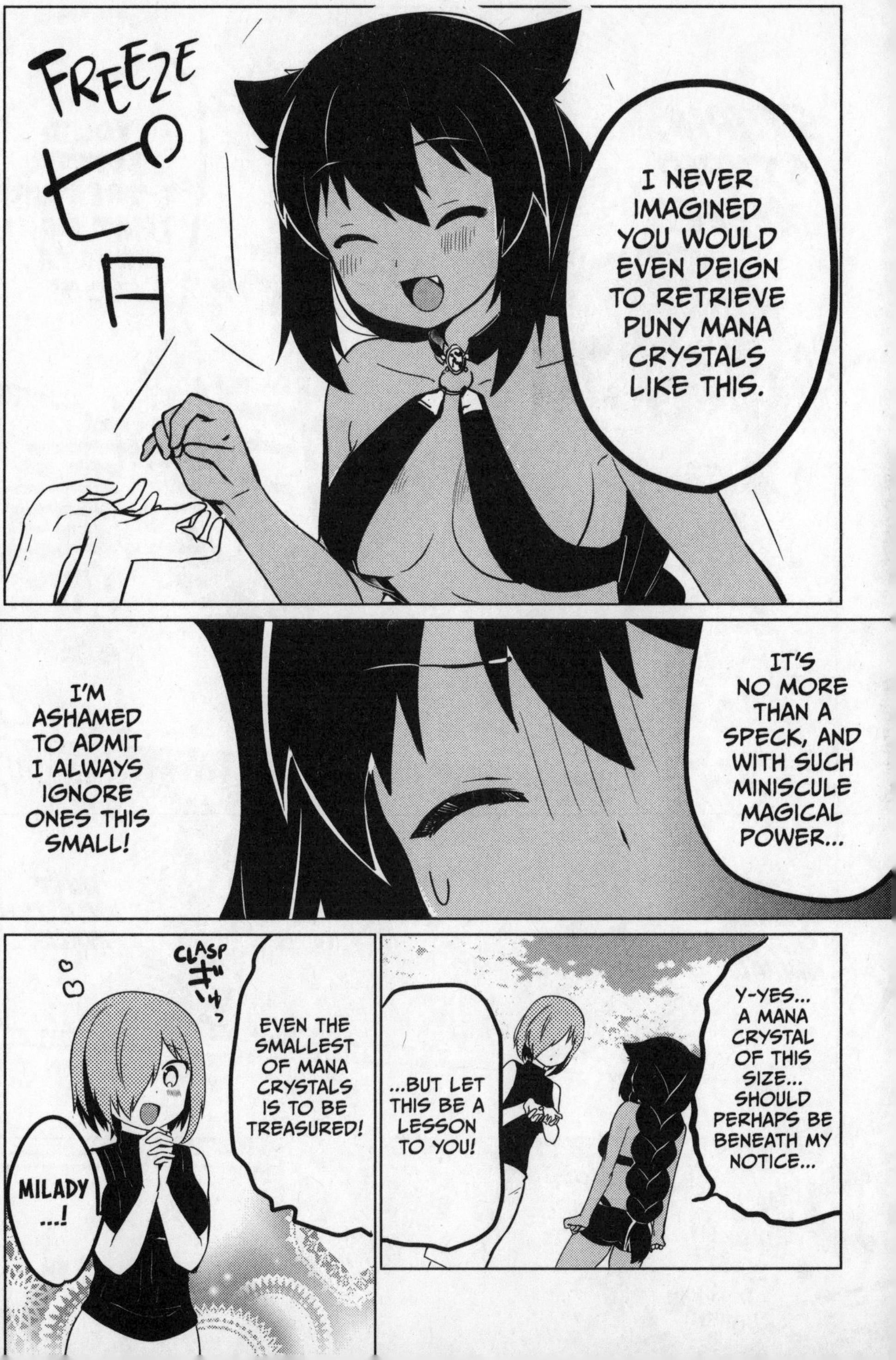
I NEVER IMAGINED YOU WOULD EVEN DEIGN TO RETRIEVE PUNY MANA CRYSTALS LIKE THIS.
FREEZE
ピタ
IT'S NO MORE THAN A SPECK, AND WITH SUCH MINISCULE MAGICAL POWER...
I'M ASHAMED TO ADMIT I ALWAYS IGNORE ONES THIS SMALL!
Y-YES... A MANA CRYSTAL OF THIS SIZE... SHOULD PERHAPS BE BENEATH MY NOTICE...
...BUT LET THIS BE A LESSON TO YOU!
CLASP
ぎゅっ
EVEN THE SMALLEST OF MANA CRYSTALS IS TO BE TREASURED!
MILADY ...!

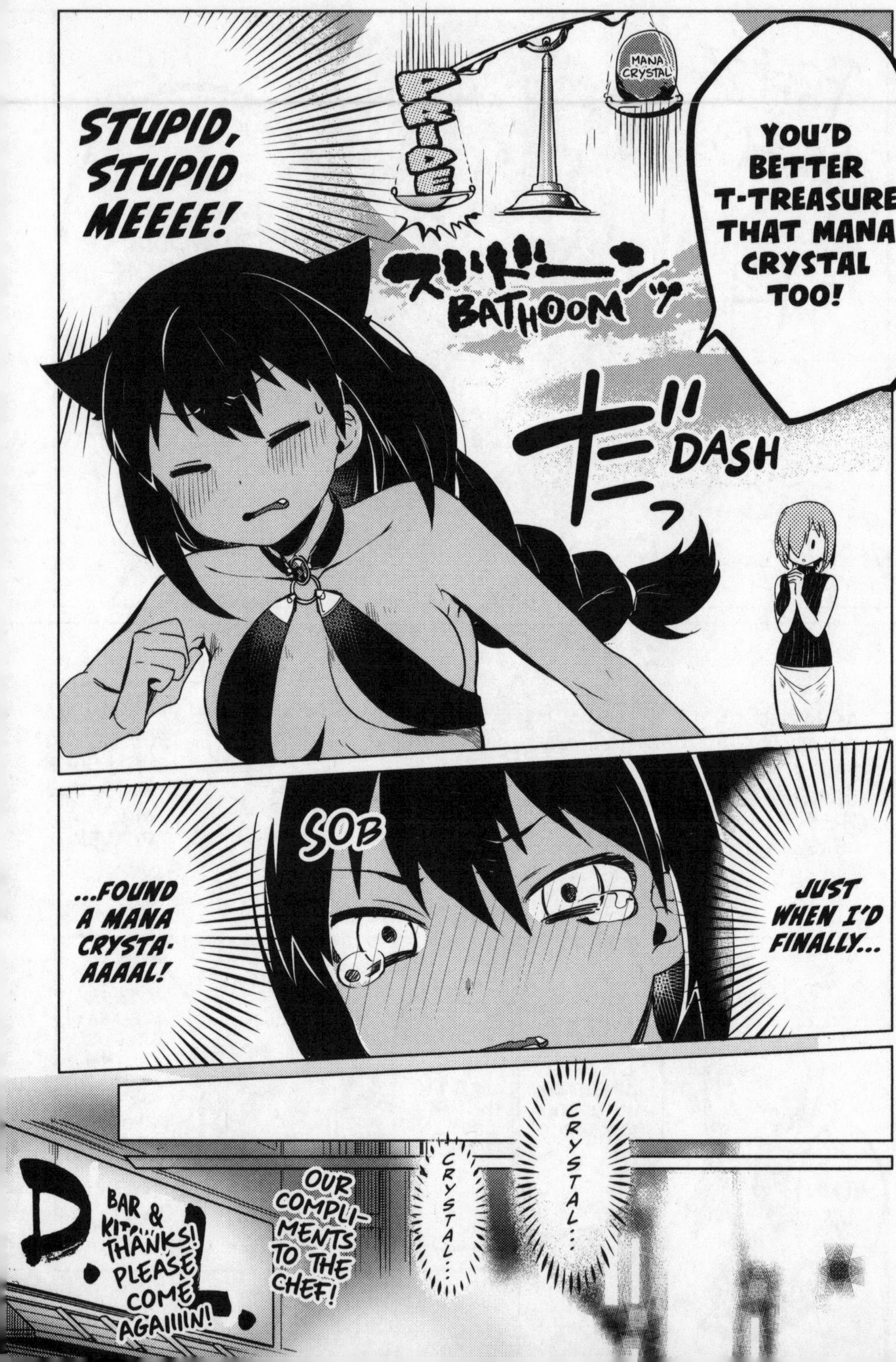
MANA CRYSTAL
YOU'D BETTER T-TREASURE THAT MANA CRYSTAL TOO!
PRIDE
STUPID, STUPID MEEEE!
BATHOOM
DASH
JUST WHEN I'D FINALLY...
SOB
...FOUND A MANA CRYSTA-AAAAL!
CRYSTAL...
CRYSTAL...
OUR COMPLI-MENTS TO THE CHEF!
BAR &
THANKS! PLEASE COME AGAIIIIN!

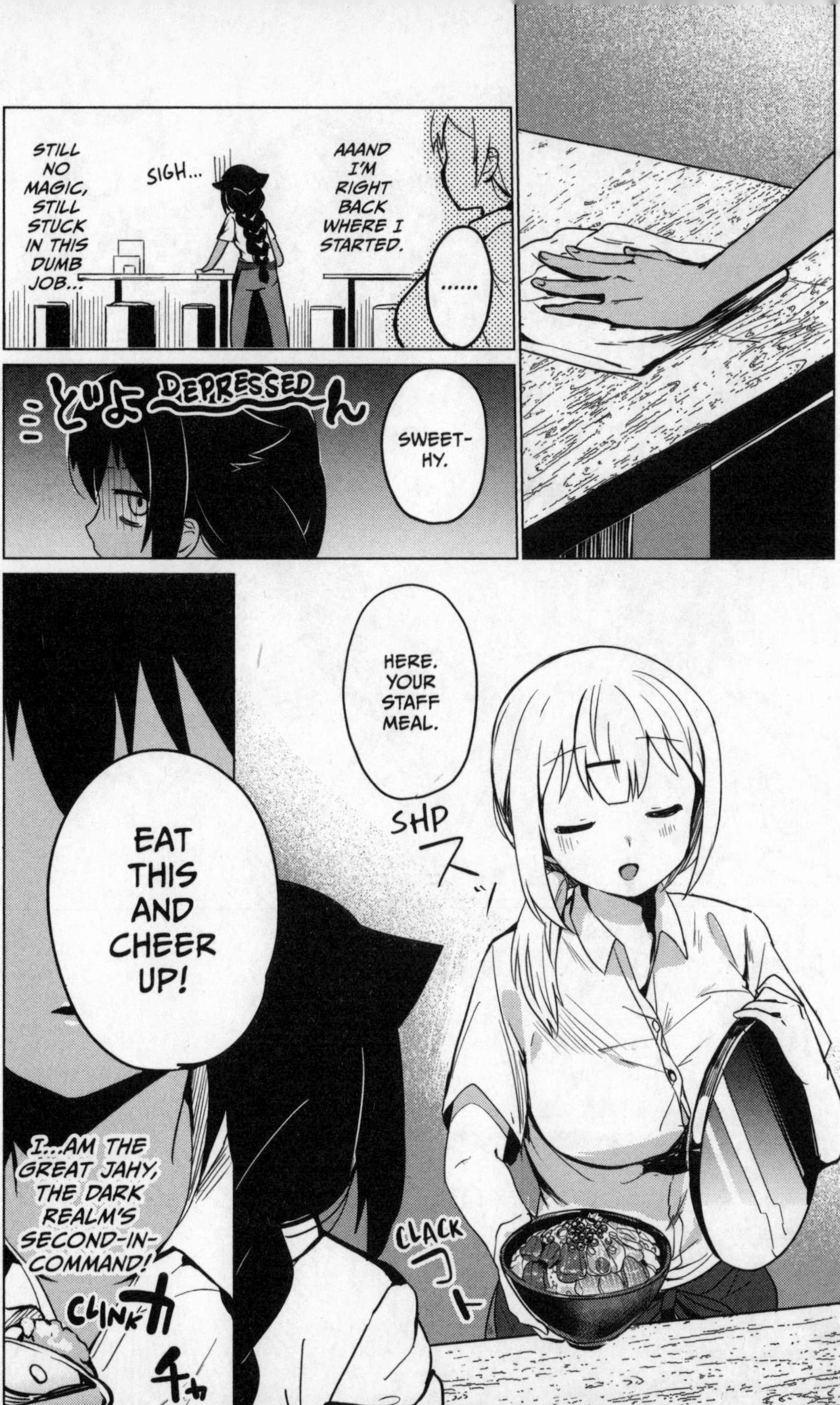
......
AAAND I'M RIGHT BACK WHERE I STARTED.
SIGH...
STILL NO MAGIC, STILL STUCK IN THIS DUMB JOB...
SWEET-HY.
どよん DEPRESSED
HERE. YOUR STAFF MEAL.
SHP スッ
EAT THIS AND CHEER UP!
CLACK コト
I...AM THE GREAT JAHY, THE DARK REALM'S SECOND-IN-COMMAND!
CLINK カチャ

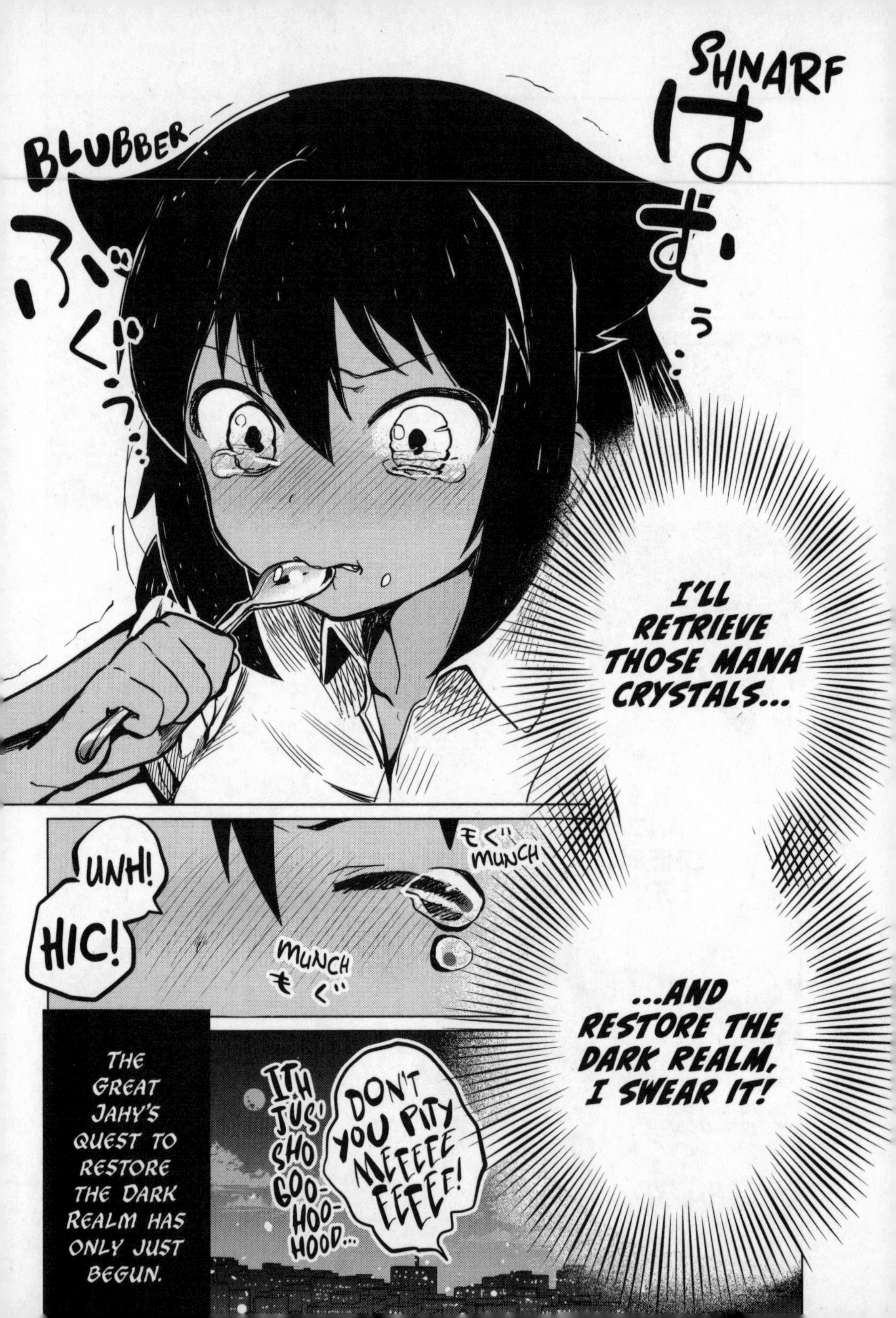
SHNARF
はむぅ…
BLUBBER
I'LL RETRIEVE THOSE MANA CRYSTALS...
モぐ MUNCH
UNH!
HIC!
MUNCH もぐ
...AND RESTORE THE DARK REALM, I SWEAR IT!
DON'T YOU PITY MEEEEE EEEEE!
ITH JUS' SHO GOO-HOO-HOOD...
THE GREAT JAHY'S QUEST TO RESTORE THE DARK REALM HAS ONLY JUST BEGUN.

← THE MAIN SERIES STARTS
FROM THE NEXT CHAPTER!

The GREAT JAHY Will NOT Be DEFEATED!

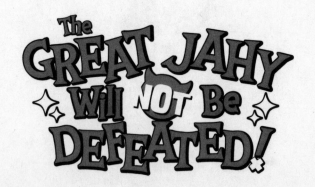

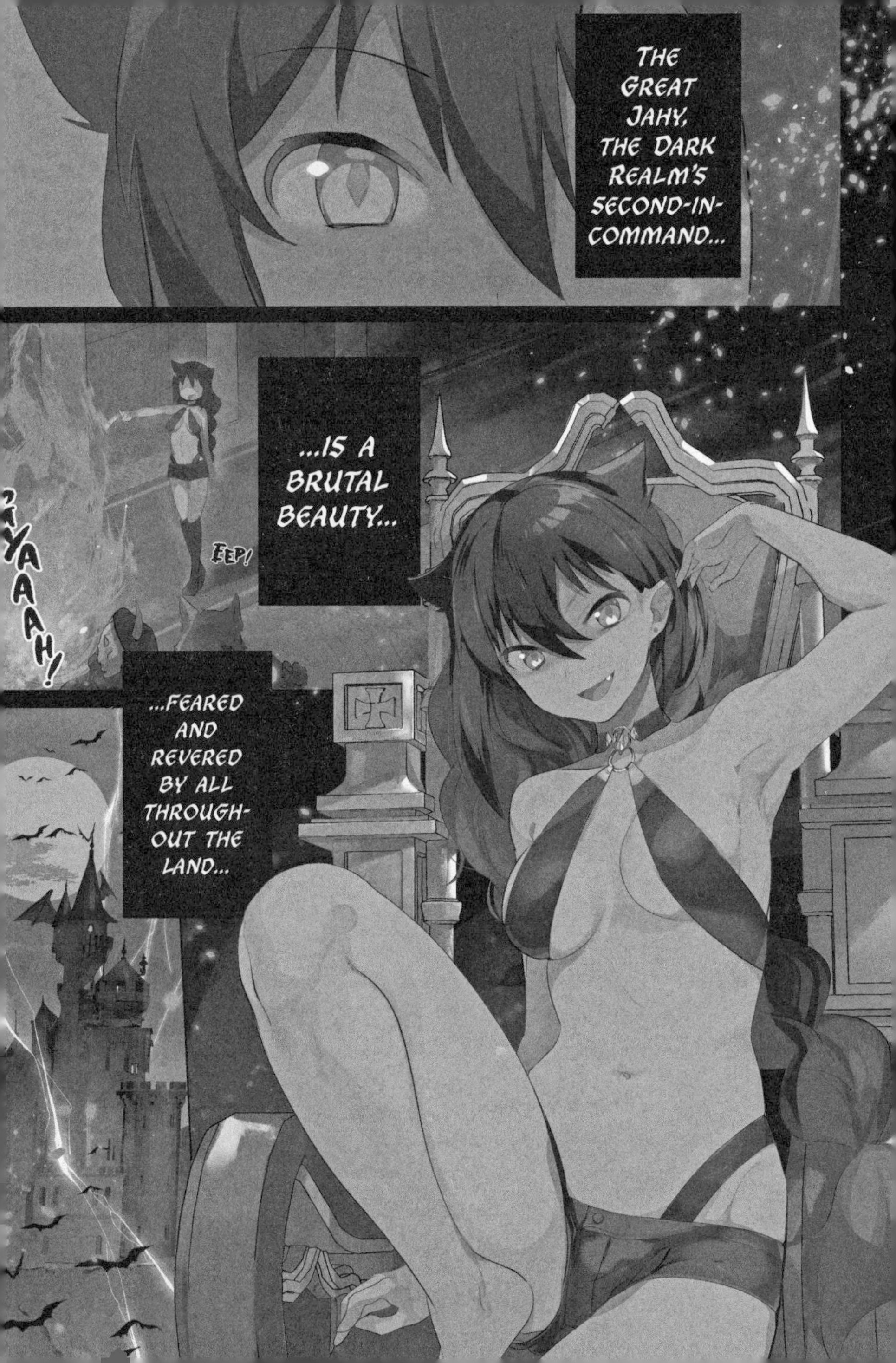
THE GREAT JAHY, THE DARK REALM'S SECOND-IN-COMMAND...
...IS A BRUTAL BEAUTY...
EEP!
YAAAH!
...FEARED AND REVERED BY ALL THROUGHOUT THE LAND...

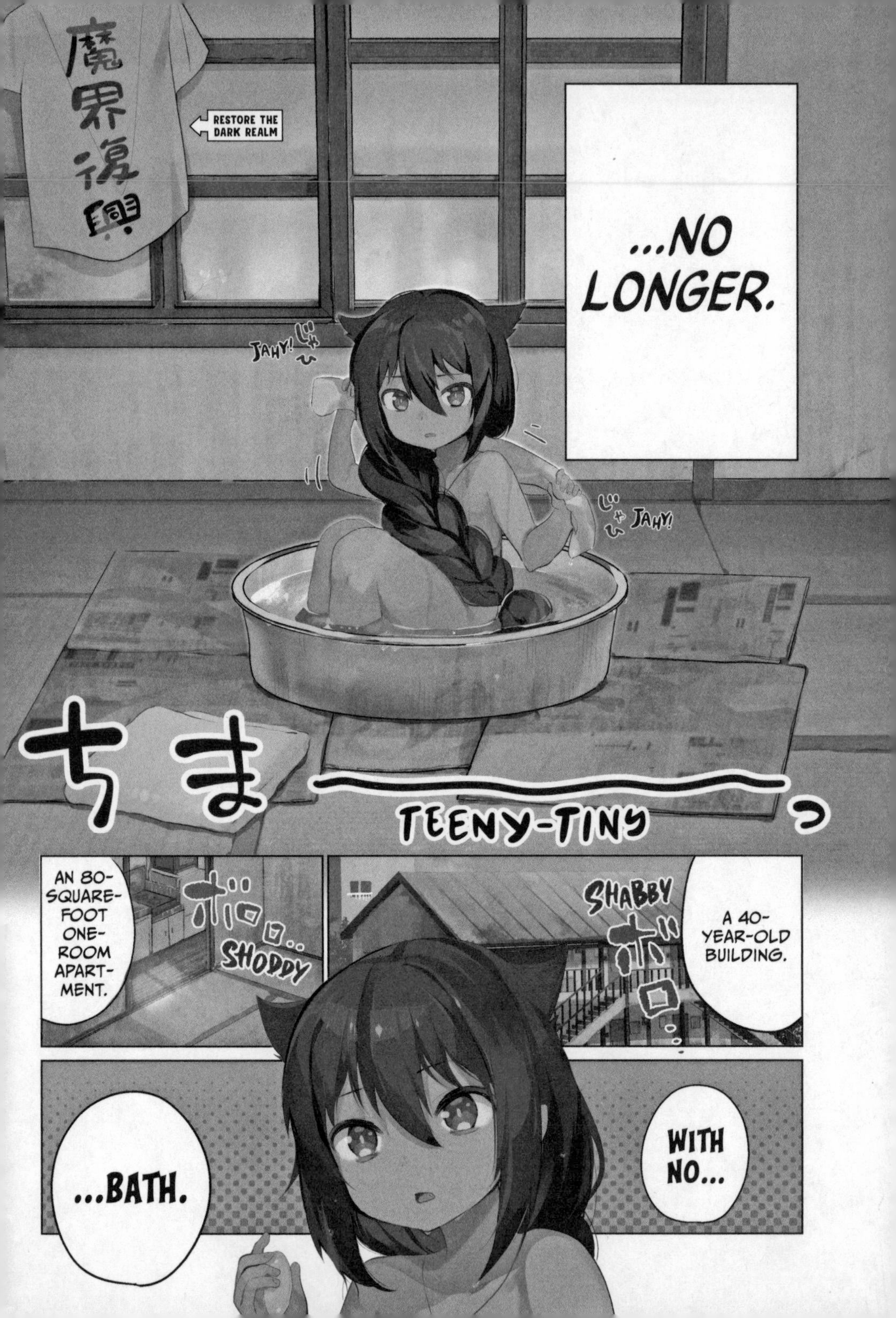
...NO LONGER.
魔界復興
RESTORE THE DARK REALM
JAHY!
JAHY!
ちまーーーっ
TEENY-TINY
A 40-YEAR-OLD BUILDING.
SHABBY
AN 80-SQUARE-FOOT ONE-ROOM APARTMENT.
SHODDY
WITH NO...
...BATH.

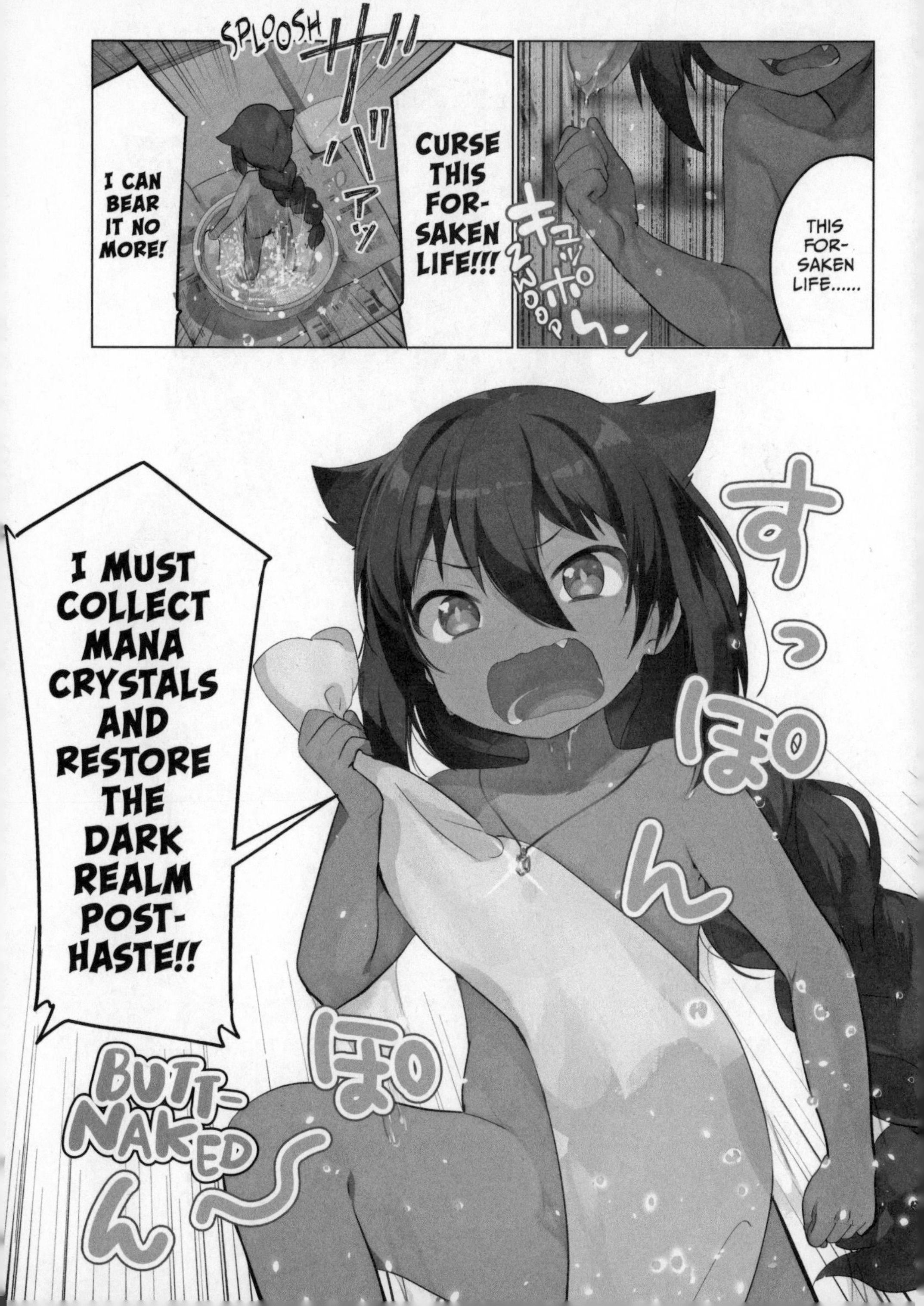
THIS FOR-SAKEN LIFE......
ZWOOP
CURSE THIS FOR-SAKEN LIFE!!!
SPLOOSH
I CAN BEAR IT NO MORE!
すっぽん
I MUST COLLECT MANA CRYSTALS AND RESTORE THE DARK REALM POST-HASTE!!
ぽん～
BUTT-NAKED

RESTORATION PLAN No. 1

The Great Jahy & the Part-Time Job

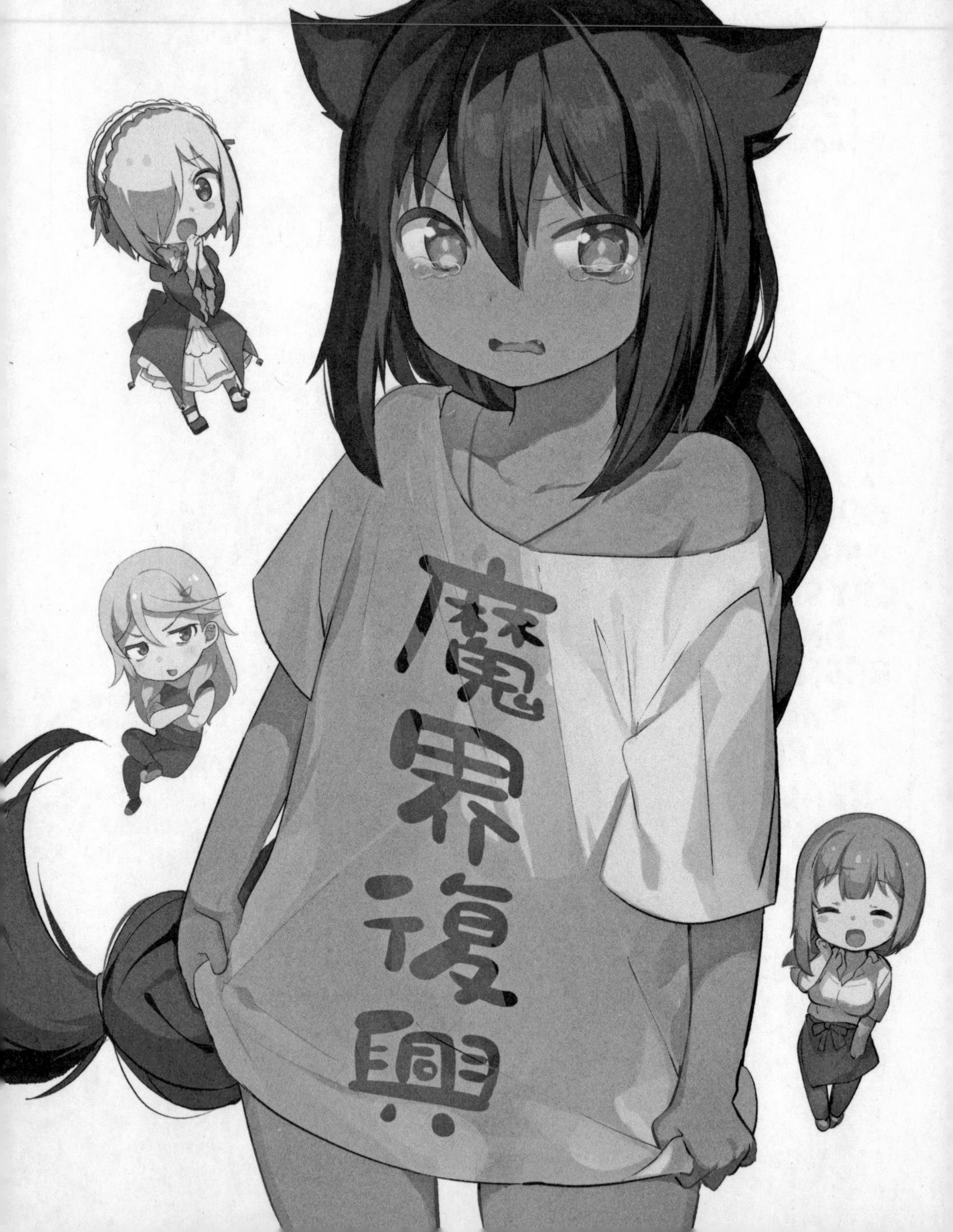
魔界復興

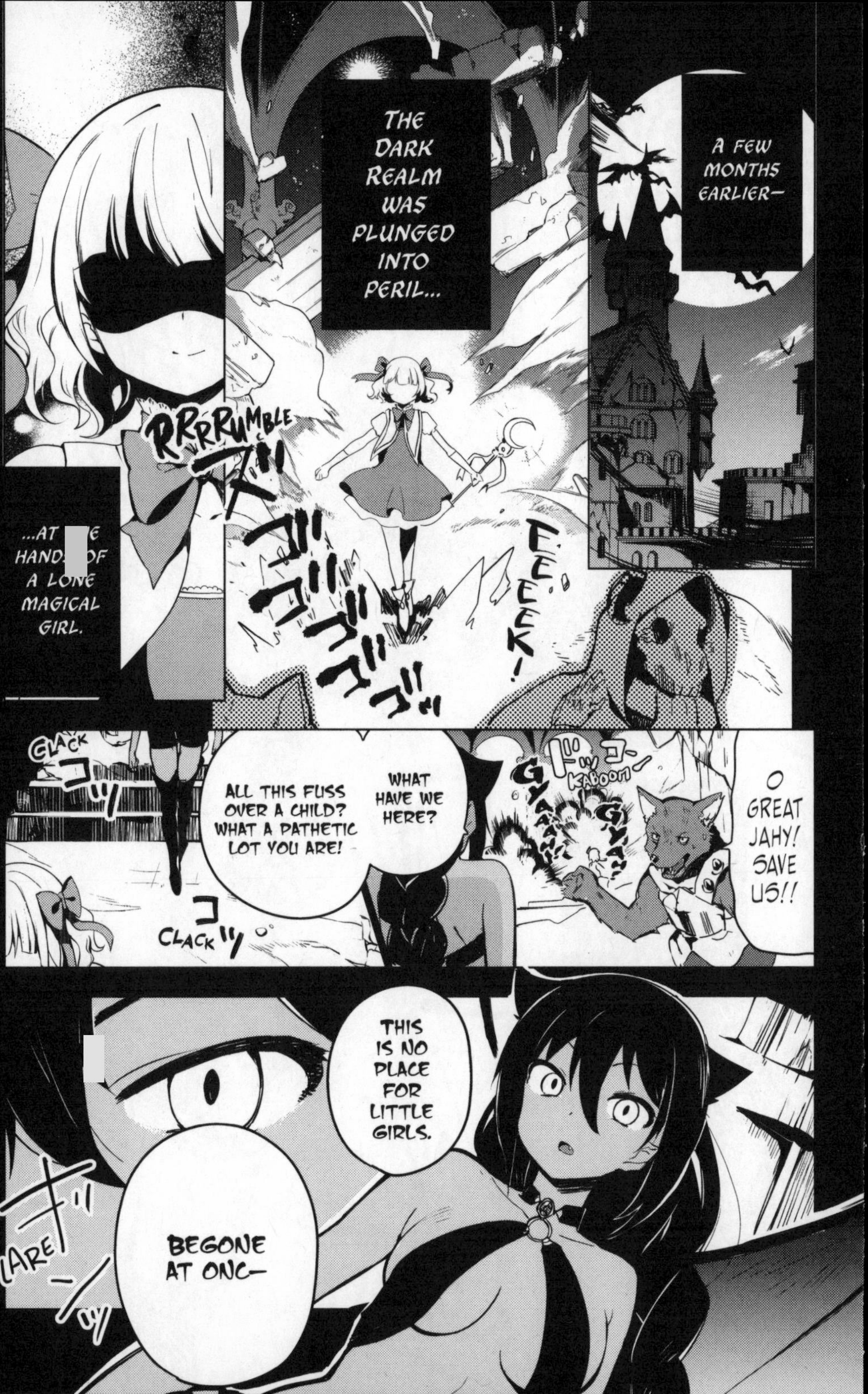
A FEW MONTHS EARLIER—
THE DARK REALM WAS PLUNGED INTO PERIL...
RRRRUMBLE
EEEEK!
...AT E HANDS OF A LONE MAGICAL GIRL.
O GREAT JAHY! SAVE US!!
KABOOM
GYAAAH!!
GYAAAH!!
WHAT HAVE WE HERE?
ALL THIS FUSS OVER A CHILD? WHAT A PATHETIC LOT YOU ARE!
CLACK
CLACK
THIS IS NO PLACE FOR LITTLE GIRLS.
BEGONE AT ONC—
GLARE

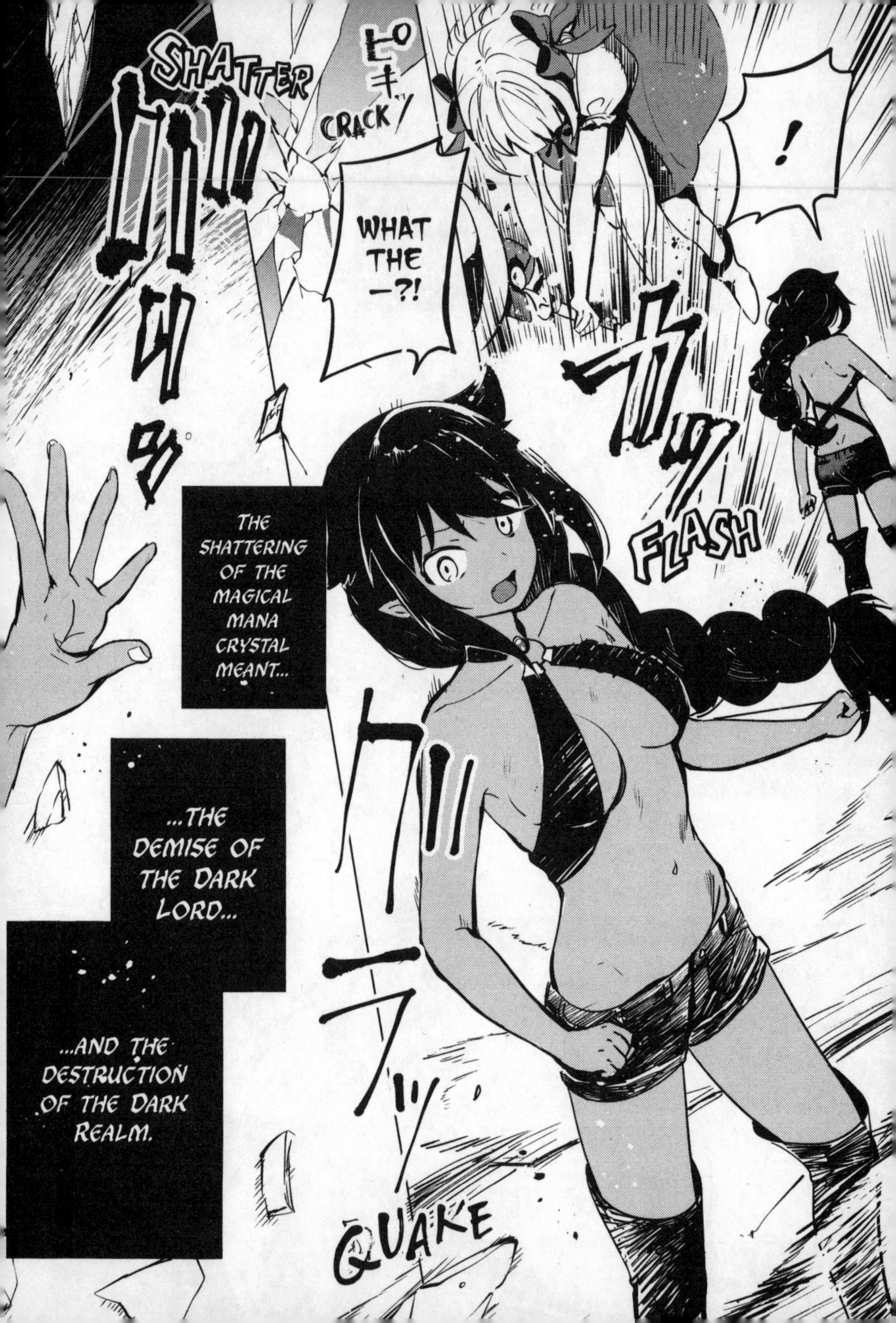
!
CRACK
WHAT THE —?!
SHATTER
FLASH
THE SHATTERING OF THE MAGICAL MANA CRYSTAL MEANT...
...THE DEMISE OF THE DARK LORD...
...AND THE DESTRUCTION OF THE DARK REALM.
QUAKE

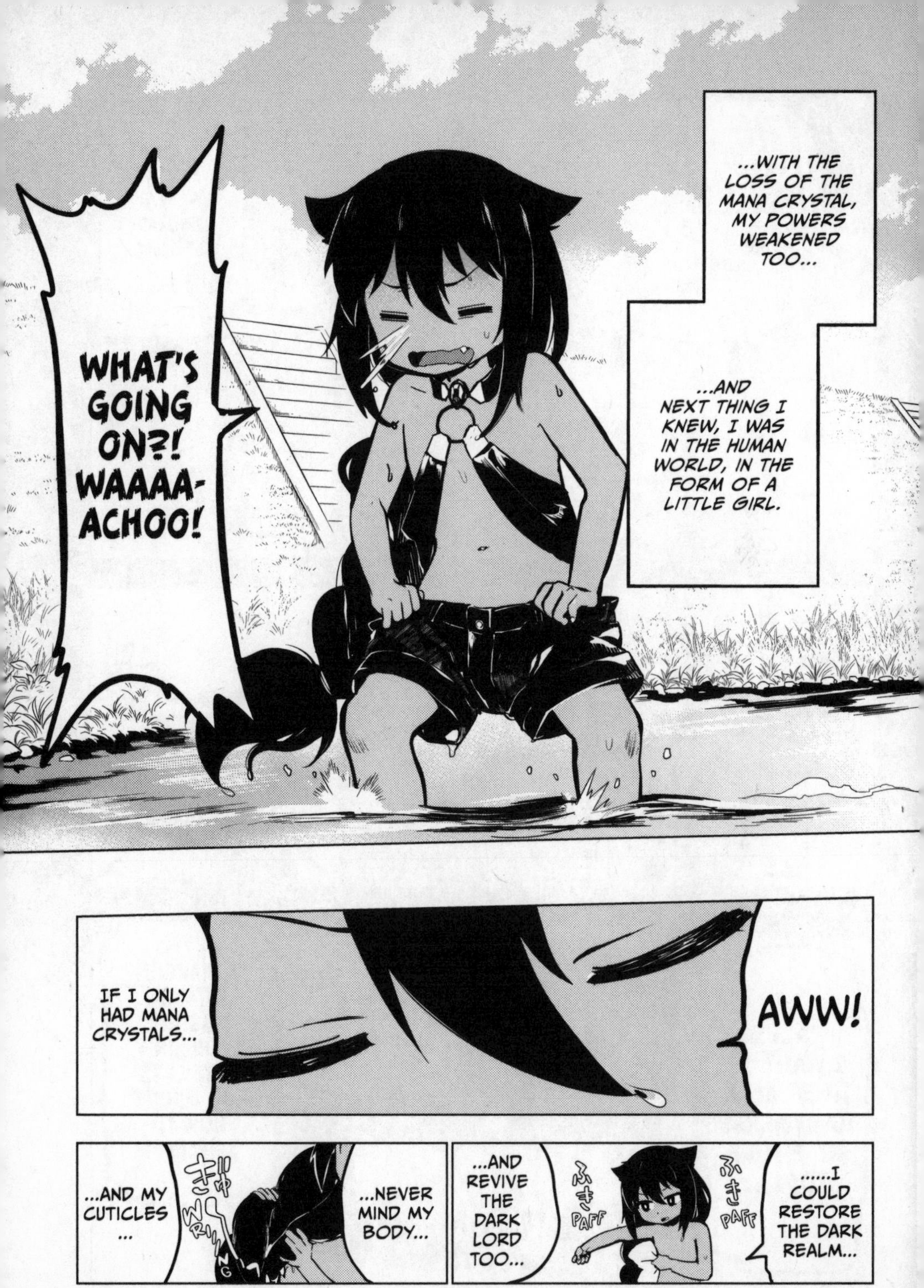

...WITH THE LOSS OF THE MANA CRYSTAL, MY POWERS WEAKENED TOO...
...AND NEXT THING I KNEW, I WAS IN THE HUMAN WORLD, IN THE FORM OF A LITTLE GIRL.
WHAT'S GOING ON?! WAAAA-ACHOO!
AWW!
IF I ONLY HAD MANA CRYSTALS...
......I COULD RESTORE THE DARK REALM...
ふき
PAFF
ふき
PAFF
...AND REVIVE THE DARK LORD TOO...
...NEVER MIND MY BODY...
ぎゅ
WRIIING
...AND MY CUTICLES ...

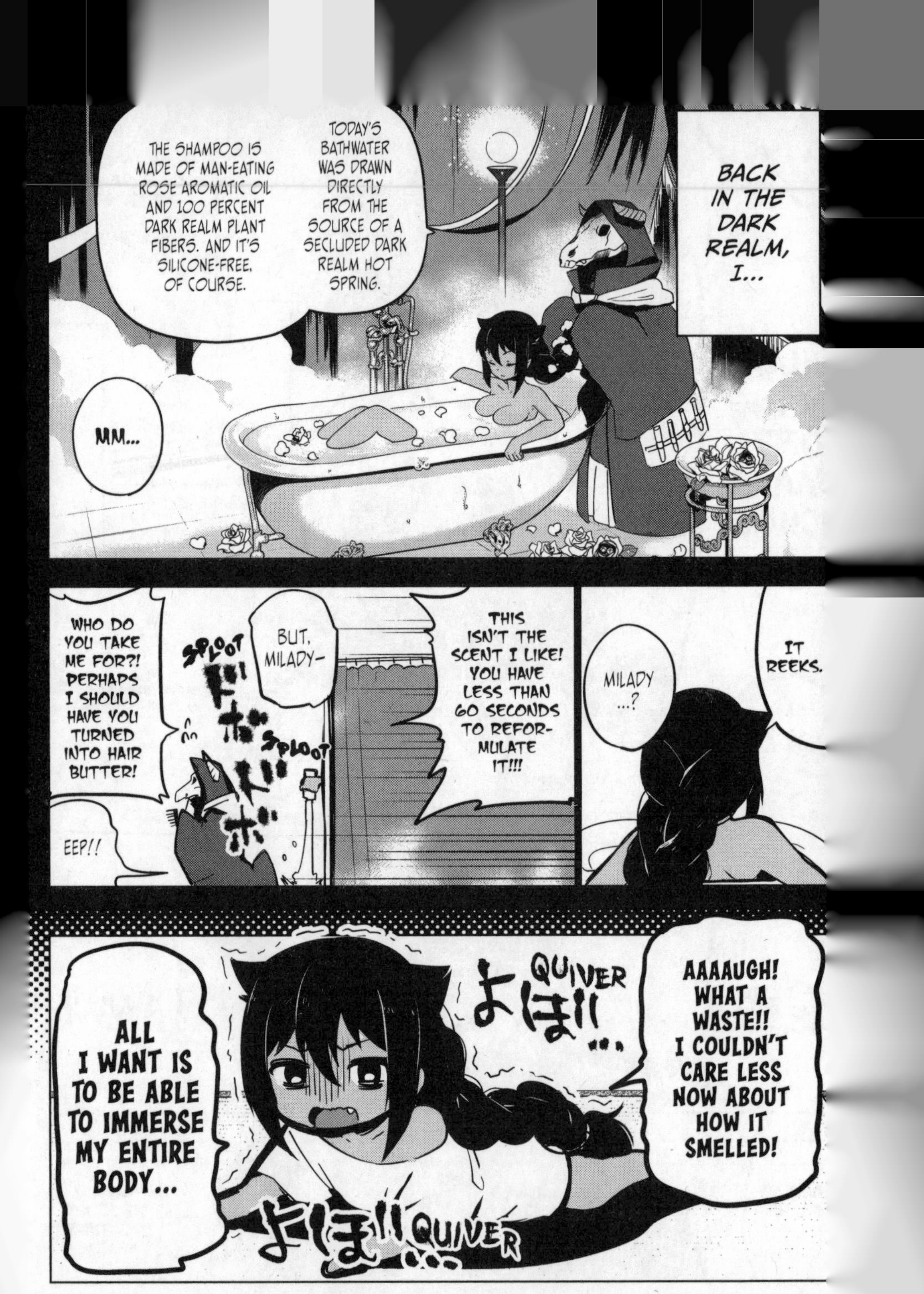
BACK IN THE DARK REALM, I...
TODAY'S BATHWATER WAS DRAWN DIRECTLY FROM THE SOURCE OF A SECLUDED DARK REALM HOT SPRING.
THE SHAMPOO IS MADE OF MAN-EATING ROSE AROMATIC OIL AND 100 PERCENT DARK REALM PLANT FIBERS. AND IT'S SILICONE-FREE, OF COURSE.
MM...
IT REEKS.
MILADY ...?
THIS ISN'T THE SCENT I LIKE! YOU HAVE LESS THAN 60 SECONDS TO REFORMULATE IT!!!
BUT, MILADY-
SPLOOT
SPLOOT
WHO DO YOU TAKE ME FOR?! PERHAPS I SHOULD HAVE YOU TURNED INTO HAIR BUTTER!
EEP!!
AAAAUGH! WHAT A WASTE!! I COULDN'T CARE LESS NOW ABOUT HOW IT SMELLED!
QUIVER
ALL I WANT IS TO BE ABLE TO IMMERSE MY ENTIRE BODY...
QUIVER

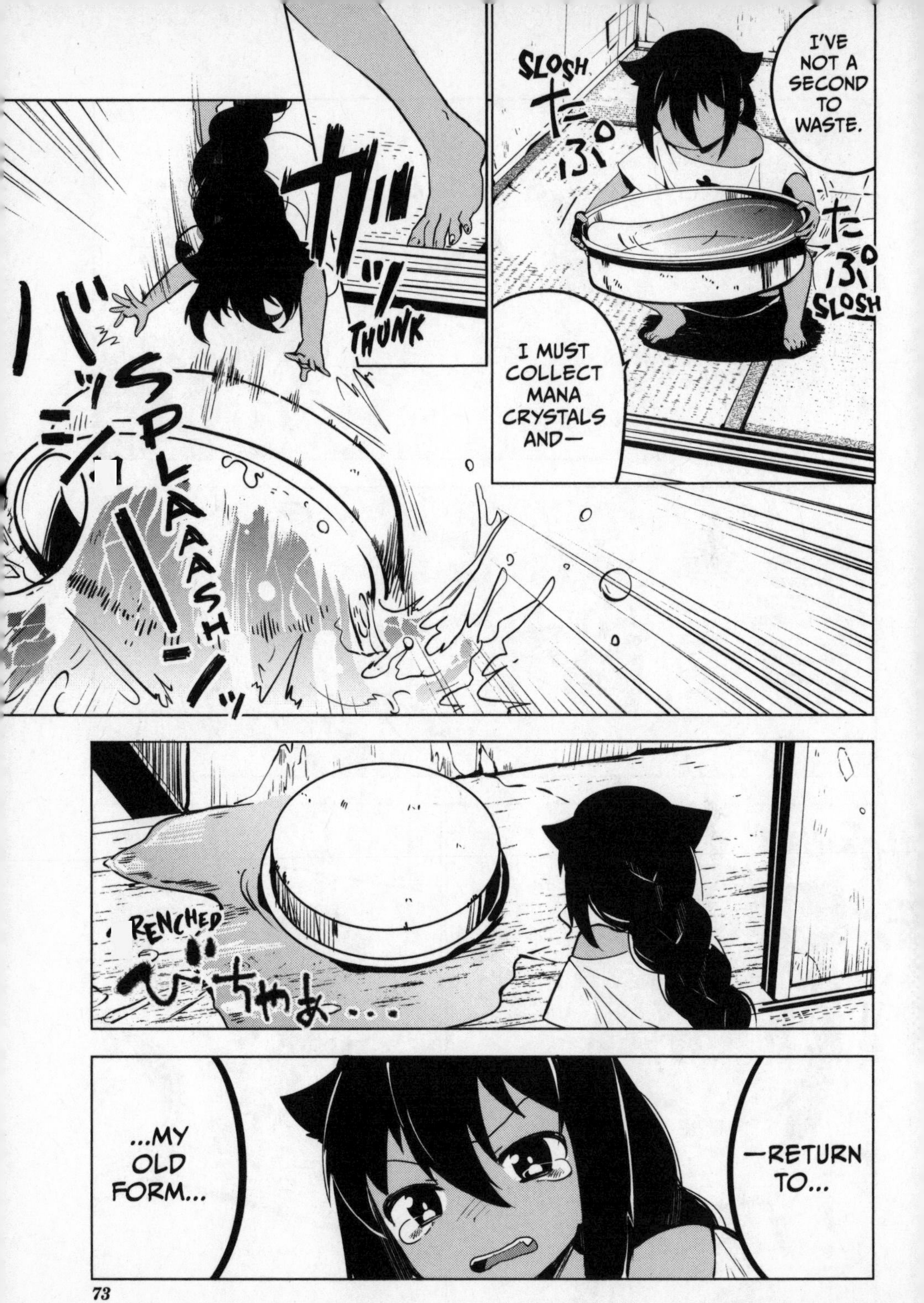
SLOSH
たぷ
I'VE NOT A SECOND TO WASTE.
たぷ
SLOSH
I MUST COLLECT MANA CRYSTALS AND—
ガッ
THUNK
バッ
SPLAAASH
RENCHED
びちゃぁ...
—RETURN TO...
...MY OLD FORM...

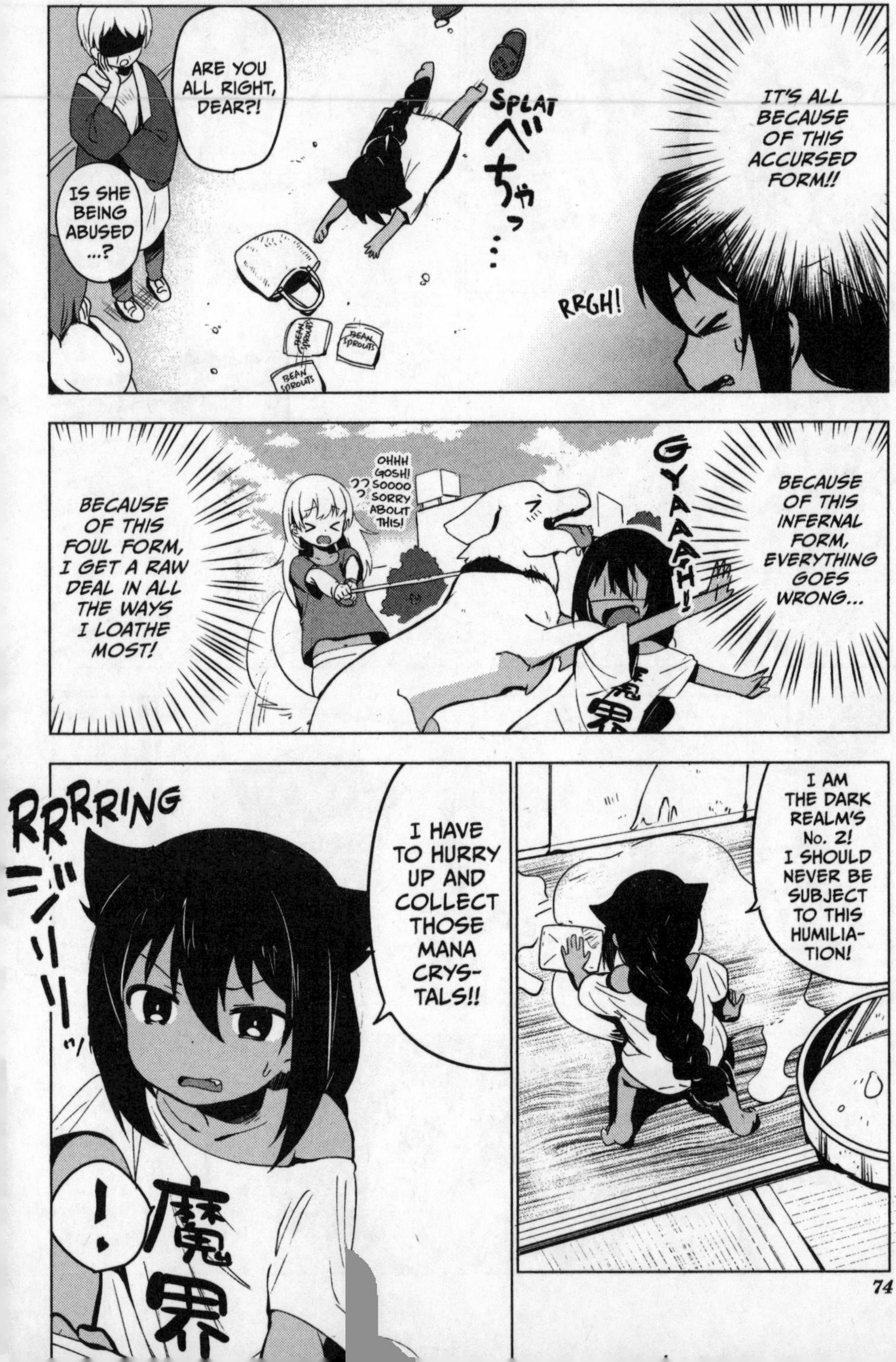
IT'S ALL BECAUSE OF THIS ACCURSED FORM!!
RRGH!
SPLAT
べちゃっ…
ARE YOU ALL RIGHT, DEAR?!
IS SHE BEING ABUSED ...?
BEAN SPROUTS
BEAN SPROUTS
BEAN SPROUTS
BECAUSE OF THIS INFERNAL FORM, EVERYTHING GOES WRONG...
GYAAAAH!!
OHHH GOSH! SOOOO SORRY ABOUT THIS!
BECAUSE OF THIS FOUL FORM, I GET A RAW DEAL IN ALL THE WAYS I LOATHE MOST!
I AM THE DARK REALM'S No. 2! I SHOULD NEVER BE SUBJECT TO THIS HUMILIATION!
I HAVE TO HURRY UP AND COLLECT THOSE MANA CRYSTALS!!
RRRRING
ジリリ
!
魔界

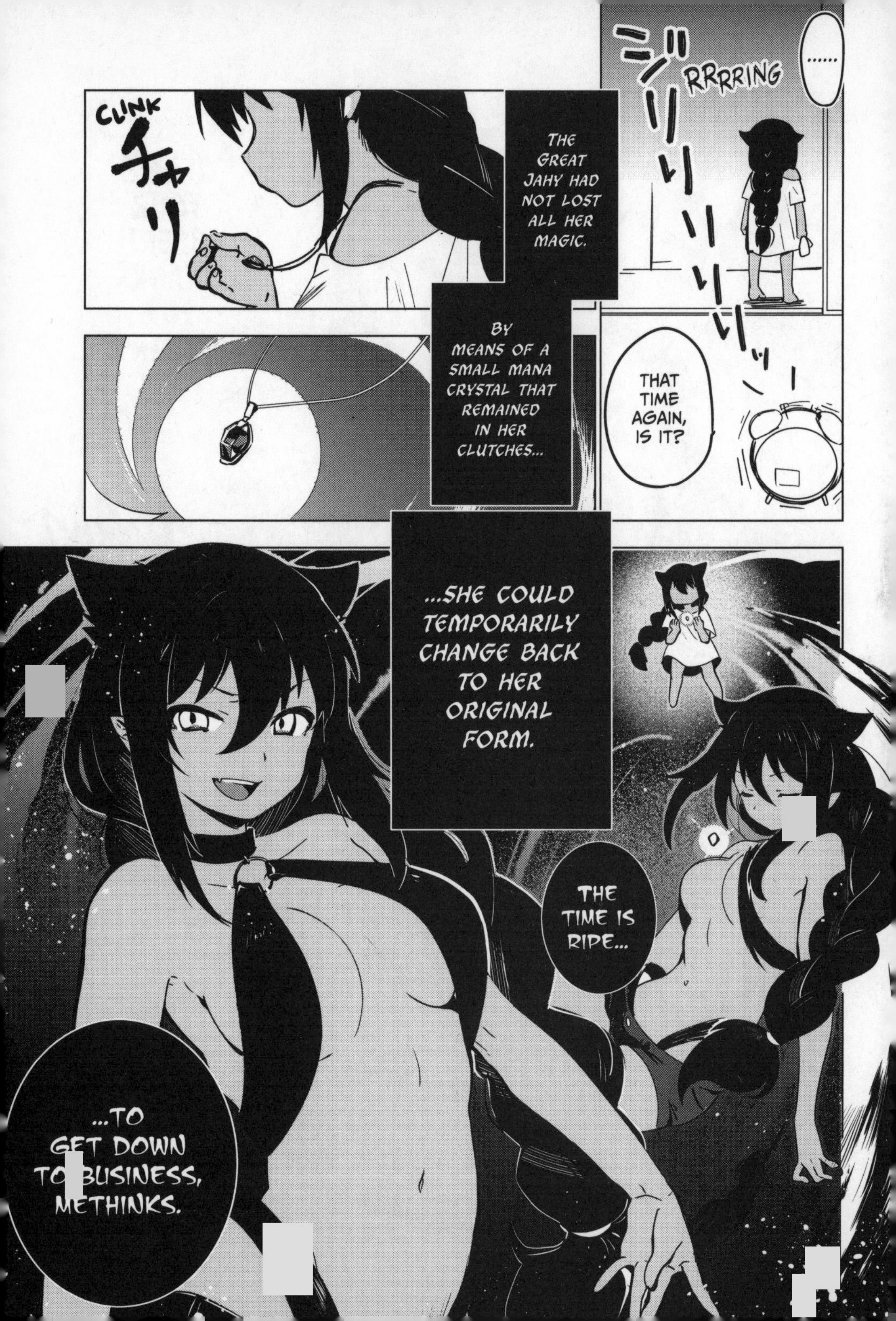
......
ジリリリリリリッ
RRRRING
THAT TIME AGAIN, IS IT?
CLINK
チャリ
THE GREAT JAHY HAD NOT LOST ALL HER MAGIC.
BY MEANS OF A SMALL MANA CRYSTAL THAT REMAINED IN HER CLUTCHES...
...SHE COULD TEMPORARILY CHANGE BACK TO HER ORIGINAL FORM.
THE TIME IS RIPE...
...TO GET DOWN TO BUSINESS, METHINKS.

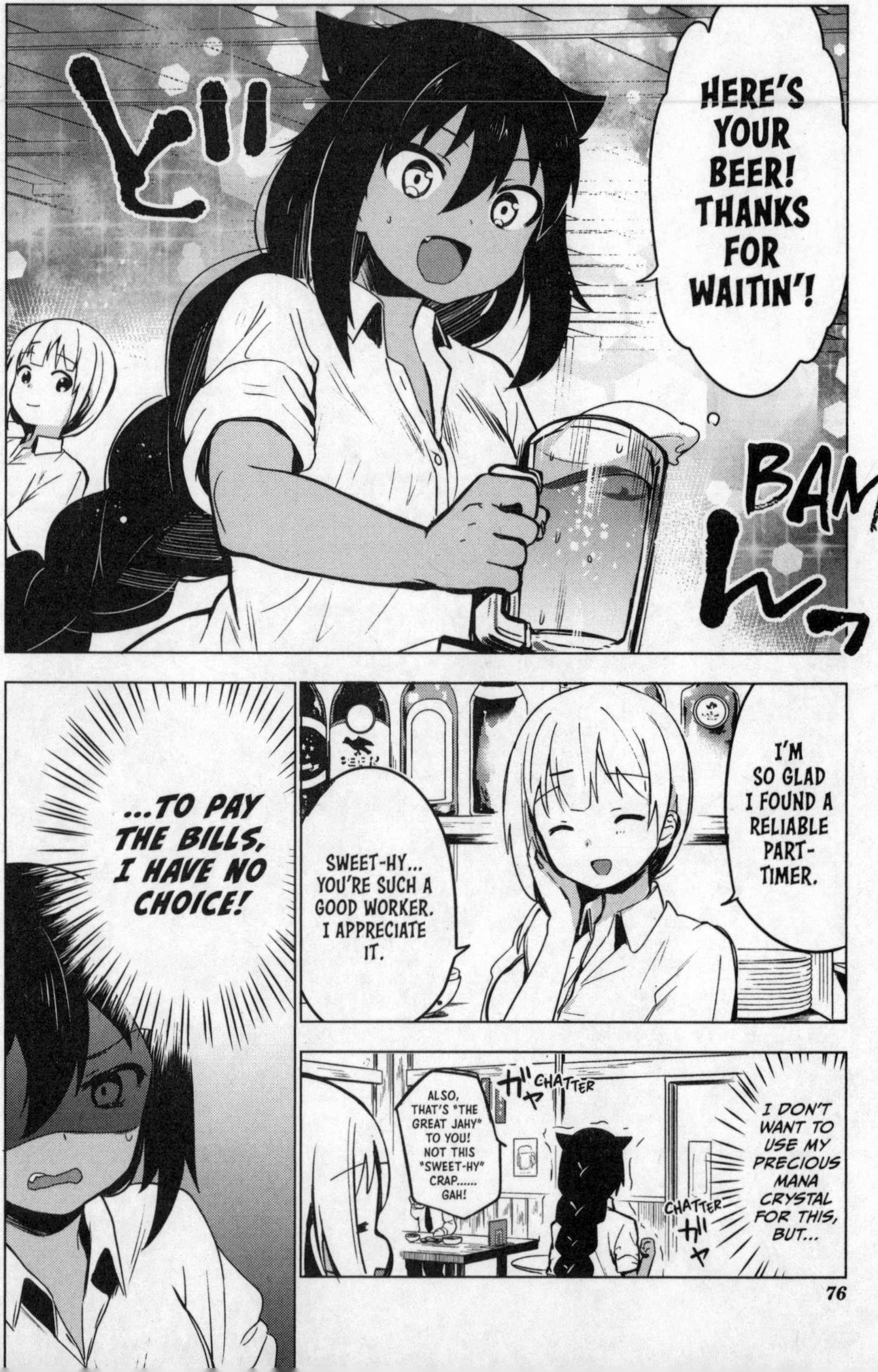
HERE'S YOUR BEER! THANKS FOR WAITIN'!
BAM
I'M SO GLAD I FOUND A RELIABLE PART-TIMER.
SWEET-HY... YOU'RE SUCH A GOOD WORKER. I APPRECIATE IT.
I DON'T WANT TO USE MY PRECIOUS MANA CRYSTAL FOR THIS, BUT...
CHATTER
CHATTER
ALSO, THAT'S "THE GREAT JAHY" TO YOU! NOT THIS "SWEET-HY" CRAP...... GAH!
...TO PAY THE BILLS, I HAVE NO CHOICE!

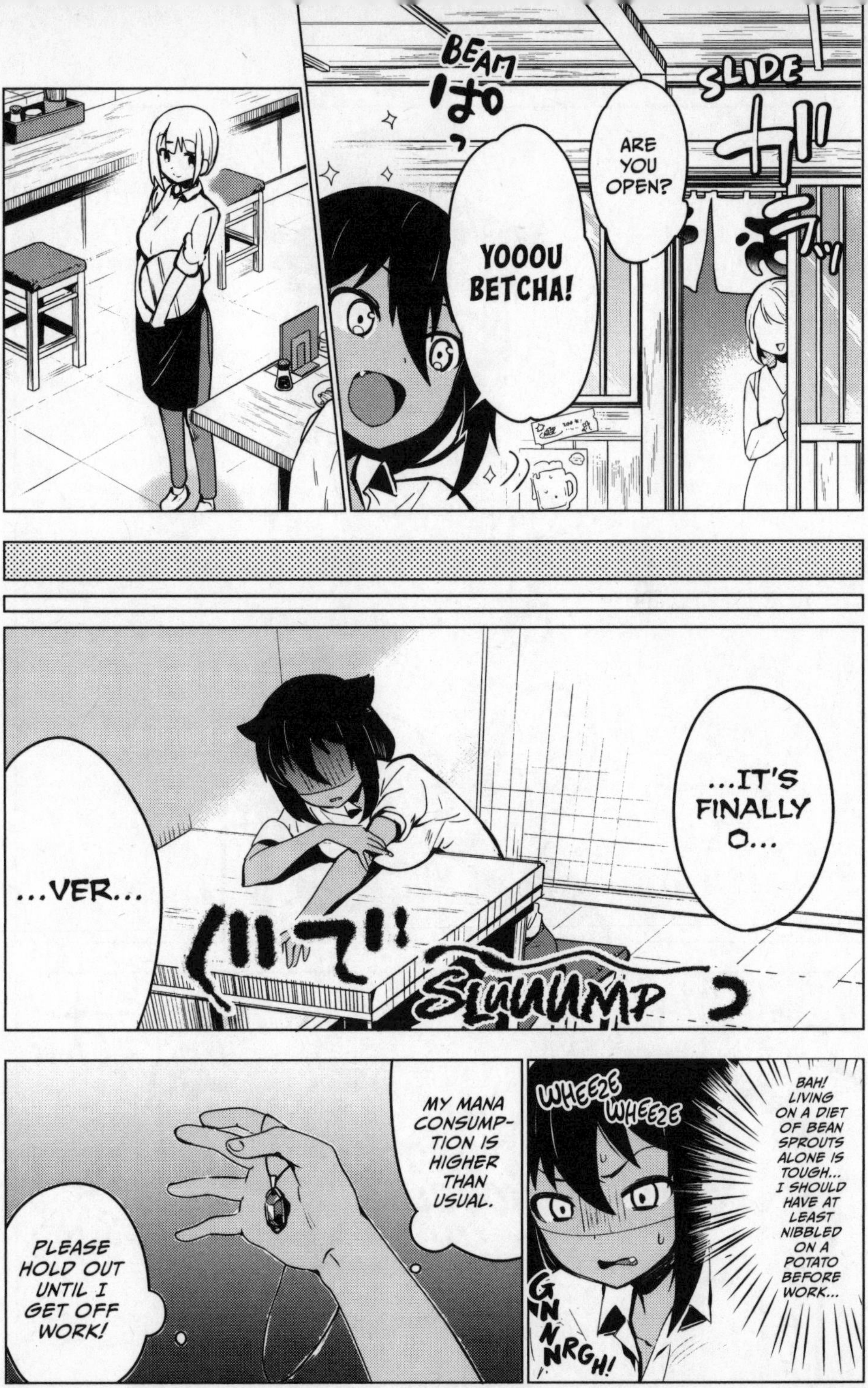
SLIDE
ARE YOU OPEN?
BEAM
YOOOU BETCHA!
...IT'S FINALLY O...
...VER...
SLUUUMP
BAH! LIVING ON A DIET OF BEAN SPROUTS ALONE IS TOUGH... I SHOULD HAVE AT LEAST NIBBLED ON A POTATO BEFORE WORK...
WHEEZE WHEEZE
GNNNRGH!
MY MANA CONSUMPTION IS HIGHER THAN USUAL.
PLEASE HOLD OUT UNTIL I GET OFF WORK!

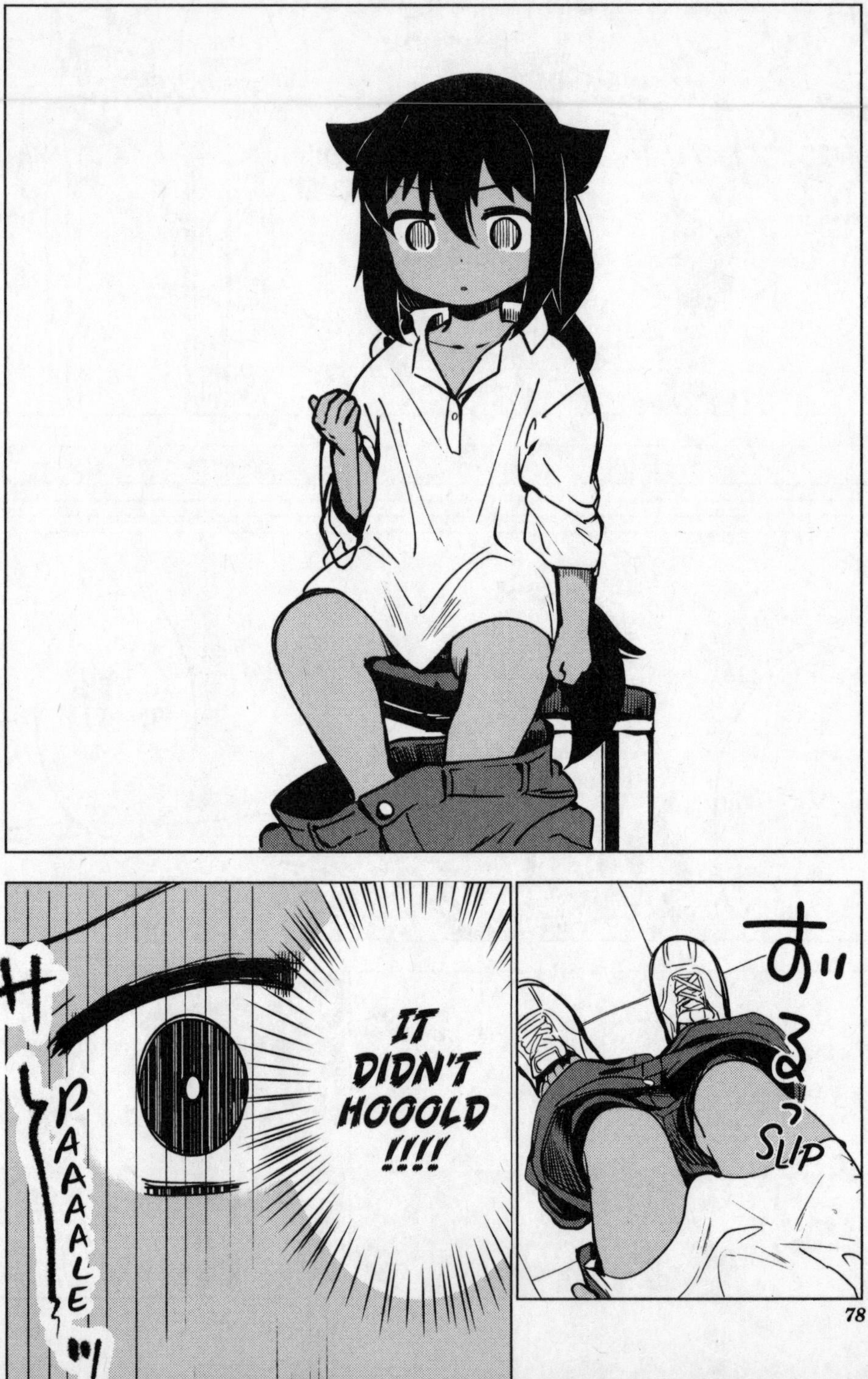
すぃるっ
SLIP
サ
PAAAALE
IT DIDN'T HOOOLD !!!!

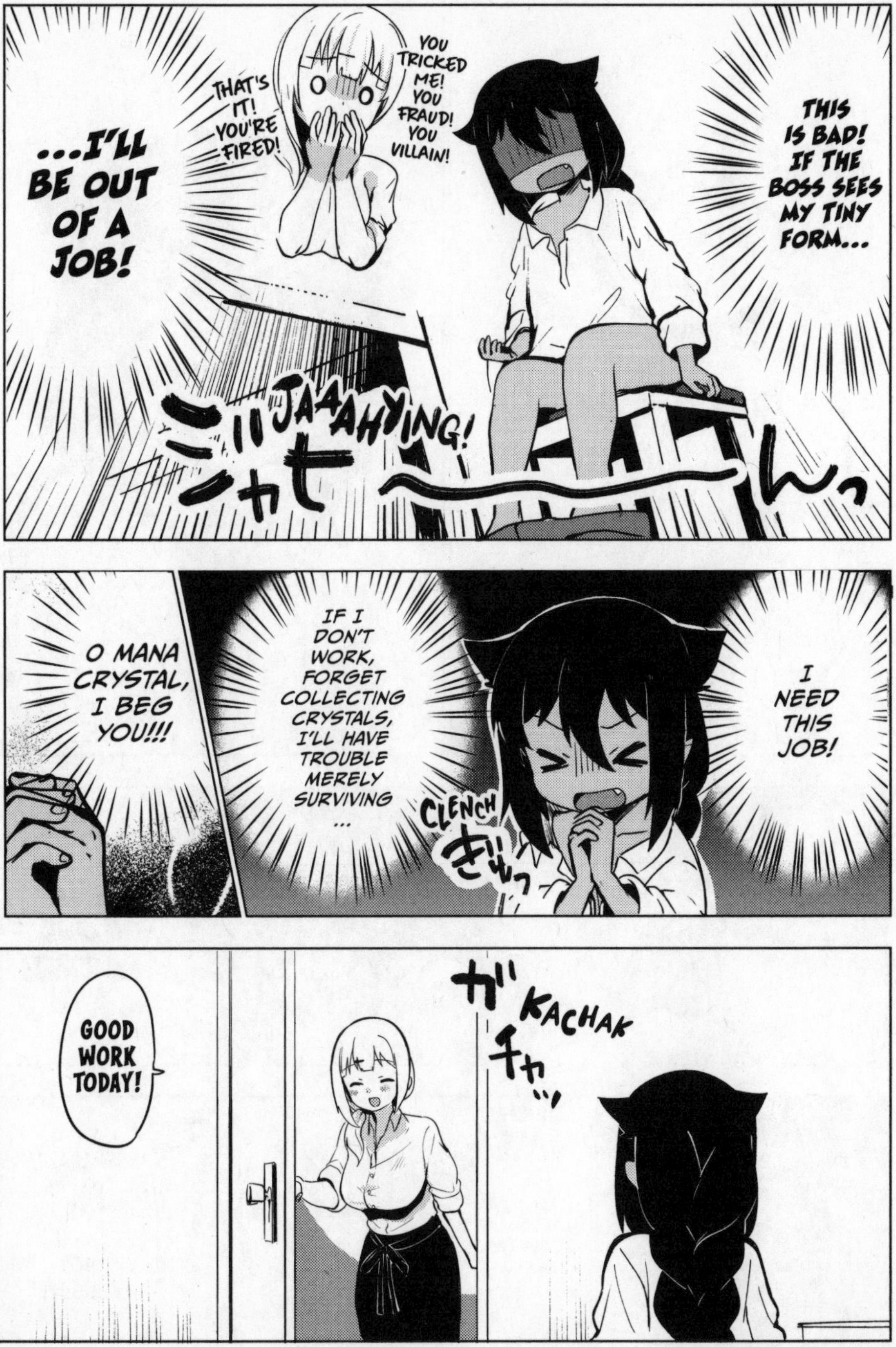
THIS IS BAD! IF THE BOSS SEES MY TINY FORM...
YOU TRICKED ME! YOU FRAUD! YOU VILLAIN!
THAT'S IT! YOU'RE FIRED!
...I'LL BE OUT OF A JOB!
JAAAAHYING!
I NEED THIS JOB!
IF I DON'T WORK, FORGET COLLECTING CRYSTALS, I'LL HAVE TROUBLE MERELY SURVIVING ...
CLENCH
ぎゅっ
O MANA CRYSTAL, I BEG YOU!!!
KACHAK
ガチャッ
GOOD WORK TODAY!

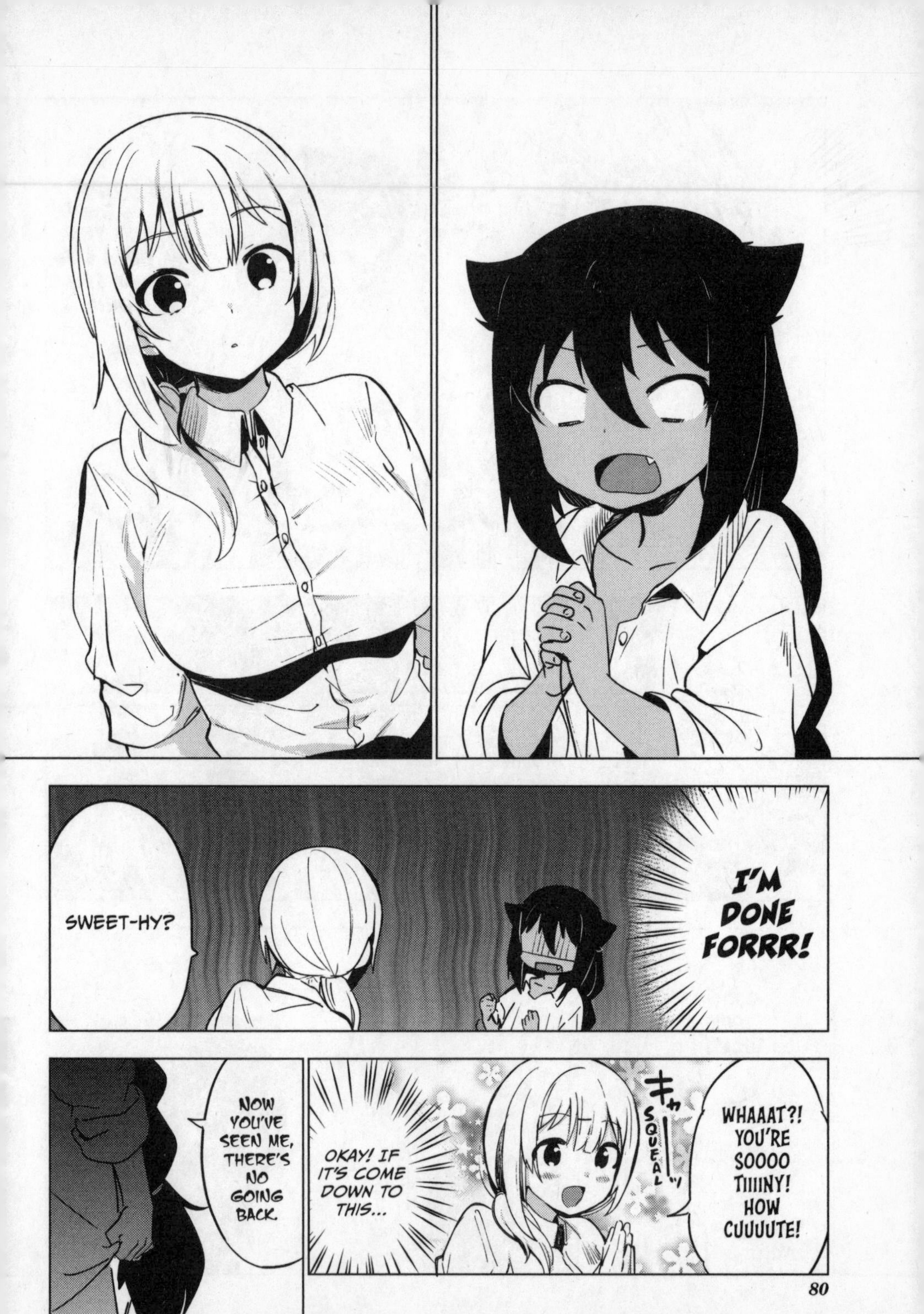
I'M DONE FORRR!
SWEET-HY?
WHAAAT?! YOU'RE SOOOO TIIIINY! HOW CUUUUTE!
キャー SQUEAL
OKAY! IF IT'S COME DOWN TO THIS...
NOW YOU'VE SEEN ME, THERE'S NO GOING BACK.

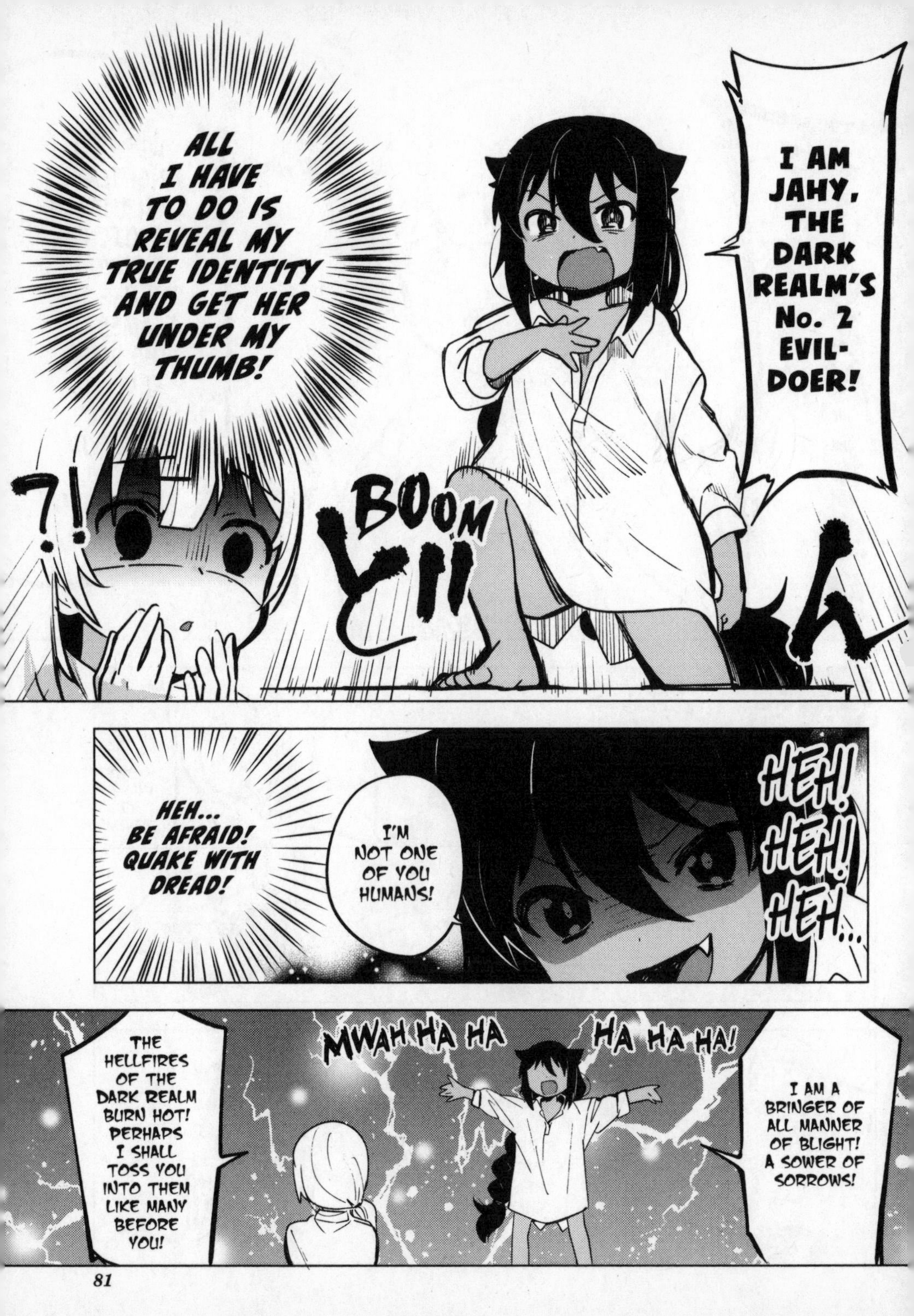
I AM JAHY, THE DARK REALM'S No. 2 EVIL-DOER!
ALL I HAVE TO DO IS REVEAL MY TRUE IDENTITY AND GET HER UNDER MY THUMB!
BOOM
?!
HEH! HEH! HEH...
I'M NOT ONE OF YOU HUMANS!
HEH... BE AFRAID! QUAKE WITH DREAD!
I AM A BRINGER OF ALL MANNER OF BLIGHT! A SOWER OF SORROWS!
MWAH HA HA
HA HA HA!
THE HELLFIRES OF THE DARK REALM BURN HOT! PERHAPS I SHALL TOSS YOU INTO THEM LIKE MANY BEFORE YOU!

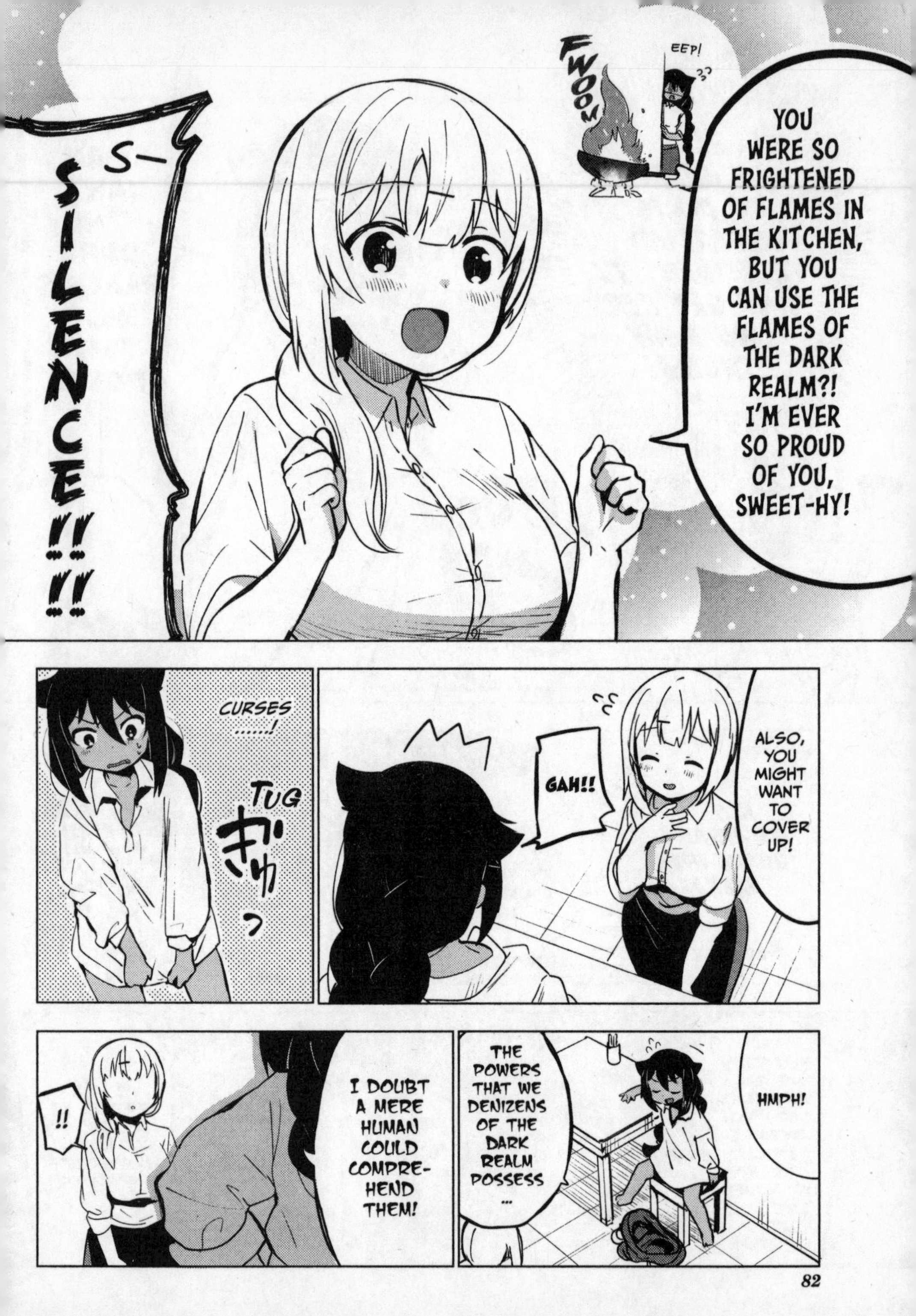
YOU WERE SO FRIGHTENED OF FLAMES IN THE KITCHEN, BUT YOU CAN USE THE FLAMES OF THE DARK REALM?! I'M EVER SO PROUD OF YOU, SWEET-HY!
EEP!
FWOOM
S—
SILENCE!!!!
ALSO, YOU MIGHT WANT TO COVER UP!
GAH!!
CURSES ......!
TUG
きゅっ
HMPH!
THE POWERS THAT WE DENIZENS OF THE DARK REALM POSSESS...
I DOUBT A MERE HUMAN COULD COMPREHEND THEM!
!!

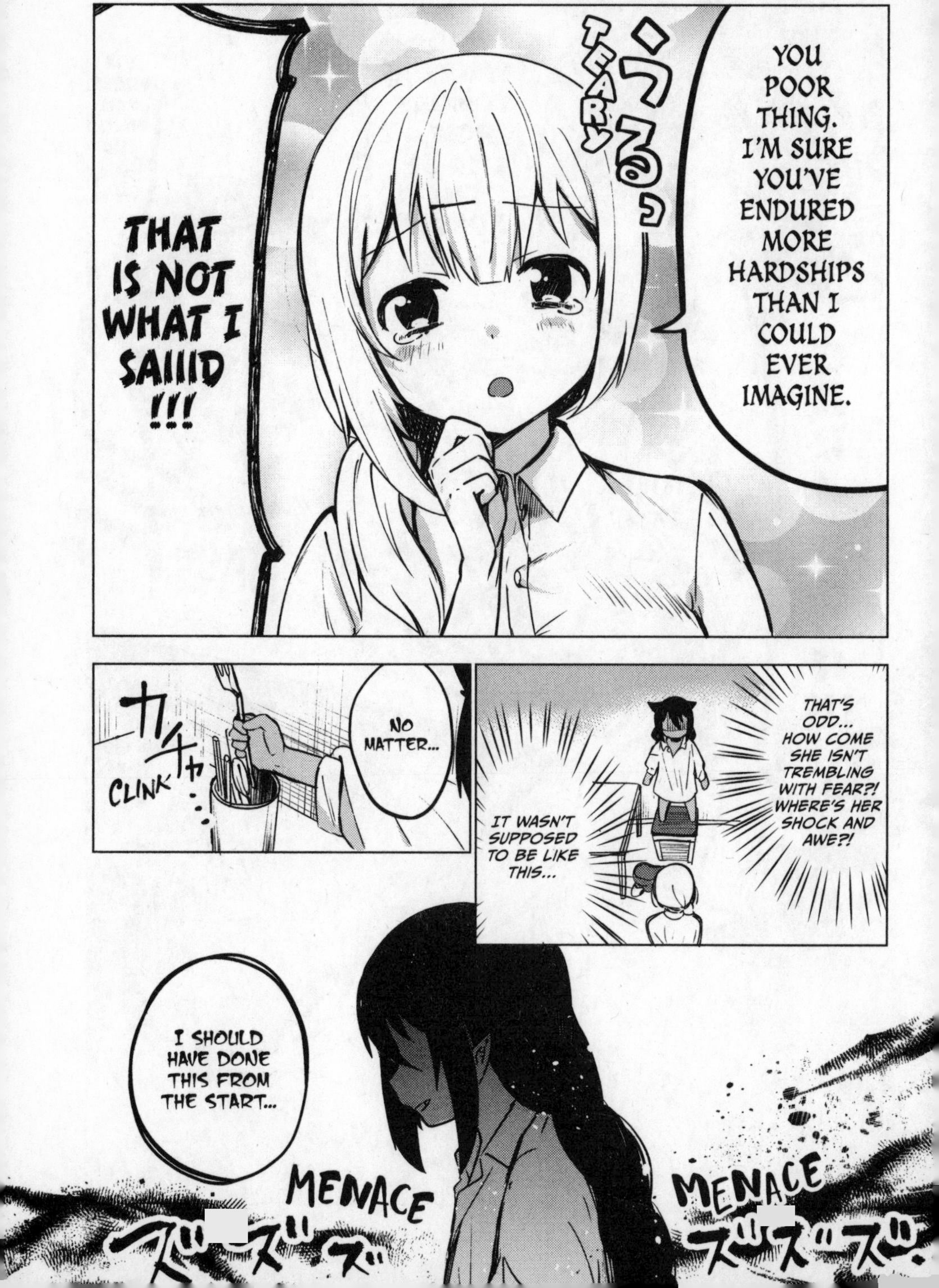
うるっ
TEARY
YOU POOR THING. I'M SURE YOU'VE ENDURED MORE HARDSHIPS THAN I COULD EVER IMAGINE.
THAT IS NOT WHAT I SAIIID !!!
THAT'S ODD... HOW COME SHE ISN'T TREMBLING WITH FEAR?! WHERE'S HER SHOCK AND AWE?!
IT WASN'T SUPPOSED TO BE LIKE THIS...
NO MATTER...
カチャ
CLINK
I SHOULD HAVE DONE THIS FROM THE START...
MENACE
MENACE

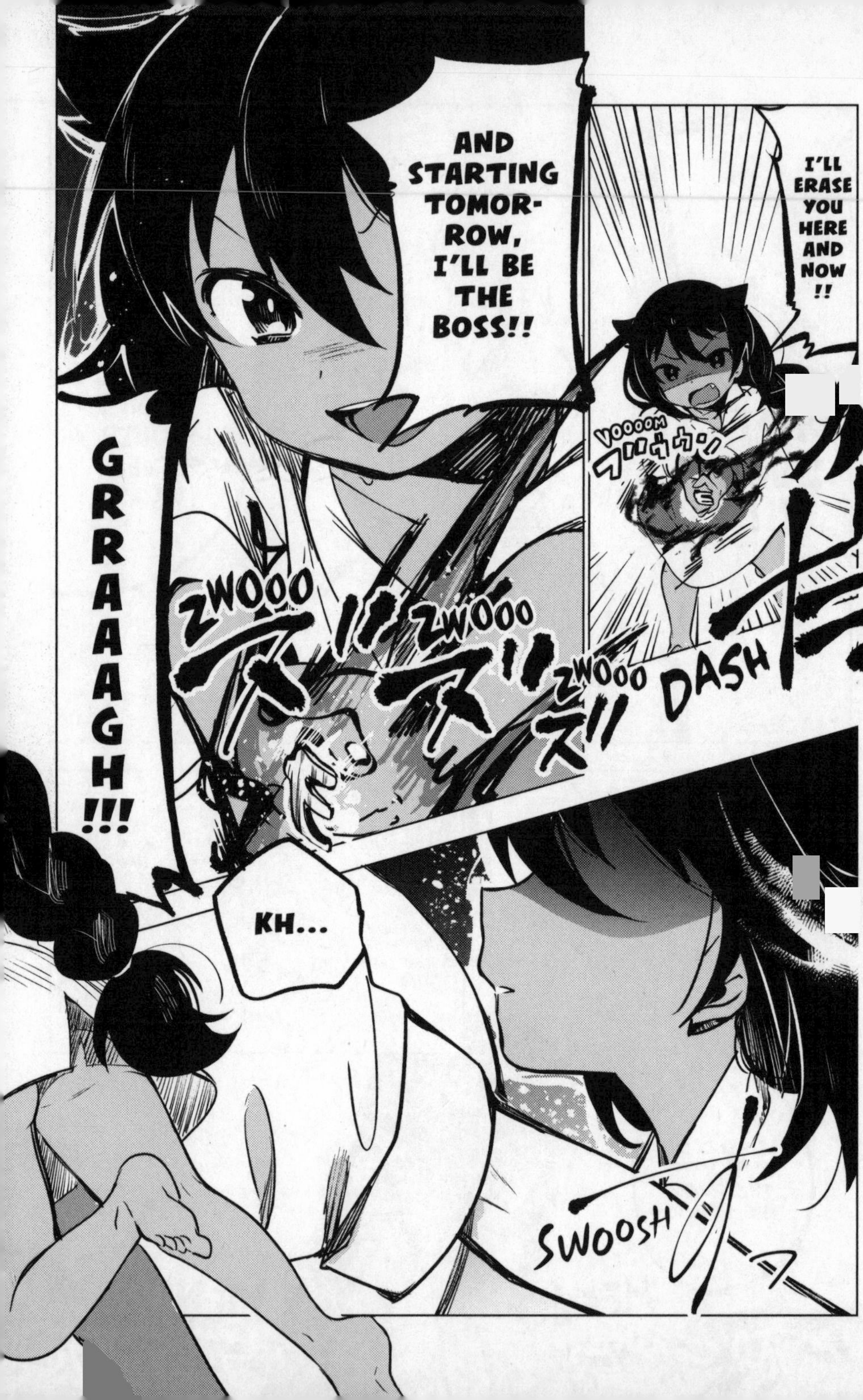
I'LL ERASE YOU HERE AND NOW!!
VOOOOM
DASH
AND STARTING TOMORROW, I'LL BE THE BOSS!!
GRRAAAAGH!!!
ZWOOO
ZWOOO
ZWOOO
KH...
SWOOSH

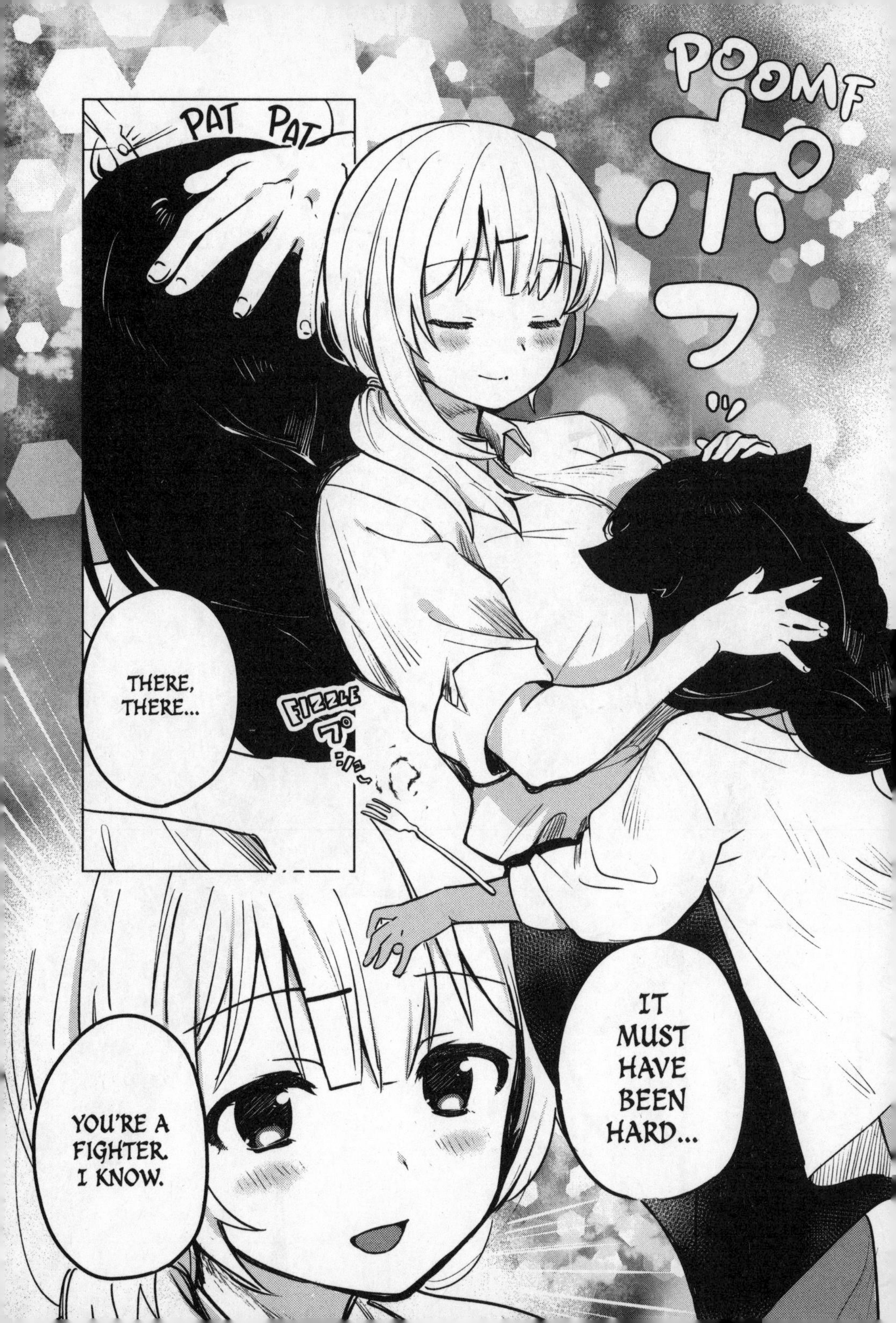
POOMF
ポフ
PAT PAT
THERE, THERE...
FIZZLE
IT MUST HAVE BEEN HARD...
YOU'RE A FIGHTER. I KNOW.

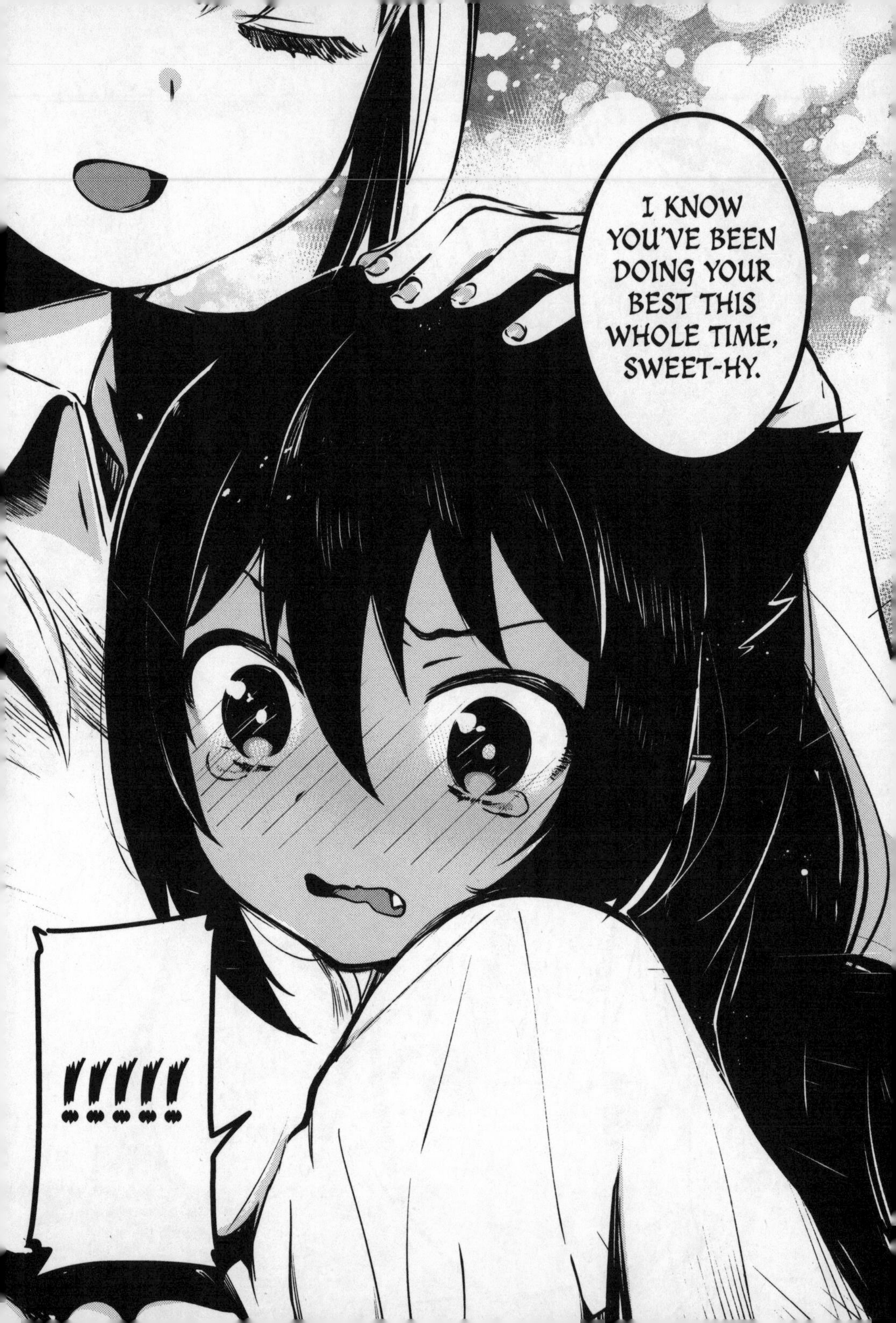
I KNOW YOU'VE BEEN DOING YOUR BEST THIS WHOLE TIME, SWEET-HY.
!!!!!

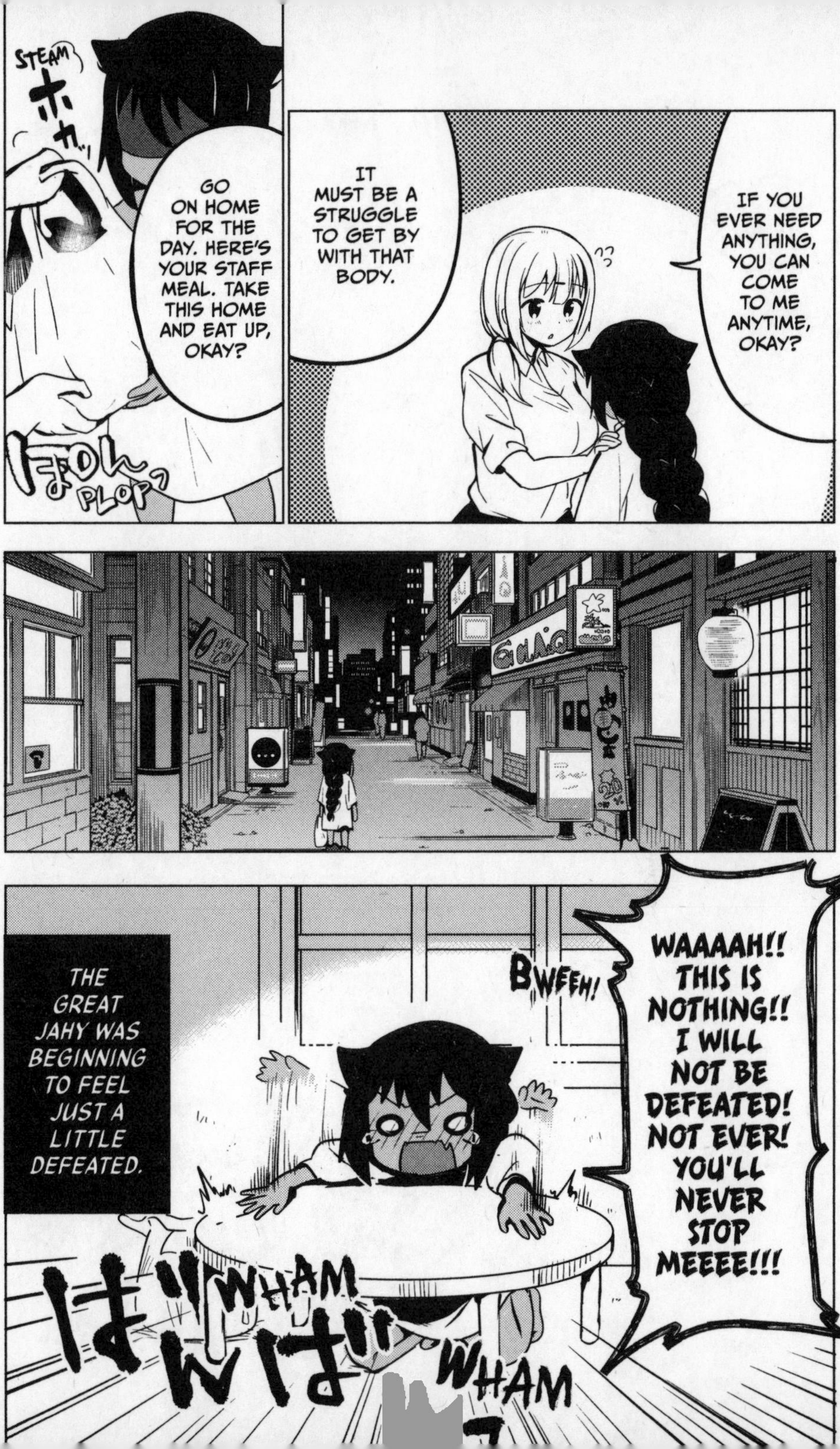
IF YOU EVER NEED ANYTHING, YOU CAN COME TO ME ANYTIME, OKAY?
IT MUST BE A STRUGGLE TO GET BY WITH THAT BODY.
STEAM
GO ON HOME FOR THE DAY. HERE'S YOUR STAFF MEAL. TAKE THIS HOME AND EAT UP, OKAY?
PLOP
WAAAAH!! THIS IS NOTHING!! I WILL NOT BE DEFEATED! NOT EVER! YOU'LL NEVER STOP MEEEE!!!
BWEEH!
THE GREAT JAHY WAS BEGINNING TO FEEL JUST A LITTLE DEFEATED.
WHAM
WHAM

The GREAT JAHY Will NOT Be DEFEATED!

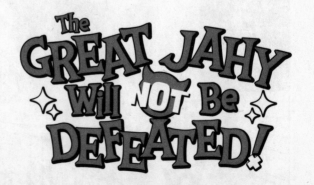

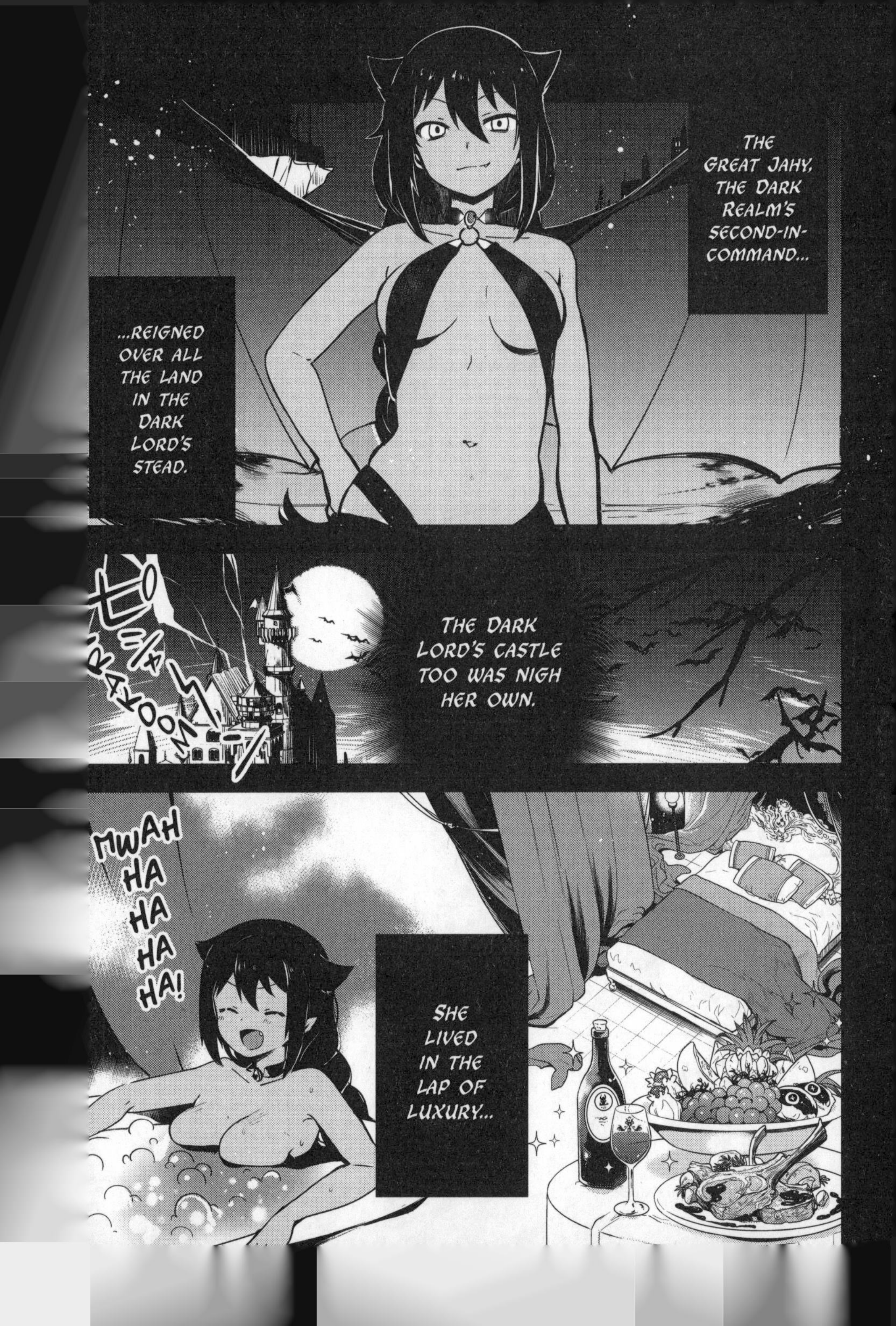
THE GREAT JAHY, THE DARK REALM'S SECOND-IN-COMMAND...
...REIGNED OVER ALL THE LAND IN THE DARK LORD'S STEAD.
THE DARK LORD'S CASTLE TOO WAS NIGH HER OWN.
RAKOOM
SHE LIVED IN THE LAP OF LUXURY...
MWAH HA HA HA HA HA!

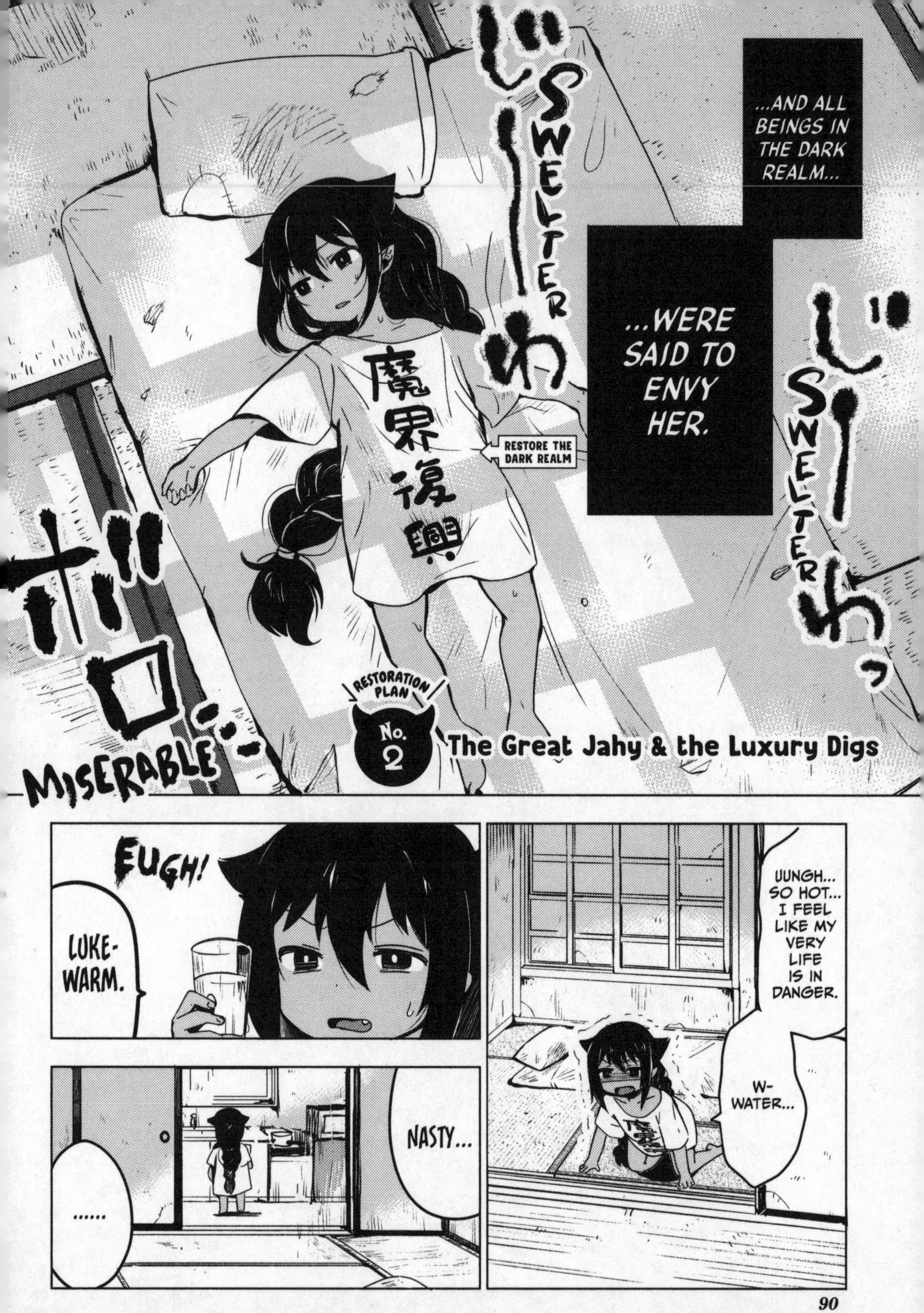
...AND ALL BEINGS IN THE DARK REALM...
...WERE SAID TO ENVY HER.
じわっ
SWELTER
じわ
SWELTER
魔界復興
RESTORE THE DARK REALM
ボロ…
MISERABLE
RESTORATION PLAN
No. 2
The Great Jahy & the Luxury Digs
UUNGH... SO HOT... I FEEL LIKE MY VERY LIFE IS IN DANGER.
W-WATER...
EUGH!
LUKE-WARM.
NASTY...
......

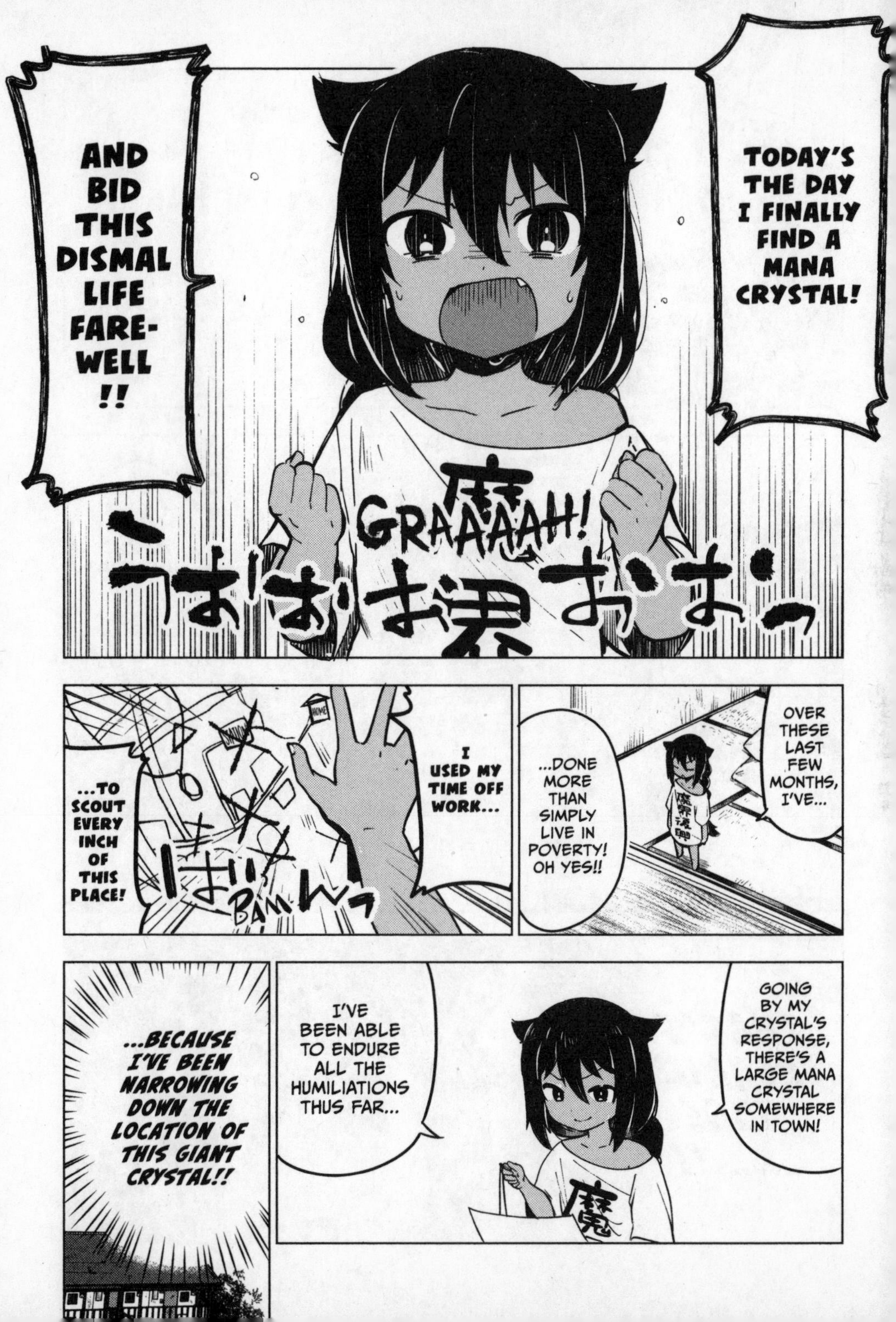
TODAY'S THE DAY I FINALLY FIND A MANA CRYSTAL!
AND BID THIS DISMAL LIFE FARE-WELL!!
GRAAAAH!
OVER THESE LAST FEW MONTHS, I'VE...
...DONE MORE THAN SIMPLY LIVE IN POVERTY! OH YES!!
I USED MY TIME OFF WORK...
...TO SCOUT EVERY INCH OF THIS PLACE!
BAM
GOING BY MY CRYSTAL'S RESPONSE, THERE'S A LARGE MANA CRYSTAL SOMEWHERE IN TOWN!
I'VE BEEN ABLE TO ENDURE ALL THE HUMILIATIONS THUS FAR...
...BECAUSE I'VE BEEN NARROWING DOWN THE LOCATION OF THIS GIANT CRYSTAL!!

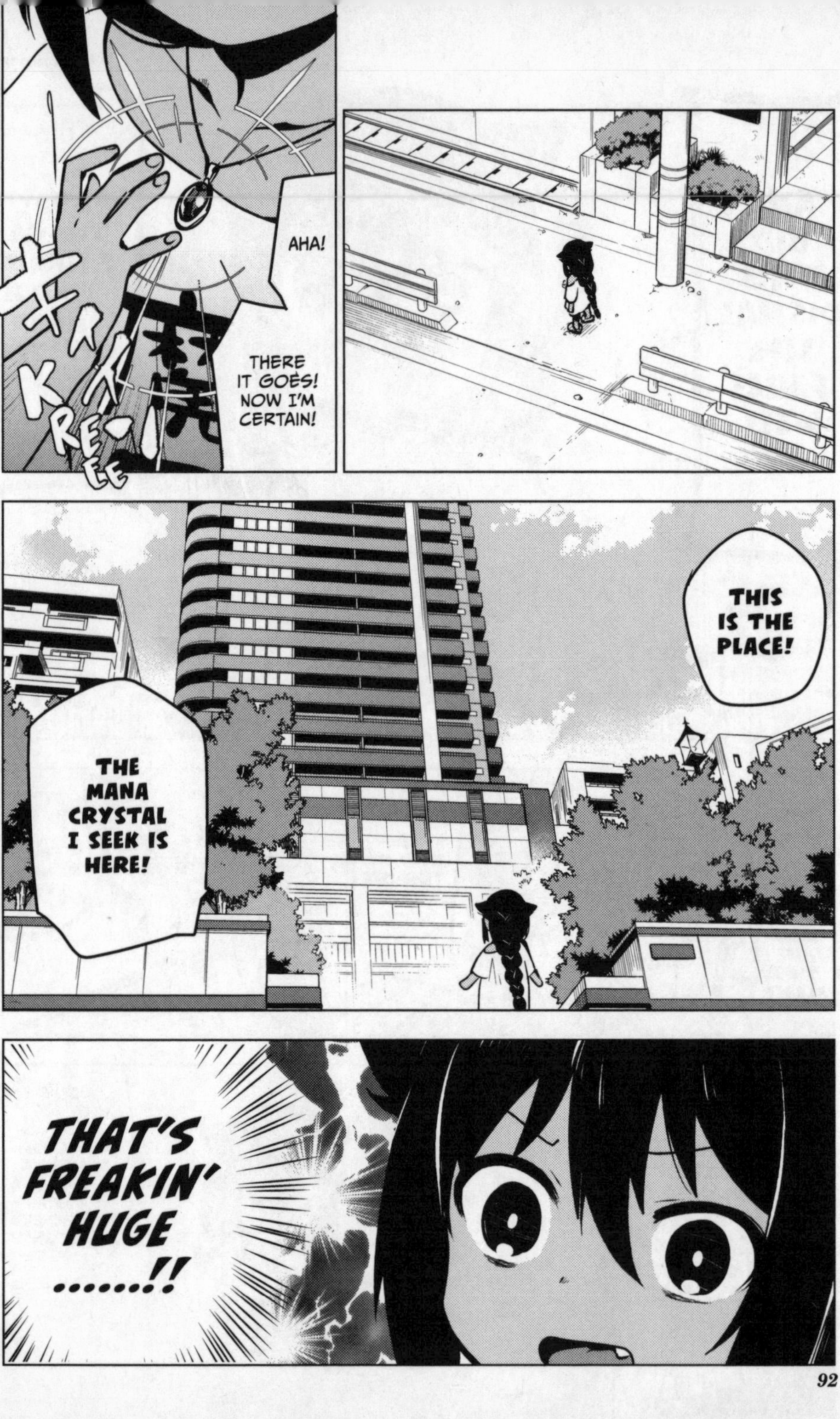
AHA!
THERE IT GOES! NOW I'M CERTAIN!
KREEE
THIS IS THE PLACE!
THE MANA CRYSTAL I SEEK IS HERE!
THAT'S FREAKIN' HUGE ......!!

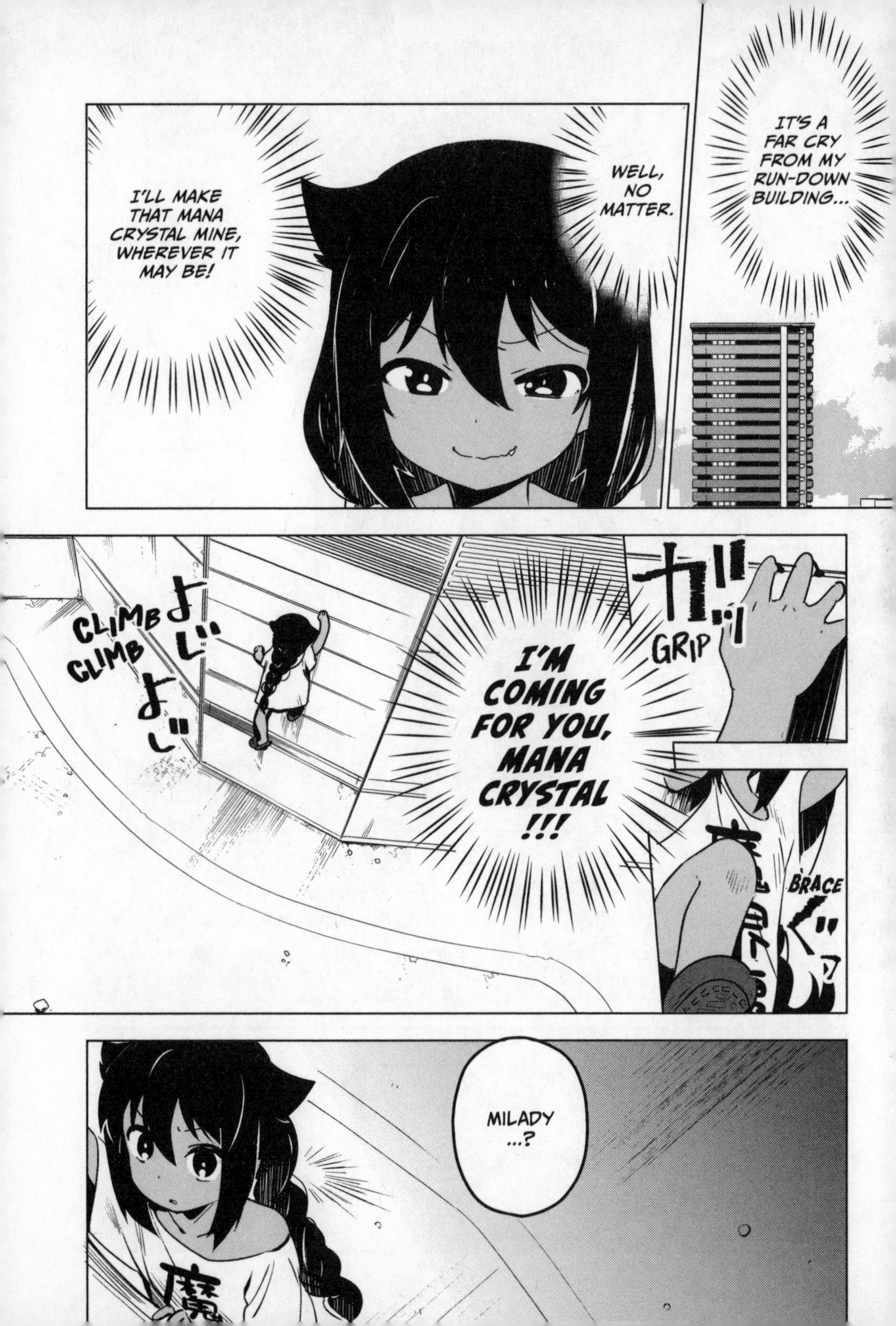
IT'S A FAR CRY FROM MY RUN-DOWN BUILDING...
WELL, NO MATTER.
I'LL MAKE THAT MANA CRYSTAL MINE, WHEREVER IT MAY BE!
ガッ
GRIP
ぐっ
BRACE
I'M COMING FOR YOU, MANA CRYSTAL!!!
よじよじ
CLIMB CLIMB
MILADY ...?

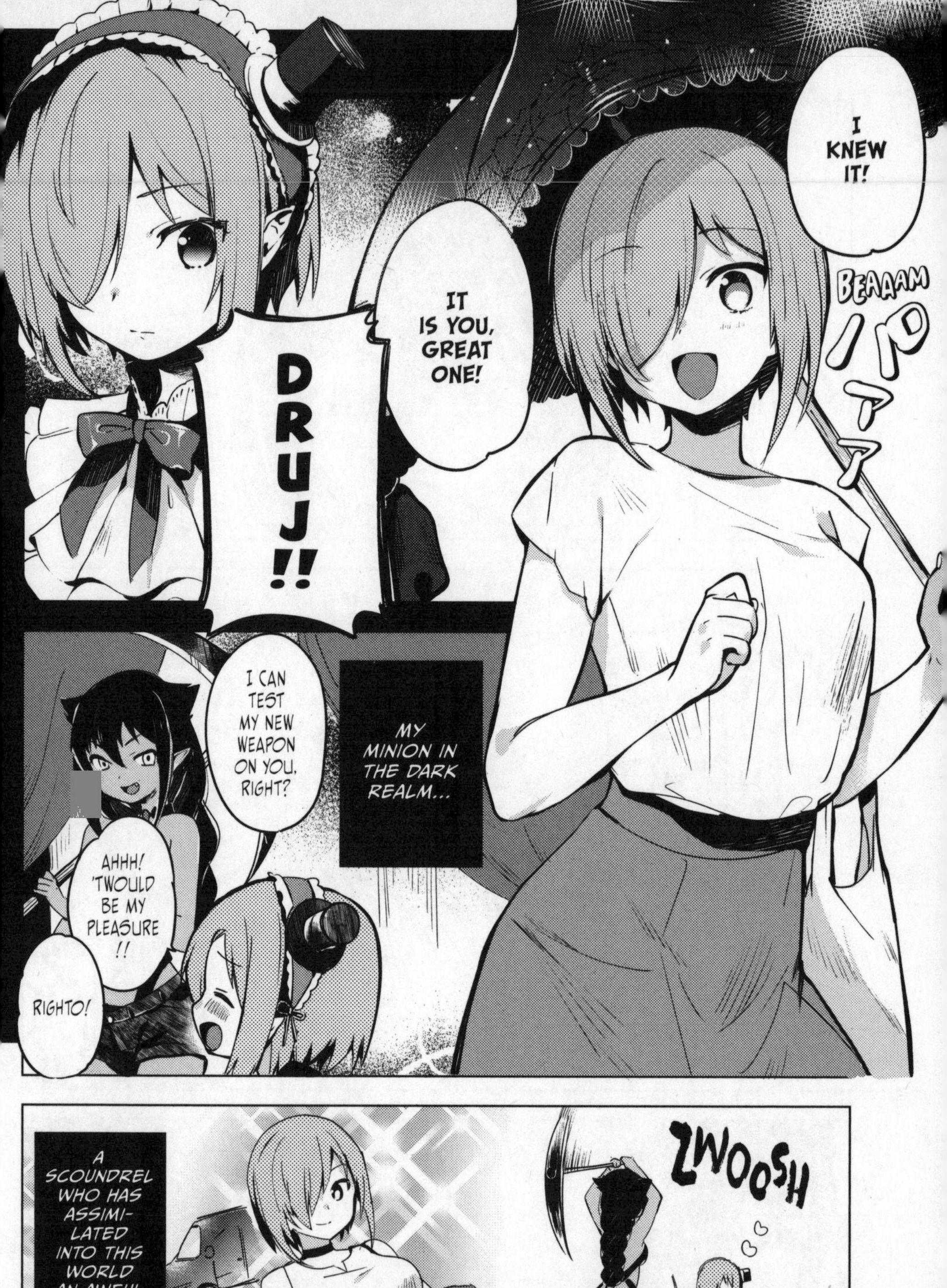
I KNEW IT!
BEAAAM
パァア
IT IS YOU, GREAT ONE!
DRUJ!!
MY MINION IN THE DARK REALM...
I CAN TEST MY NEW WEAPON ON YOU, RIGHT?
AHHH! 'TWOULD BE MY PLEASURE !!
RIGHTO!
ZWOOSH
A SCOUNDREL WHO HAS ASSIMI-LATED INTO THIS WORLD AN AWFUL LOT!

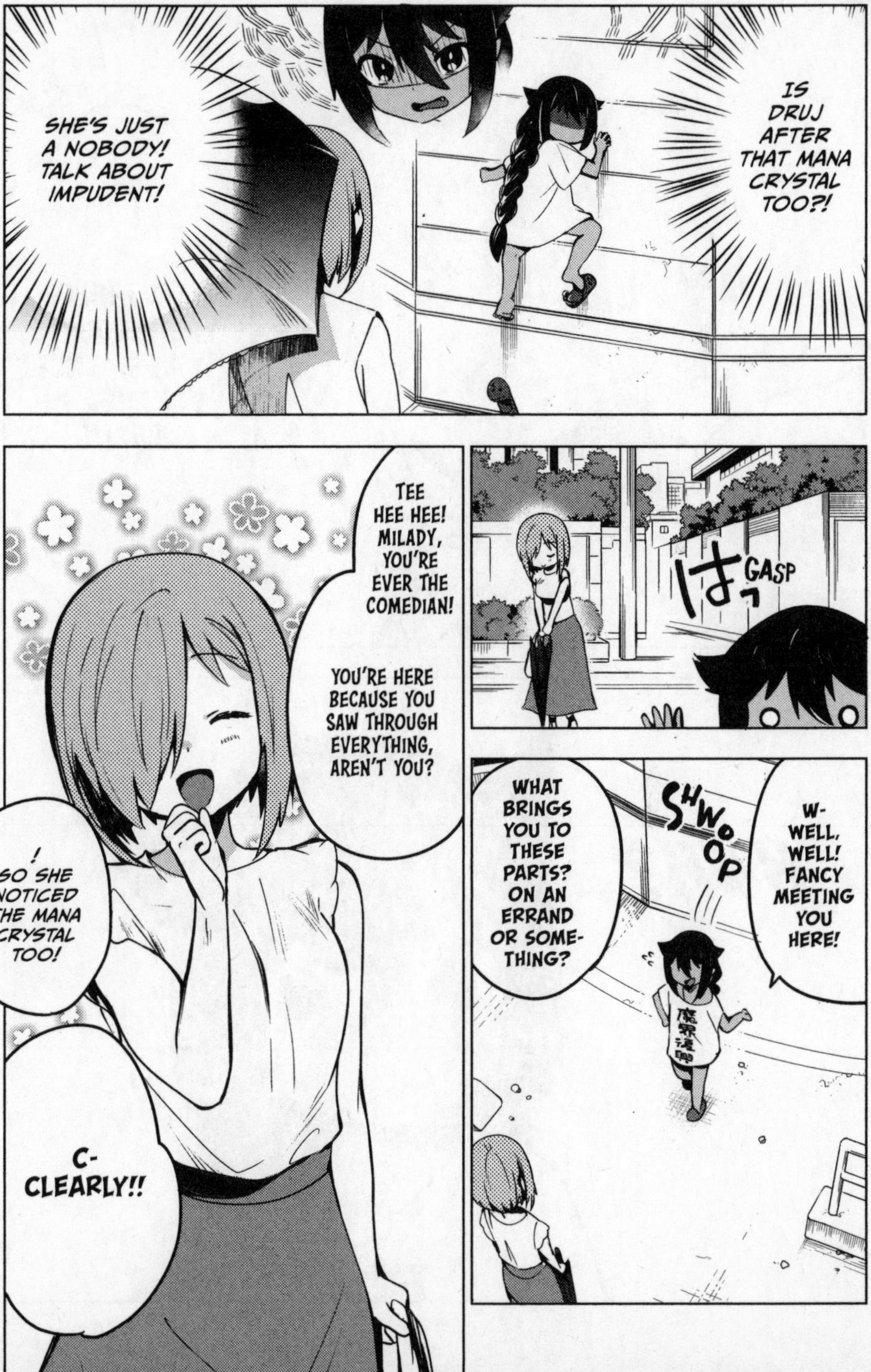
IS DRUJ AFTER THAT MANA CRYSTAL TOO?!
SHE'S JUST A NOBODY! TALK ABOUT IMPUDENT!
はっ GASP
W-WELL, WELL! FANCY MEETING YOU HERE!
SHWOOP
WHAT BRINGS YOU TO THESE PARTS? ON AN ERRAND OR SOMETHING?
TEE HEE HEE! MILADY, YOU'RE EVER THE COMEDIAN!
YOU'RE HERE BECAUSE YOU SAW THROUGH EVERYTHING, AREN'T YOU?
! SO SHE NOTICED THE MANA CRYSTAL TOO!
C-CLEARLY!!

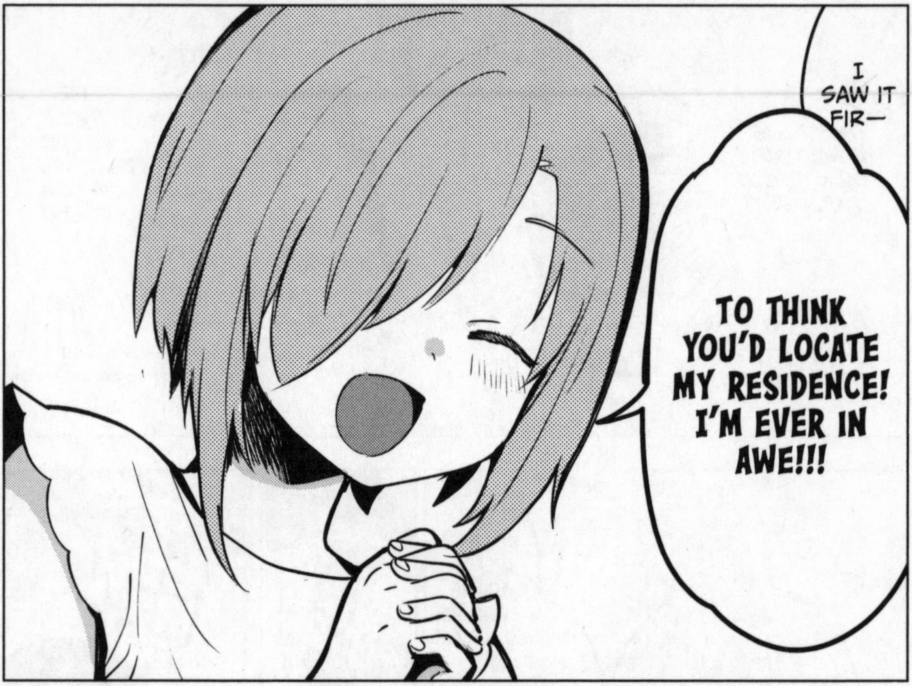
I SAW IT FIR—
TO THINK YOU'D LOCATE MY RESIDENCE! I'M EVER IN AWE!!!

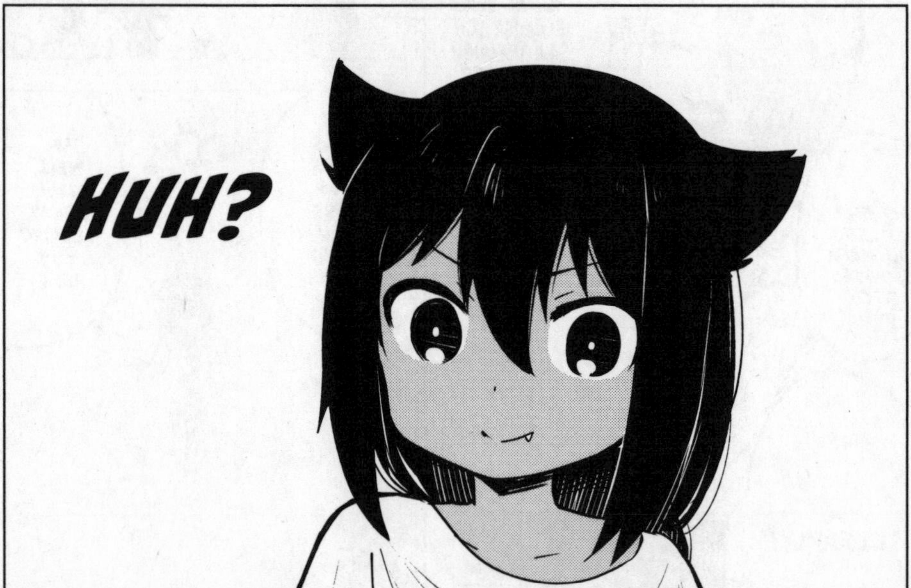
HUH?

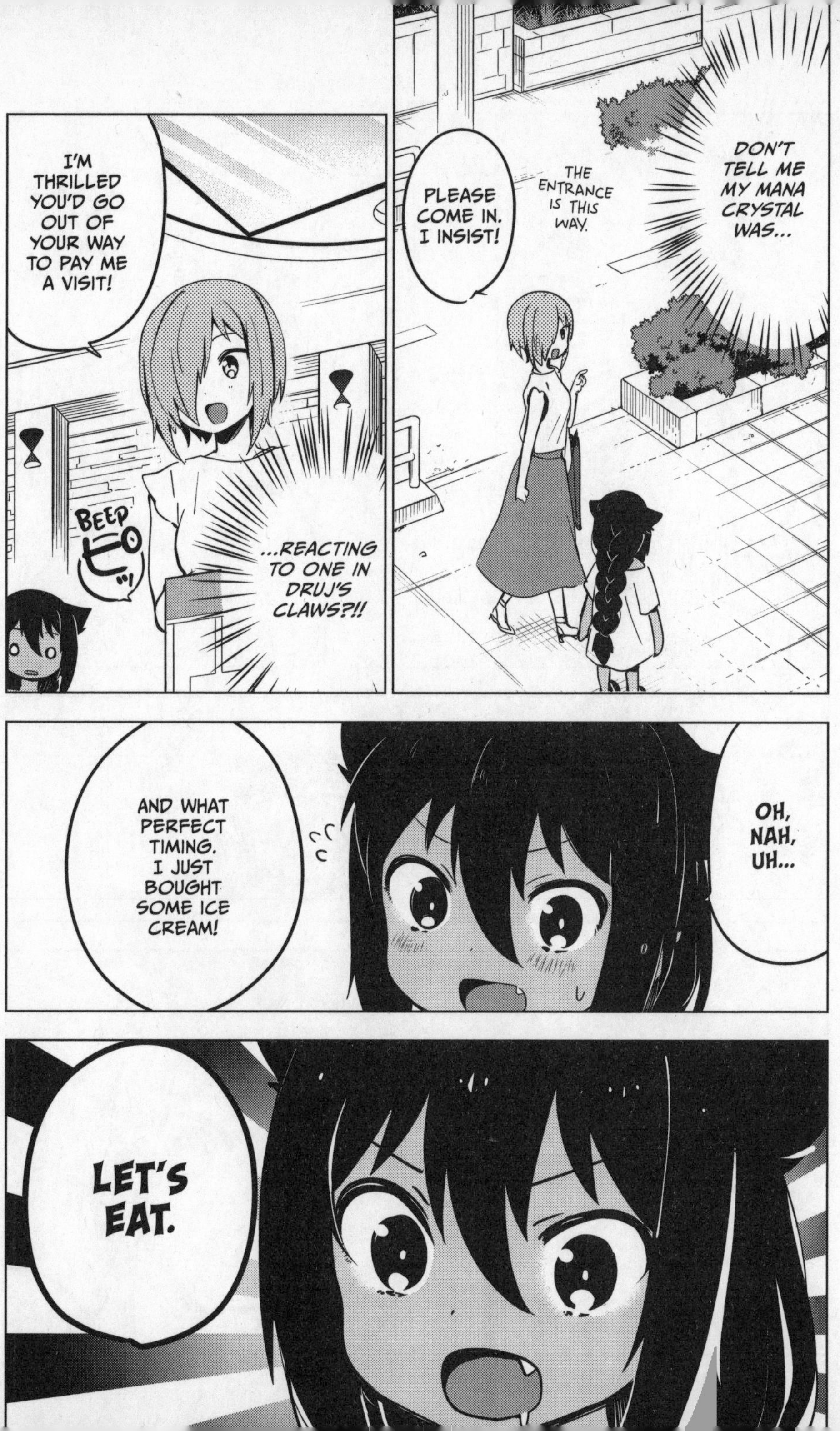
DON'T TELL ME MY MANA CRYSTAL WAS...
THE ENTRANCE IS THIS WAY.
PLEASE COME IN. I INSIST!
I'M THRILLED YOU'D GO OUT OF YOUR WAY TO PAY ME A VISIT!
...REACTING TO ONE IN DRUJ'S CLAWS?!!
BEEP
ピッ
OH, NAH, UH...
AND WHAT PERFECT TIMING. I JUST BOUGHT SOME ICE CREAM!
LET'S EAT.

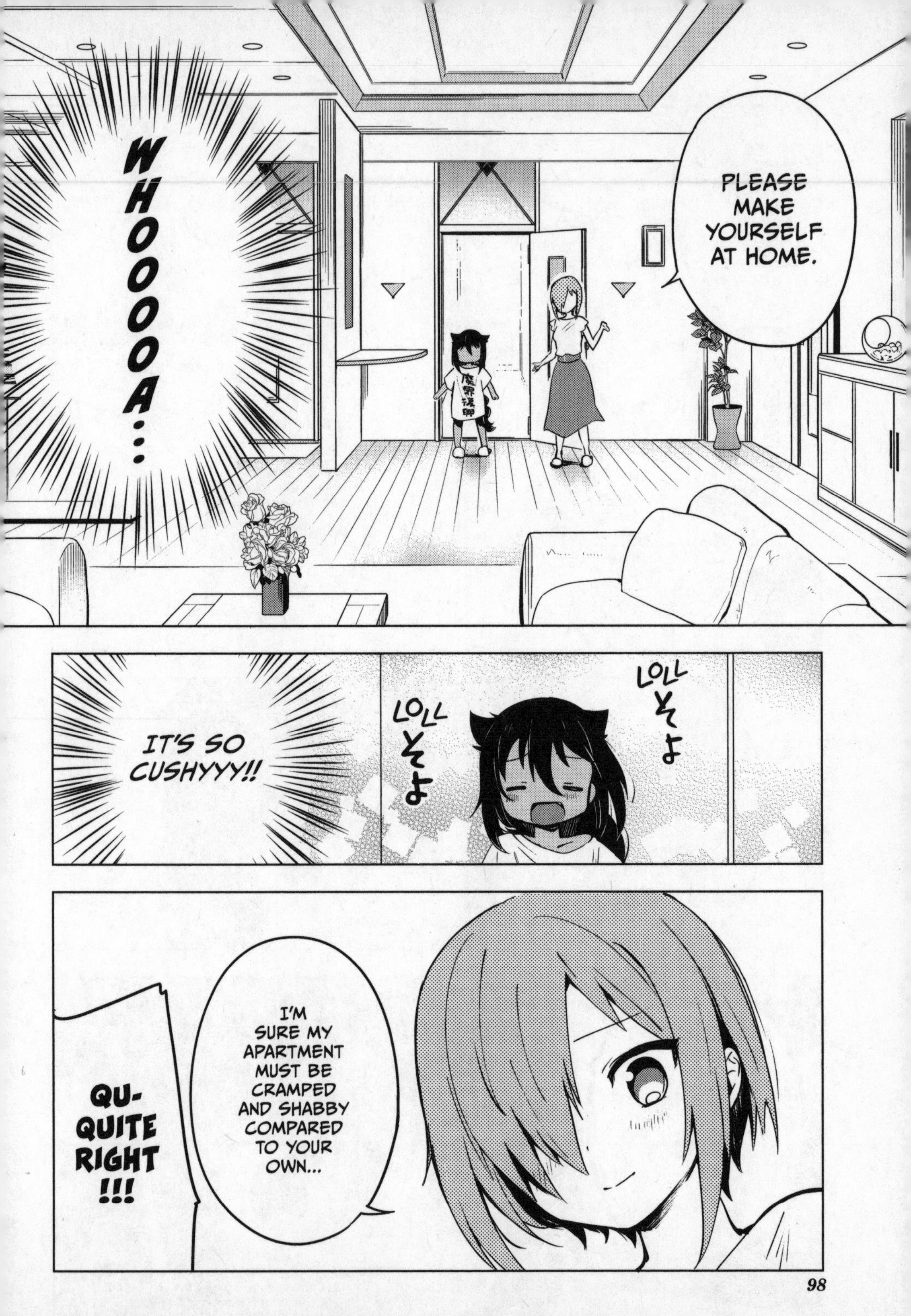
PLEASE MAKE YOURSELF AT HOME.
WHOOOOOA...
LOLL そよ
LOLL そよ
IT'S SO CUSHYYY!!
I'M SURE MY APARTMENT MUST BE CRAMPED AND SHABBY COMPARED TO YOUR OWN...
QU-QUITE RIGHT!!!

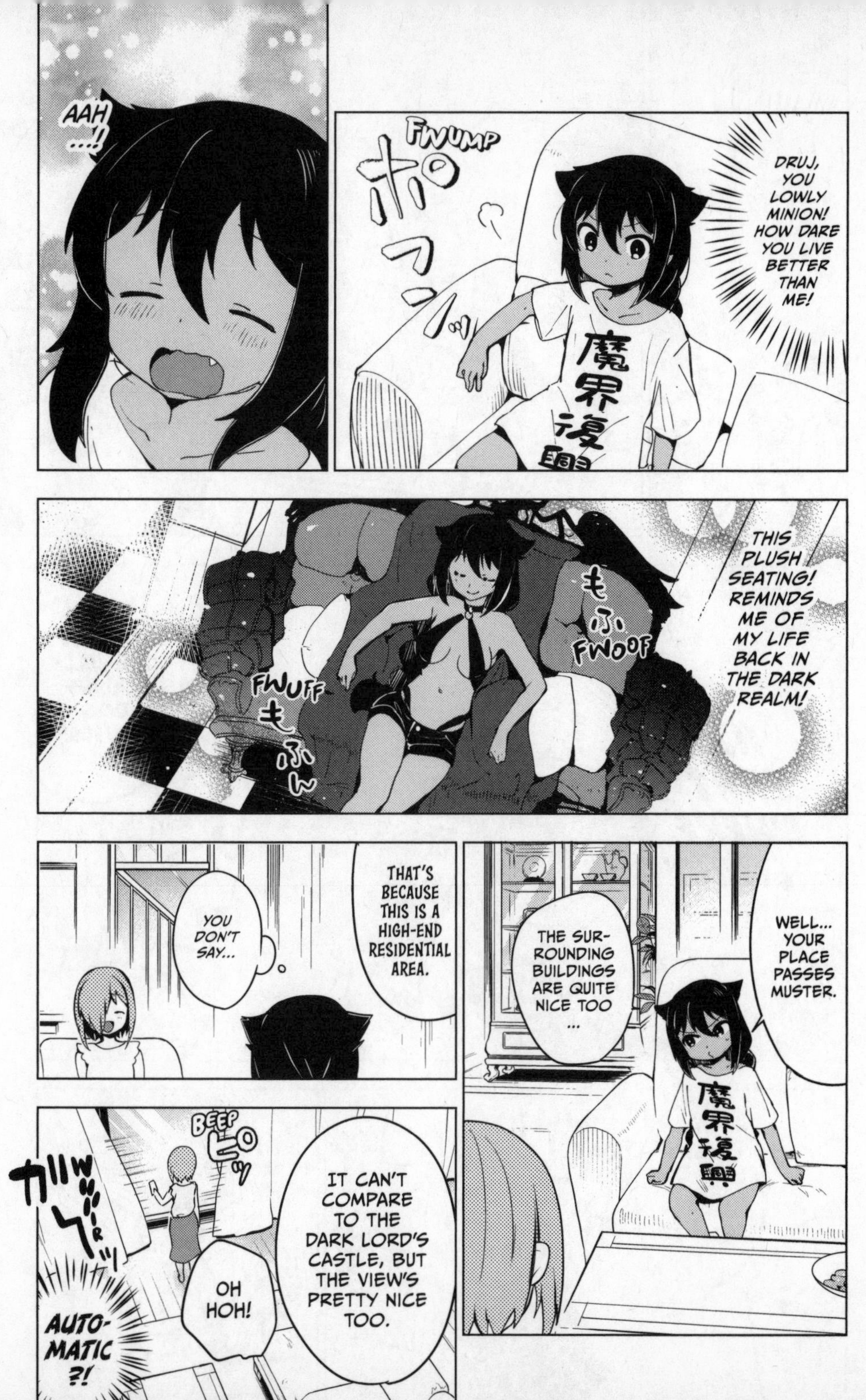
FWUMP
ポフッ
DRUJ, YOU LOWLY MINION! HOW DARE YOU LIVE BETTER THAN ME!
AAH ...!
THIS PLUSH SEATING! REMINDS ME OF MY LIFE BACK IN THE DARK REALM!
もふ
FWOOF
FWUFF
もふん
WELL... YOUR PLACE PASSES MUSTER.
THE SUR-ROUNDING BUILDINGS ARE QUITE NICE TOO ...
THAT'S BECAUSE THIS IS A HIGH-END RESIDENTIAL AREA.
YOU DON'T SAY...
IT CAN'T COMPARE TO THE DARK LORD'S CASTLE, BUT THE VIEW'S PRETTY NICE TOO.
BEEP
ピッ
OH HOH!
WHIRR
ガーッ
AUTO-MATIC ?!

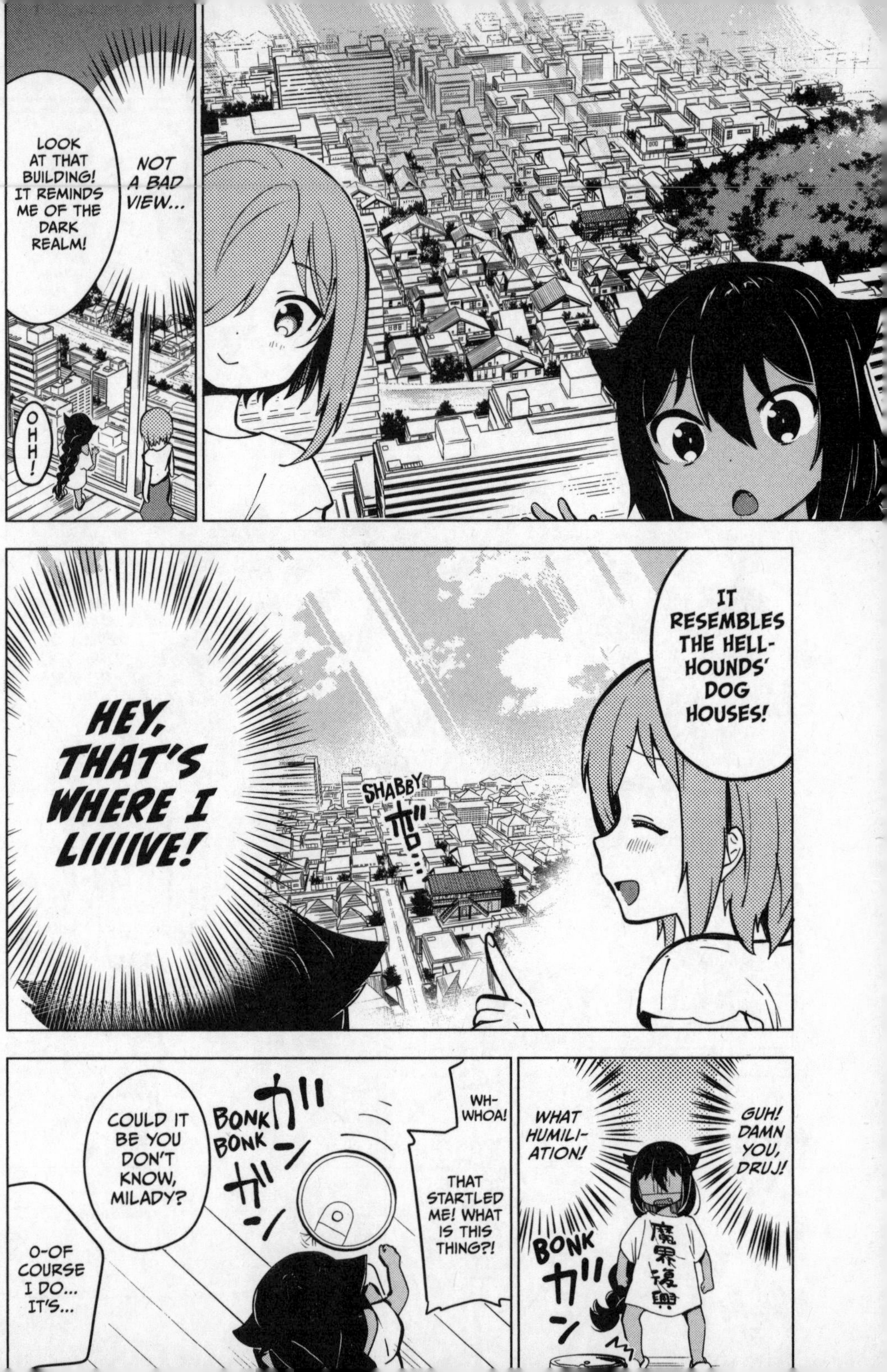
NOT A BAD VIEW...
LOOK AT THAT BUILDING! IT REMINDS ME OF THE DARK REALM!
OHH!
IT RESEMBLES THE HELL-HOUNDS' DOG HOUSES!
SHABBY
HEY, THAT'S WHERE I LIIIIVE!
GUH! DAMN YOU, DRUJ!
WHAT HUMILI-ATION!
魔界復興
BONK
WH-WHOA!
THAT STARTLED ME! WHAT IS THIS THING?!
BONK BONK
COULD IT BE YOU DON'T KNOW, MILADY?
O-OF COURSE I DO... IT'S...

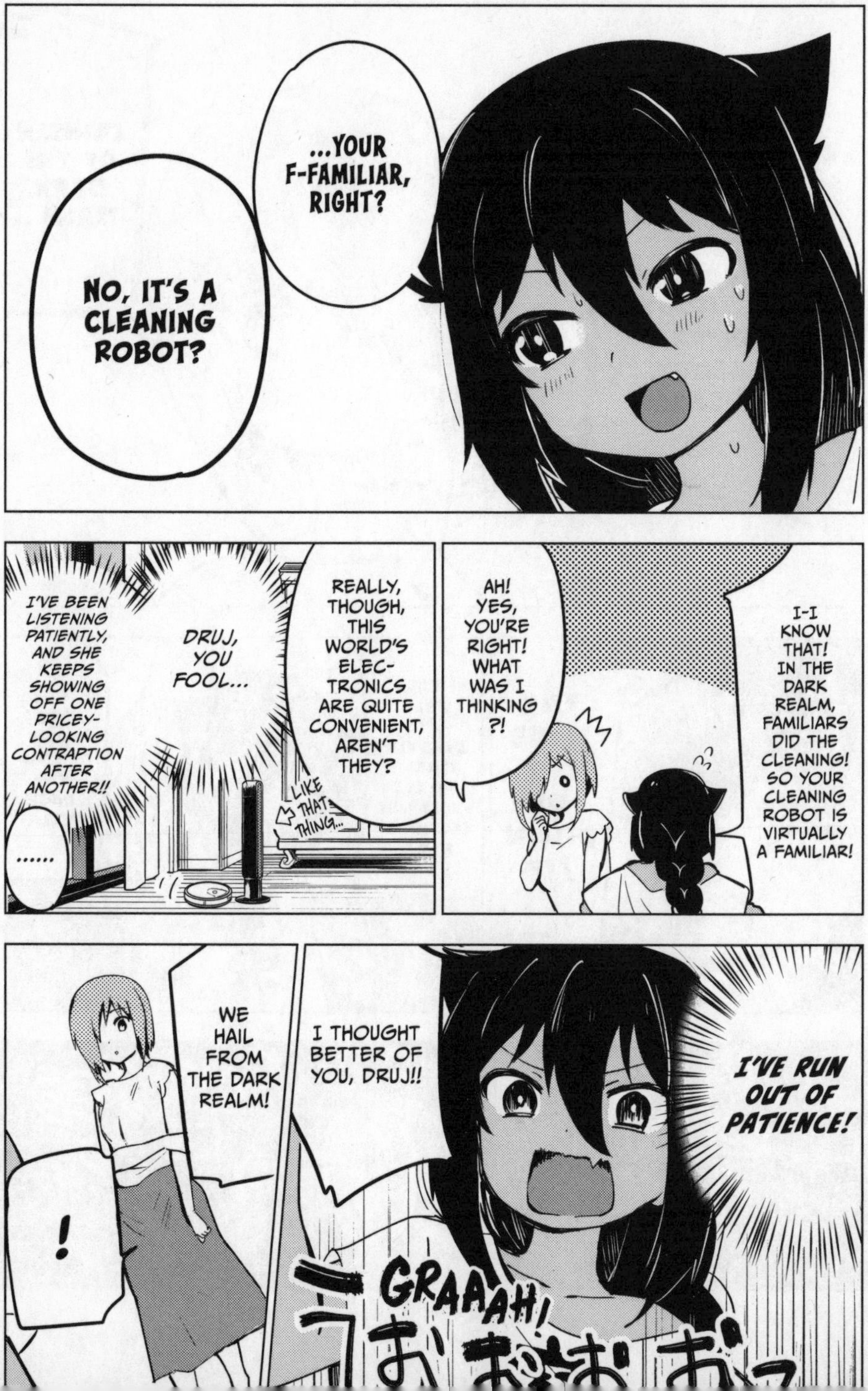
...YOUR F-FAMILIAR, RIGHT?
NO, IT'S A CLEANING ROBOT?
I-I KNOW THAT! IN THE DARK REALM, FAMILIARS DID THE CLEANING! SO YOUR CLEANING ROBOT IS VIRTUALLY A FAMILIAR!
AH! YES, YOU'RE RIGHT! WHAT WAS I THINKING?!
REALLY, THOUGH, THIS WORLD'S ELEC-TRONICS ARE QUITE CONVENIENT, AREN'T THEY?
LIKE THAT THING...
DRUJ, YOU FOOL...
I'VE BEEN LISTENING PATIENTLY, AND SHE KEEPS SHOWING OFF ONE PRICEY-LOOKING CONTRAPTION AFTER ANOTHER!!
......
I'VE RUN OUT OF PATIENCE!
GRAAAH!
I THOUGHT BETTER OF YOU, DRUJ!!
WE HAIL FROM THE DARK REALM!
!

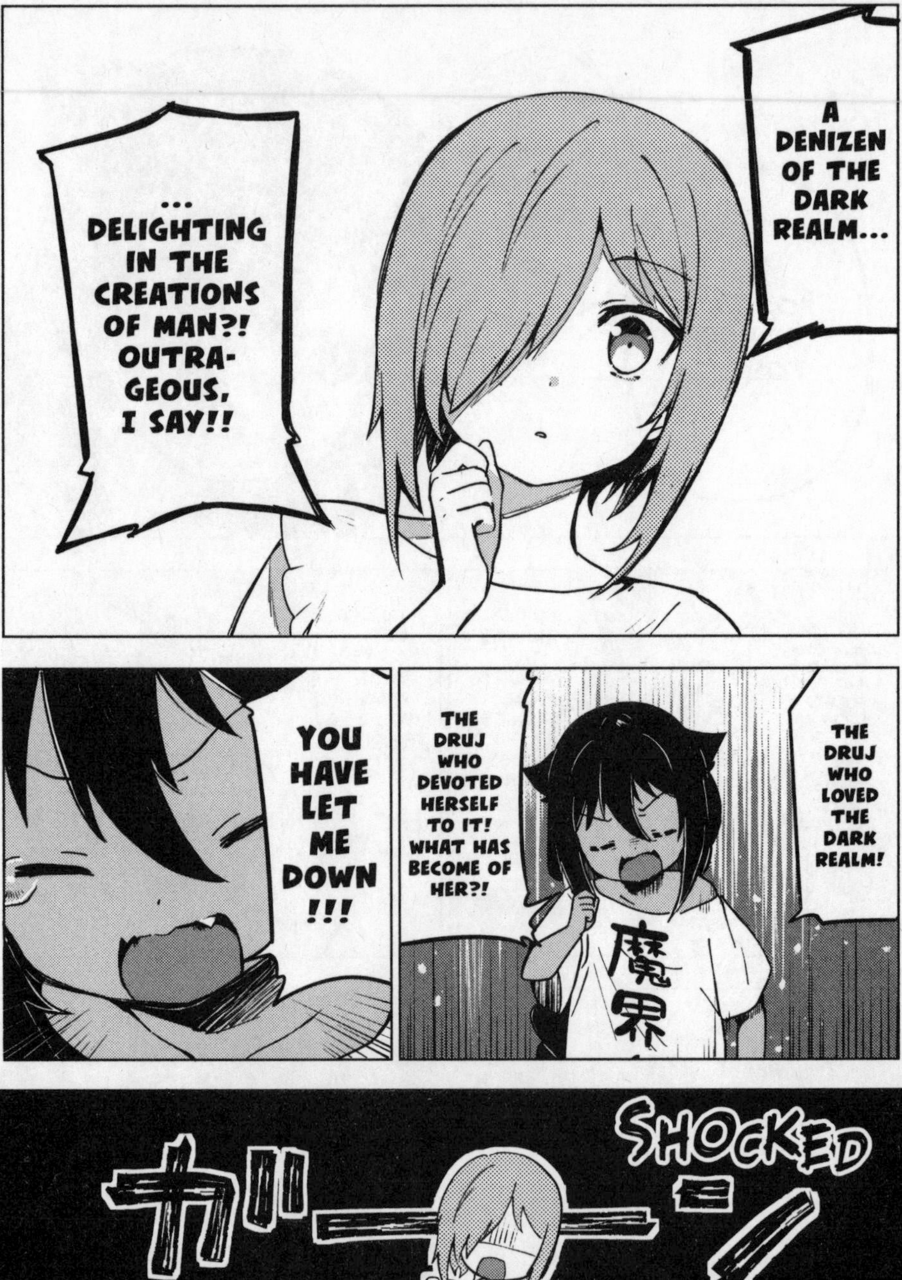
A DENIZEN OF THE DARK REALM...
... DELIGHTING IN THE CREATIONS OF MAN?! OUTRAGEOUS, I SAY!!
THE DRUJ WHO LOVED THE DARK REALM!
THE DRUJ WHO DEVOTED HERSELF TO IT! WHAT HAS BECOME OF HER?!
魔界
YOU HAVE LET ME DOWN!!!
ガーーン
SHOCKED

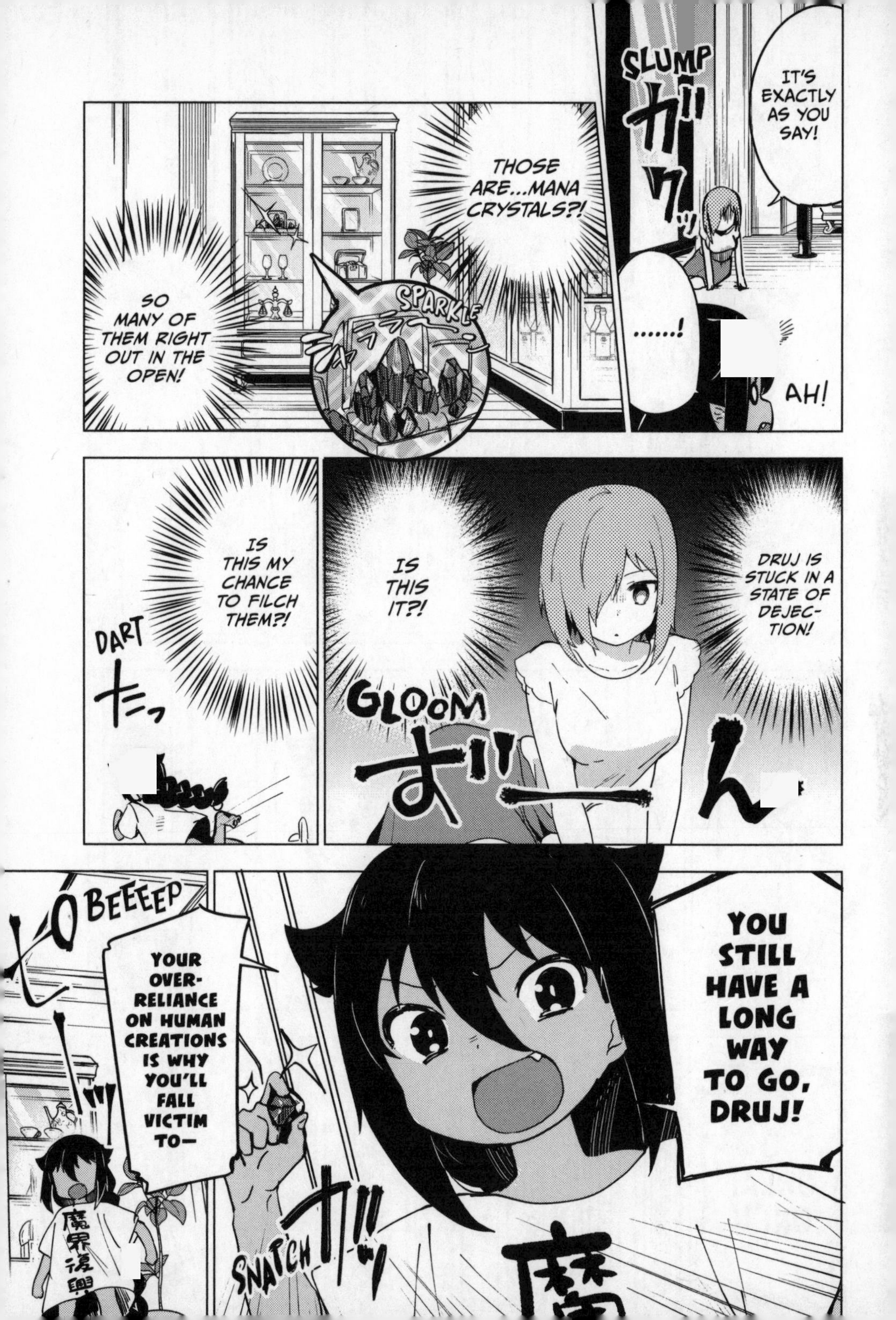
SLUMP
IT'S EXACTLY AS YOU SAY!
......!
AH!
THOSE ARE...MANA CRYSTALS?!
SPARKLE
SO MANY OF THEM RIGHT OUT IN THE OPEN!
DRUJ IS STUCK IN A STATE OF DEJECTION!
IS THIS IT?!
GLOOM
IS THIS MY CHANCE TO FILCH THEM?!
DART
YOU STILL HAVE A LONG WAY TO GO, DRUJ!
BEEEEP
YOUR OVER-RELIANCE ON HUMAN CREATIONS IS WHY YOU'LL FALL VICTIM TO—
SNATCH
魔界復興

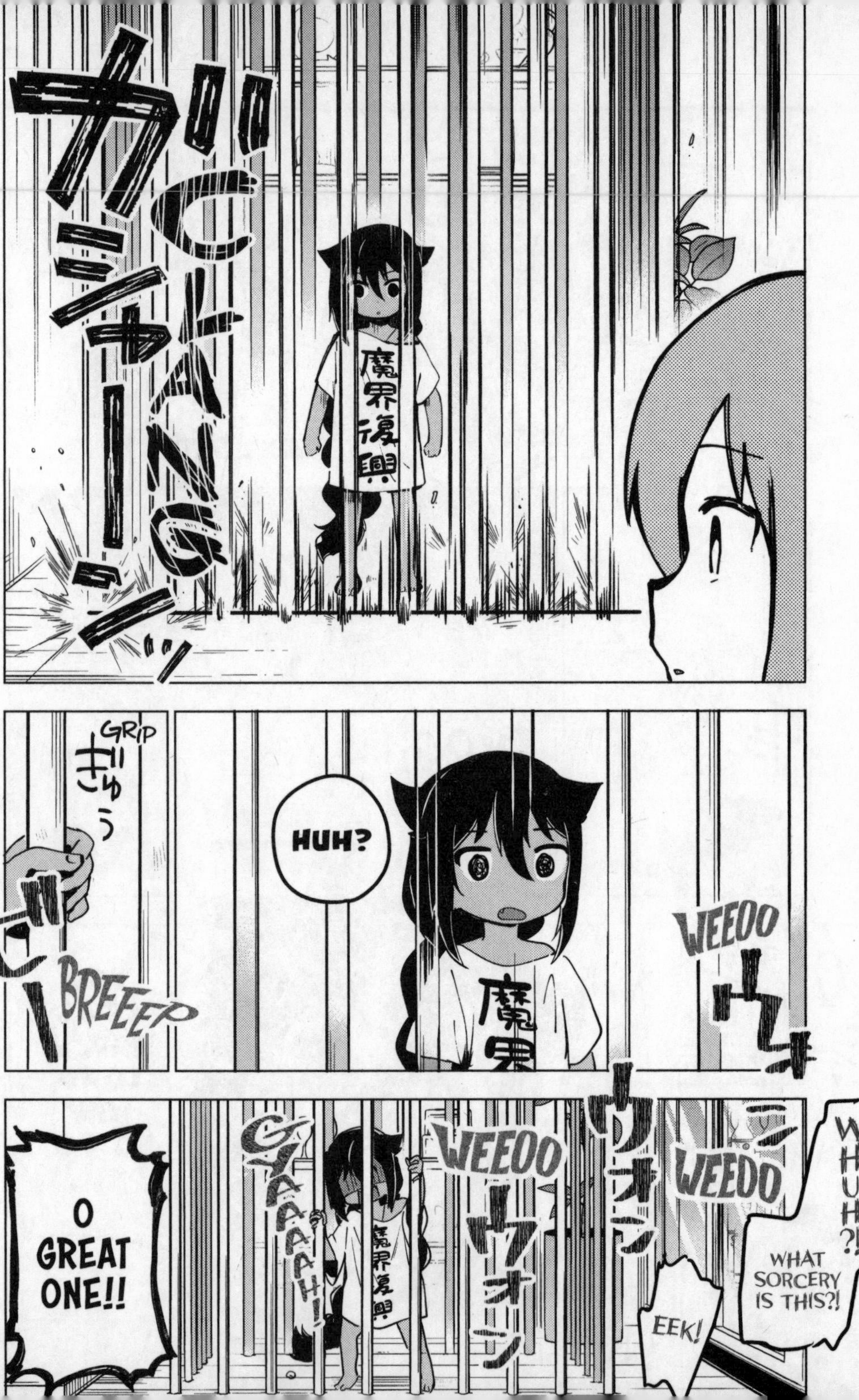

カシャーン
CLANG
魔界復興
HUH?
WEEOO
GRIP
ぎゅう
BREEEP
WHUH?!
WHAT SORCERY IS THIS?!
EEK!
WEEOO
WEEOO
GYAAAAH!
O GREAT ONE!!

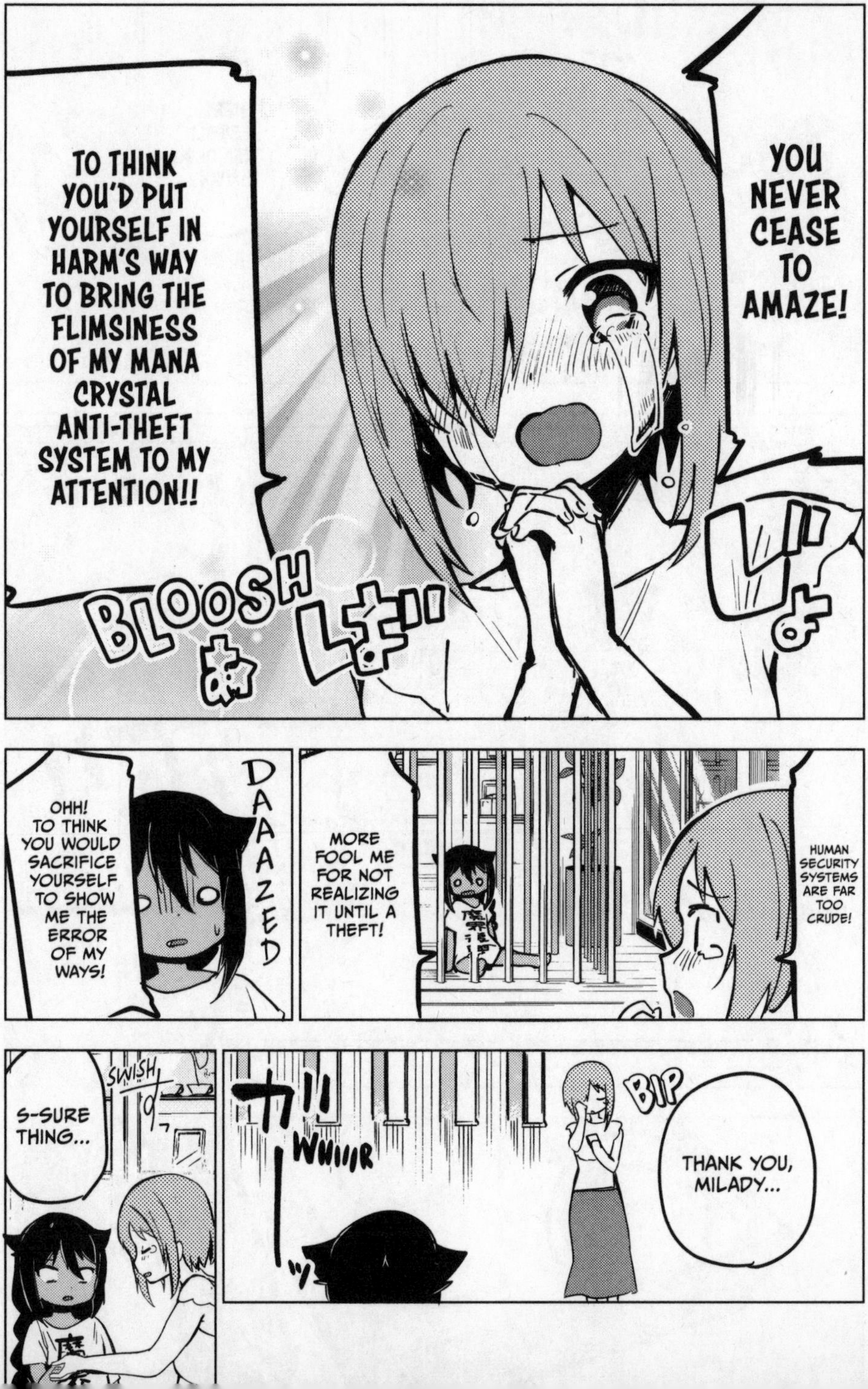
YOU NEVER CEASE TO AMAZE!
TO THINK YOU'D PUT YOURSELF IN HARM'S WAY TO BRING THE FLIMSINESS OF MY MANA CRYSTAL ANTI-THEFT SYSTEM TO MY ATTENTION!!
BLOOSH
HUMAN SECURITY SYSTEMS ARE FAR TOO CRUDE!
MORE FOOL ME FOR NOT REALIZING IT UNTIL A THEFT!
DAAAZED
OHH! TO THINK YOU WOULD SACRIFICE YOURSELF TO SHOW ME THE ERROR OF MY WAYS!
BIP
THANK YOU, MILADY...
WHIIIR
SWISH
S-SURE THING...

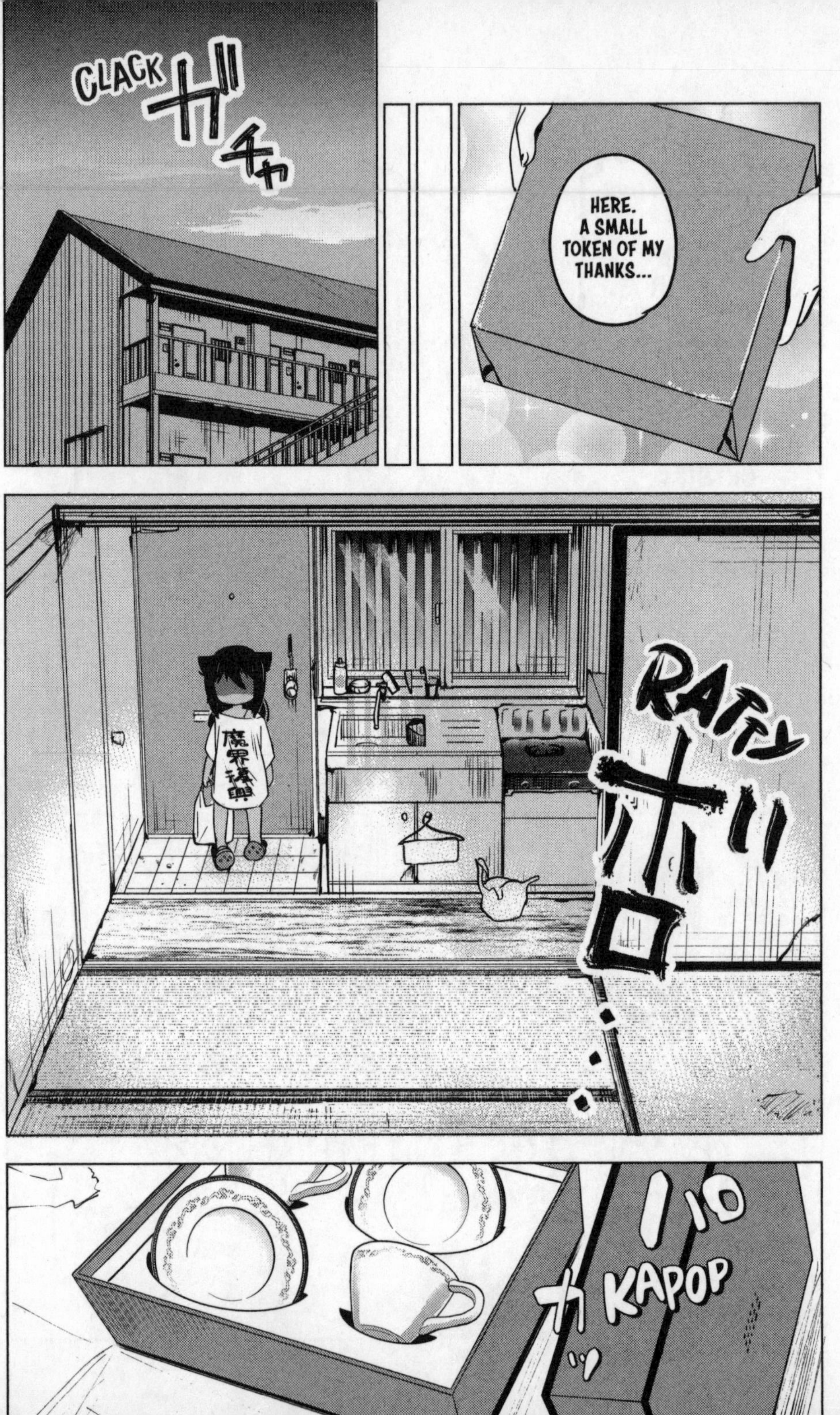
HERE. A SMALL TOKEN OF MY THANKS...
CLACK
ガチャ
RATTY
ボロ
KAPOP
パカッ

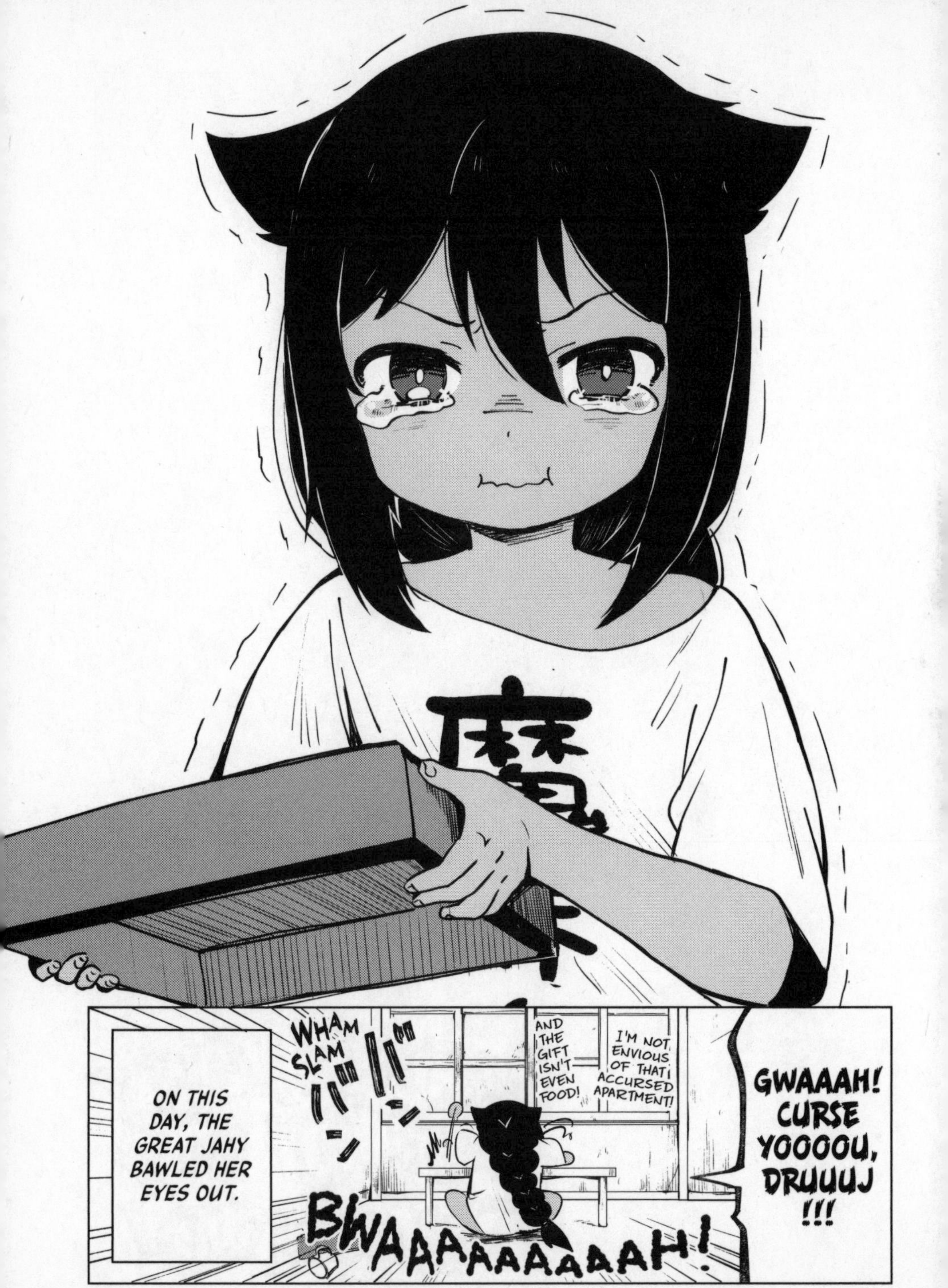
GWAAAH! CURSE YOOOOU, DRUUUJ!!!
I'M NOT ENVIOUS OF THAT ACCURSED APARTMENT!
AND THE GIFT ISN'T EVEN FOOD!
WHAM SLAM
BWAAAAAAAAAAH!
ON THIS DAY, THE GREAT JAHY BAWLED HER EYES OUT.

The GREAT JAHY Will NOT Be DEFEATED!

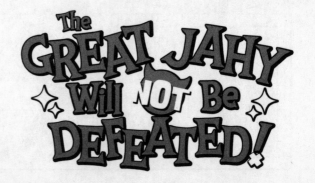

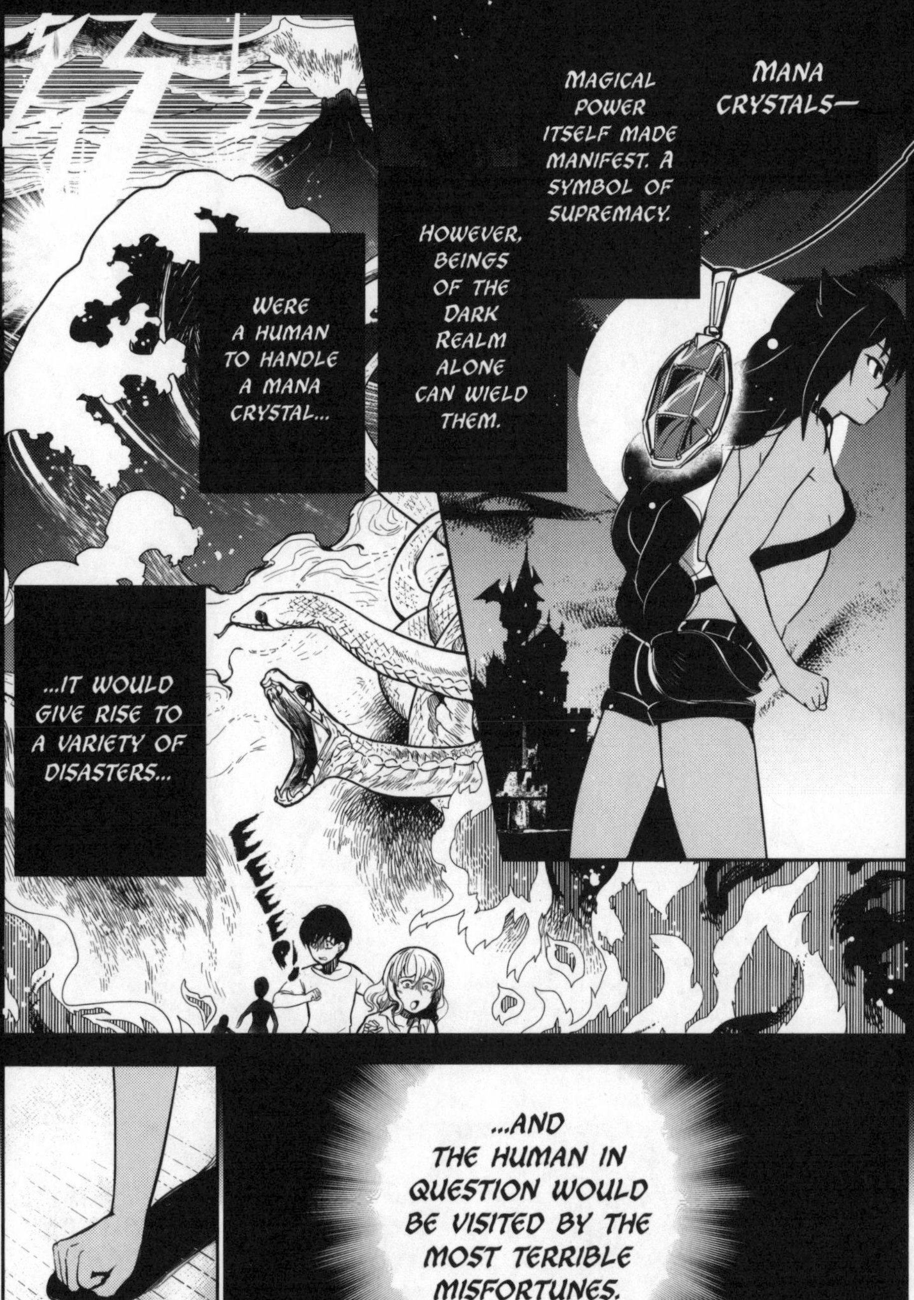
MANA CRYSTALS—
MAGICAL POWER ITSELF MADE MANIFEST. A SYMBOL OF SUPREMACY.
HOWEVER, BEINGS OF THE DARK REALM ALONE CAN WIELD THEM.
WERE A HUMAN TO HANDLE A MANA CRYSTAL...
...IT WOULD GIVE RISE TO A VARIETY OF DISASTERS...
EEEEP!
...AND THE HUMAN IN QUESTION WOULD BE VISITED BY THE MOST TERRIBLE MISFORTUNES.

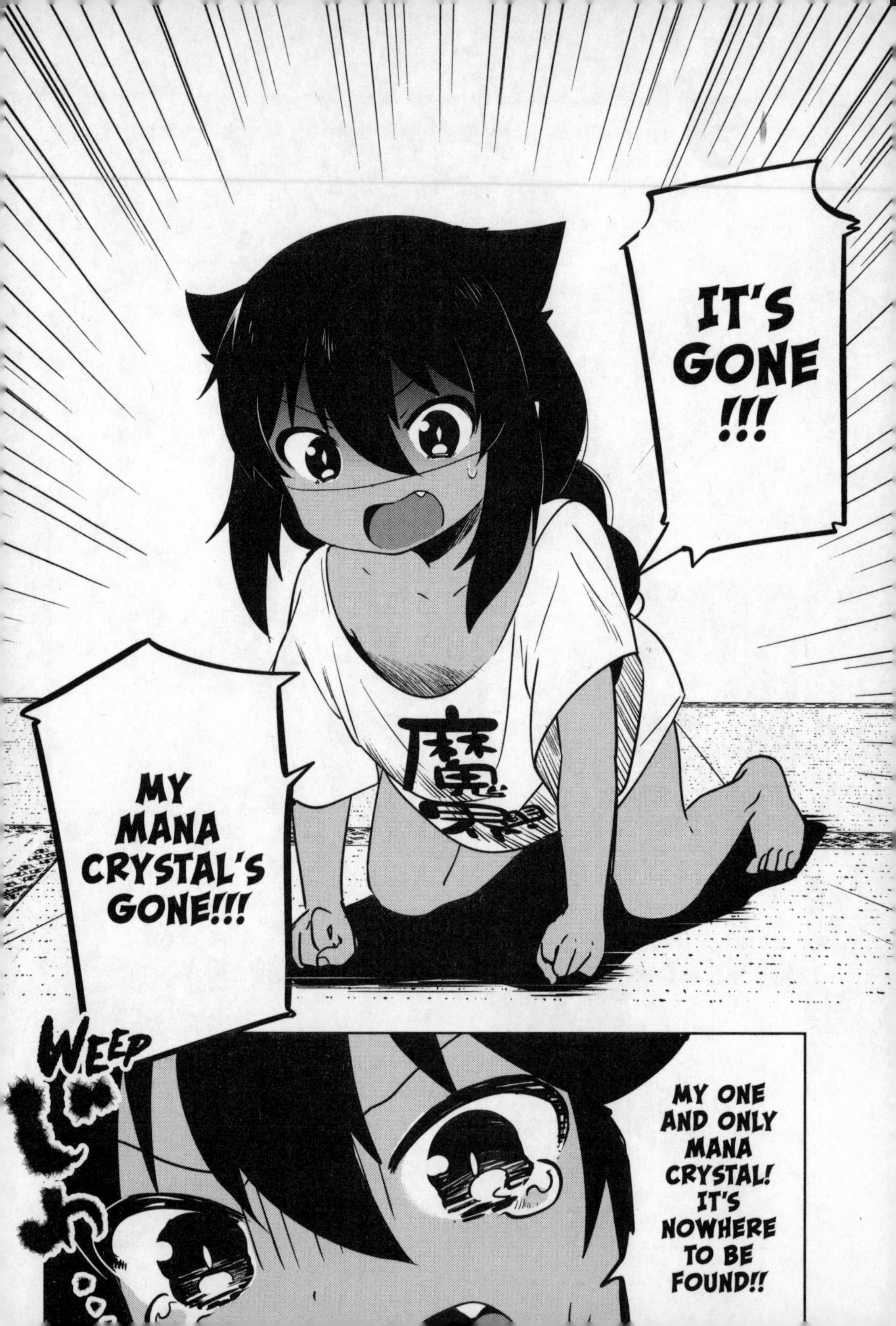
IT'S GONE!!!
MY MANA CRYSTAL'S GONE!!!
MY ONE AND ONLY MANA CRYSTAL! IT'S NOWHERE TO BE FOUND!!
WEEP

RESTORATION PLAN No. 3

The Great Jahy & the Precious Mana Crystal

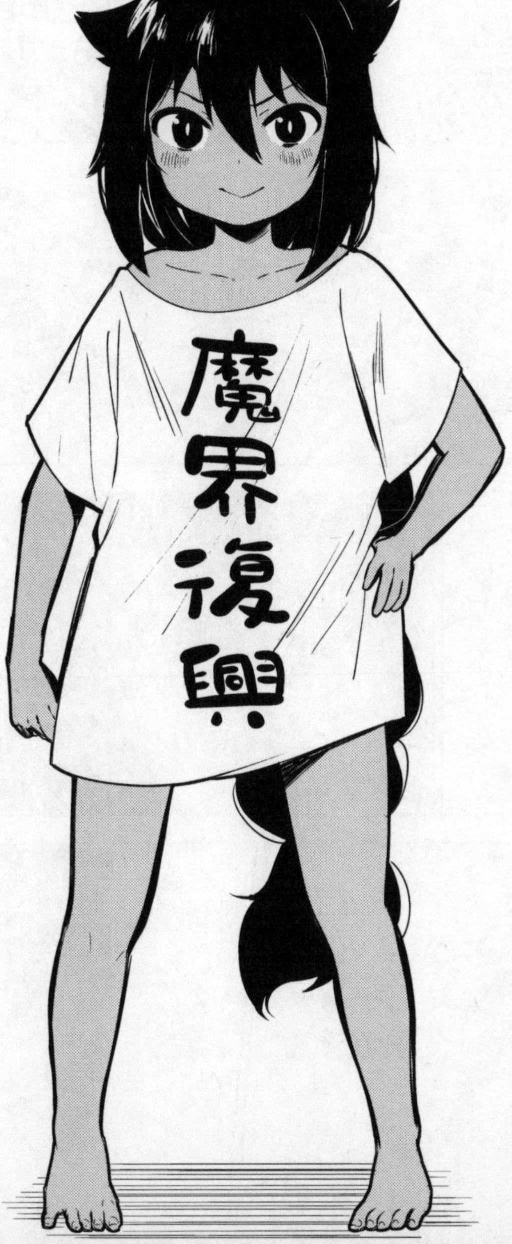
魔界復興

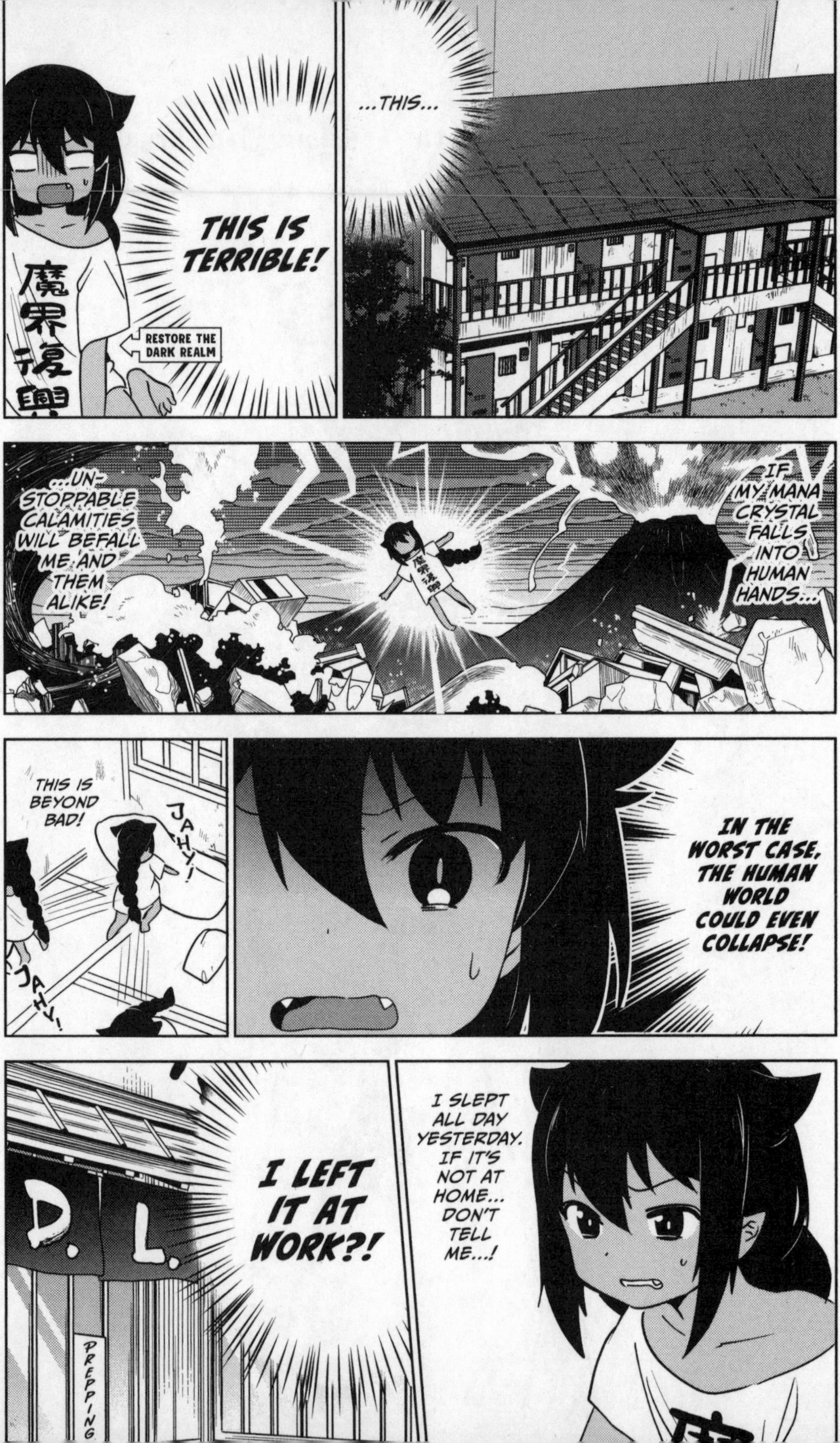
...THIS...
THIS IS TERRIBLE!
魔界復興
RESTORE THE DARK REALM
IF MY MANA CRYSTAL FALLS INTO HUMAN HANDS...
...UN-STOPPABLE CALAMITIES WILL BEFALL ME AND THEM ALIKE!
IN THE WORST CASE, THE HUMAN WORLD COULD EVEN COLLAPSE!
THIS IS BEYOND BAD!
JAHY!
JAHY!
I SLEPT ALL DAY YESTERDAY. IF IT'S NOT AT HOME... DON'T TELL ME...!
I LEFT IT AT WORK?!
D.L.
PREPPING

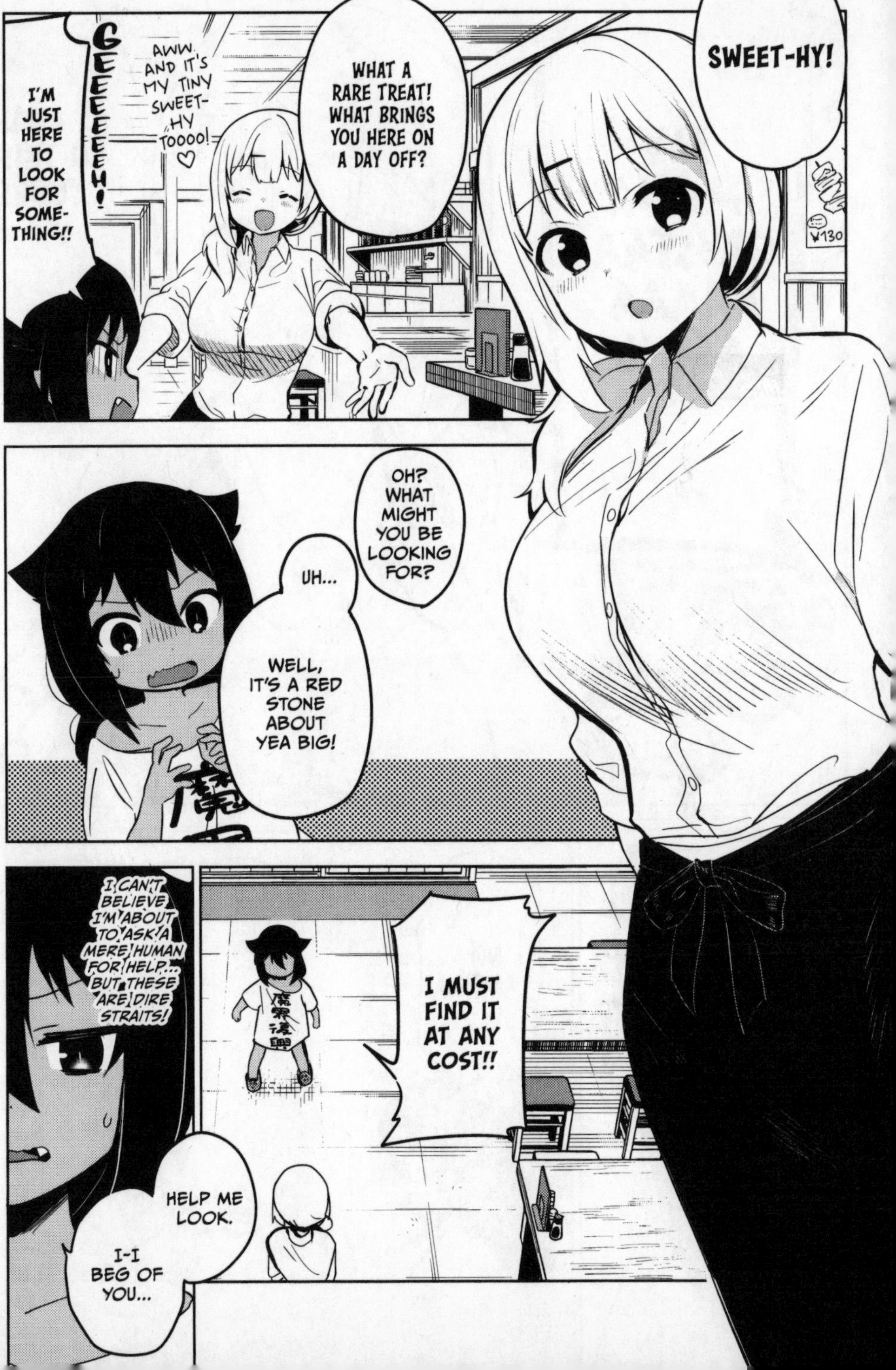
SWEET-HY!
WHAT A RARE TREAT! WHAT BRINGS YOU HERE ON A DAY OFF?
AWW. AND IT'S MY TINY SWEET-HY TOOOO! ♡
GEEEEEEH!
I'M JUST HERE TO LOOK FOR SOME-THING!!
OH? WHAT MIGHT YOU BE LOOKING FOR?
UH...
WELL, IT'S A RED STONE ABOUT YEA BIG!
I MUST FIND IT AT ANY COST!!
I CAN'T BELIEVE I'M ABOUT TO ASK A MERE HUMAN FOR HELP... BUT THESE ARE DIRE STRAITS!
HELP ME LOOK.
I-I BEG OF YOU...

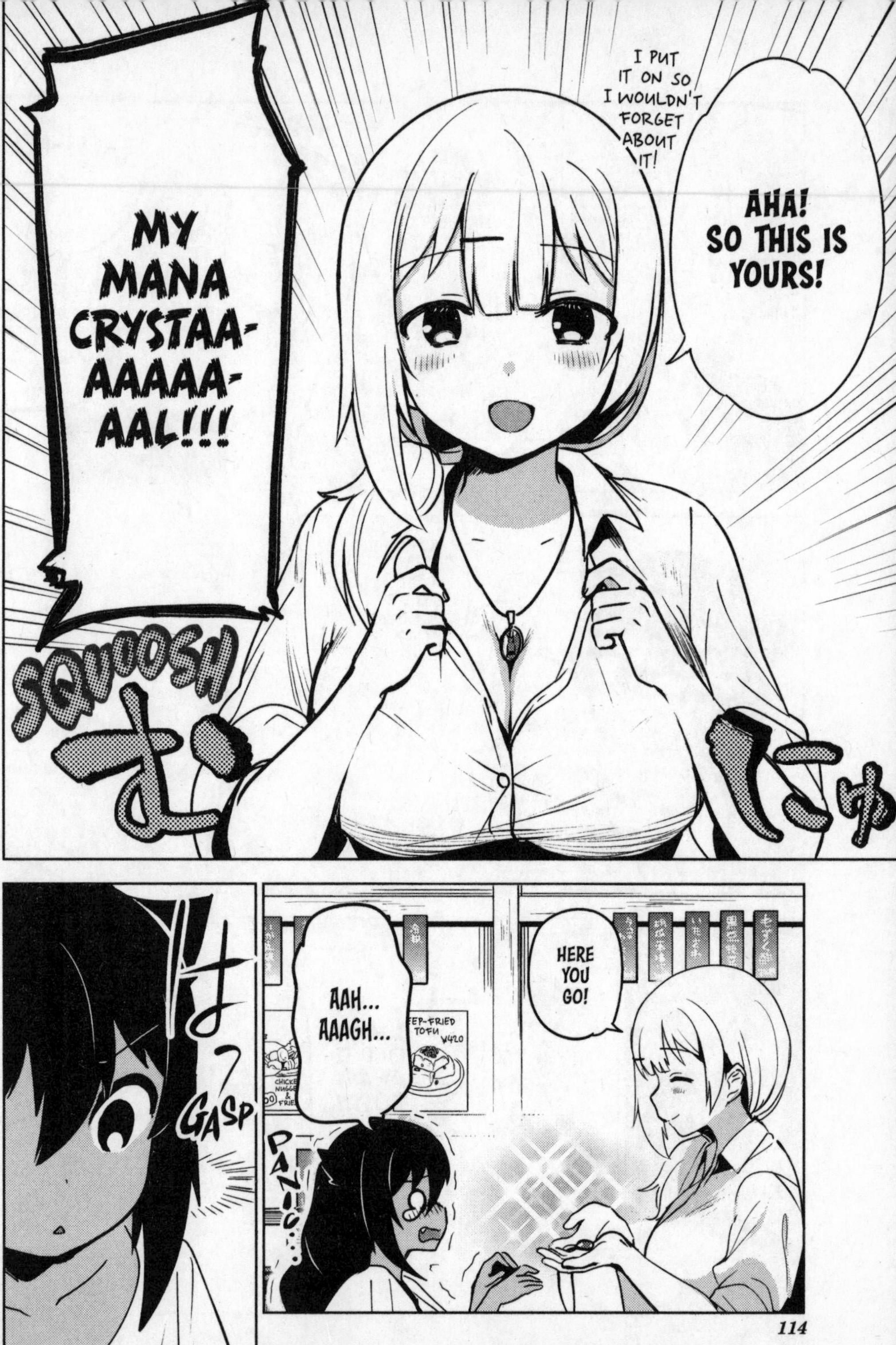
AHA! SO THIS IS YOURS!
I PUT IT ON SO I WOULDN'T FORGET ABOUT IT!
MY MANA CRYSTAA-AAAAA-AAL!!!
SQUOOSH
HERE YOU GO!
AAH... AAAGH...
TOFU ¥420
PANIC...
GASP

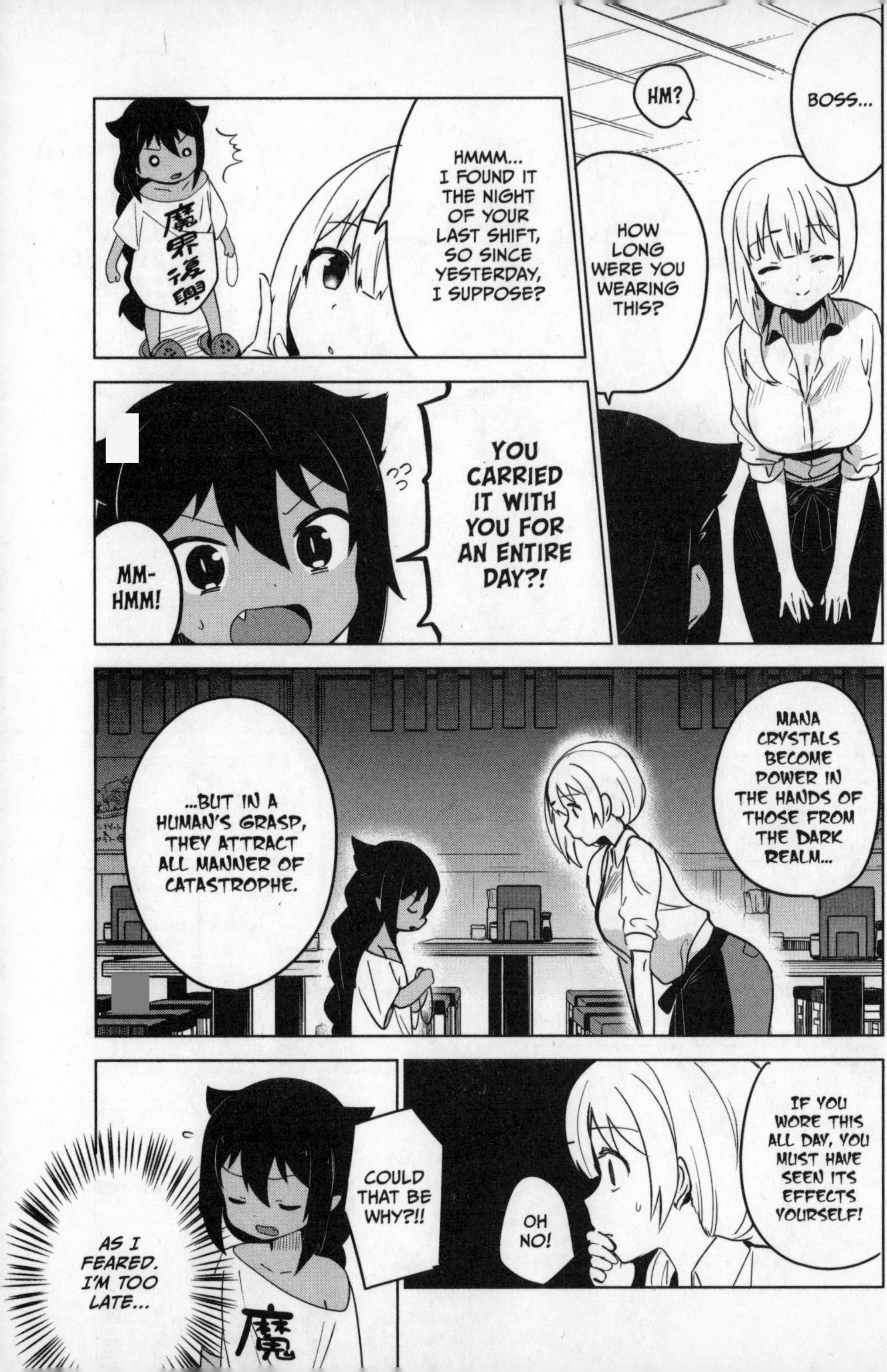
BOSS...
HM?
HOW LONG WERE YOU WEARING THIS?
HMMM... I FOUND IT THE NIGHT OF YOUR LAST SHIFT, SO SINCE YESTERDAY, I SUPPOSE?
魔界復興
YOU CARRIED IT WITH YOU FOR AN ENTIRE DAY?!
MM-HMM!
MANA CRYSTALS BECOME POWER IN THE HANDS OF THOSE FROM THE DARK REALM...
...BUT IN A HUMAN'S GRASP, THEY ATTRACT ALL MANNER OF CATASTROPHE.
IF YOU WORE THIS ALL DAY, YOU MUST HAVE SEEN ITS EFFECTS YOURSELF!
OH NO!
COULD THAT BE WHY?!!
AS I FEARED. I'M TOO LATE...
魔

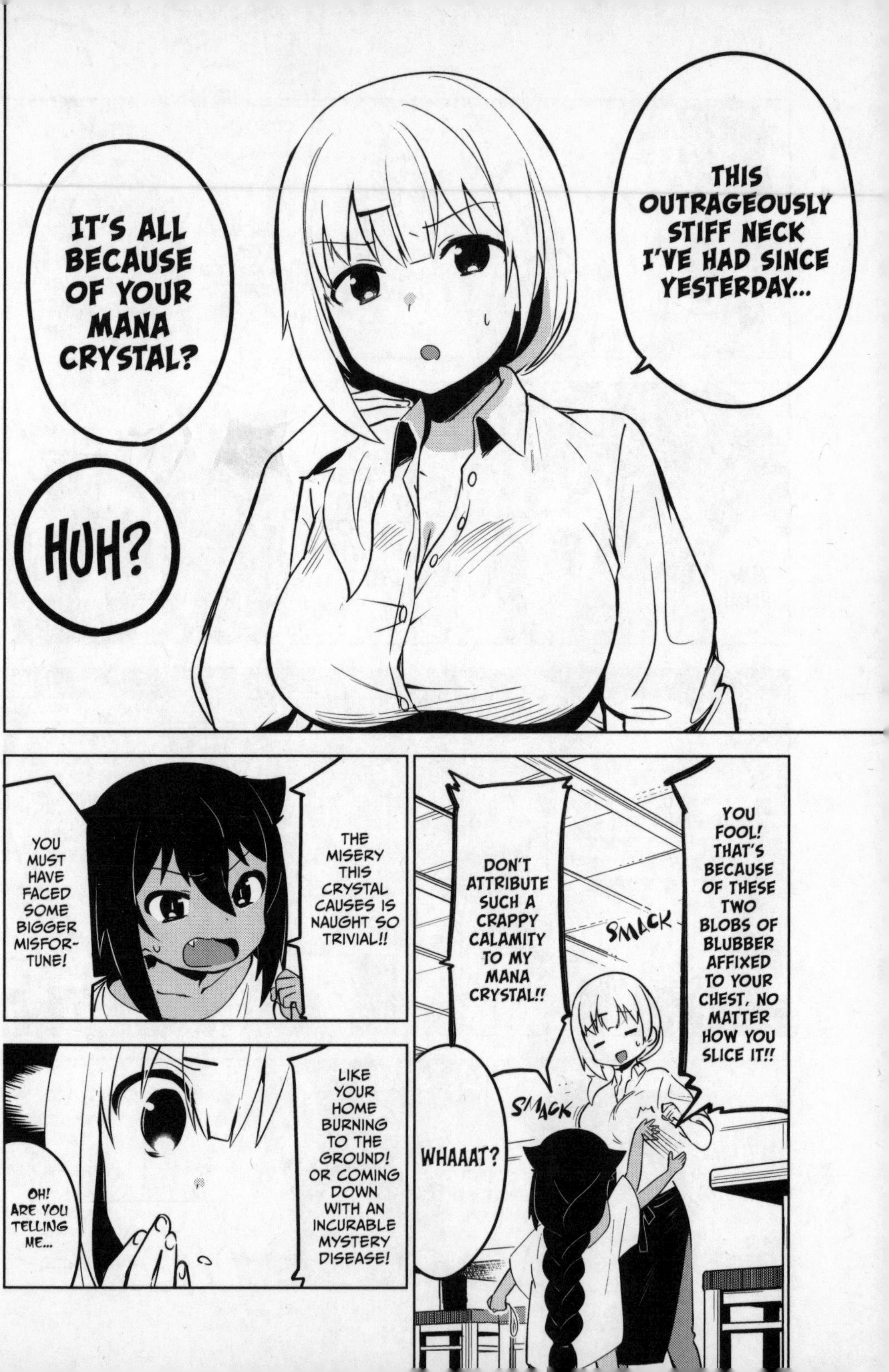
THIS OUTRAGEOUSLY STIFF NECK I'VE HAD SINCE YESTERDAY...
IT'S ALL BECAUSE OF YOUR MANA CRYSTAL?
HUH?
YOU FOOL! THAT'S BECAUSE OF THESE TWO BLOBS OF BLUBBER AFFIXED TO YOUR CHEST, NO MATTER HOW YOU SLICE IT!!
SMACK
DON'T ATTRIBUTE SUCH A CRAPPY CALAMITY TO MY MANA CRYSTAL!!
SMACK
WHAAAT?
THE MISERY THIS CRYSTAL CAUSES IS NAUGHT SO TRIVIAL!!
YOU MUST HAVE FACED SOME BIGGER MISFOR-TUNE!
LIKE YOUR HOME BURNING TO THE GROUND! OR COMING DOWN WITH AN INCURABLE MYSTERY DISEASE!
OH! ARE YOU TELLING ME...

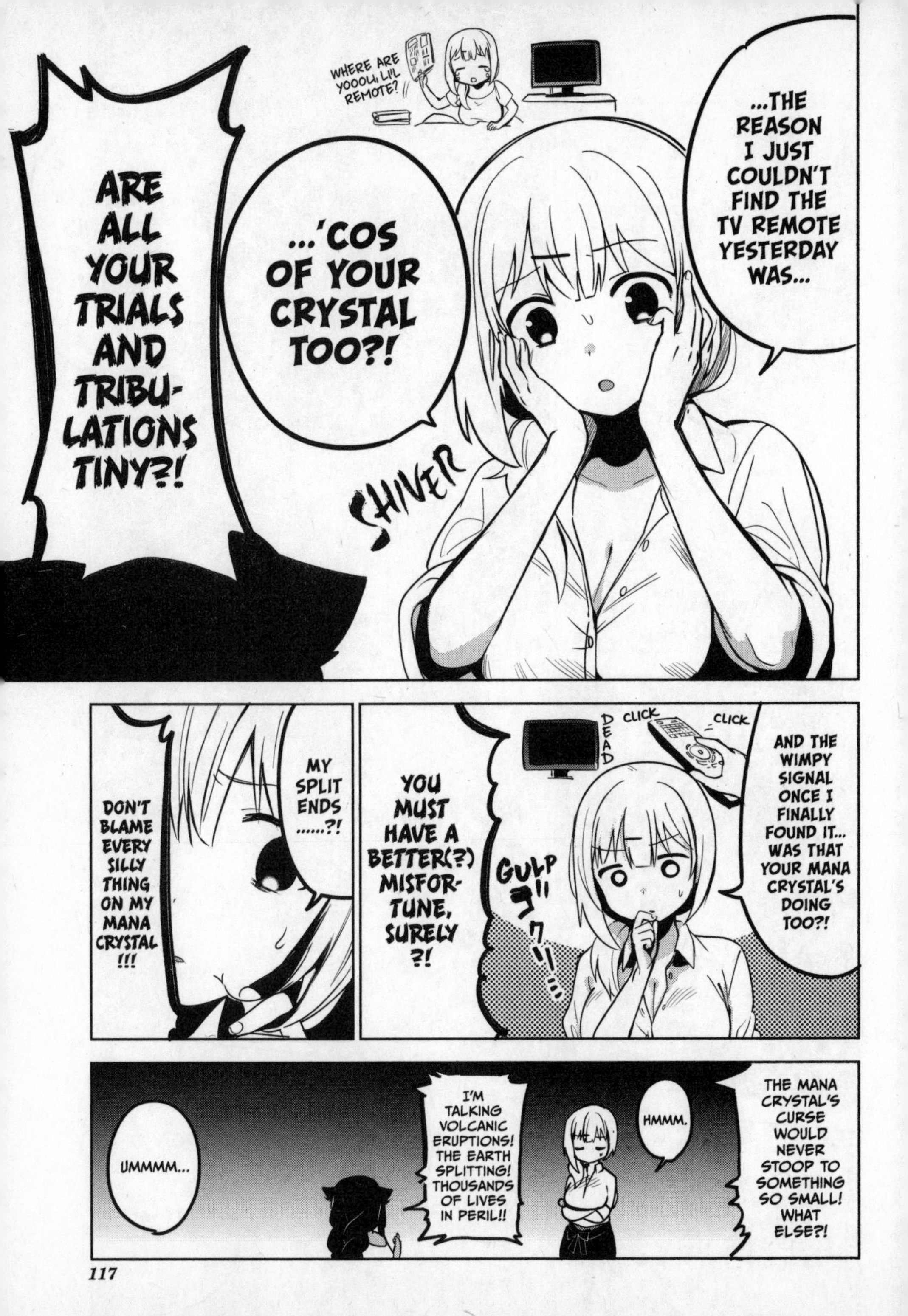
WHERE ARE YOOOU, LI'L REMOTE?
...THE REASON I JUST COULDN'T FIND THE TV REMOTE YESTERDAY WAS...
...'COS OF YOUR CRYSTAL TOO?!
ARE ALL YOUR TRIALS AND TRIBU-LATIONS TINY?!
SHIVER
DEAD
CLICK
CLICK
AND THE WIMPY SIGNAL ONCE I FINALLY FOUND IT... WAS THAT YOUR MANA CRYSTAL'S DOING TOO?!
GULP
YOU MUST HAVE A BETTER(?) MISFOR-TUNE, SURELY ?!
MY SPLIT ENDS ......?!
DON'T BLAME EVERY SILLY THING ON MY MANA CRYSTAL !!!
THE MANA CRYSTAL'S CURSE WOULD NEVER STOOP TO SOMETHING SO SMALL! WHAT ELSE?!
HMMM.
I'M TALKING VOLCANIC ERUPTIONS! THE EARTH SPLITTING! THOUSANDS OF LIVES IN PERIL!!
UMMMM...

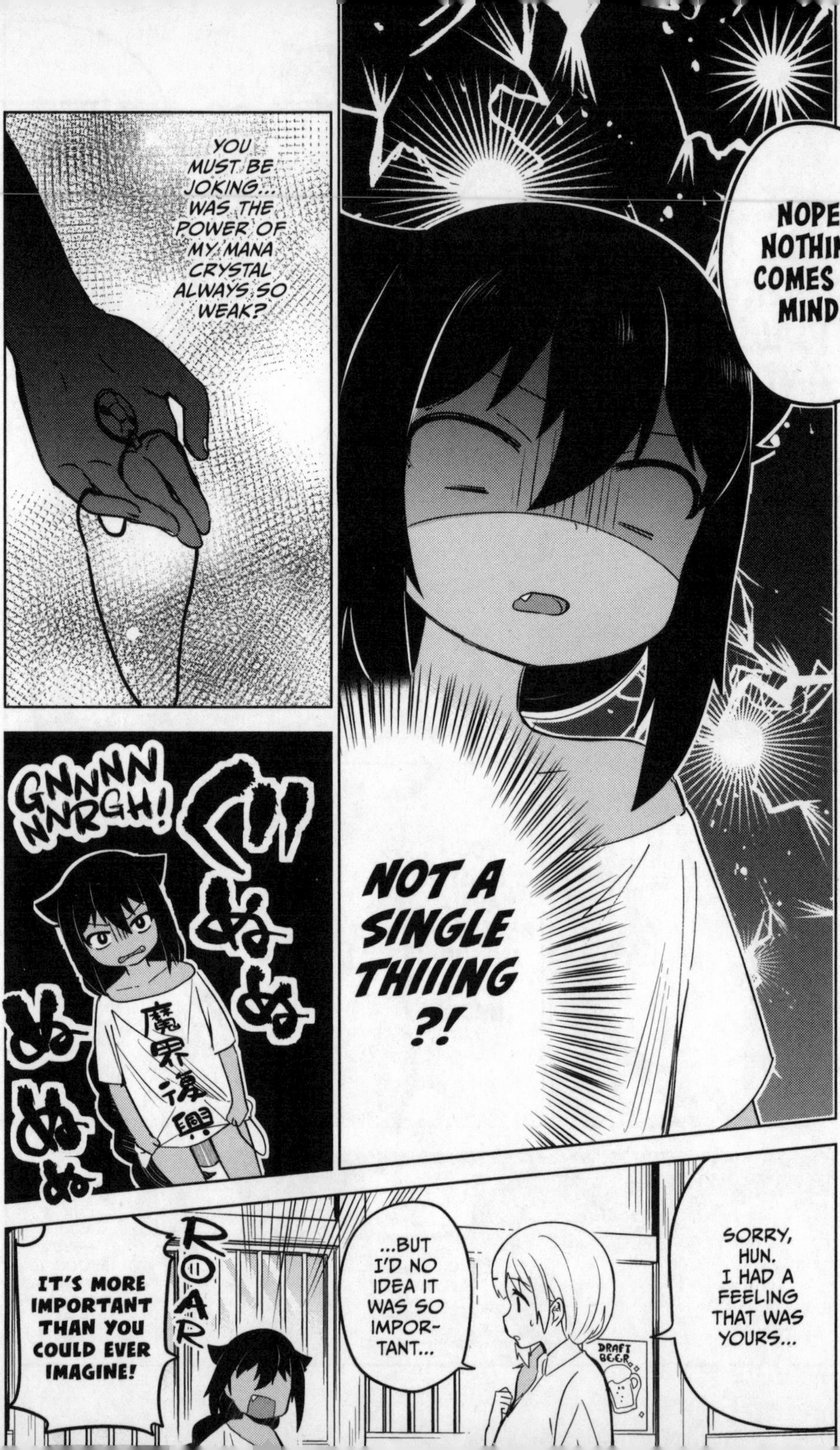
NOPE, NOTHING COMES TO MIND!
NOT A SINGLE THIIING?!
YOU MUST BE JOKING... WAS THE POWER OF MY MANA CRYSTAL ALWAYS SO WEAK?
GNNNNNNRGH!
魔界復興
SORRY, HUN. I HAD A FEELING THAT WAS YOURS...
...BUT I'D NO IDEA IT WAS SO IMPORTANT...
DRAFT BEER
ROAR
IT'S MORE IMPORTANT THAN YOU COULD EVER IMAGINE!

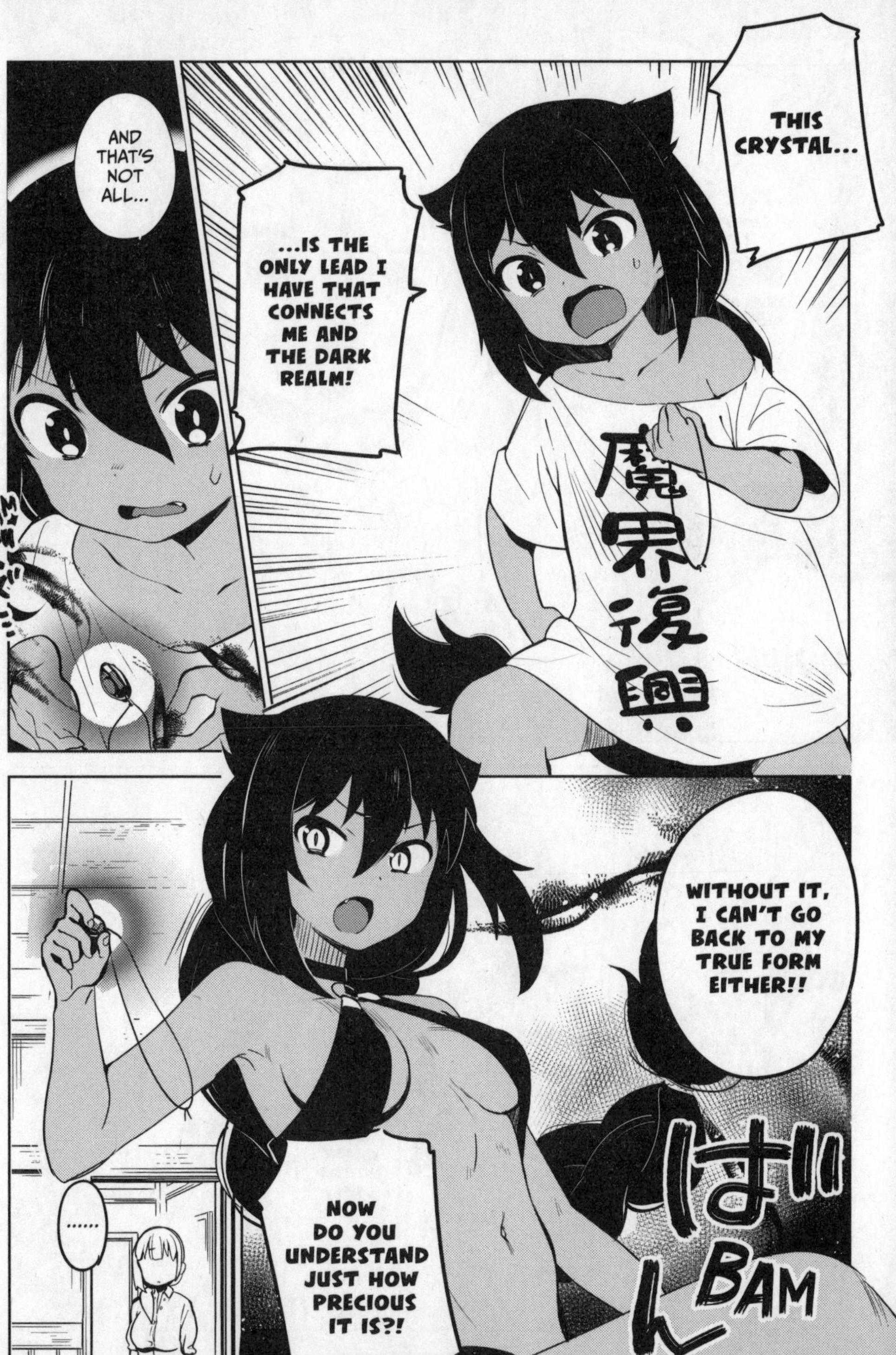
THIS CRYSTAL...
...IS THE ONLY LEAD I HAVE THAT CONNECTS ME AND THE DARK REALM!
魔界復興
AND THAT'S NOT ALL...
ZMMM
ズズ…
WITHOUT IT, I CAN'T GO BACK TO MY TRUE FORM EITHER!!
はんっ
BAM
NOW DO YOU UNDERSTAND JUST HOW PRECIOUS IT IS?!
......

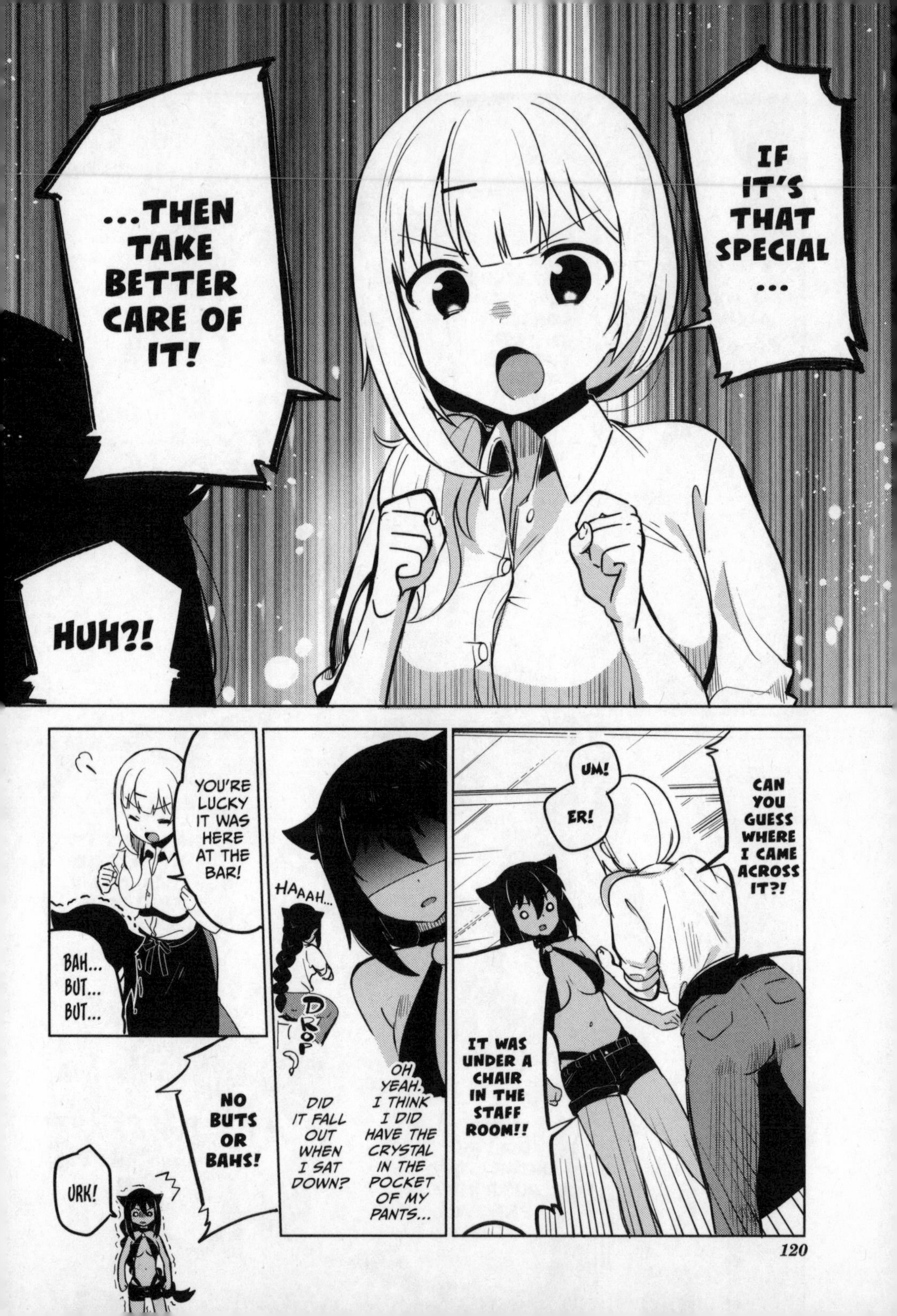
IF IT'S THAT SPECIAL...
...THEN TAKE BETTER CARE OF IT!
HUH?!
CAN YOU GUESS WHERE I CAME ACROSS IT?!
UM!
ER!
IT WAS UNDER A CHAIR IN THE STAFF ROOM!!
HAAAH...
DROP
OH YEAH. I THINK I DID HAVE THE CRYSTAL IN THE POCKET OF MY PANTS...
DID IT FALL OUT WHEN I SAT DOWN?
YOU'RE LUCKY IT WAS HERE AT THE BAR!
BAH... BUT... BUT...
NO BUTS OR BAHS!
URK!

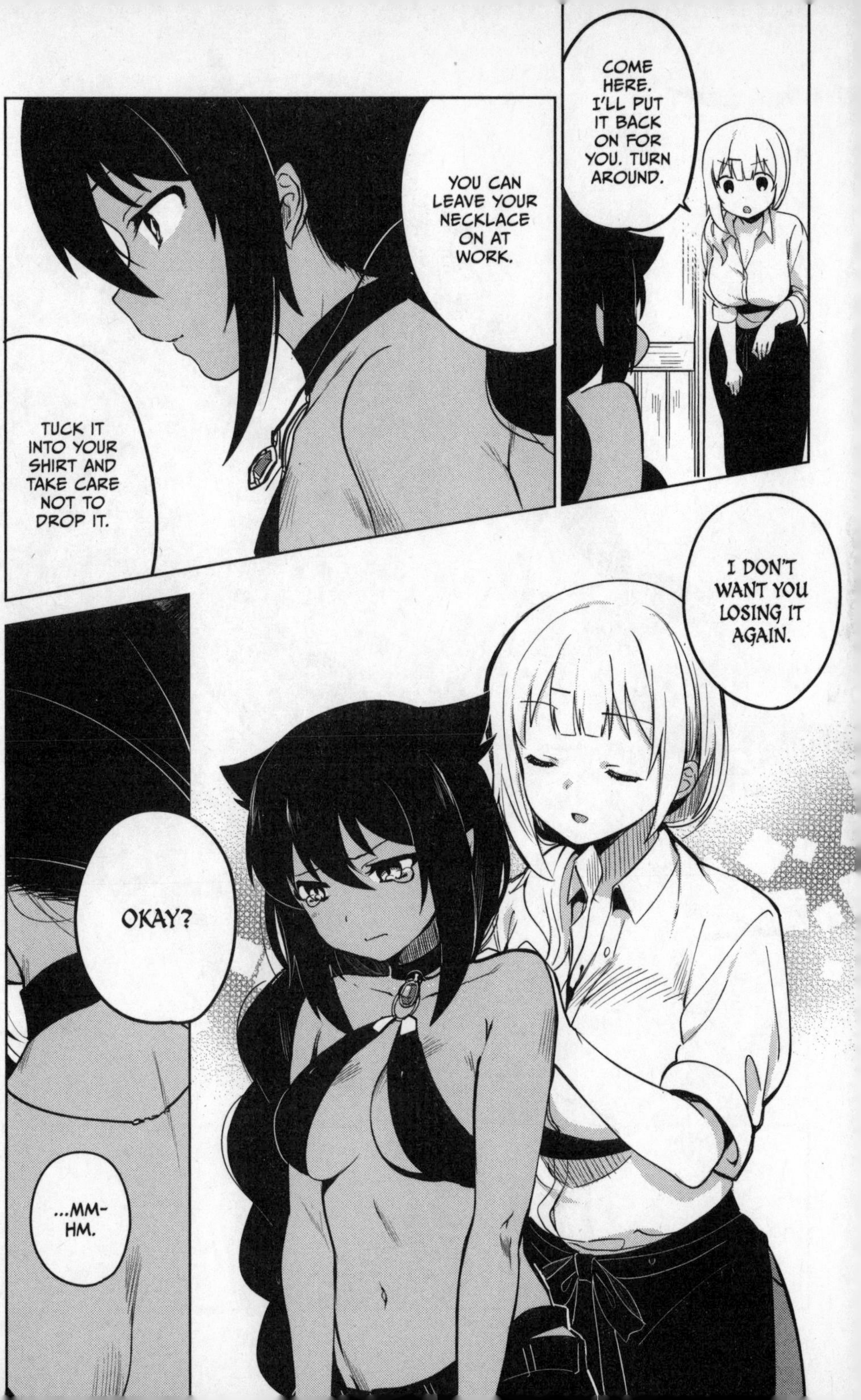
COME HERE. I'LL PUT IT BACK ON FOR YOU. TURN AROUND.
YOU CAN LEAVE YOUR NECKLACE ON AT WORK.
TUCK IT INTO YOUR SHIRT AND TAKE CARE NOT TO DROP IT.
I DON'T WANT YOU LOSING IT AGAIN.
OKAY?
...MM-HM.

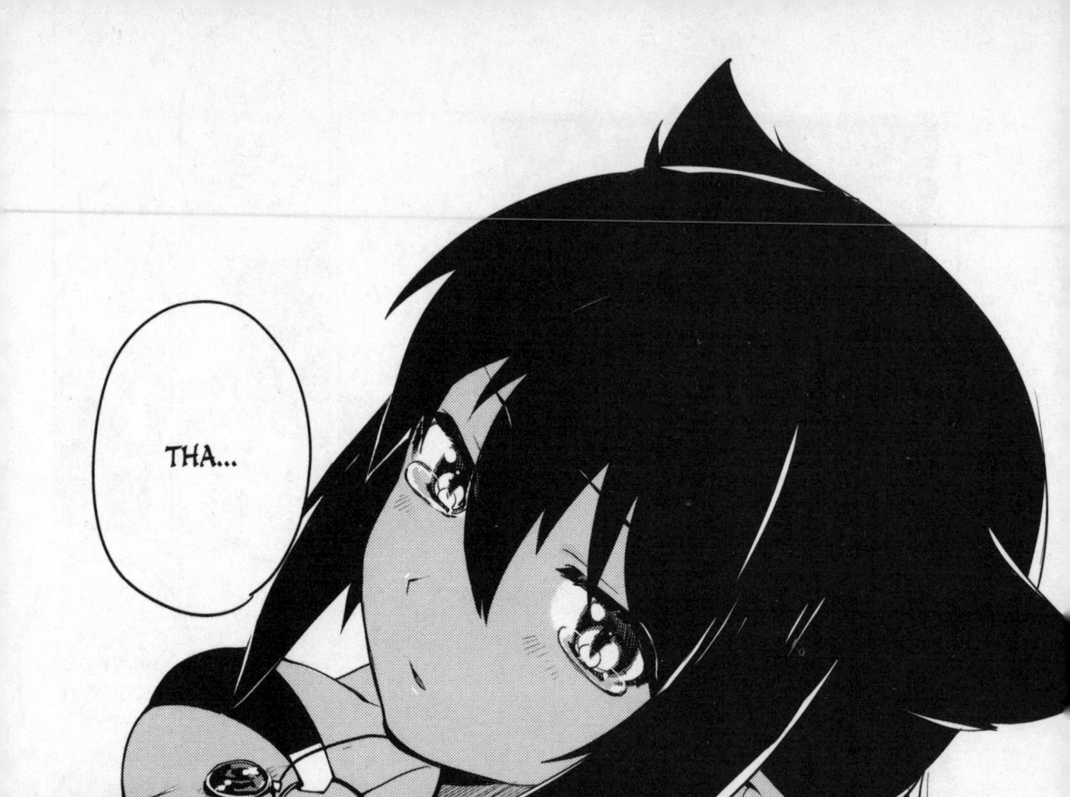
THA...
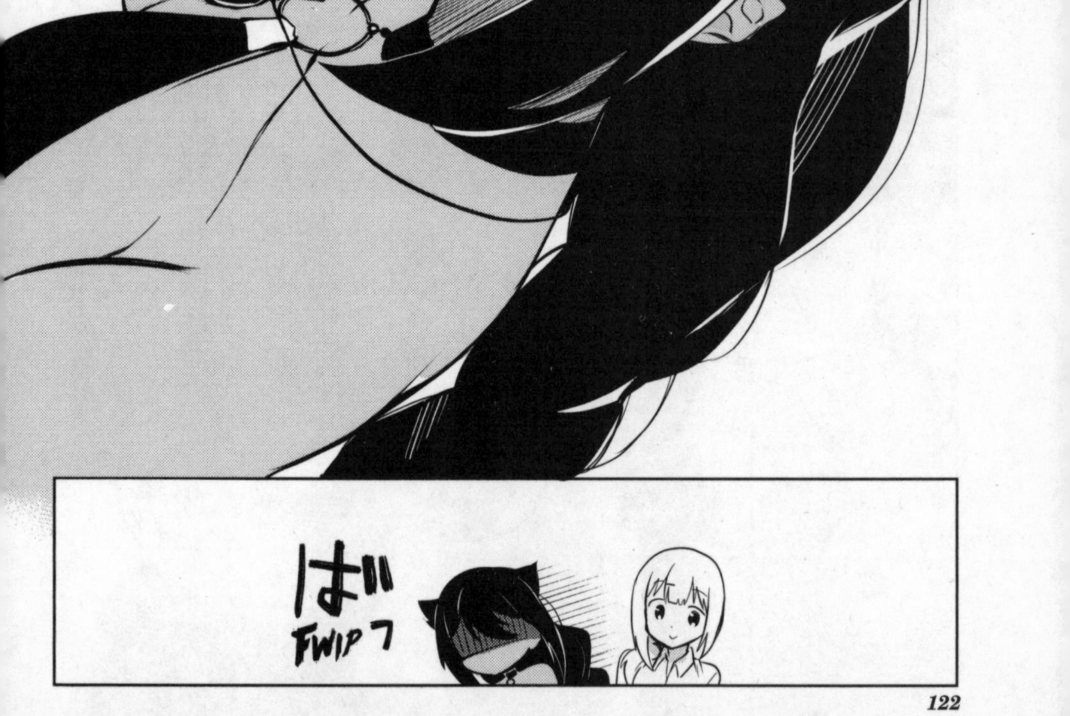
ばっ
FWIP

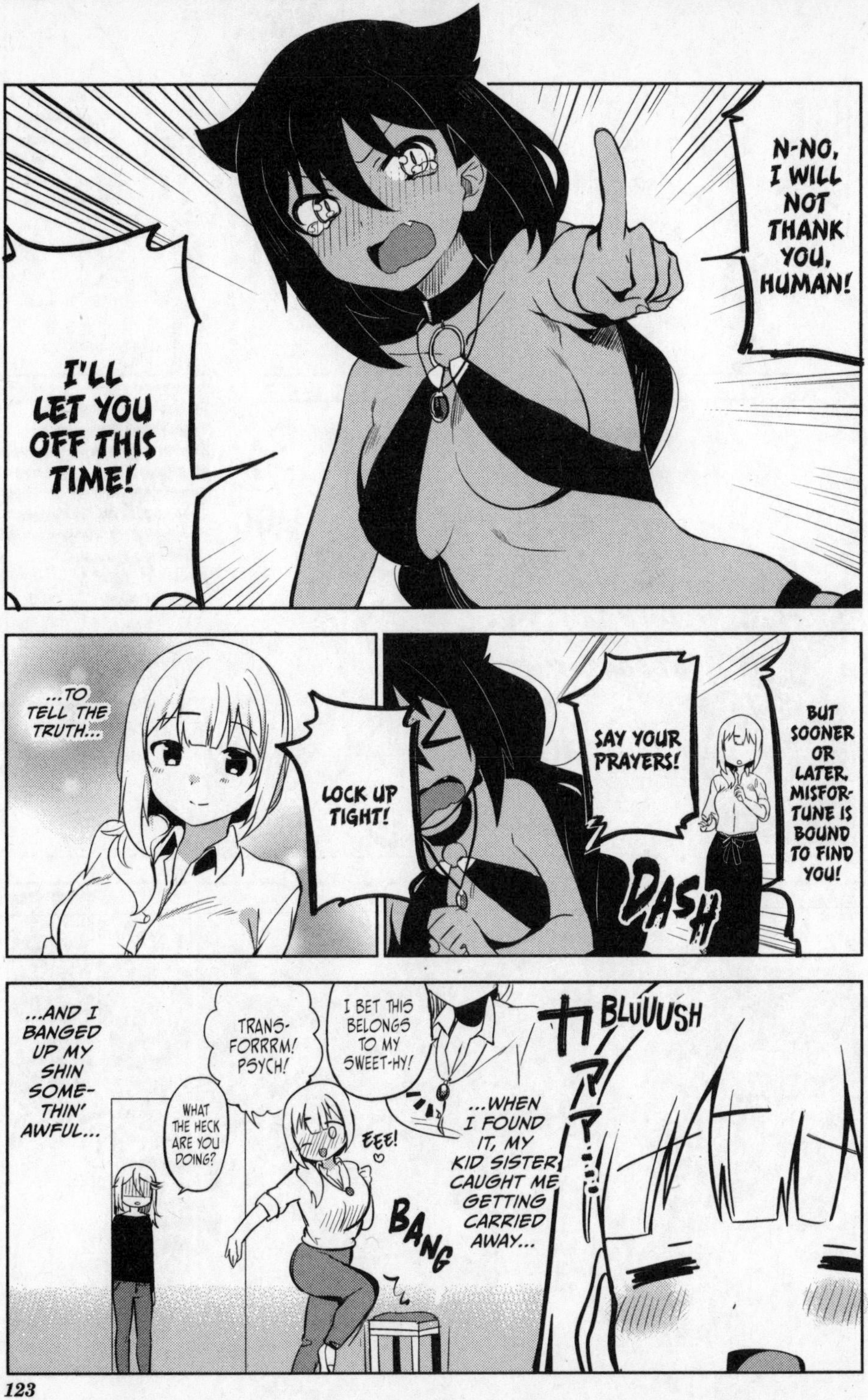
N-NO, I WILL NOT THANK YOU, HUMAN!
I'LL LET YOU OFF THIS TIME!
BUT SOONER OR LATER, MISFORTUNE IS BOUND TO FIND YOU!
SAY YOUR PRAYERS!
DASH
LOCK UP TIGHT!
...TO TELL THE TRUTH...
BLUUUSH
...WHEN I FOUND IT, MY KID SISTER CAUGHT ME GETTING CARRIED AWAY...
I BET THIS BELONGS TO MY SWEET-HY!
EEE!
BANG
TRANS-FORRRM! PSYCH!
WHAT THE HECK ARE YOU DOING?
...AND I BANGED UP MY SHIN SOMETHIN' AWFUL...

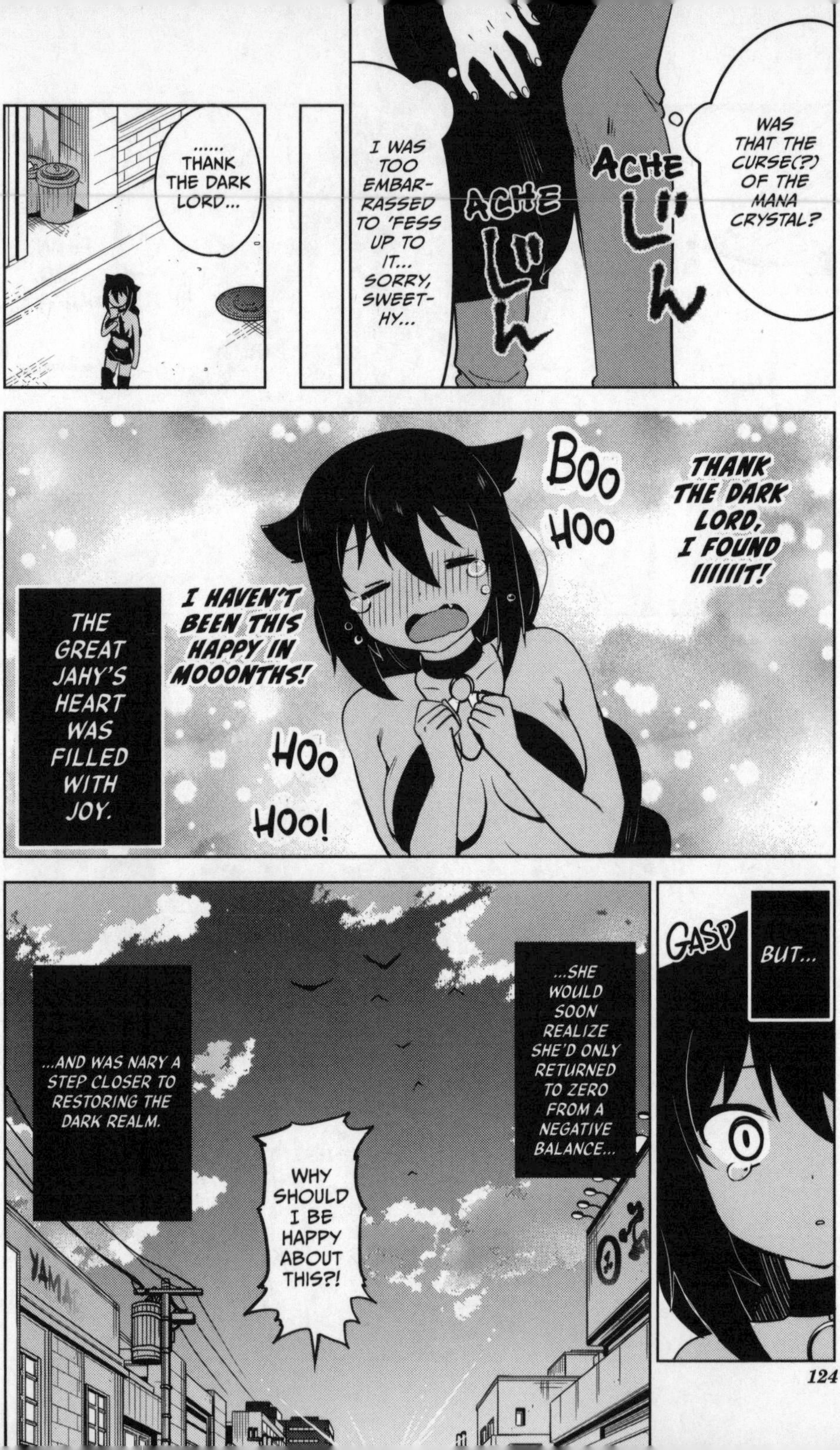
WAS THAT THE CURSE(?) OF THE MANA CRYSTAL?
ACHE じん
ACHE じん
I WAS TOO EMBAR-RASSED TO 'FESS UP TO IT... SORRY, SWEETHY...
...... THANK THE DARK LORD...
THANK THE DARK LORD, I FOUND IIIIIIIT!
BOO HOO
I HAVEN'T BEEN THIS HAPPY IN MOOONTHS!
HOO HOO!
THE GREAT JAHY'S HEART WAS FILLED WITH JOY.
GASP
BUT...
...SHE WOULD SOON REALIZE SHE'D ONLY RETURNED TO ZERO FROM A NEGATIVE BALANCE...
...AND WAS NARY A STEP CLOSER TO RESTORING THE DARK REALM.
WHY SHOULD I BE HAPPY ABOUT THIS?!

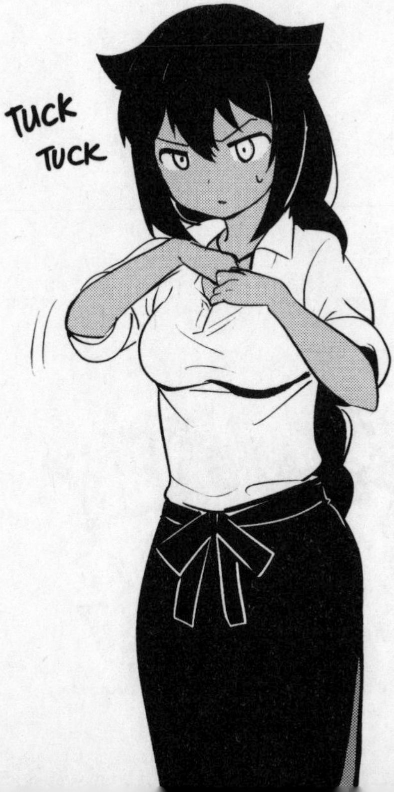
TUCK
TUCK

The GREAT JAHY Will NOT Be DEFEATED!

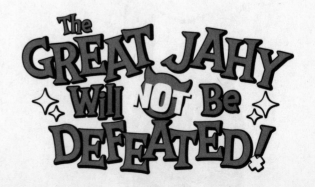

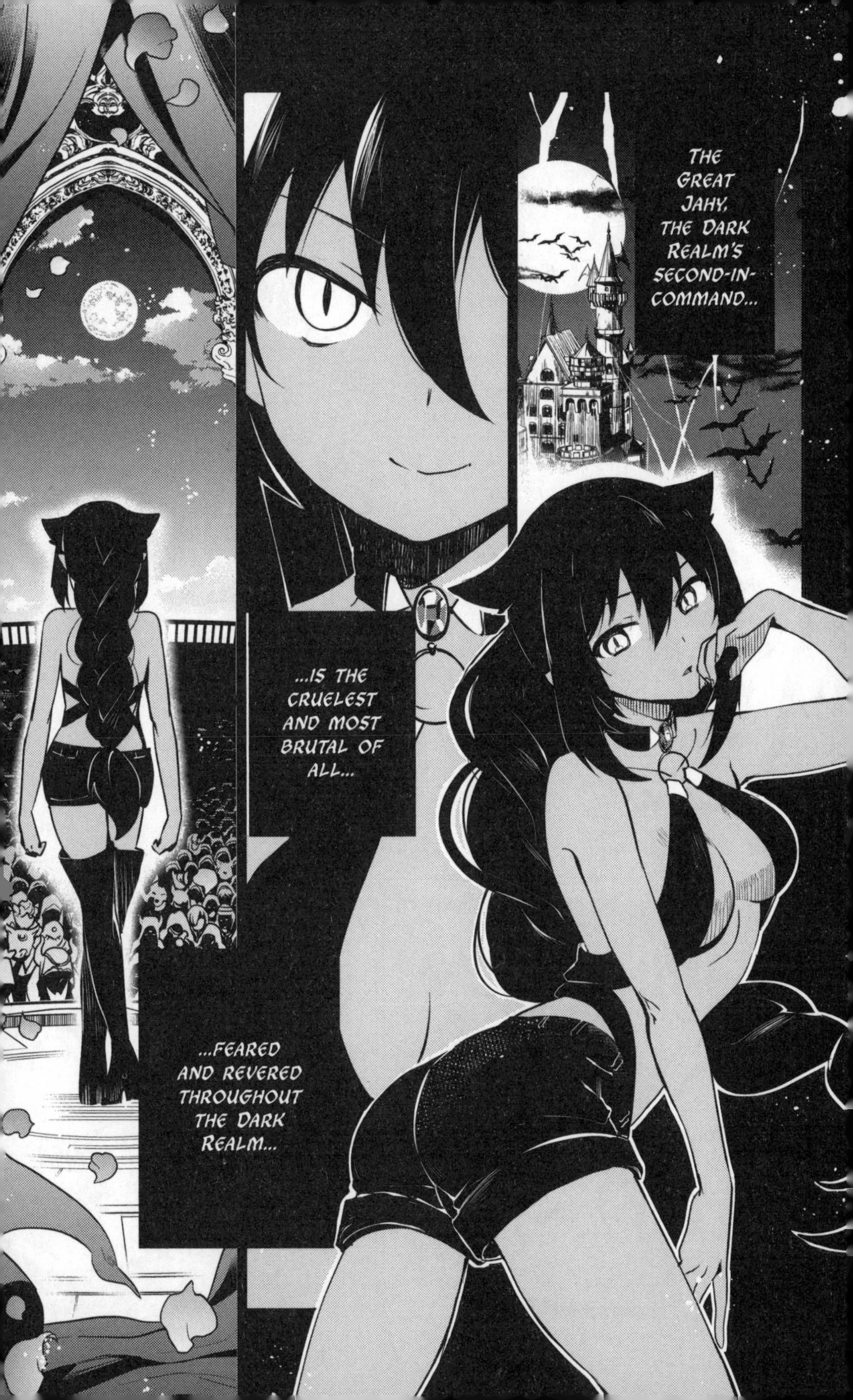
THE GREAT JAHY, THE DARK REALM'S SECOND-IN-COMMAND...
...IS THE CRUELEST AND MOST BRUTAL OF ALL...
...FEARED AND REVERED THROUGHOUT THE DARK REALM...

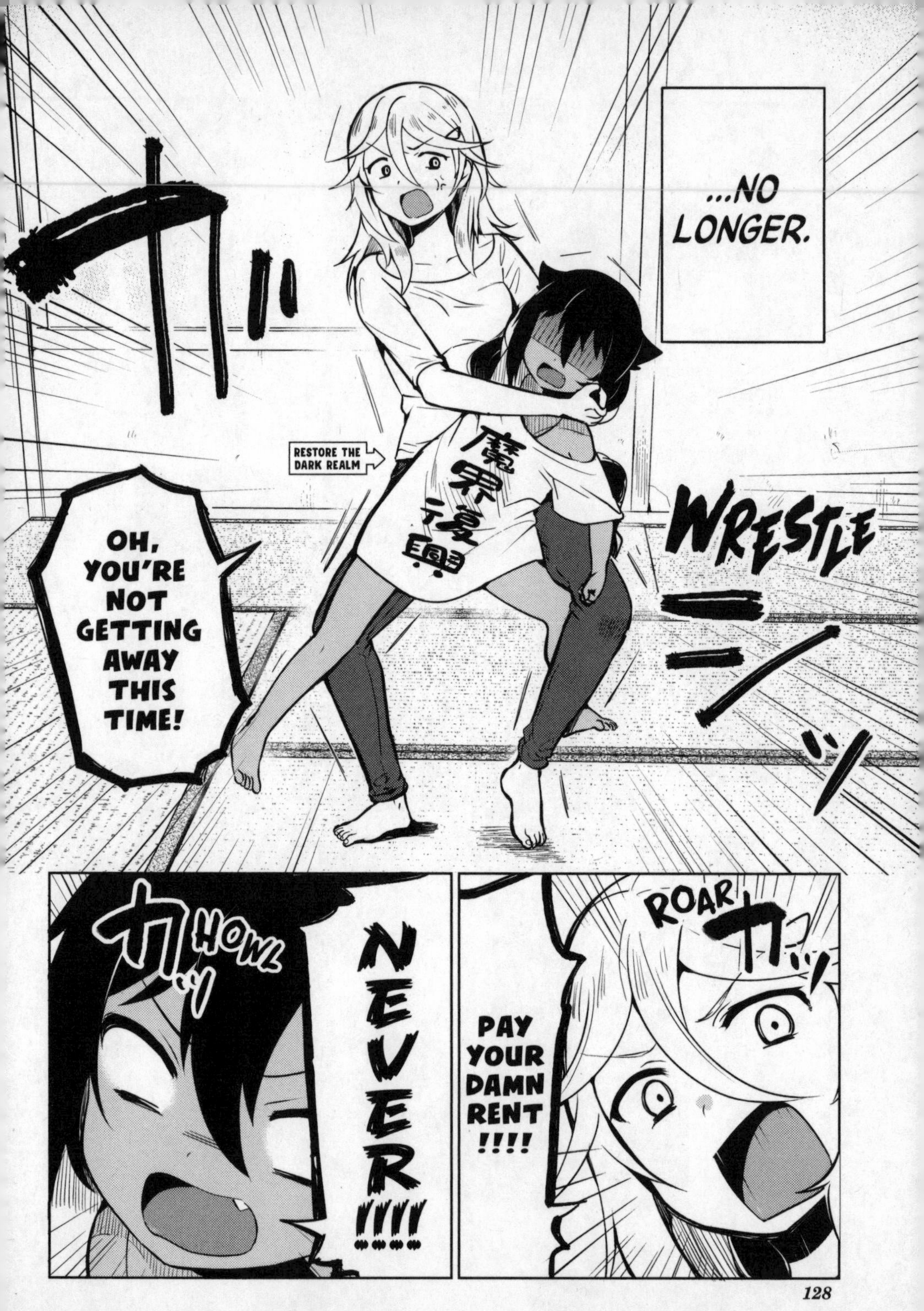
...NO LONGER.
WRESTLE
RESTORE THE DARK REALM
OH, YOU'RE NOT GETTING AWAY THIS TIME!
ROAR
PAY YOUR DAMN RENT!!!!
HOWL
NEVER!!!!!

RESTORATION PLAN No. 4

The Great Jahy & the Landlady

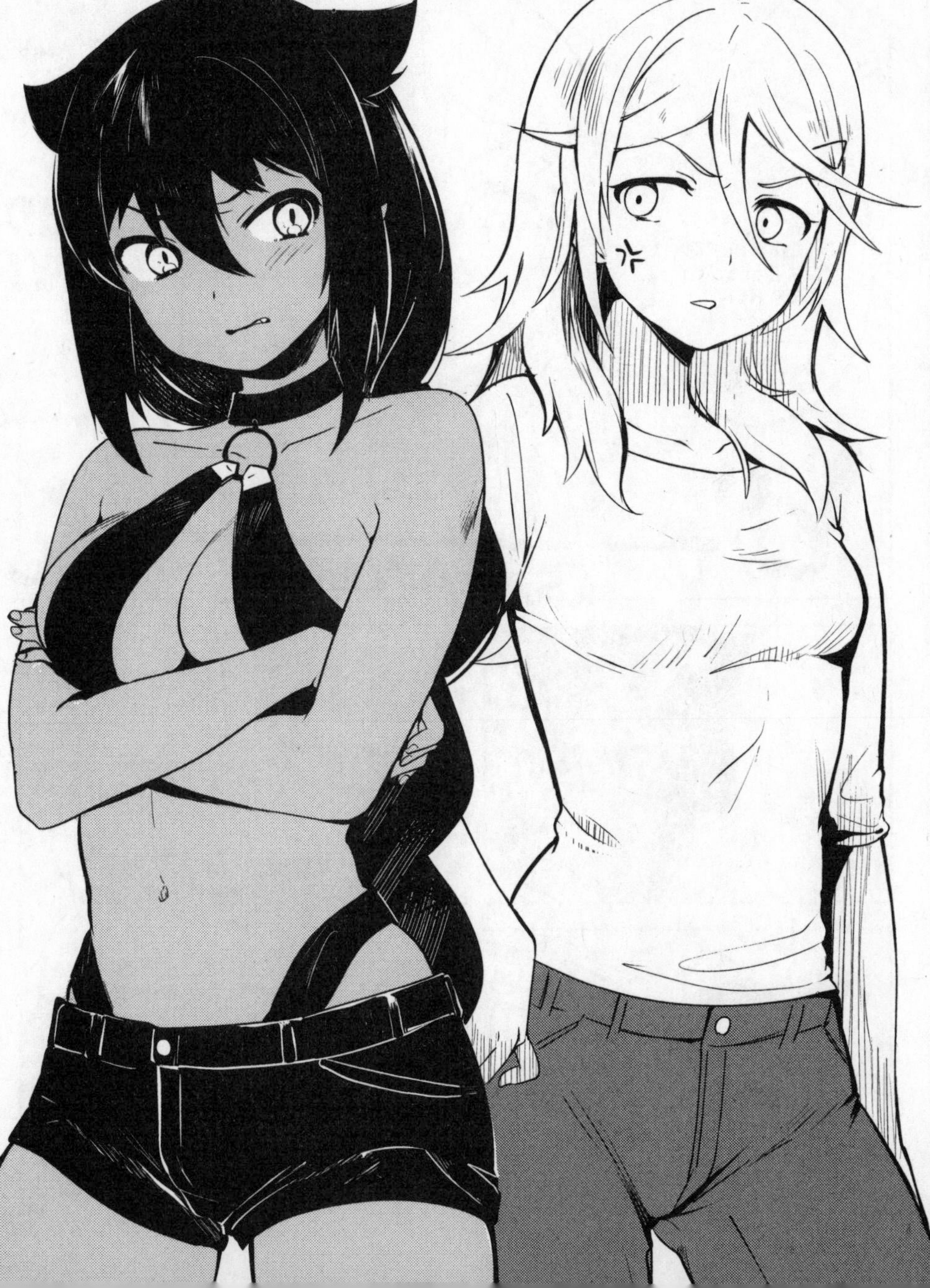

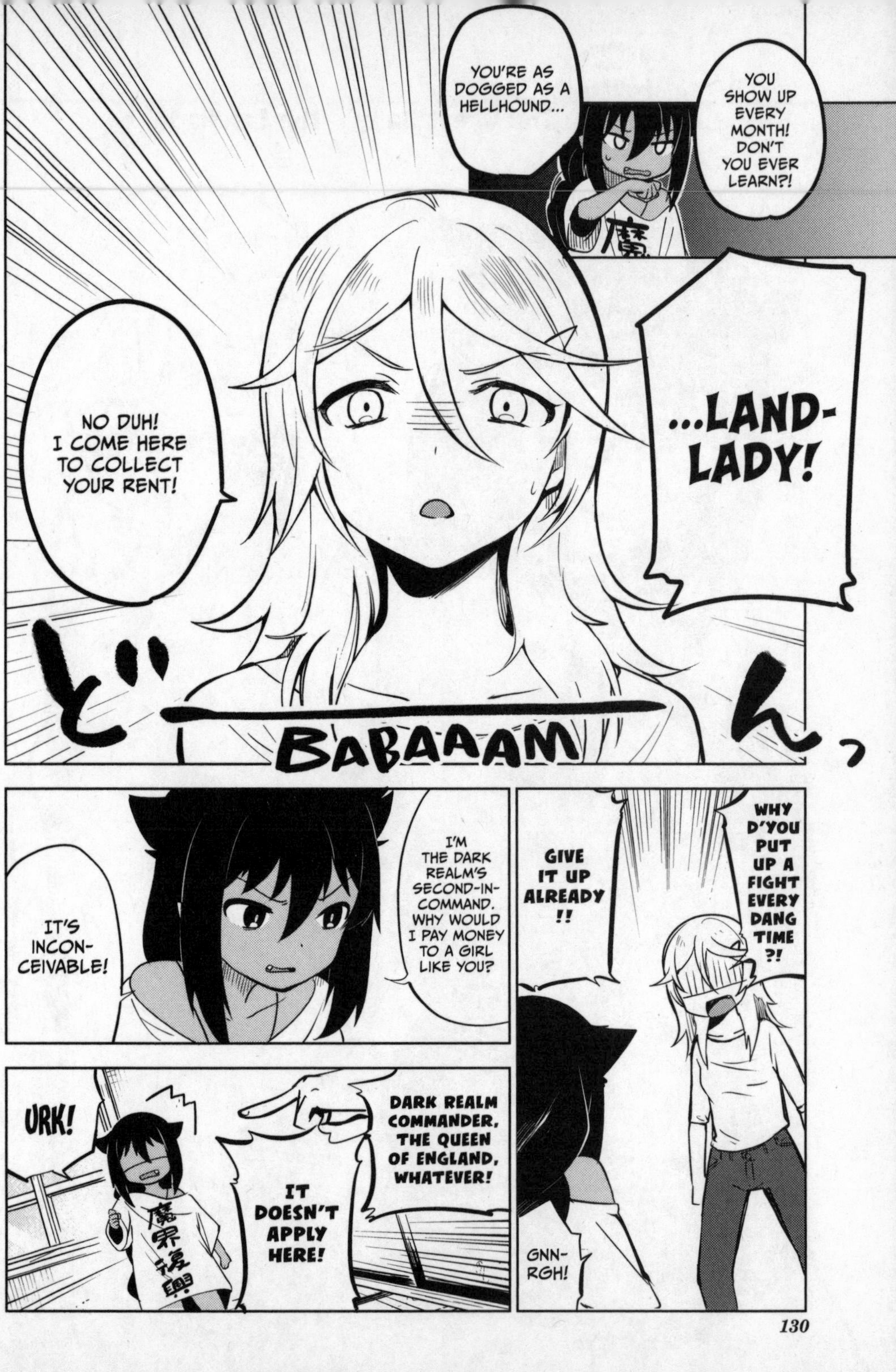
YOU SHOW UP EVERY MONTH! DON'T YOU EVER LEARN?!
YOU'RE AS DOGGED AS A HELLHOUND...
...LAND-LADY!
NO DUH! I COME HERE TO COLLECT YOUR RENT!
BABAAAM
WHY D'YOU PUT UP A FIGHT EVERY DANG TIME?!
GIVE IT UP ALREADY!!
GNN-RGH!
I'M THE DARK REALM'S SECOND-IN-COMMAND. WHY WOULD I PAY MONEY TO A GIRL LIKE YOU?
IT'S INCON-CEIVABLE!
DARK REALM COMMANDER, THE QUEEN OF ENGLAND, WHATEVER!
IT DOESN'T APPLY HERE!
URK!

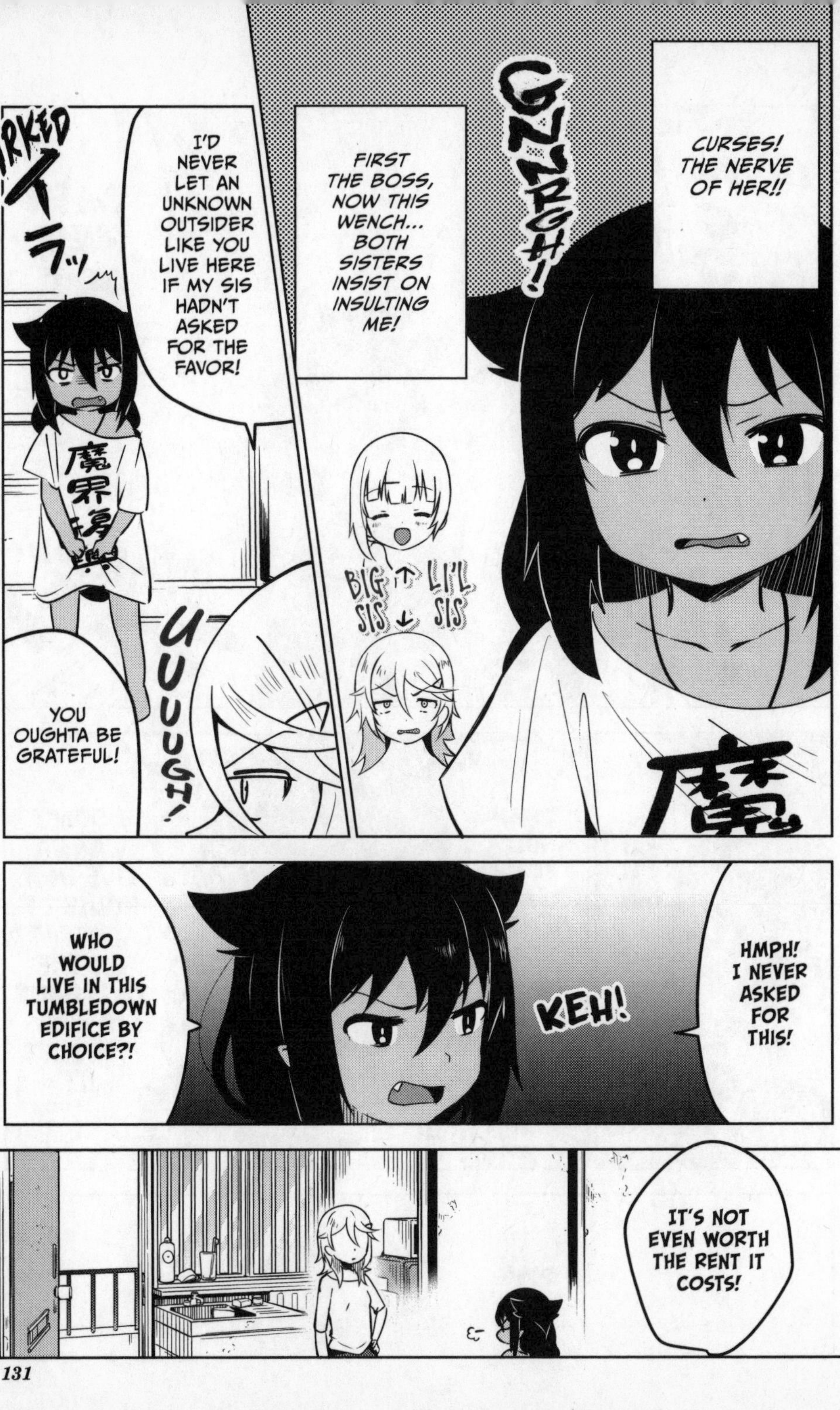
CURSES! THE NERVE OF HER!!
GNNRGH!
FIRST THE BOSS, NOW THIS WENCH... BOTH SISTERS INSIST ON INSULTING ME!
BIG SIS ↑ LI'L SIS ↓
IRKED イラッ
I'D NEVER LET AN UNKNOWN OUTSIDER LIKE YOU LIVE HERE IF MY SIS HADN'T ASKED FOR THE FAVOR!
UUUUUGH!
YOU OUGHTA BE GRATEFUL!
HMPH! I NEVER ASKED FOR THIS!
KEH!
WHO WOULD LIVE IN THIS TUMBLEDOWN EDIFICE BY CHOICE?!
IT'S NOT EVEN WORTH THE RENT IT COSTS!

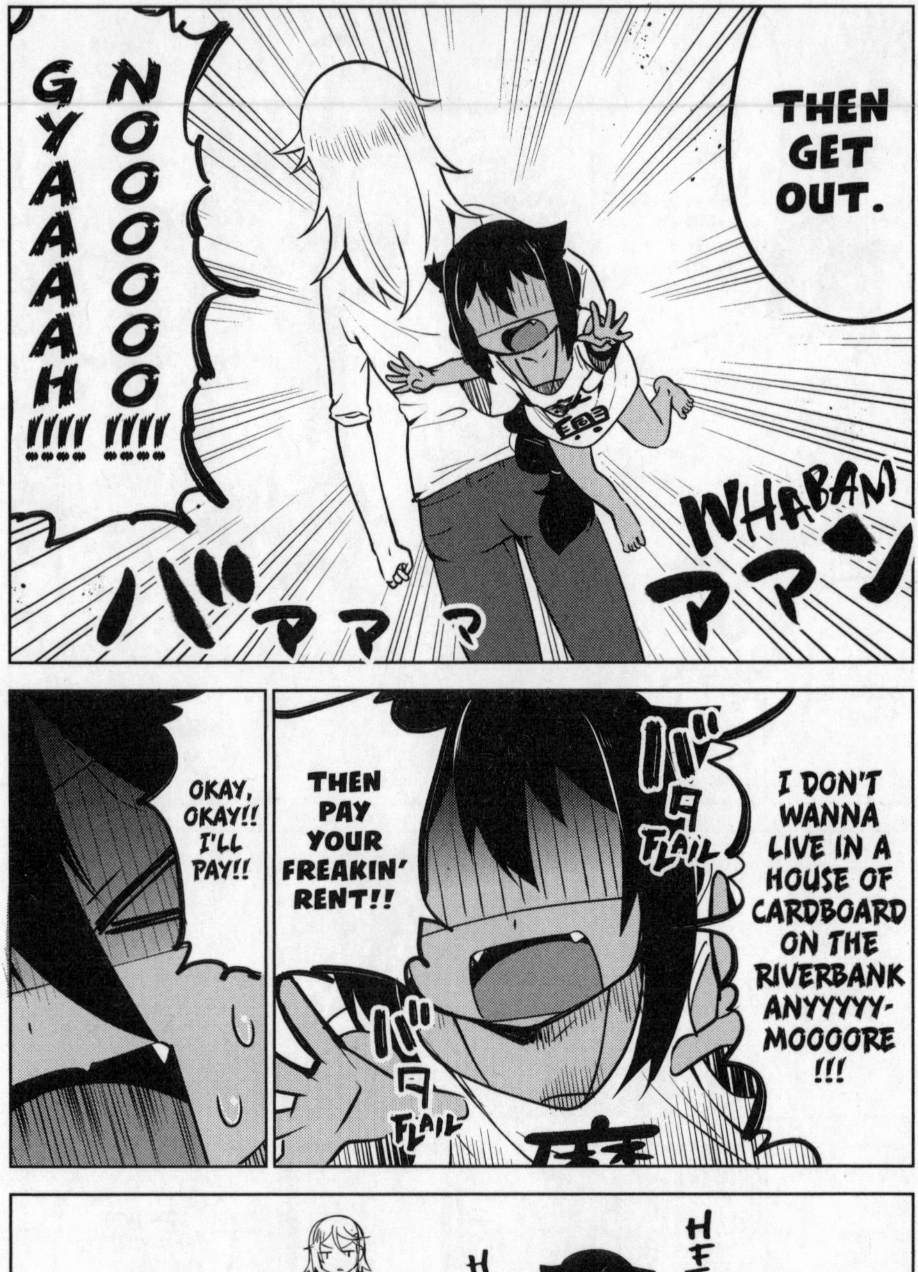
THEN GET OUT.
NOOOOOO!!!!
GYAAAAAH!!!!
WHABAM
バアアア アアーン
I DON'T WANNA LIVE IN A HOUSE OF CARDBOARD ON THE RIVERBANK ANYYYYY-MOOOORE!!!
バタ FLAIL
バタ FLAIL
THEN PAY YOUR FREAKIN' RENT!!
OKAY, OKAY!! I'LL PAY!!
HFFFF!
HFFFF!

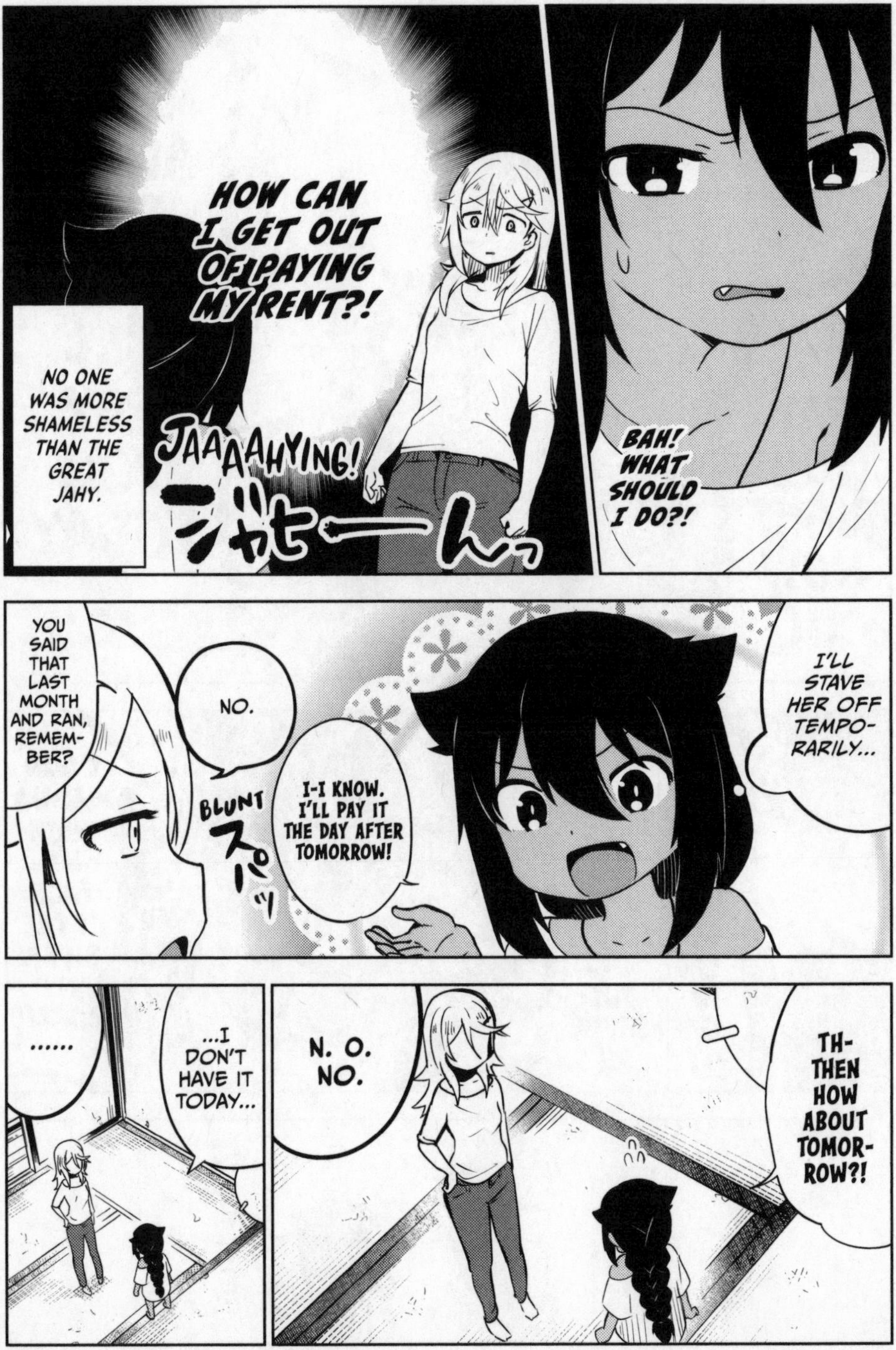
BAH! WHAT SHOULD I DO?!
HOW CAN I GET OUT OF PAYING MY RENT?!
NO ONE WAS MORE SHAMELESS THAN THE GREAT JAHY.
JAAAAHYING!
ジャーーんっ
I'LL STAVE HER OFF TEMPO-RARILY...
I-I KNOW. I'LL PAY IT THE DAY AFTER TOMORROW!
NO.
BLUNT
スパッ
YOU SAID THAT LAST MONTH AND RAN, REMEMBER?
TH-THEN HOW ABOUT TOMOR-ROW?!
N. O. NO.
...I DON'T HAVE IT TODAY...
......

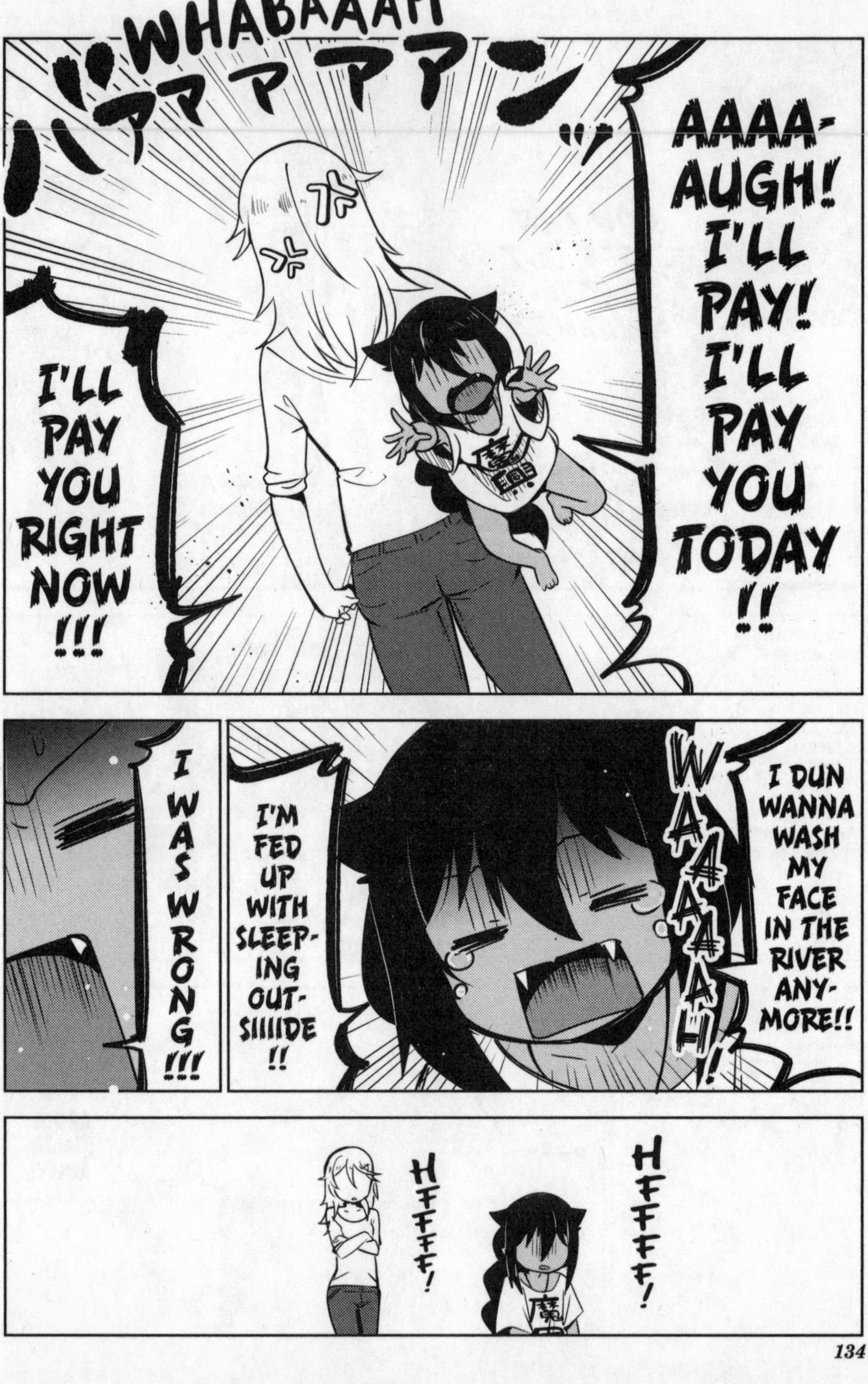
WHABAAAM
バァァアァン
AAAA-AUGH! I'LL PAY! I'LL PAY YOU TODAY!!
I'LL PAY YOU RIGHT NOW!!!
I DUN WANNA WASH MY FACE IN THE RIVER ANYMORE!!
WAAAAAH!
I'M FED UP WITH SLEEP-ING OUT-SIIIIDE!!
I WAS WRONG!!!
HFFFFF!
HFFFF!

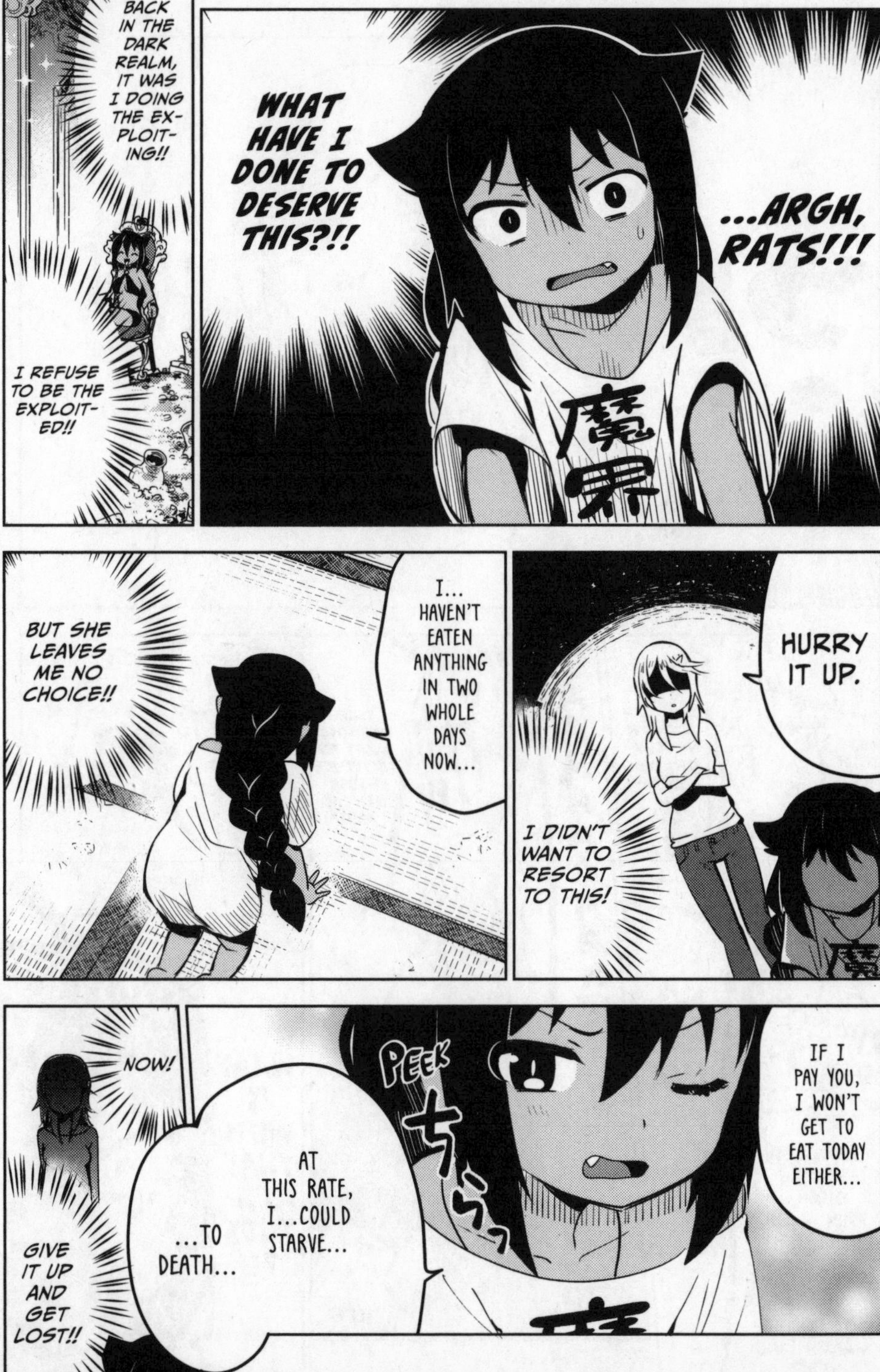
...ARGH, RATS!!!
WHAT HAVE I DONE TO DESERVE THIS?!!
魔界
BACK IN THE DARK REALM, IT WAS I DOING THE EX-PLOIT-ING!!
I REFUSE TO BE THE EXPLOIT-ED!!
HURRY IT UP.
I DIDN'T WANT TO RESORT TO THIS!
I... HAVEN'T EATEN ANYTHING IN TWO WHOLE DAYS NOW...
BUT SHE LEAVES ME NO CHOICE!!
IF I PAY YOU, I WON'T GET TO EAT TODAY EITHER...
PEEK
AT THIS RATE, I...COULD STARVE...
...TO DEATH...
NOW!
GIVE IT UP AND GET LOST!!

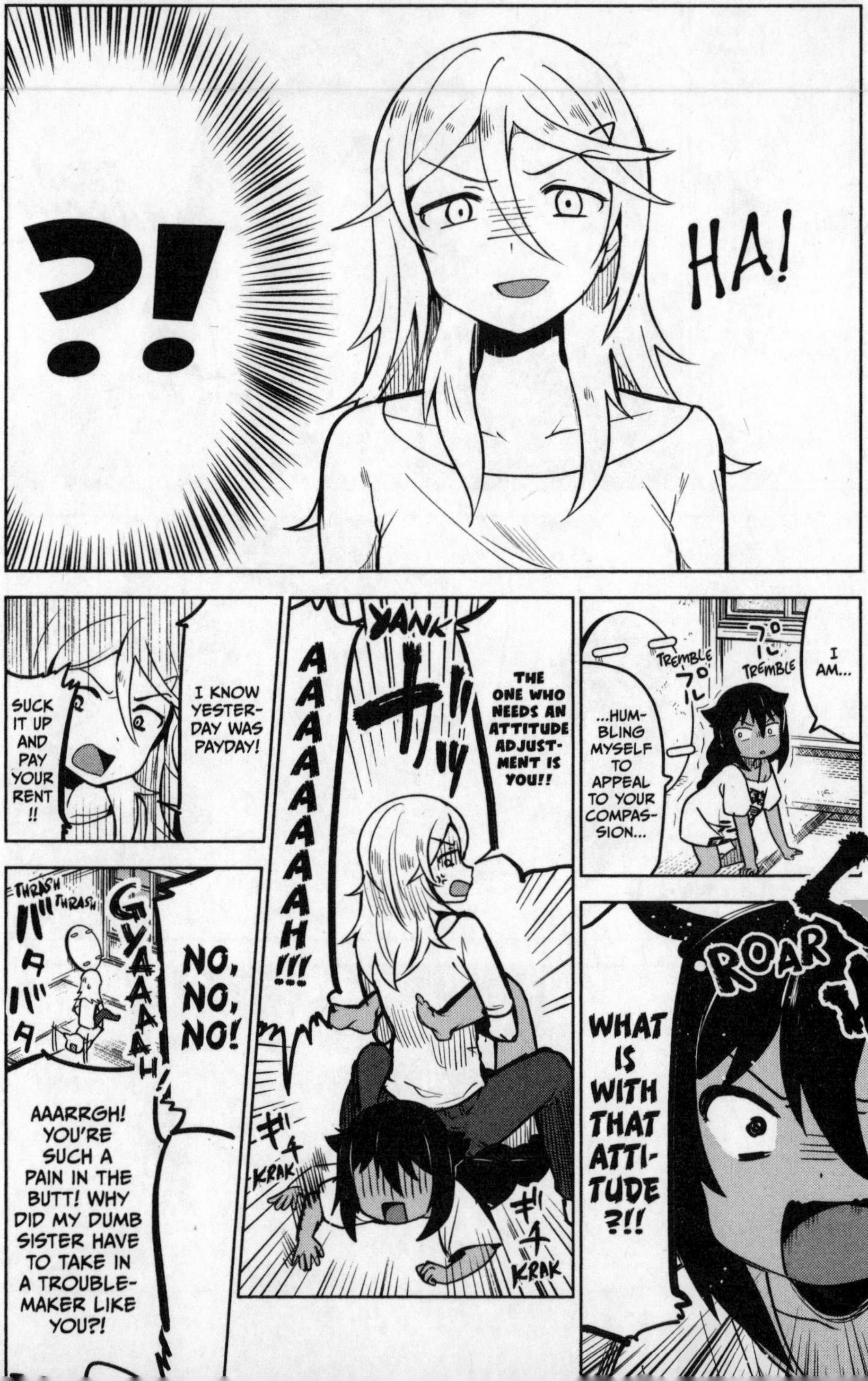
HA!
?!
TREMBLE
TREMBLE
I AM...
...HUMBLING MYSELF TO APPEAL TO YOUR COMPASSION...
ROAR
WHAT IS WITH THAT ATTITUDE?!!
YANK
AAAAAAAAAAAAH!!!
THE ONE WHO NEEDS AN ATTITUDE ADJUSTMENT IS YOU!!
KRAK
KRAK
I KNOW YESTERDAY WAS PAYDAY!
SUCK IT UP AND PAY YOUR RENT!!
NO, NO, NO!
GYAAAAH
THRASH
THRASH
AAARRGH! YOU'RE SUCH A PAIN IN THE BUTT! WHY DID MY DUMB SISTER HAVE TO TAKE IN A TROUBLE-MAKER LIKE YOU?!

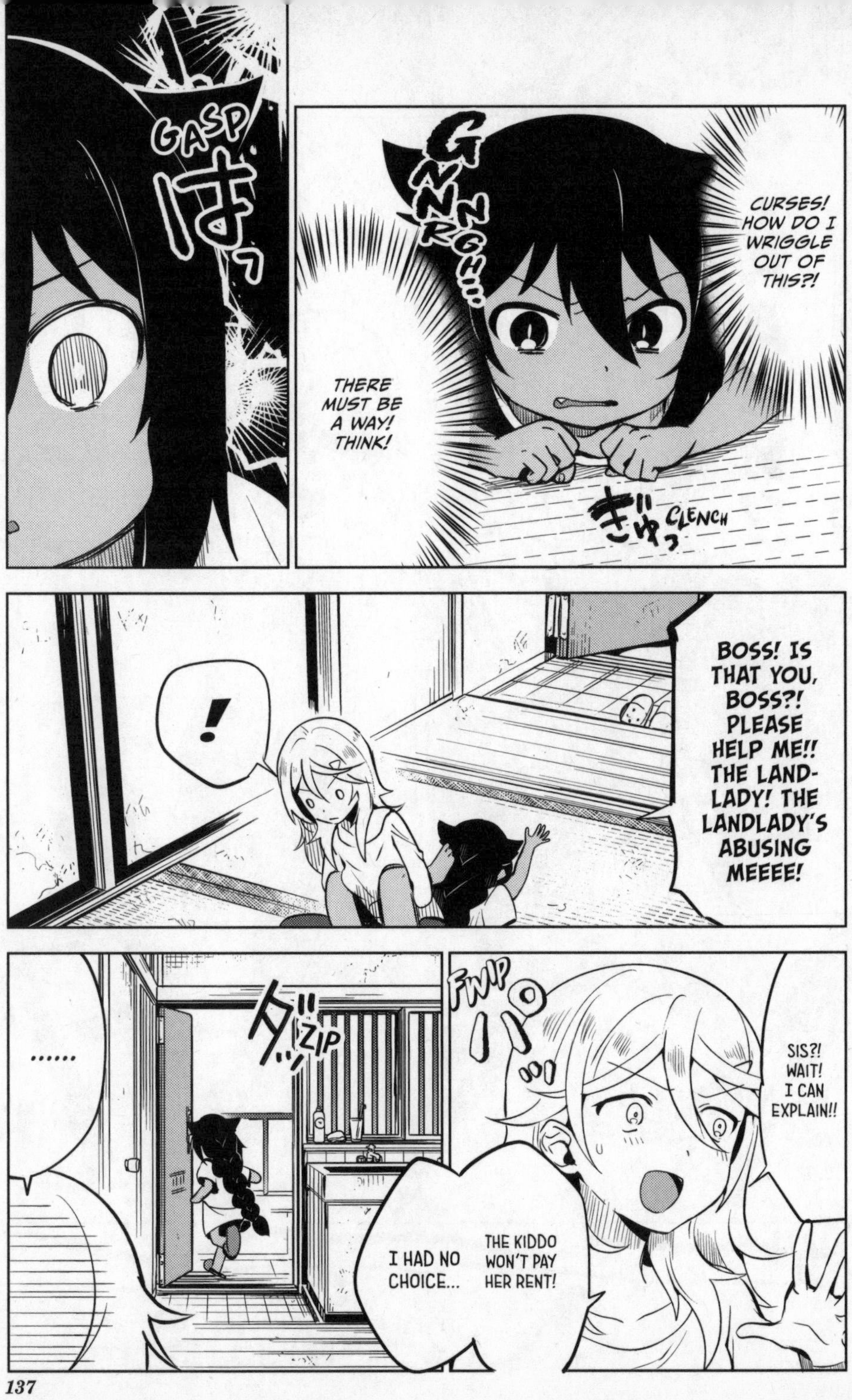
GNNNRGH...
CURSES! HOW DO I WRIGGLE OUT OF THIS?!
THERE MUST BE A WAY! THINK!
ぎゅっ CLENCH
GASP
はっ
BOSS! IS THAT YOU, BOSS?! PLEASE HELP ME!! THE LAND-LADY! THE LANDLADY'S ABUSING MEEEE!
!
FWIP
パッ
SIS?! WAIT! I CAN EXPLAIN!!
THE KIDDO WON'T PAY HER RENT!
I HAD NO CHOICE...
ダッ ZIP
......

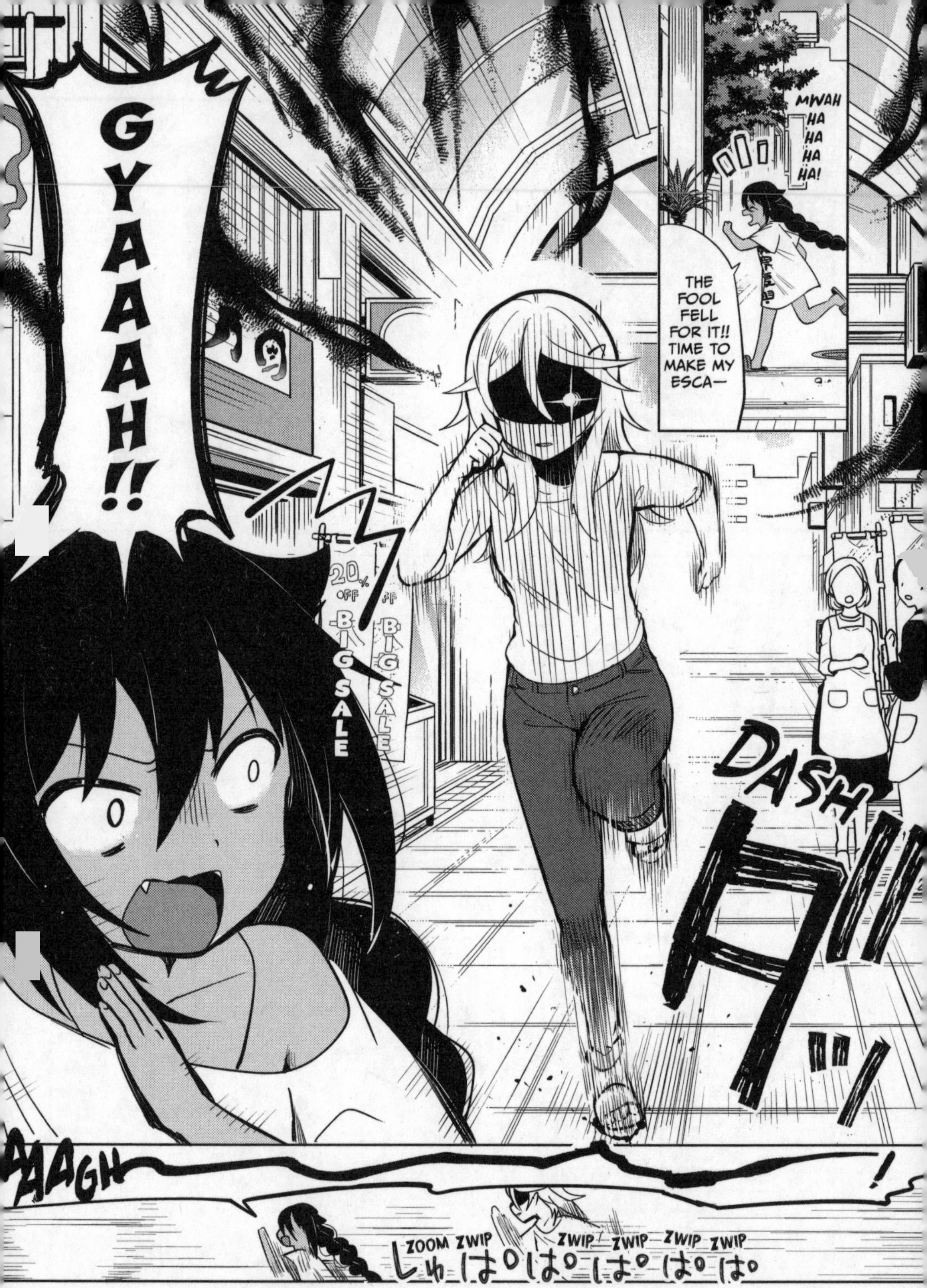
MWAH HA HA HA HA!
THE FOOL FELL FOR IT!! TIME TO MAKE MY ESCA—
GYAAAH!!
20% OFF
BIG SALE
BIG SALE
DASH
AAAGH—!
ZOOM ZWIP ZWIP ZWIP ZWIP ZWIP
しゅぱぱぱぱぱ

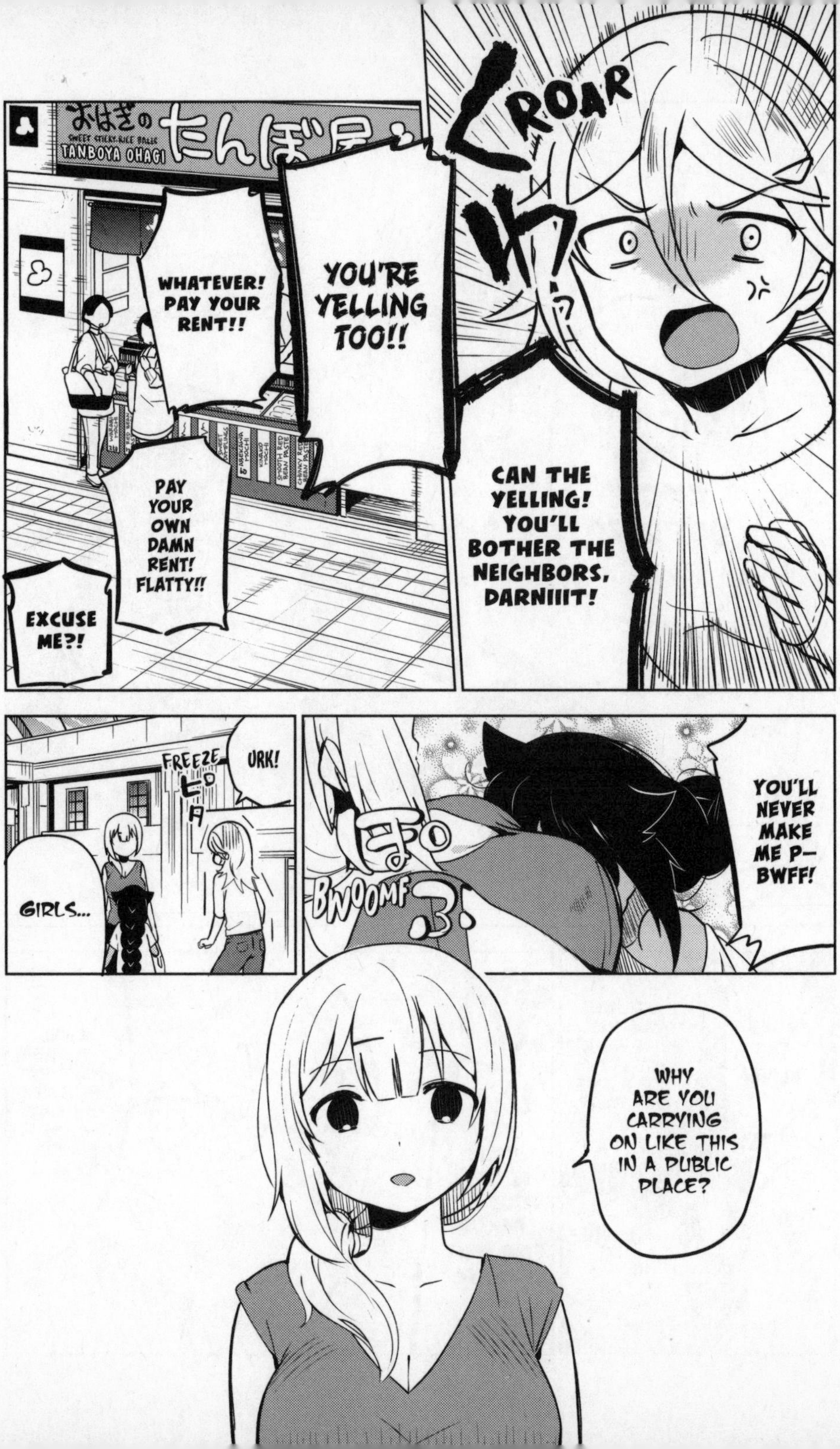
ROAR
CAN THE YELLING! YOU'LL BOTHER THE NEIGHBORS, DARNIIIT!
おはぎの たんぼ屋
SWEET STICKY-RICE BALLS
TANBOYA OHAGI
YOU'RE YELLING TOO!!
WHATEVER! PAY YOUR RENT!!
PAY YOUR OWN DAMN RENT! FLATTY!!
EXCUSE ME?!
YOU'LL NEVER MAKE ME P—BWFF!
BWOOMF
URK!
FREEZE
GIRLS...
WHY ARE YOU CARRYING ON LIKE THIS IN A PUBLIC PLACE?

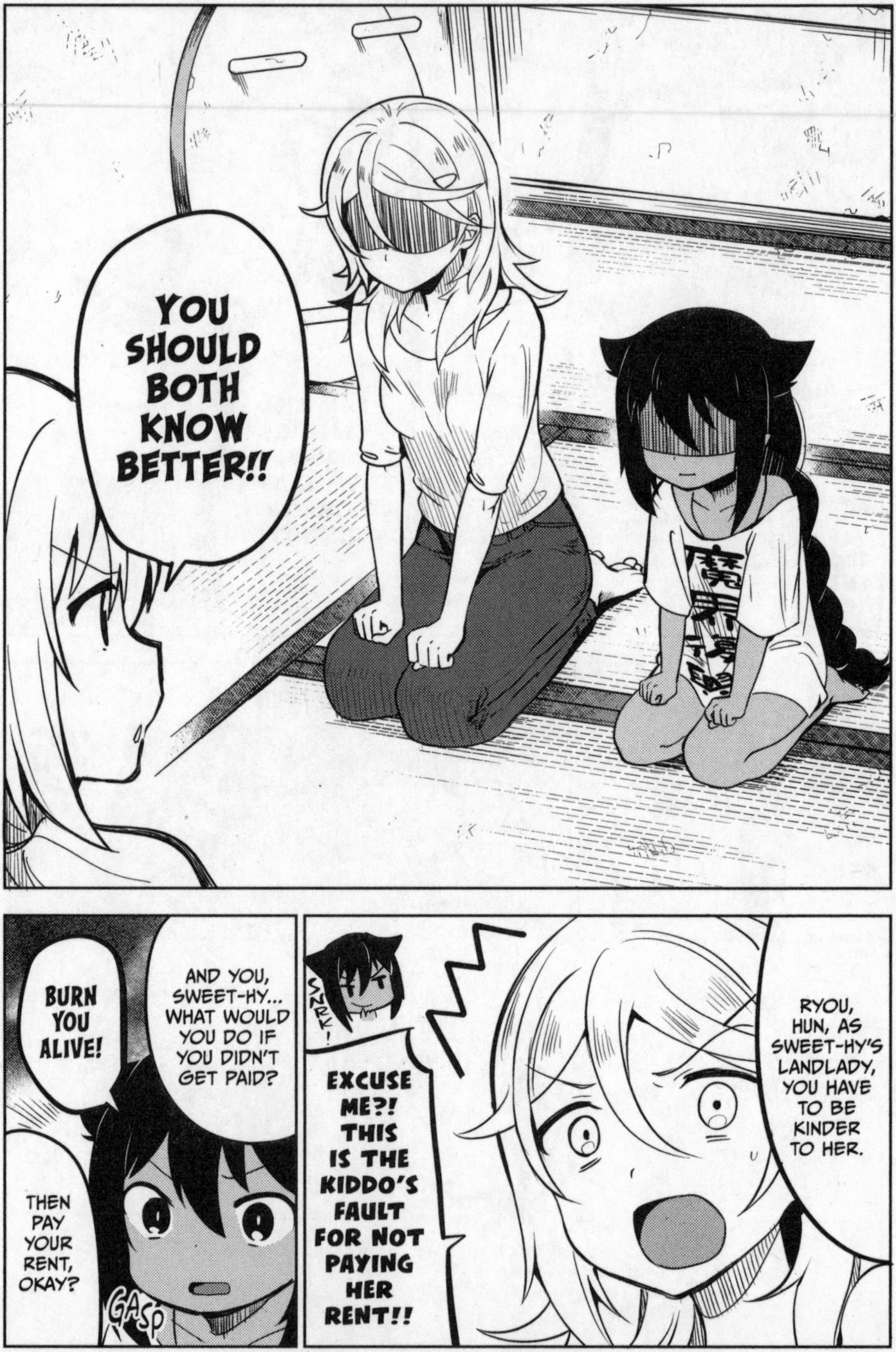
YOU SHOULD BOTH KNOW BETTER!!
RYOU, HUN, AS SWEET-HY'S LANDLADY, YOU HAVE TO BE KINDER TO HER.
EXCUSE ME?! THIS IS THE KIDDO'S FAULT FOR NOT PAYING HER RENT!!
SNRK!
AND YOU, SWEET-HY... WHAT WOULD YOU DO IF YOU DIDN'T GET PAID?
BURN YOU ALIVE!
THEN PAY YOUR RENT, OKAY?
GASP

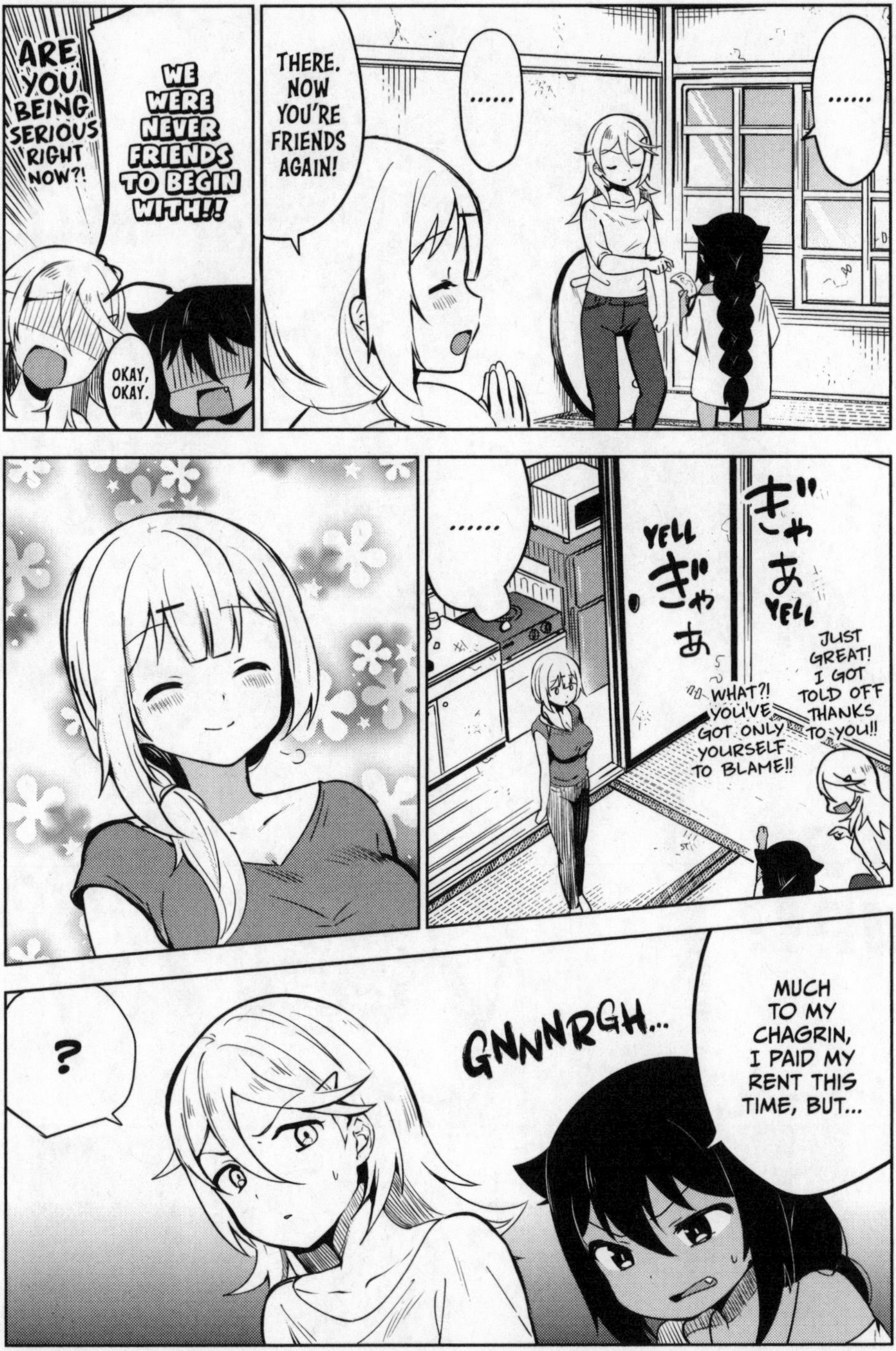
......
......
THERE. NOW YOU'RE FRIENDS AGAIN!
WE WERE NEVER FRIENDS TO BEGIN WITH!!
ARE YOU BEING SERIOUS RIGHT NOW?!
OKAY, OKAY.
......
ぎゃあ YELL
ぎゃあ YELL
JUST GREAT! I GOT TOLD OFF THANKS TO YOU!!
WHAT?! YOU'VE GOT ONLY YOURSELF TO BLAME!!
MUCH TO MY CHAGRIN, I PAID MY RENT THIS TIME, BUT...
GNNNRGH...
?

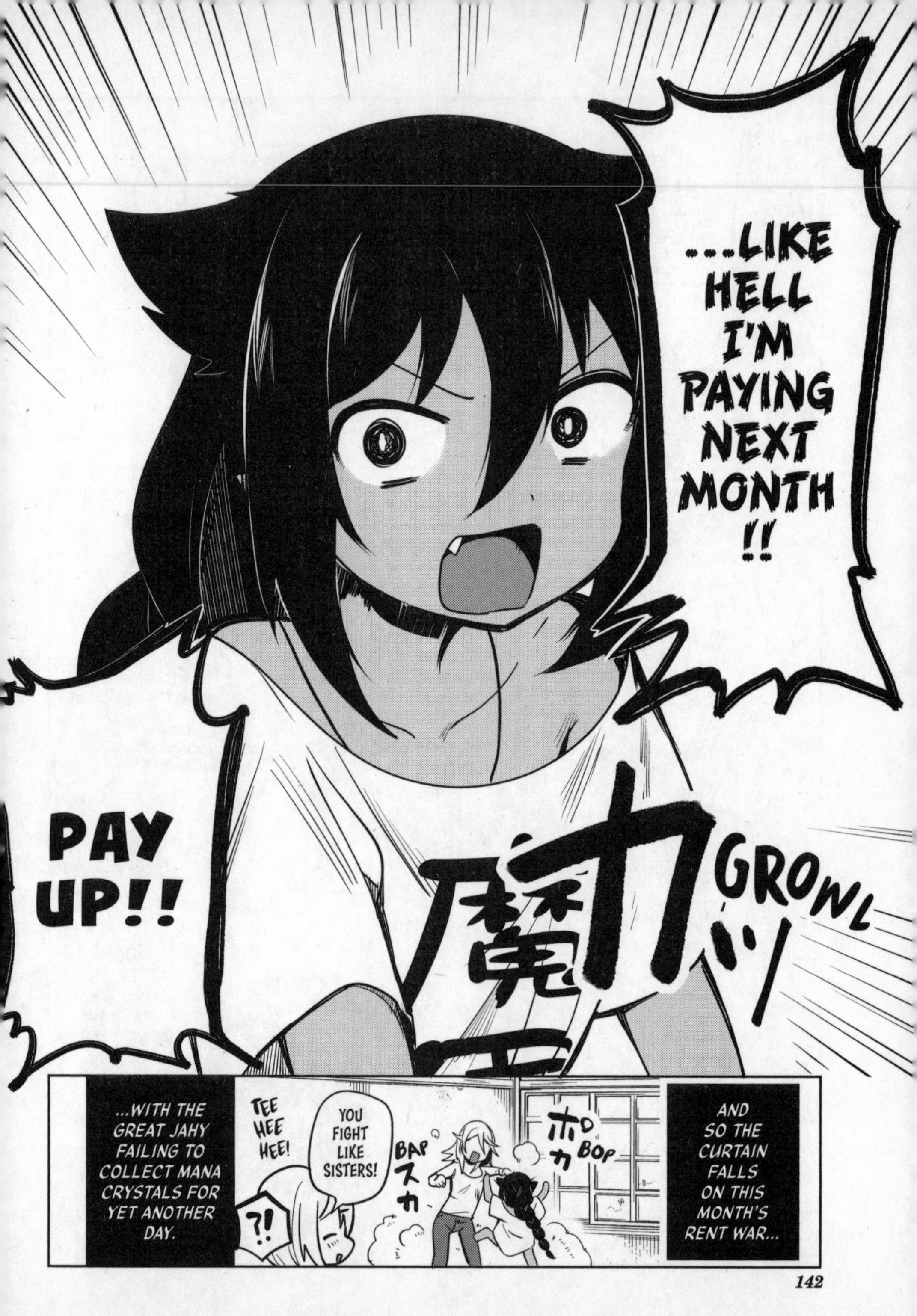
...LIKE HELL I'M PAYING NEXT MONTH!!
PAY UP!!
GROWL
AND SO THE CURTAIN FALLS ON THIS MONTH'S RENT WAR...
BOP
YOU FIGHT LIKE SISTERS!
BAP
TEE HEE HEE!
?!
...WITH THE GREAT JAHY FAILING TO COLLECT MANA CRYSTALS FOR YET ANOTHER DAY.

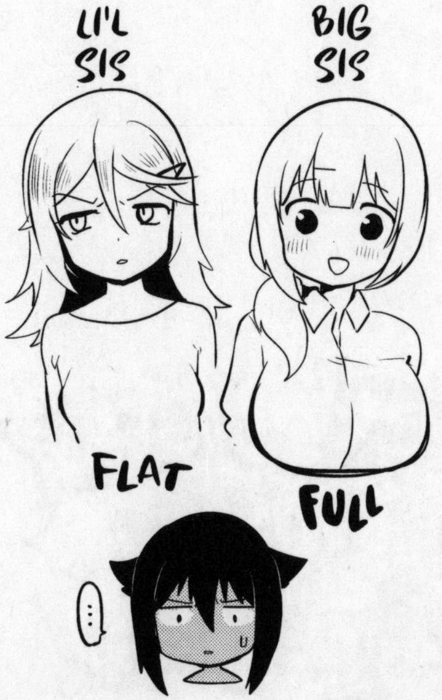
LI'L SIS
BIG SIS
FLAT
FULL
...

The GREAT JAHY Will NOT Be DEFEATED!

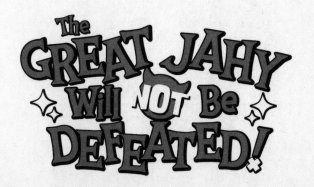

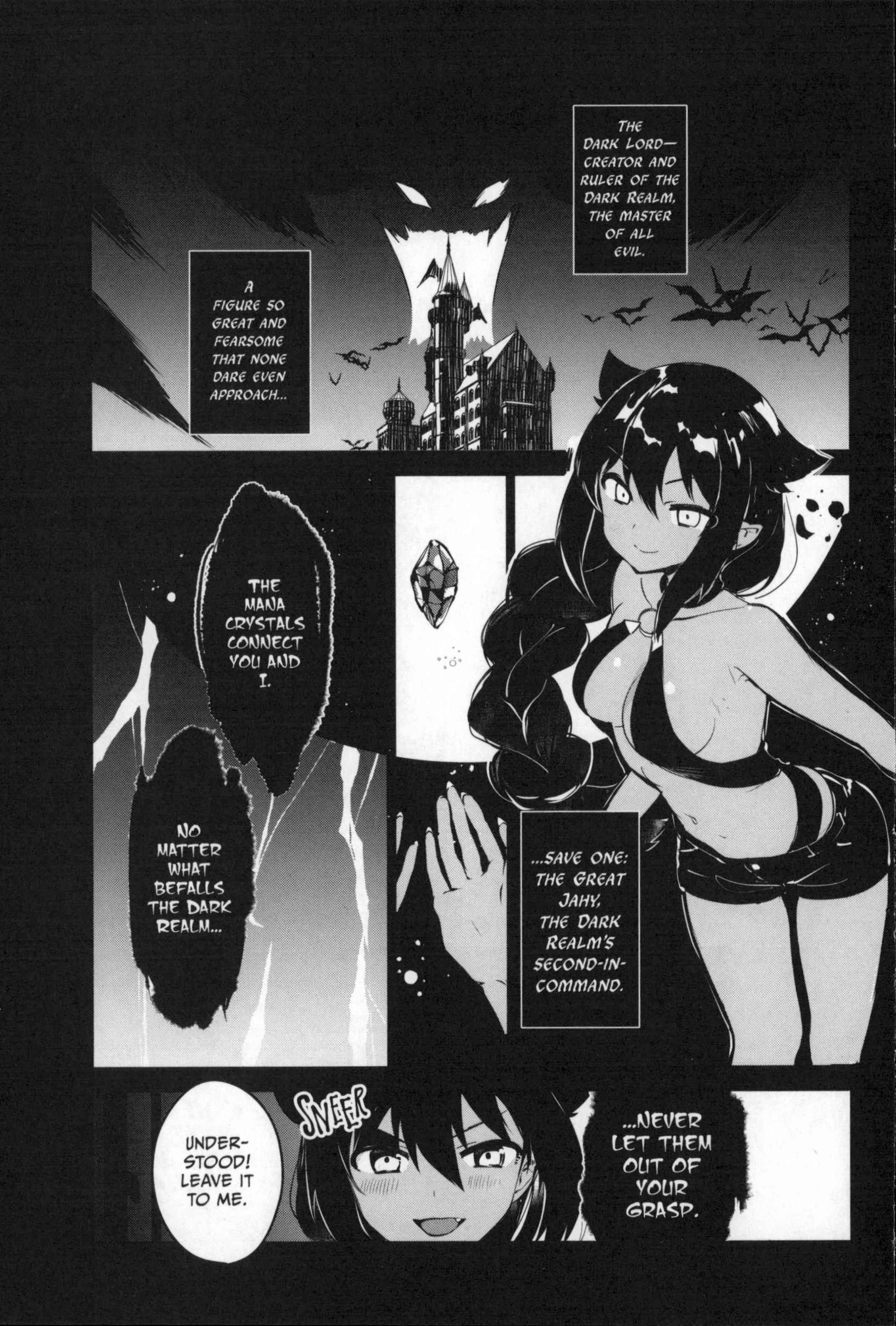
THE DARK LORD—CREATOR AND RULER OF THE DARK REALM, THE MASTER OF ALL EVIL.
A FIGURE SO GREAT AND FEARSOME THAT NONE DARE EVEN APPROACH...
...SAVE ONE: THE GREAT JAHY, THE DARK REALM'S SECOND-IN-COMMAND.
THE MANA CRYSTALS CONNECT YOU AND I.
NO MATTER WHAT BEFALLS THE DARK REALM...
...NEVER LET THEM OUT OF YOUR GRASP.
SNEER
UNDER-STOOD! LEAVE IT TO ME.

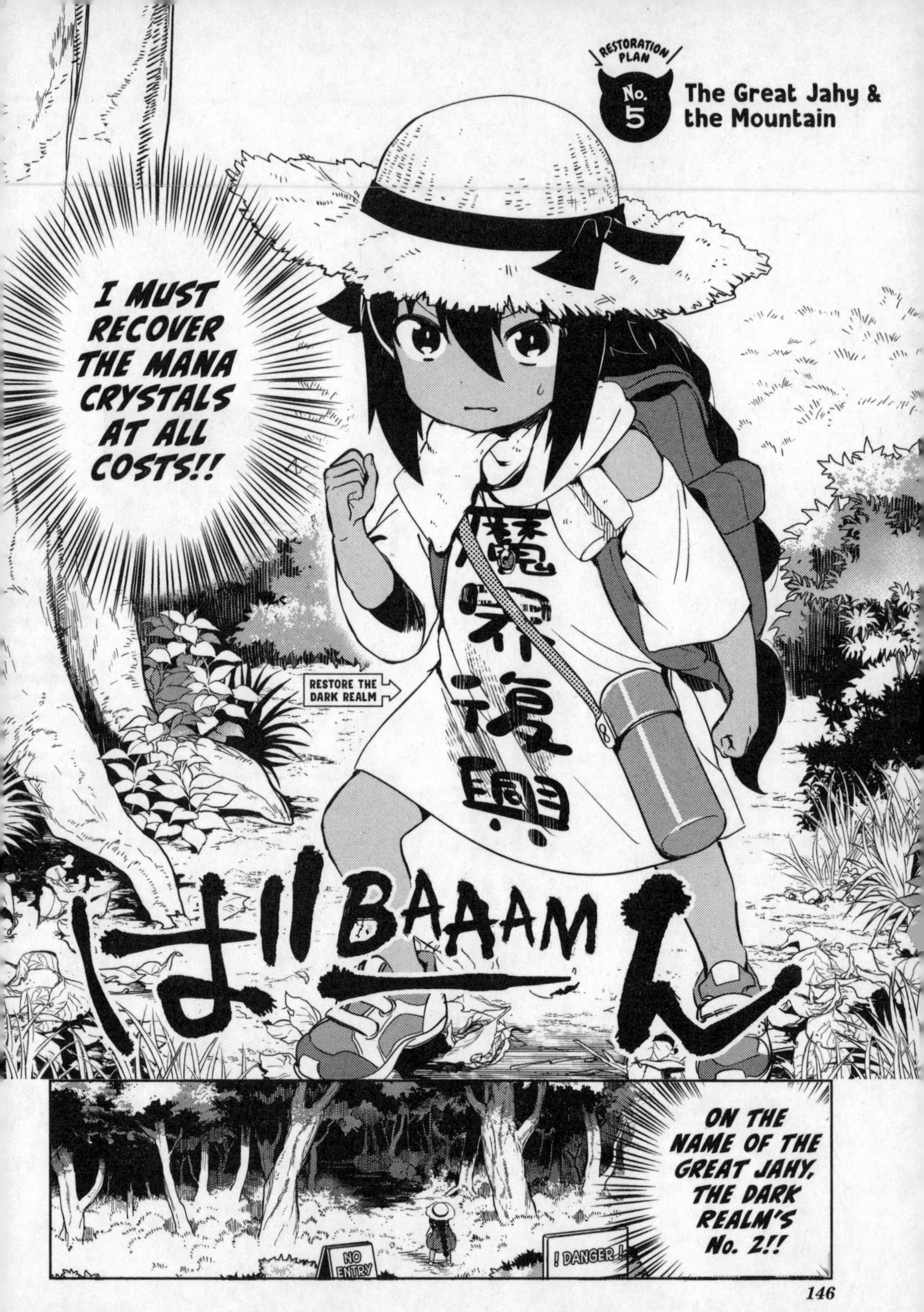
RESTORATION PLAN
No. 5
The Great Jahy & the Mountain
I MUST RECOVER THE MANA CRYSTALS AT ALL COSTS!!
魔界復興
RESTORE THE DARK REALM
ばーん
BAAAM
ON THE NAME OF THE GREAT JAHY, THE DARK REALM'S No. 2!!
NO ENTRY
! DANGER !

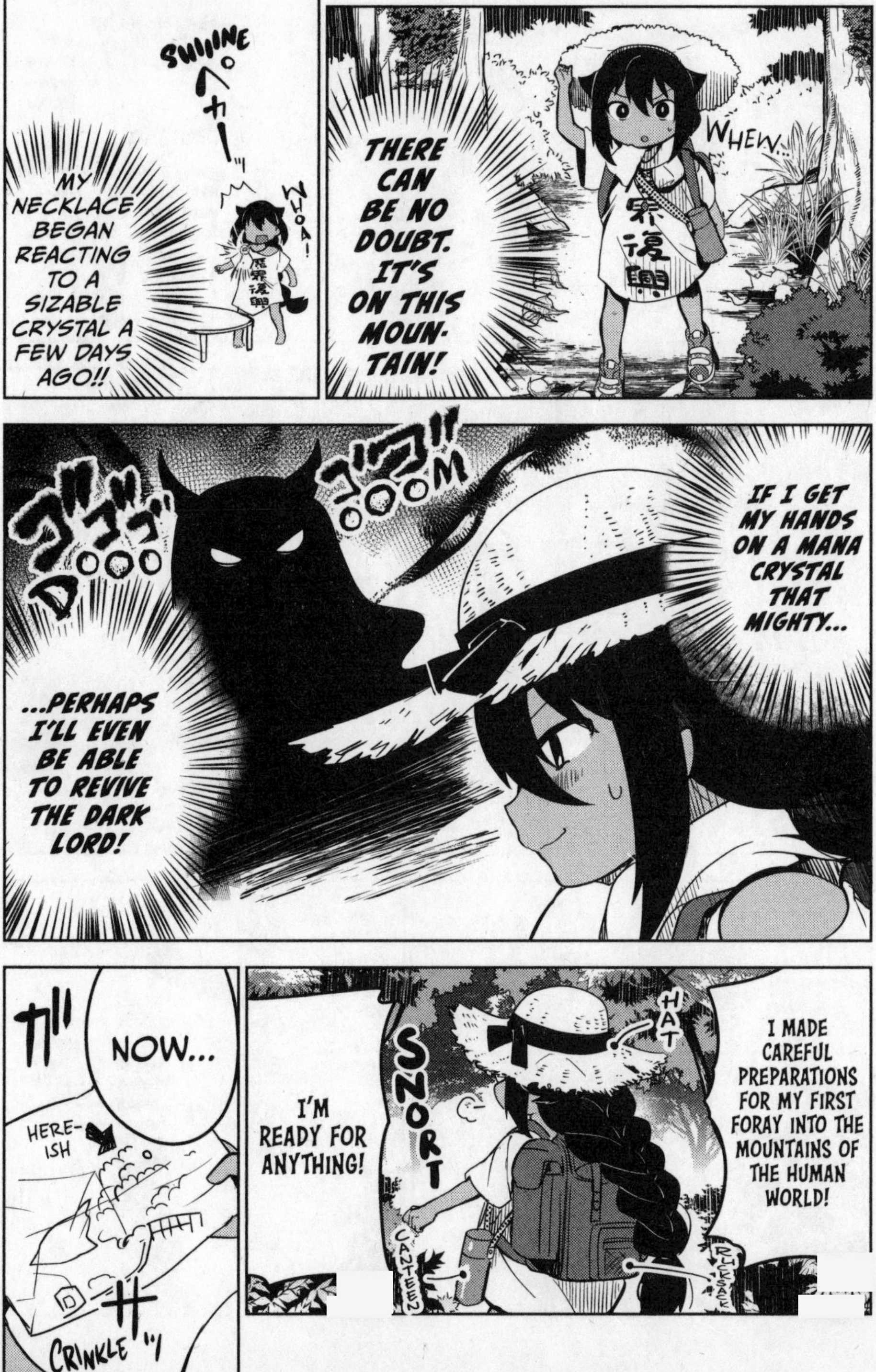
WHEW...
THERE CAN BE NO DOUBT. IT'S ON THIS MOUN-TAIN!
SHIIINE
ペカー
WHOA!
MY NECKLACE BEGAN REACTING TO A SIZABLE CRYSTAL A FEW DAYS AGO!!
ゴゴ
OOOM
ゴゴゴ
DOOOO
IF I GET MY HANDS ON A MANA CRYSTAL THAT MIGHTY...
...PERHAPS I'LL EVEN BE ABLE TO REVIVE THE DARK LORD!
I MADE CAREFUL PREPARATIONS FOR MY FIRST FORAY INTO THE MOUNTAINS OF THE HUMAN WORLD!
HAT
SNORT
I'M READY FOR ANYTHING!
CANTEEN
RUCKSACK
ガ
NOW...
HERE-ISH
CRINKLE

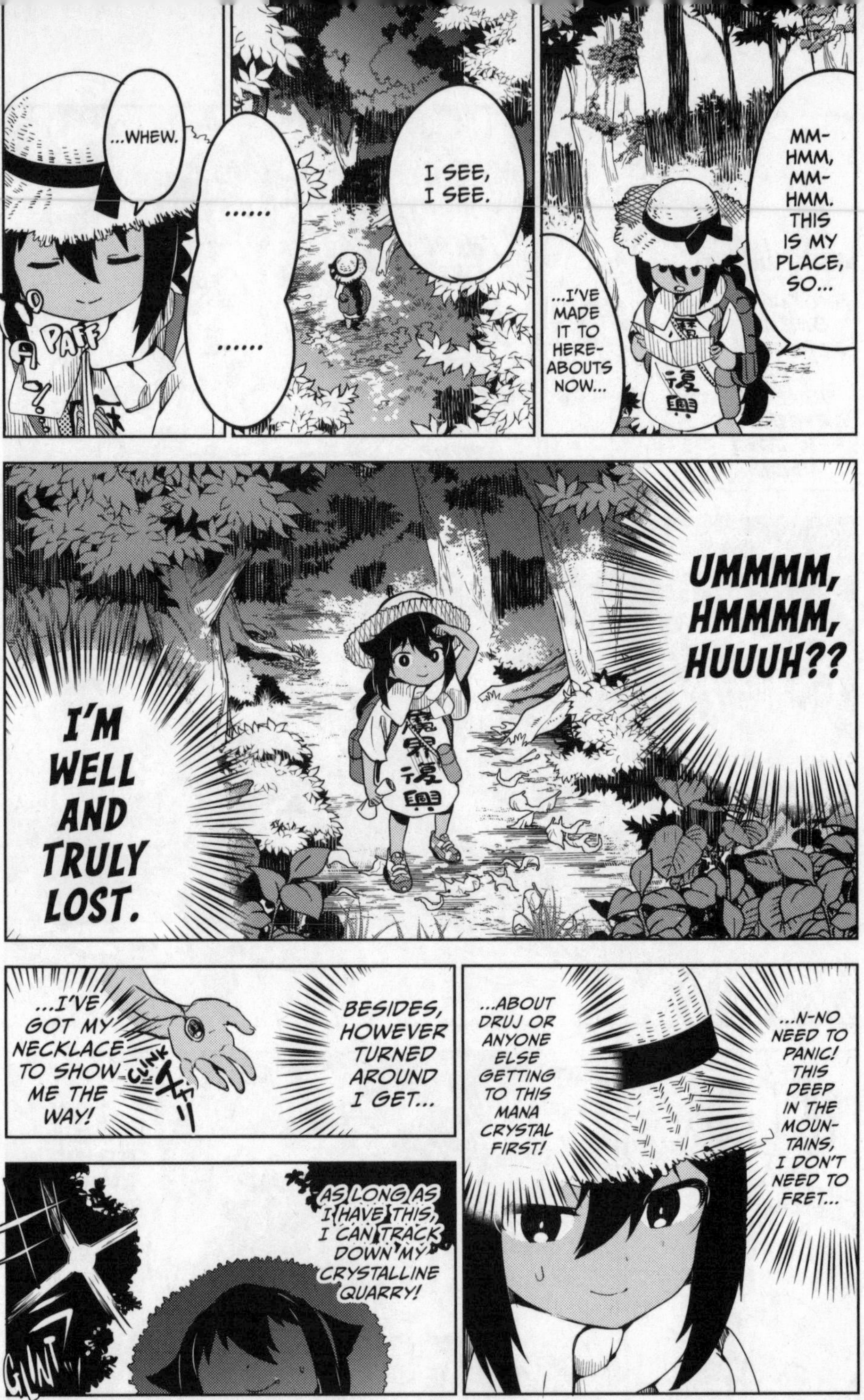
MM-HMM, MM-HMM. THIS IS MY PLACE, SO...
...I'VE MADE IT TO HERE-ABOUTS NOW...
I SEE, I SEE.
......
......
...WHEW.
PAFF
UMMMM, HMMMM, HUUUH??
I'M WELL AND TRULY LOST.
...N-NO NEED TO PANIC! THIS DEEP IN THE MOUNTAINS, I DON'T NEED TO FRET...
...ABOUT DRUJ OR ANYONE ELSE GETTING TO THIS MANA CRYSTAL FIRST!
BESIDES, HOWEVER TURNED AROUND I GET...
...I'VE GOT MY NECKLACE TO SHOW ME THE WAY!
CLINK
AS LONG AS I HAVE THIS, I CAN TRACK DOWN MY CRYSTALLINE QUARRY!
GLINT

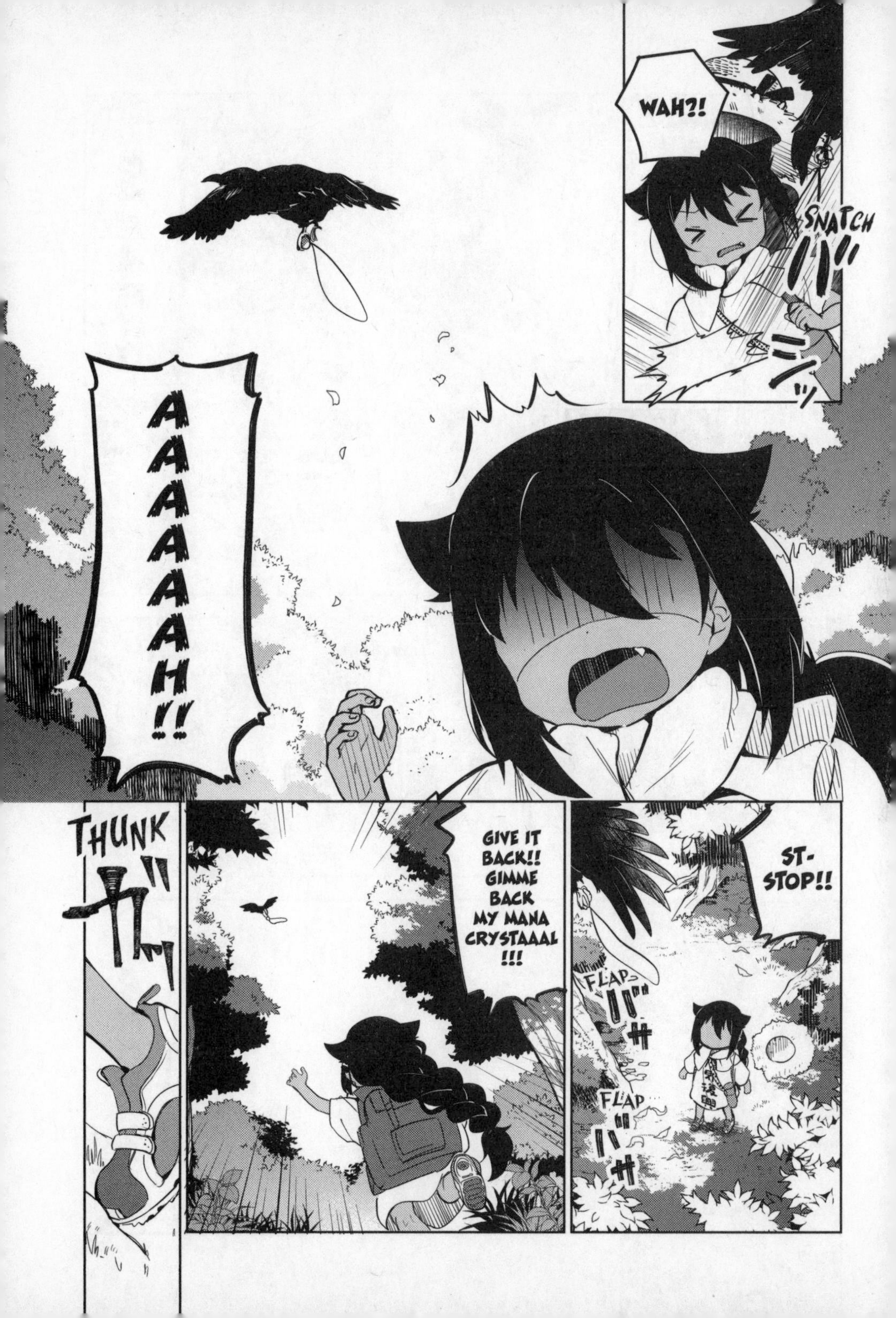
WAH?!
SNATCH
AAAAAAAH!!
ST-STOP!!
FLAP
FLAP
GIVE IT BACK!! GIMME BACK MY MANA CRYSTAAAL!!!
THUNK

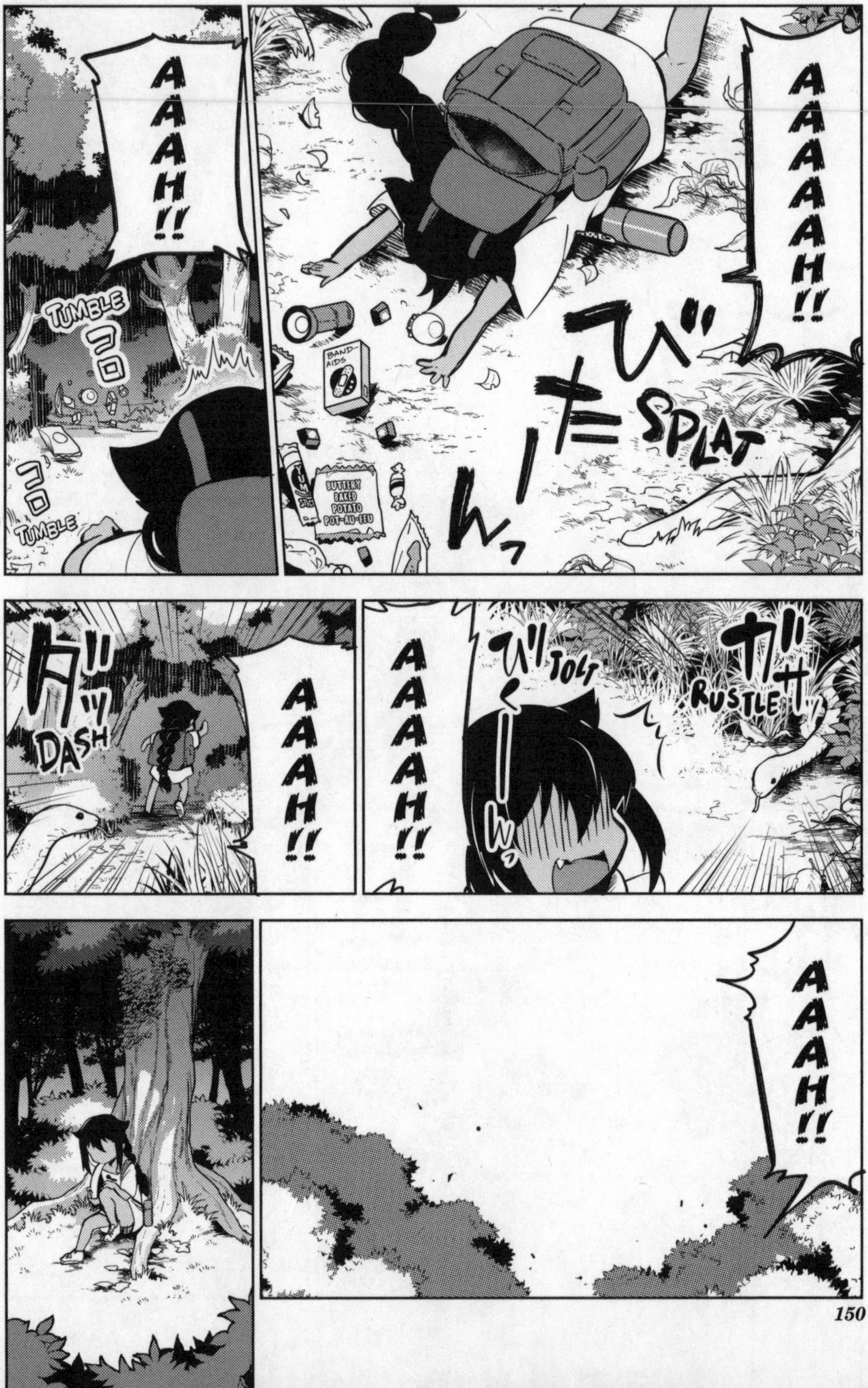
AAAAAH!!
びたーんっ
SPLAT
BAND-AIDS
YUM STICK
BUTTERY BAKED POTATO POT-AU-FEU
AAAH!!
TUMBLE コロ
コロ TUMBLE
AAAAH!!
びくーんっ
JOLT
ガサ
RUSTLE
AAAH!!
ダッ
DASH
AAAH!!

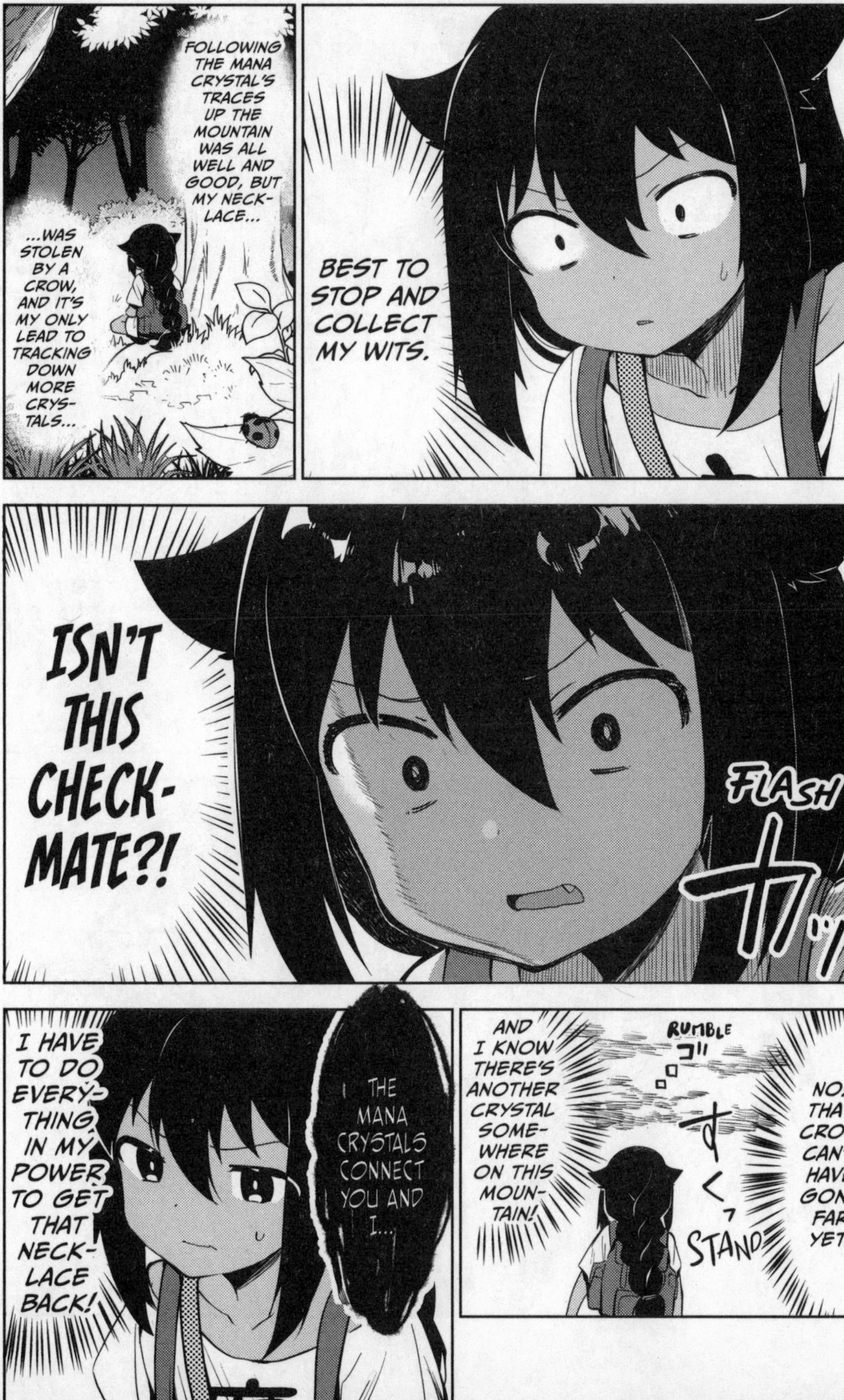
BEST TO STOP AND COLLECT MY WITS.
FOLLOWING THE MANA CRYSTAL'S TRACES UP THE MOUNTAIN WAS ALL WELL AND GOOD, BUT MY NECKLACE...
...WAS STOLEN BY A CROW, AND IT'S MY ONLY LEAD TO TRACKING DOWN MORE CRYSTALS...
FLASH
ISN'T THIS CHECKMATE?!
NO! THAT CROW CAN'T HAVE GONE FAR YET!
RUMBLE
STAND
AND I KNOW THERE'S ANOTHER CRYSTAL SOMEWHERE ON THIS MOUNTAIN!
THE MANA CRYSTALS CONNECT YOU AND I...
I HAVE TO DO EVERYTHING IN MY POWER TO GET THAT NECKLACE BACK!

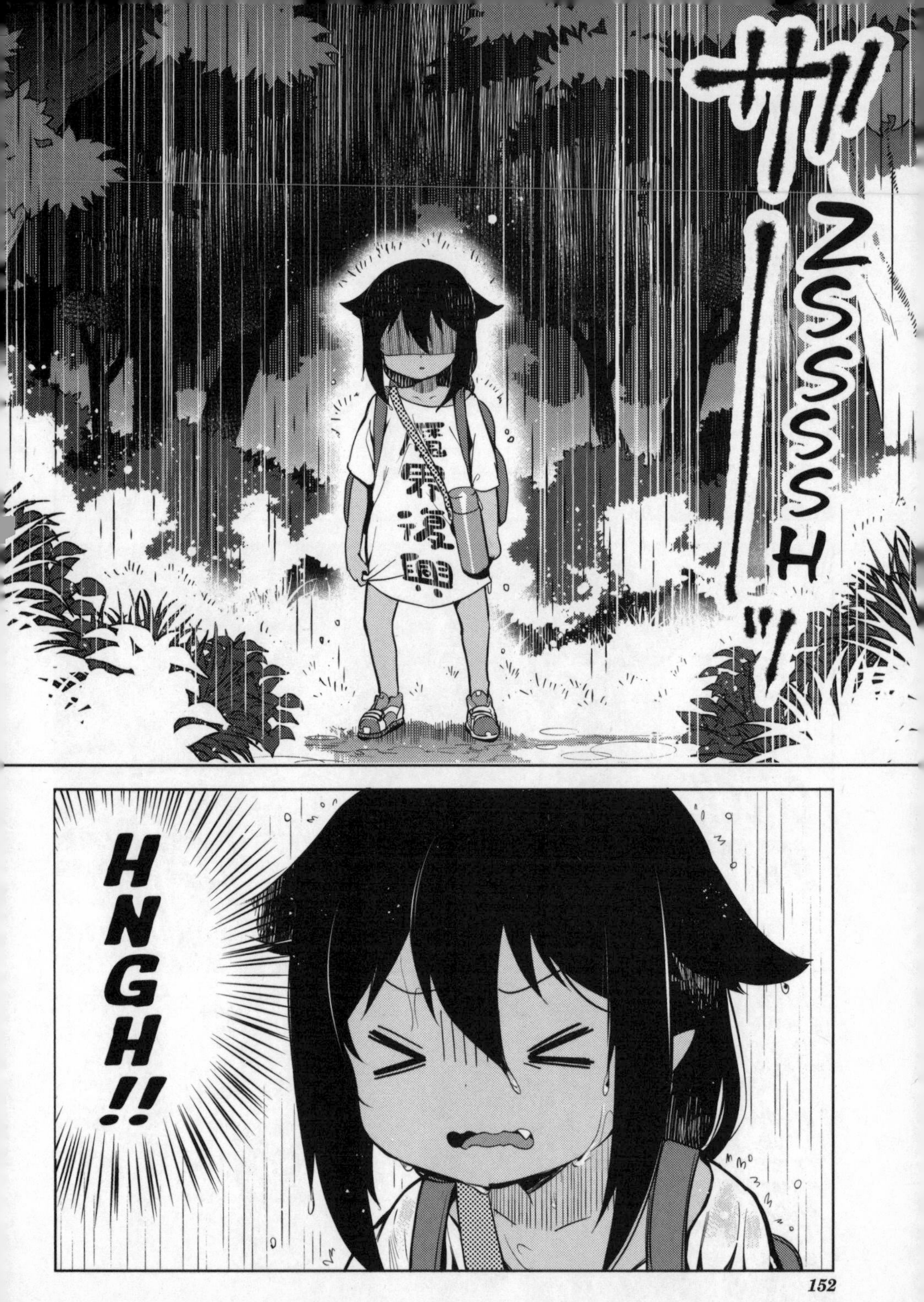
ザーーッ
ZSSSSH
HNGH!!

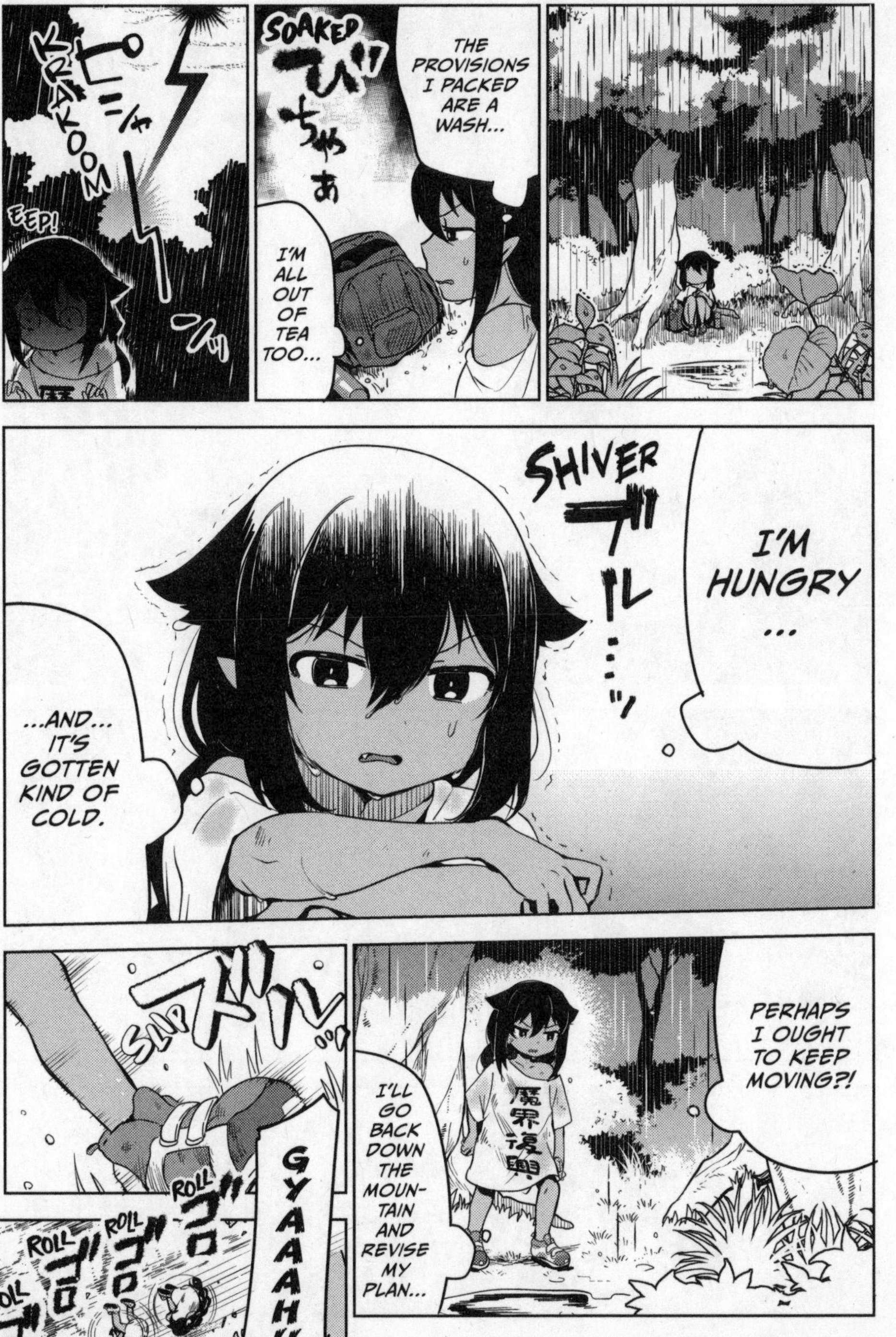
SOAKED
びちゃあ
THE PROVISIONS I PACKED ARE A WASH...
I'M ALL OUT OF TEA TOO...
KRAKOOM
EEP!
I'M HUNGRY ...
SHIVER
...AND... IT'S GOTTEN KIND OF COLD.
PERHAPS I OUGHT TO KEEP MOVING?!
魔界復興
I'LL GO BACK DOWN THE MOUN-TAIN AND REVISE MY PLAN...
SLIP
GYAAAAH!!
ROLL ゴロ
ROLL ゴロ
ROLL ゴロ
ROLL ゴロ

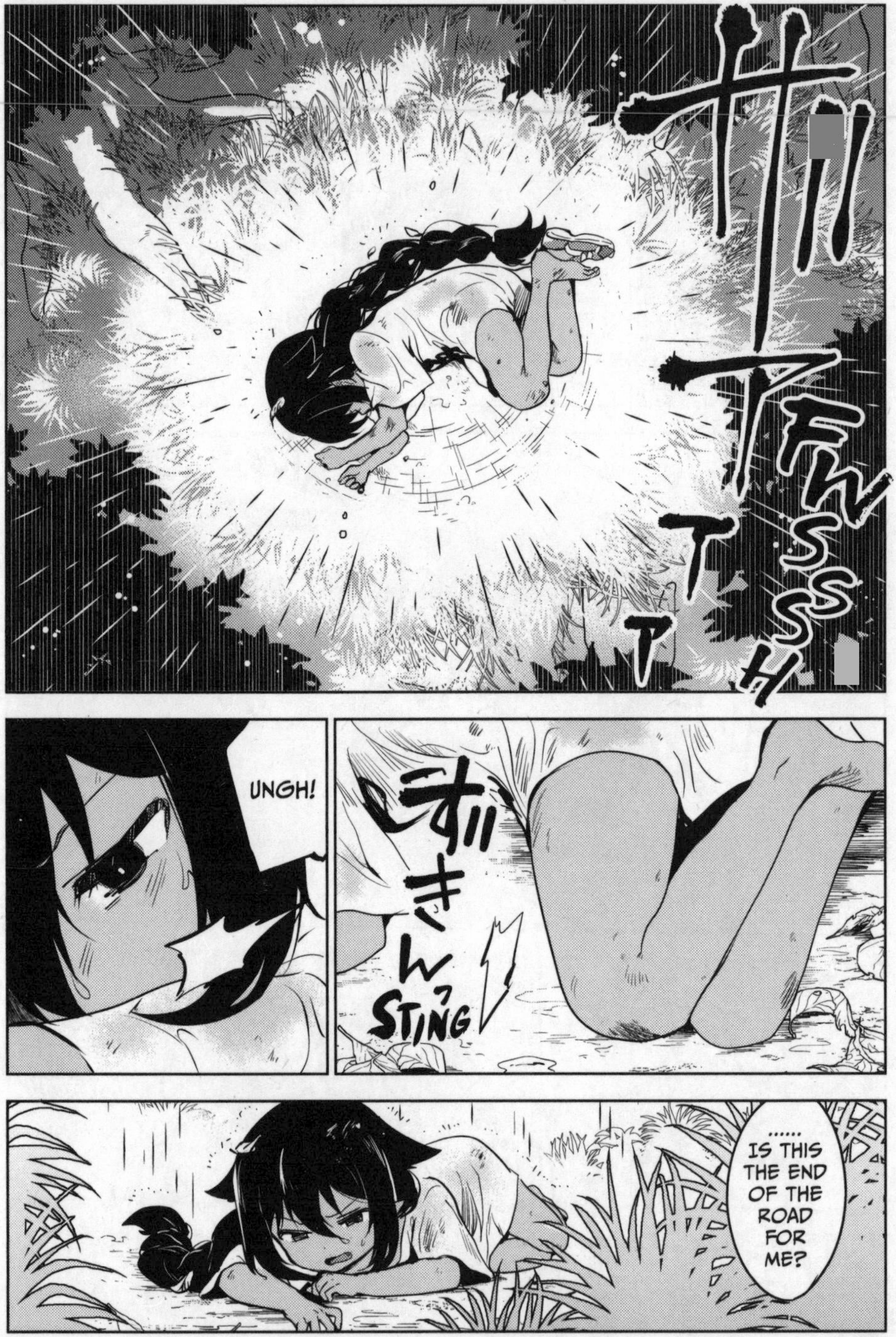
FWSSSH
ずきんっ
STING
UNGH!
......
IS THIS THE END OF THE ROAD FOR ME?

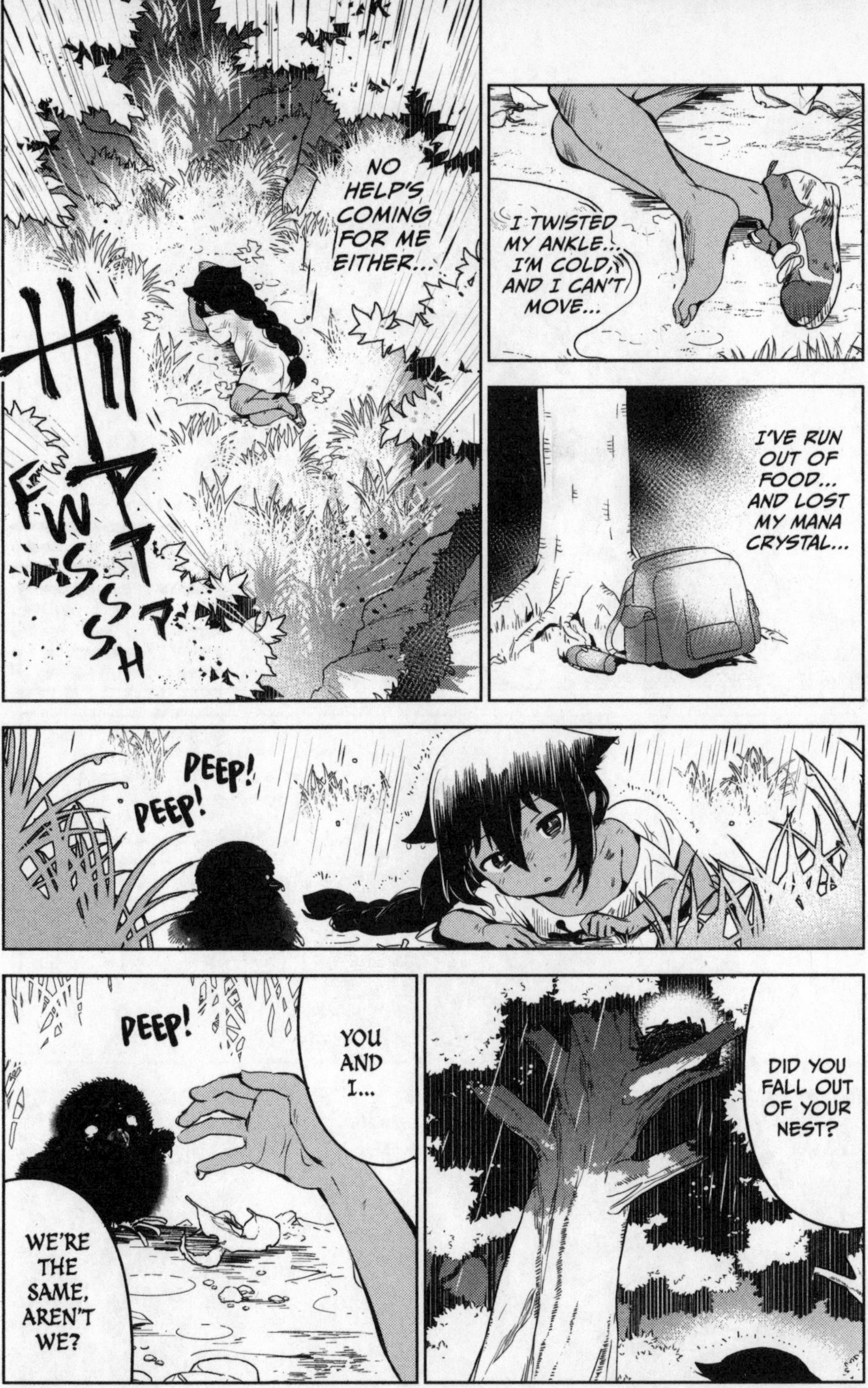
I TWISTED MY ANKLE... I'M COLD, AND I CAN'T MOVE...
I'VE RUN OUT OF FOOD... AND LOST MY MANA CRYSTAL...
NO HELP'S COMING FOR ME EITHER...
FWSSSH
PEEP!
PEEP!
DID YOU FALL OUT OF YOUR NEST?
YOU AND I...
PEEP!
WE'RE THE SAME, AREN'T WE?

FALLEN TO THE GROUND...

FATED TO GROW WEAK AND DIE...

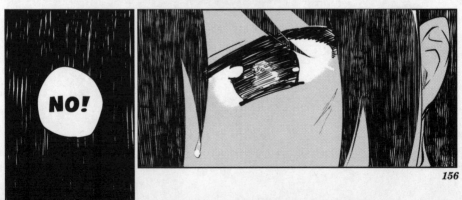

NO!

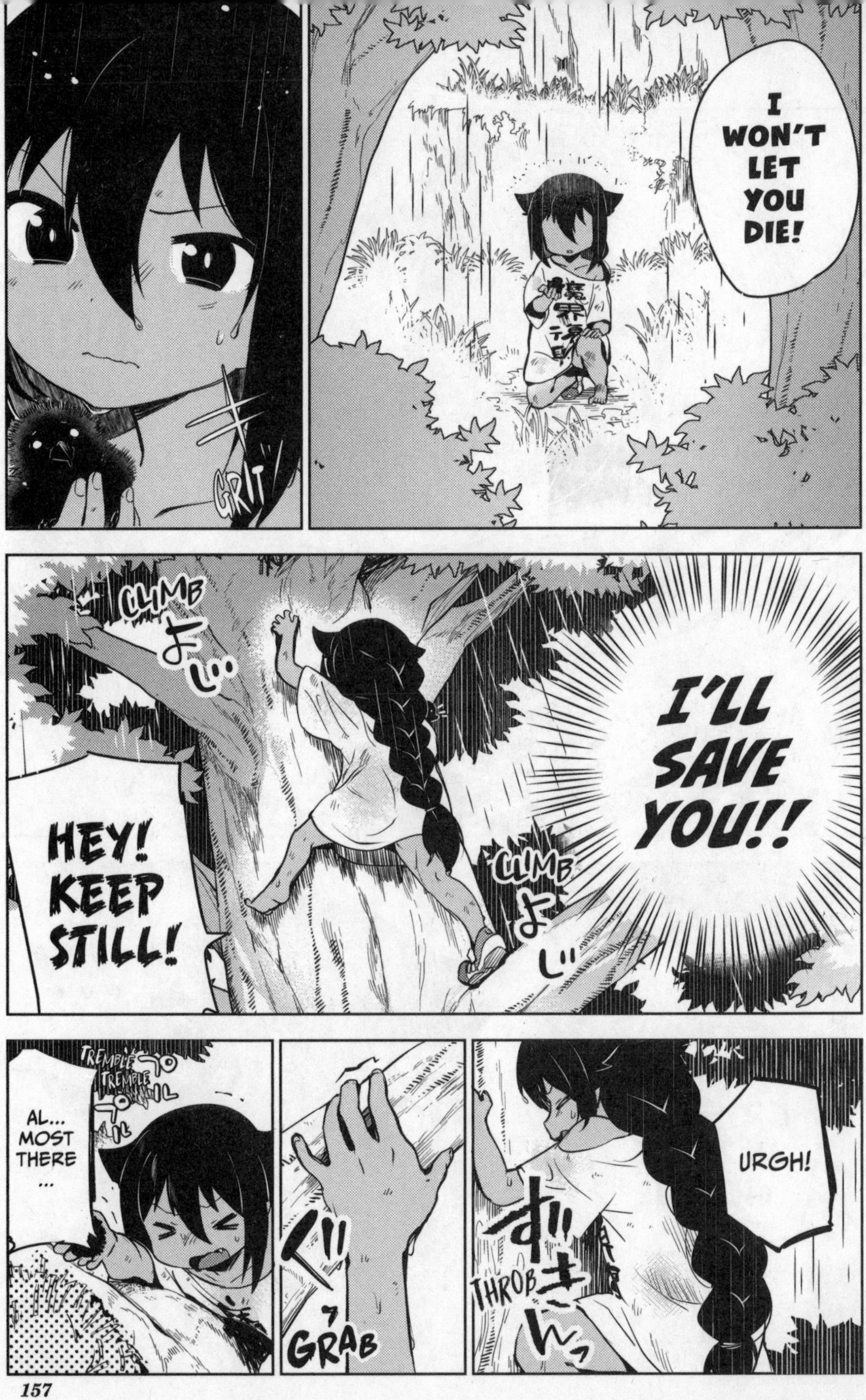
I WON'T LET YOU DIE!
GRIT
I'LL SAVE YOU!!
CLIMB
よじ
HEY! KEEP STILL!
CLIMB
よじ
URGH!
THROB
GRAB
TREMBLE
TREMBLE
AL... MOST THERE ...

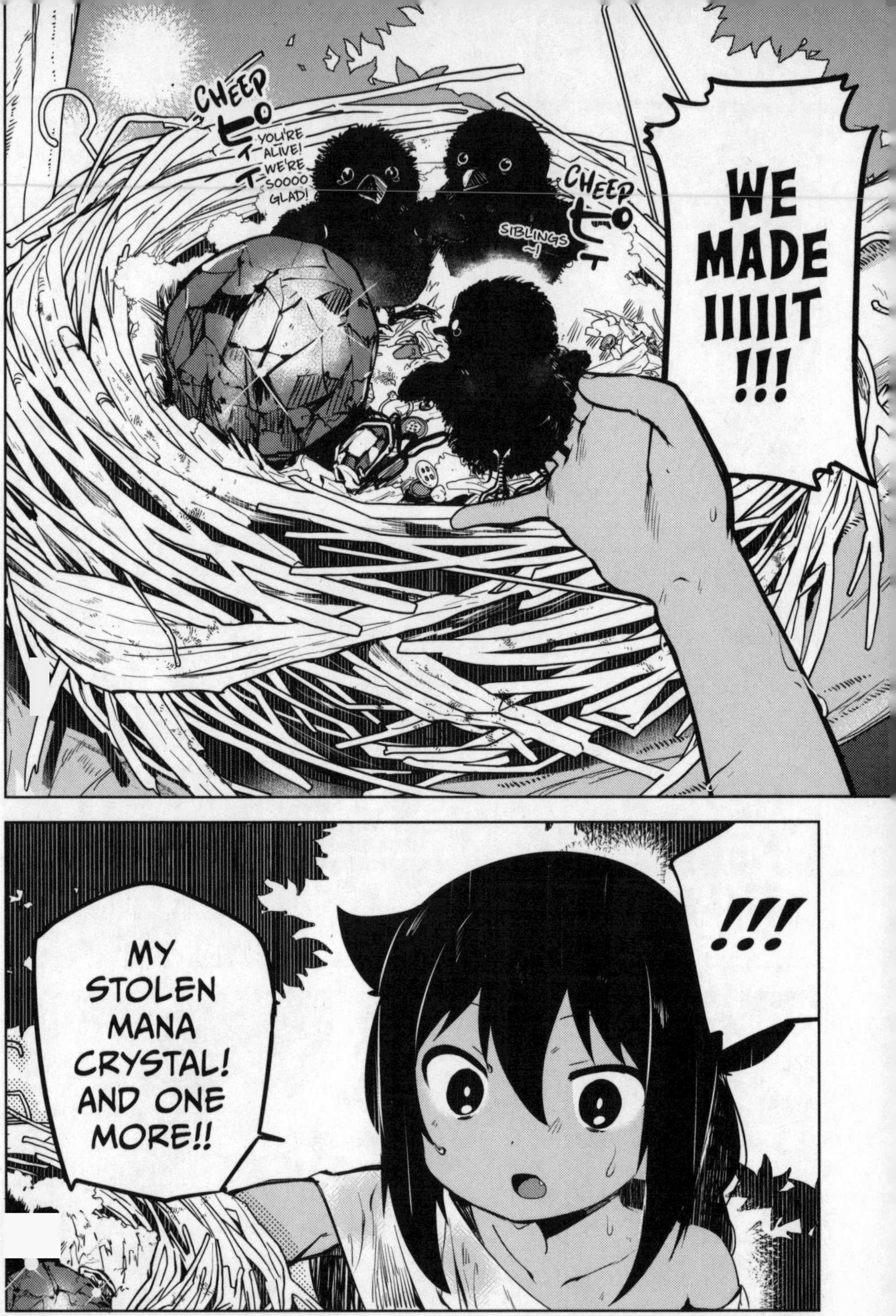
WE MADE IIIIIT!!!
CHEEP ピィ
SIBLINGS ~!
CHEEP ピィ
YOU'RE ALIVE! WE'RE SOOOO GLAD!
!!!
MY STOLEN MANA CRYSTAL! AND ONE MORE!!

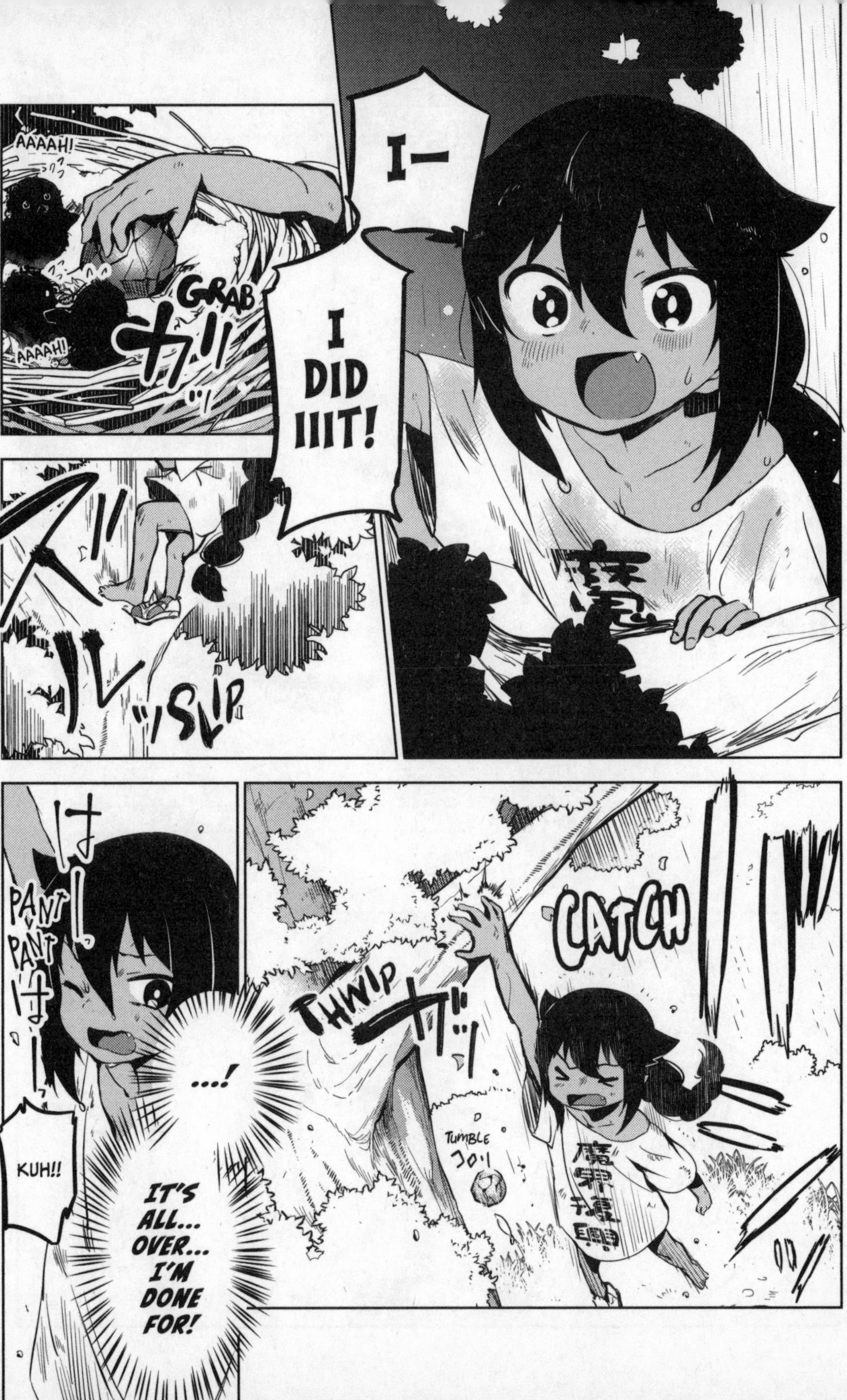
I—
I DID IIIT!
AAAAH!
GRAB
カリ
AAAAH!
SLIP
ズルッ
CATCH
THWIP
ガッ
TUMBLE
コロ
PANT PANT
はー はー
...!
KUH!!
IT'S ALL... OVER... I'M DONE FOR!

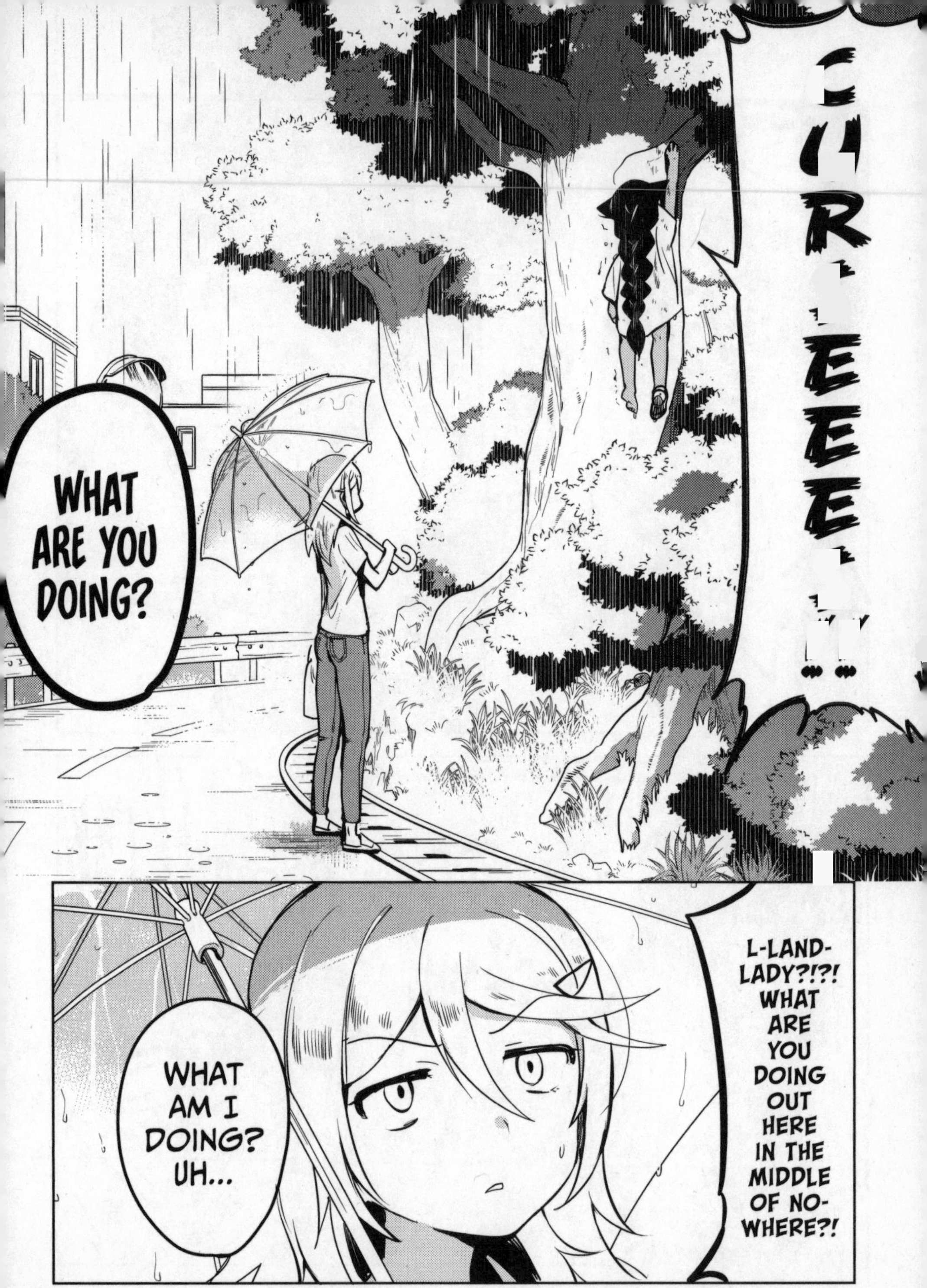
WHAT ARE YOU DOING?
L-LANDLADY?!?! WHAT ARE YOU DOING OUT HERE IN THE MIDDLE OF NOWHERE?!
WHAT AM I DOING? UH...

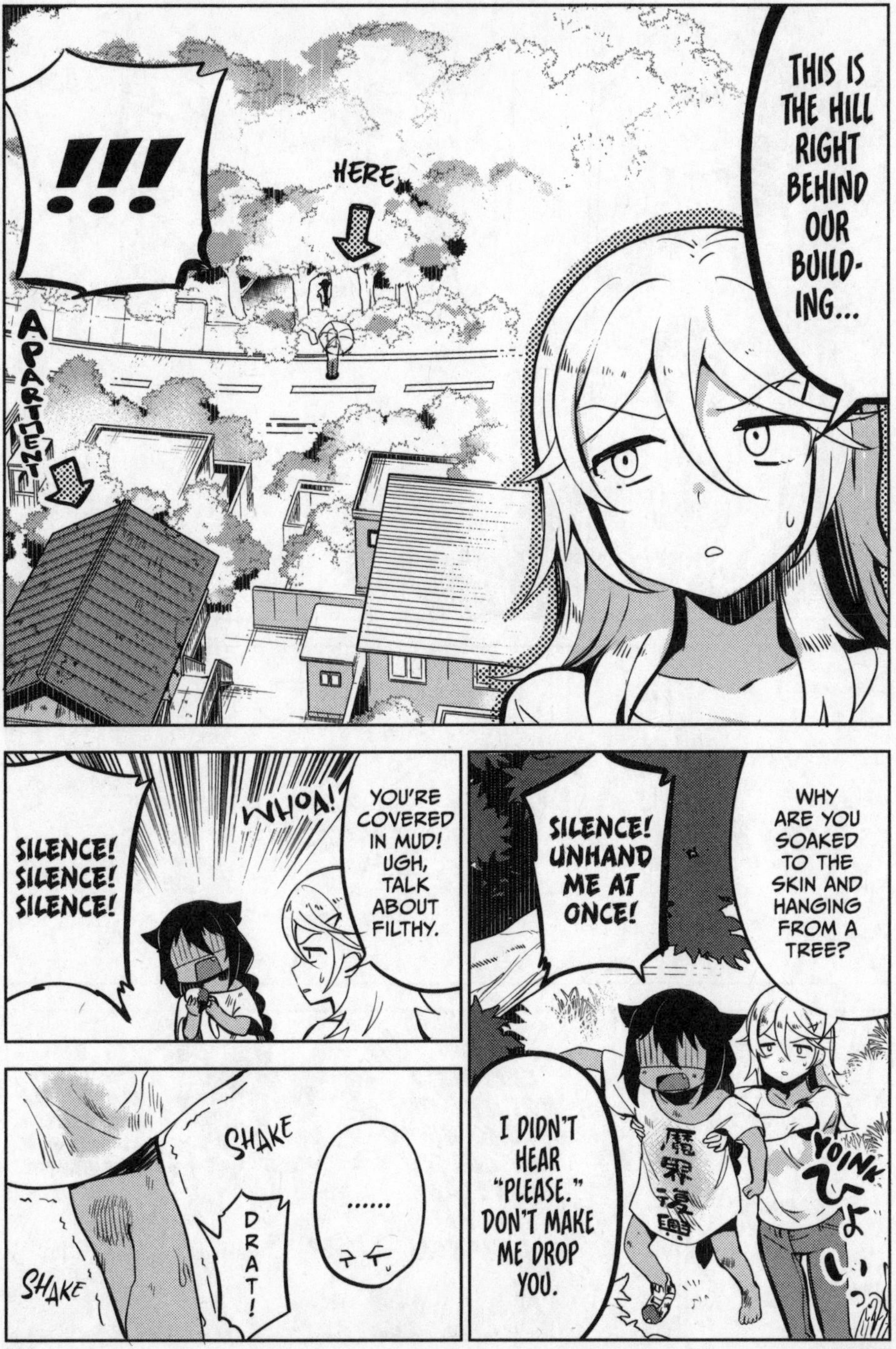
THIS IS THE HILL RIGHT BEHIND OUR BUILDING...
HERE
!!!
APARTMENT
WHY ARE YOU SOAKED TO THE SKIN AND HANGING FROM A TREE?
SILENCE! UNHAND ME AT ONCE!
I DIDN'T HEAR "PLEASE." DON'T MAKE ME DROP YOU.
YOINK
YOU'RE COVERED IN MUD! UGH, TALK ABOUT FILTHY.
WHOA!
SILENCE! SILENCE! SILENCE!
SHAKE
......
DRAT!
SHAKE

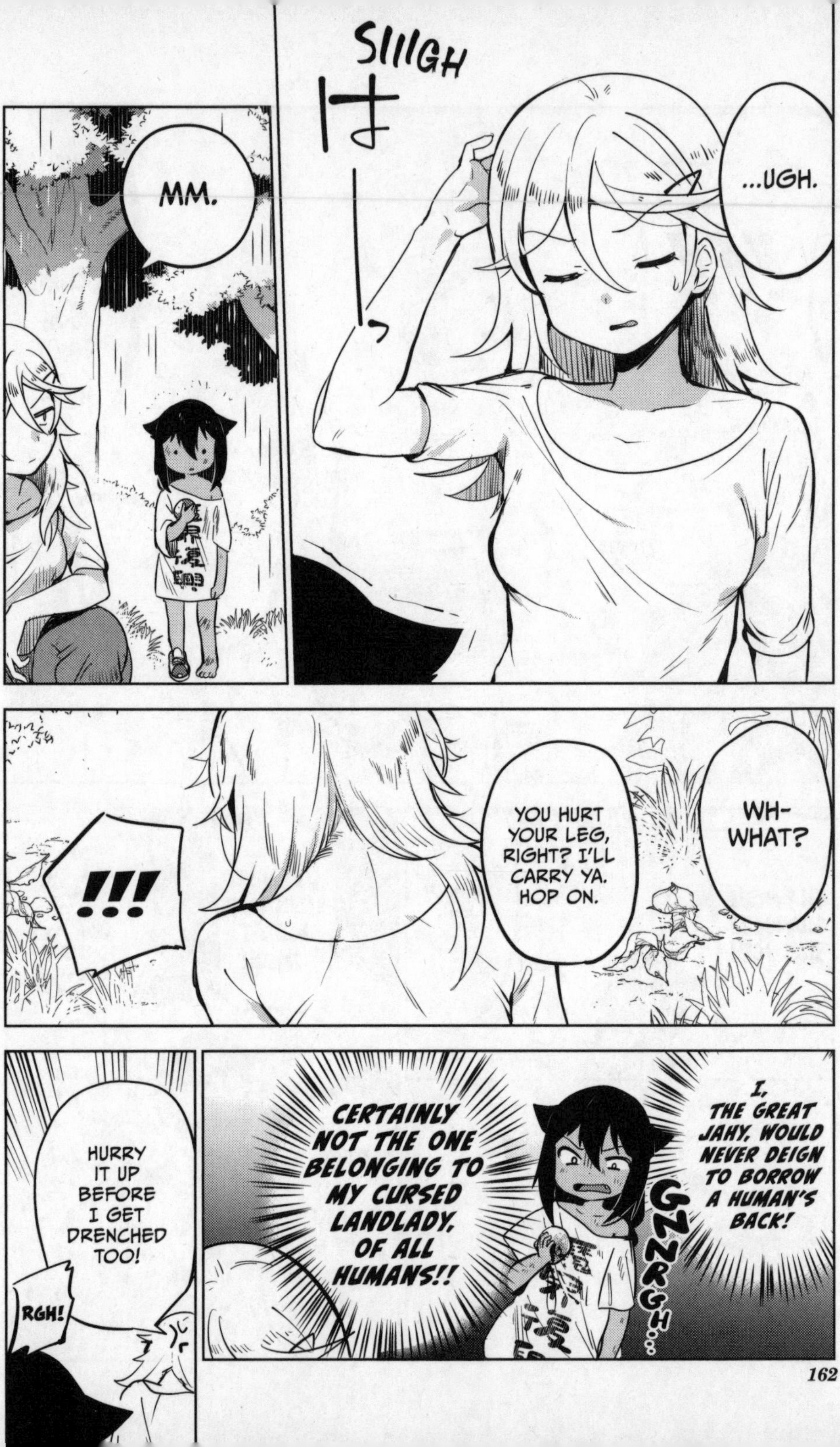
SIIIGH
はーっ
...UGH.
MM.
WH-WHAT?
YOU HURT YOUR LEG, RIGHT? I'LL CARRY YA. HOP ON.
!!!
I, THE GREAT JAHY, WOULD NEVER DEIGN TO BORROW A HUMAN'S BACK!
GNNRGH...
CERTAINLY NOT THE ONE BELONGING TO MY CURSED LANDLADY, OF ALL HUMANS!!
HURRY IT UP BEFORE I GET DRENCHED TOO!
RGH!

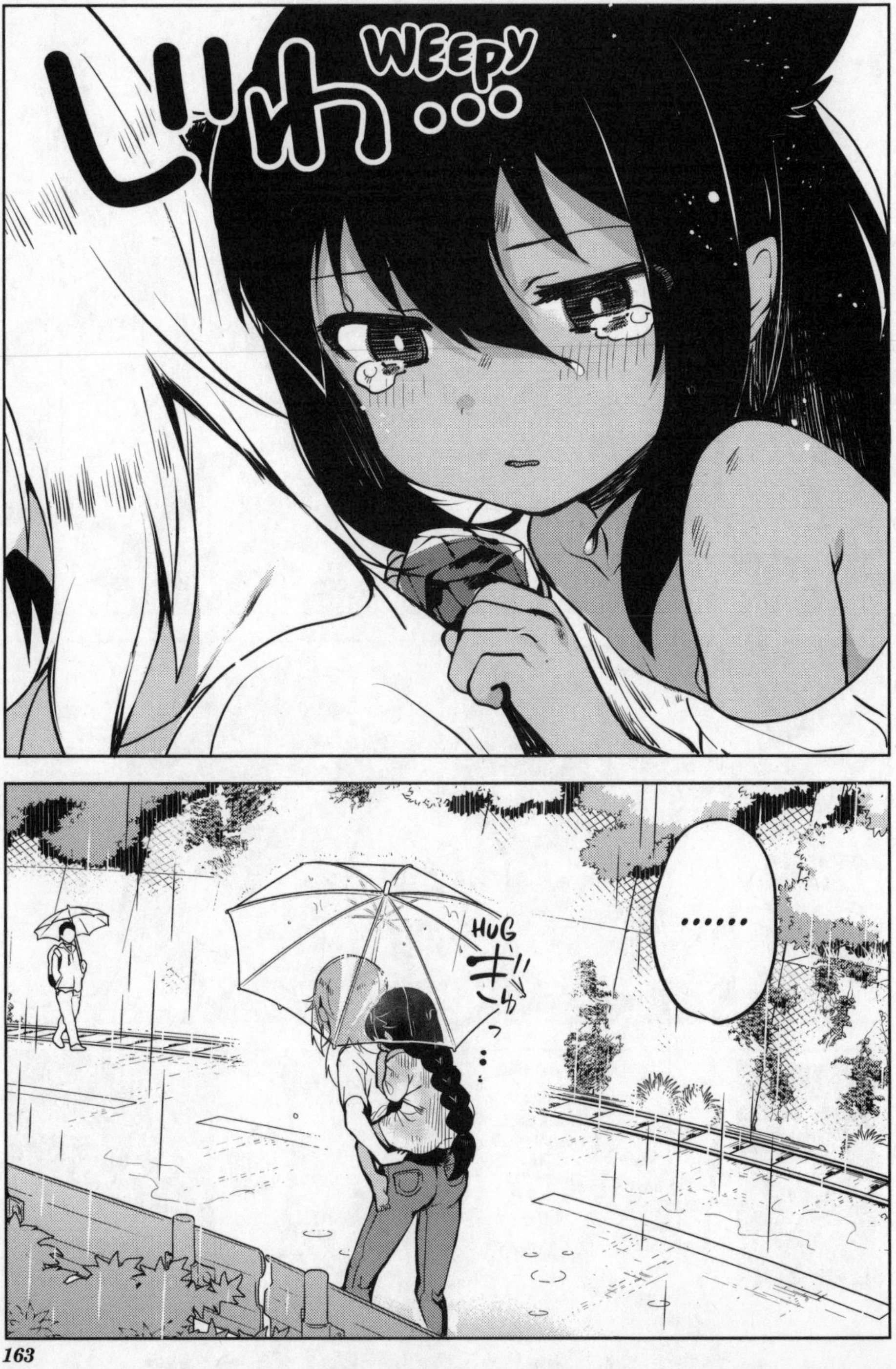
WEEPY...
HUG
......

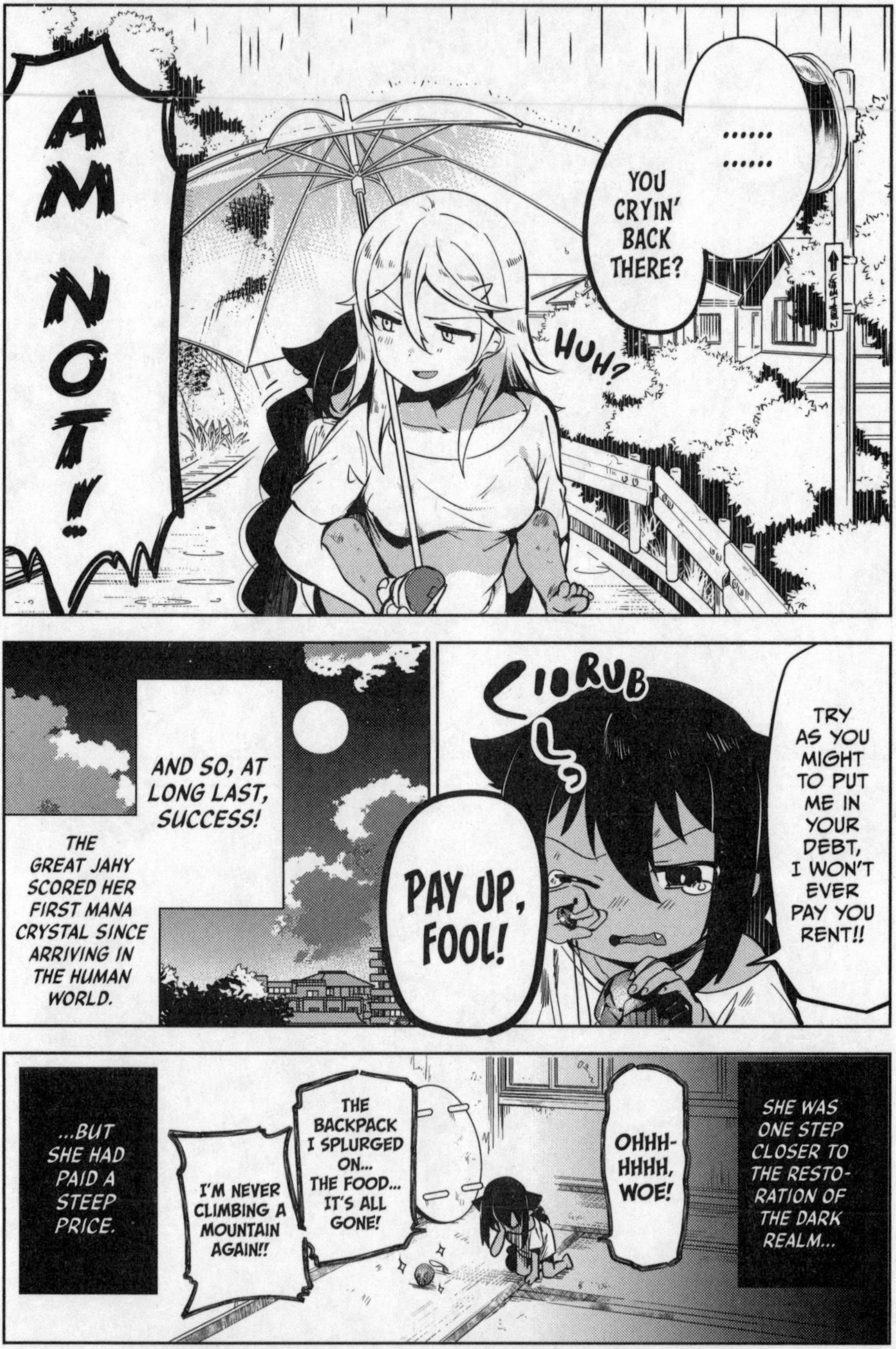

......
......
YOU CRYIN' BACK THERE?
HUH?
AM NOT!!
TRY AS YOU MIGHT TO PUT ME IN YOUR DEBT, I WON'T EVER PAY YOU RENT!!
PAY UP, FOOL!
CIORUB
AND SO, AT LONG LAST, SUCCESS!
THE GREAT JAHY SCORED HER FIRST MANA CRYSTAL SINCE ARRIVING IN THE HUMAN WORLD.
SHE WAS ONE STEP CLOSER TO THE RESTO-RATION OF THE DARK REALM...
OHHH-HHHH, WOE!
THE BACKPACK I SPLURGED ON... THE FOOD... IT'S ALL GONE!
I'M NEVER CLIMBING A MOUNTAIN AGAIN!!
...BUT SHE HAD PAID A STEEP PRICE.

The GREAT JAHY Will NOT Be DEFEATED! 1 THE END

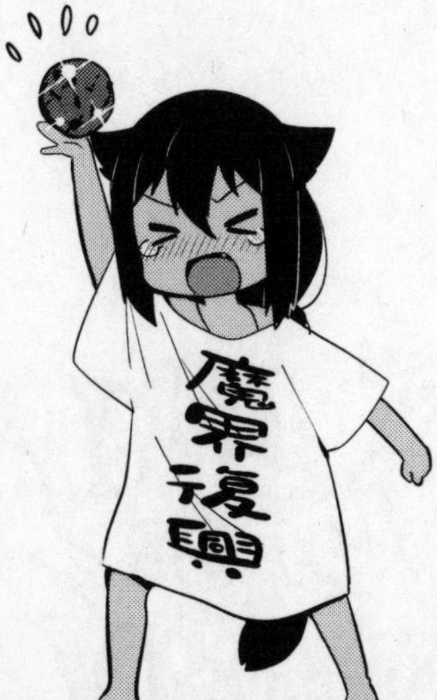
魔界復興

The GREAT JAHY Will NOT Be DEFEATED!

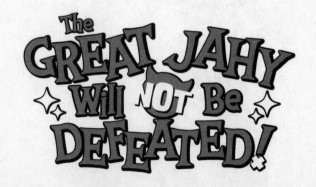

RESTORATION PLAN

BONUS STORY

The Great Jahy & the Luxe Day

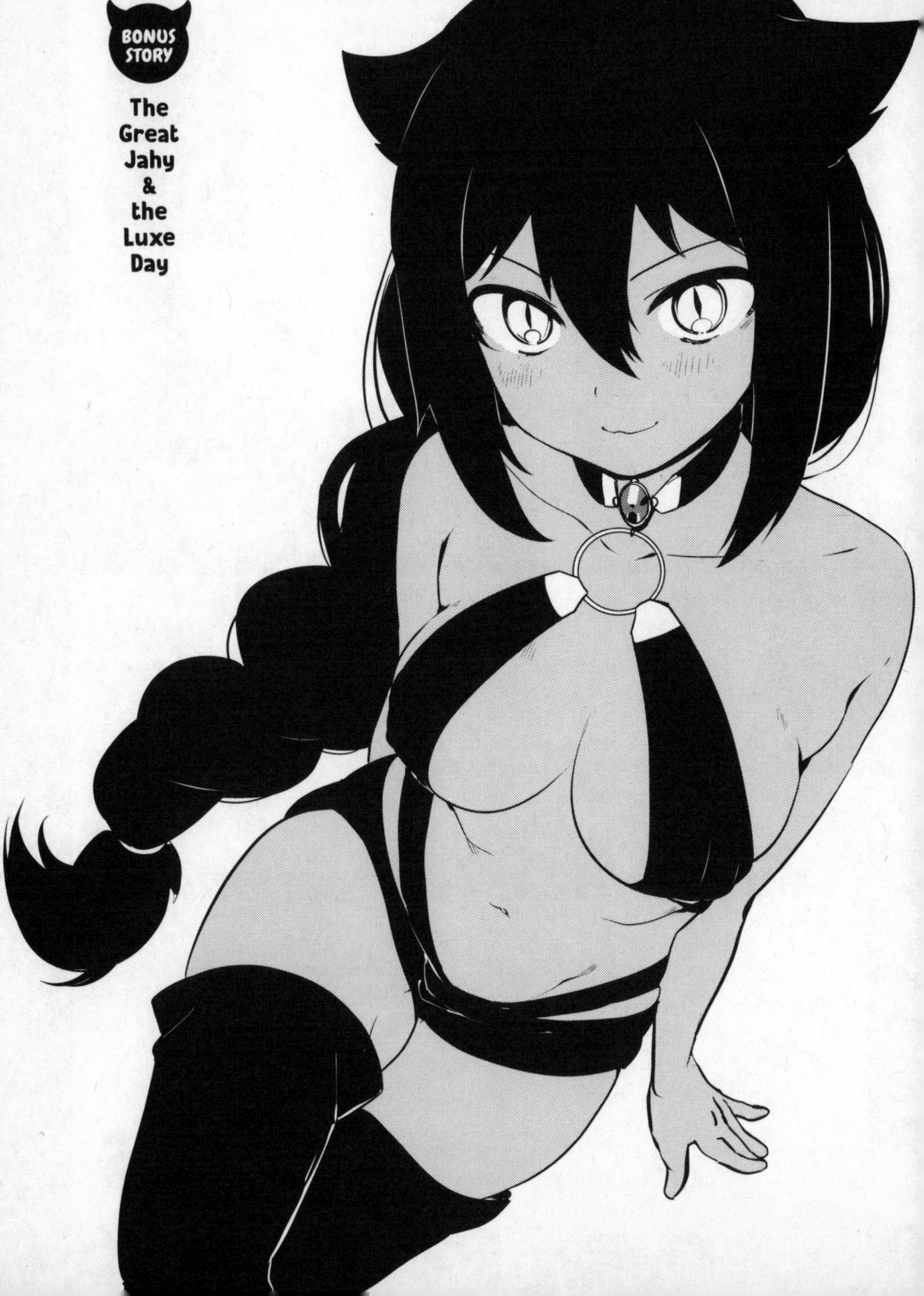

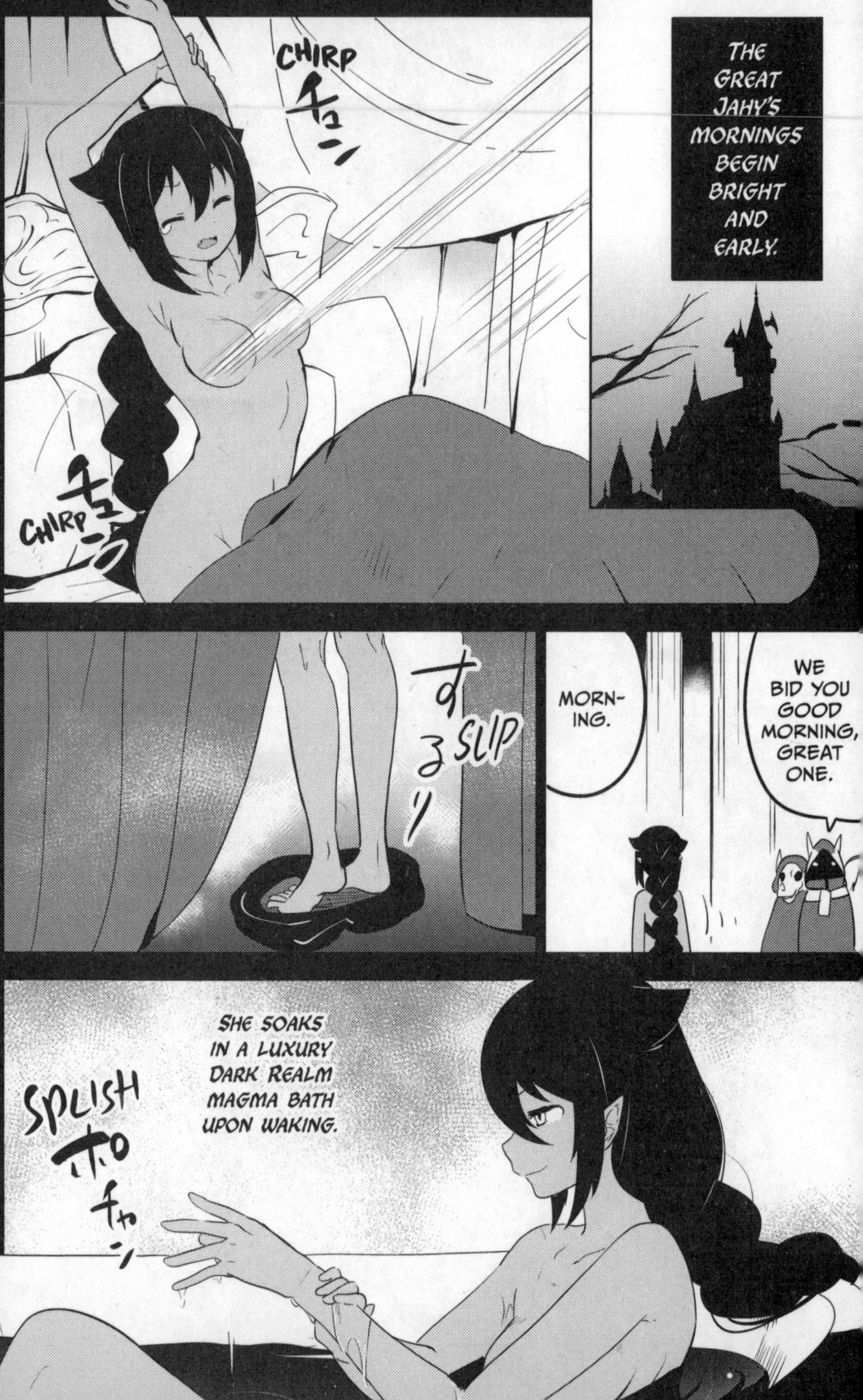
THE GREAT JAHY'S MORNINGS BEGIN BRIGHT AND EARLY.
CHIRP
チュン
CHIRP
チュン
WE BID YOU GOOD MORNING, GREAT ONE.
MORN-ING.
するり
SLIP
SHE SOAKS IN A LUXURY DARK REALM MAGMA BATH UPON WAKING.
SPLISH
ポチャン

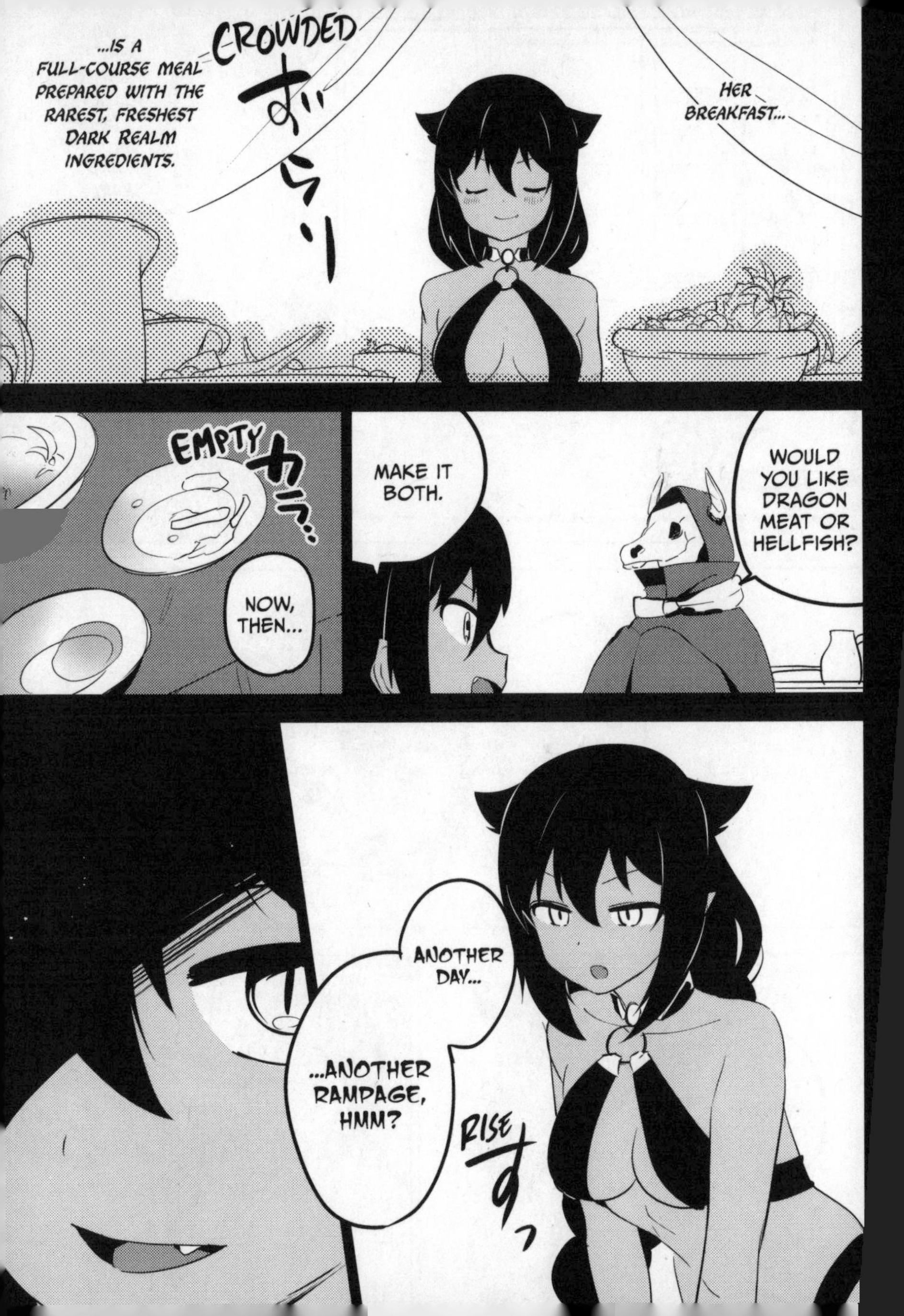
HER BREAKFAST...
CROWDED
ずらり
...IS A FULL-COURSE MEAL PREPARED WITH THE RAREST, FRESHEST DARK REALM INGREDIENTS.
WOULD YOU LIKE DRAGON MEAT OR HELLFISH?
MAKE IT BOTH.
EMPTY
カラ…
NOW, THEN...
ANOTHER DAY...
...ANOTHER RAMPAGE, HMM?
RISE
すっ

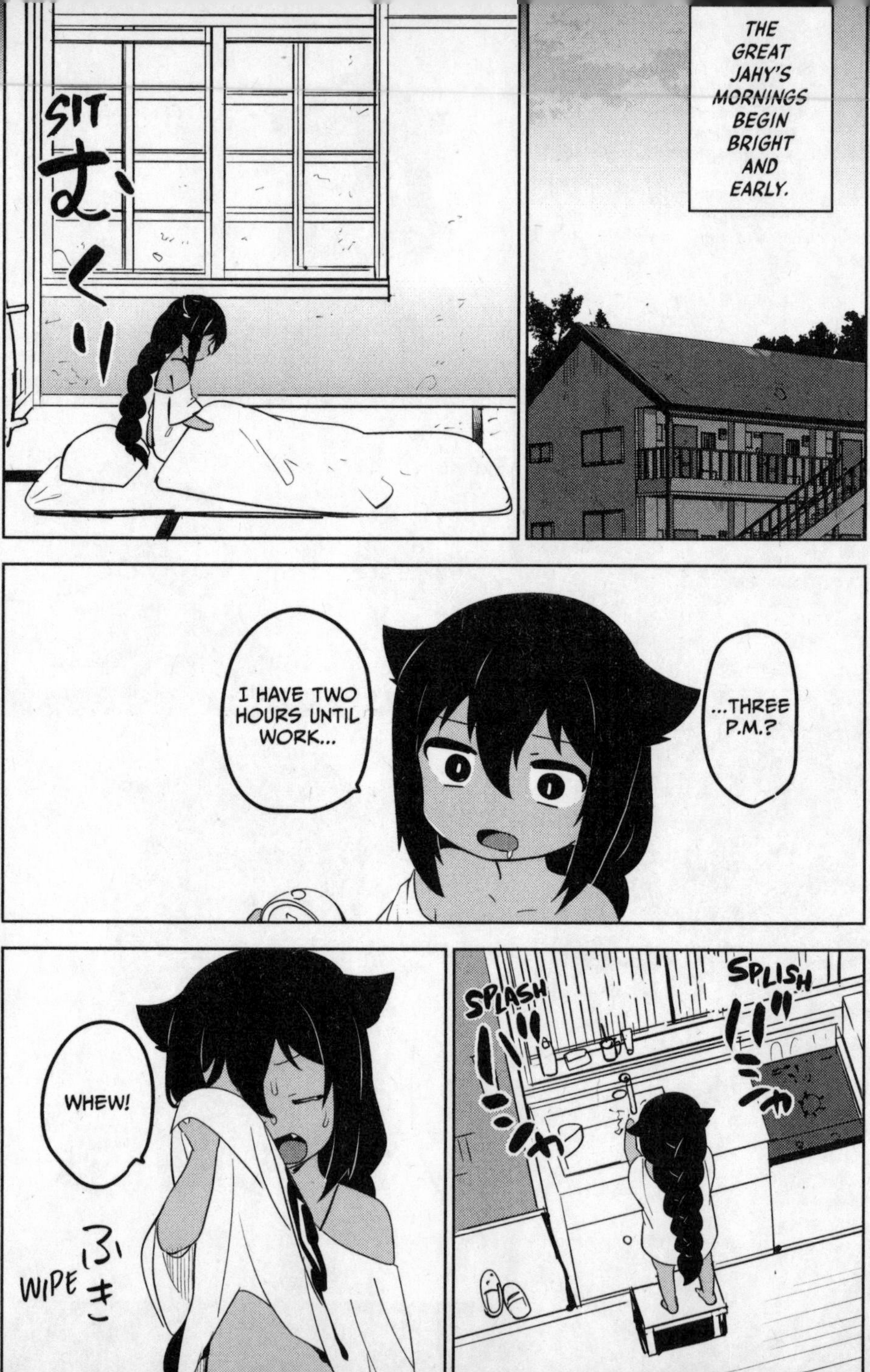
THE GREAT JAHY'S MORNINGS BEGIN BRIGHT AND EARLY.
SIT
むくり
...THREE P.M.?
I HAVE TWO HOURS UNTIL WORK...
SPLISH
ばしゃ
SPLASH
ばしゃ
WHEW!
WIPE
ふき

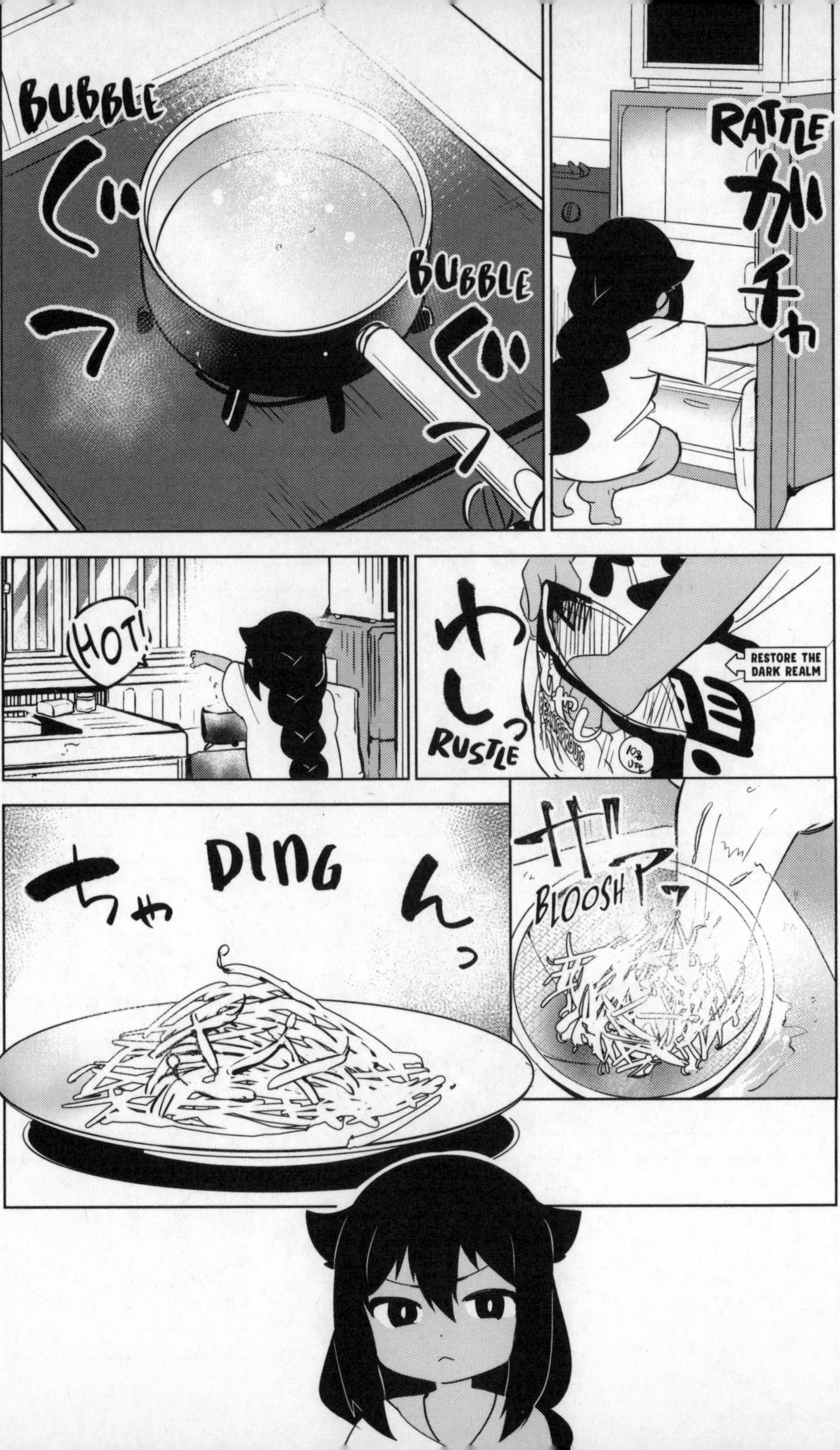
RATTLE
BUBBLE
BUBBLE
RESTORE THE DARK REALM
RUSTLE
HOT!
BLOOSH
DING

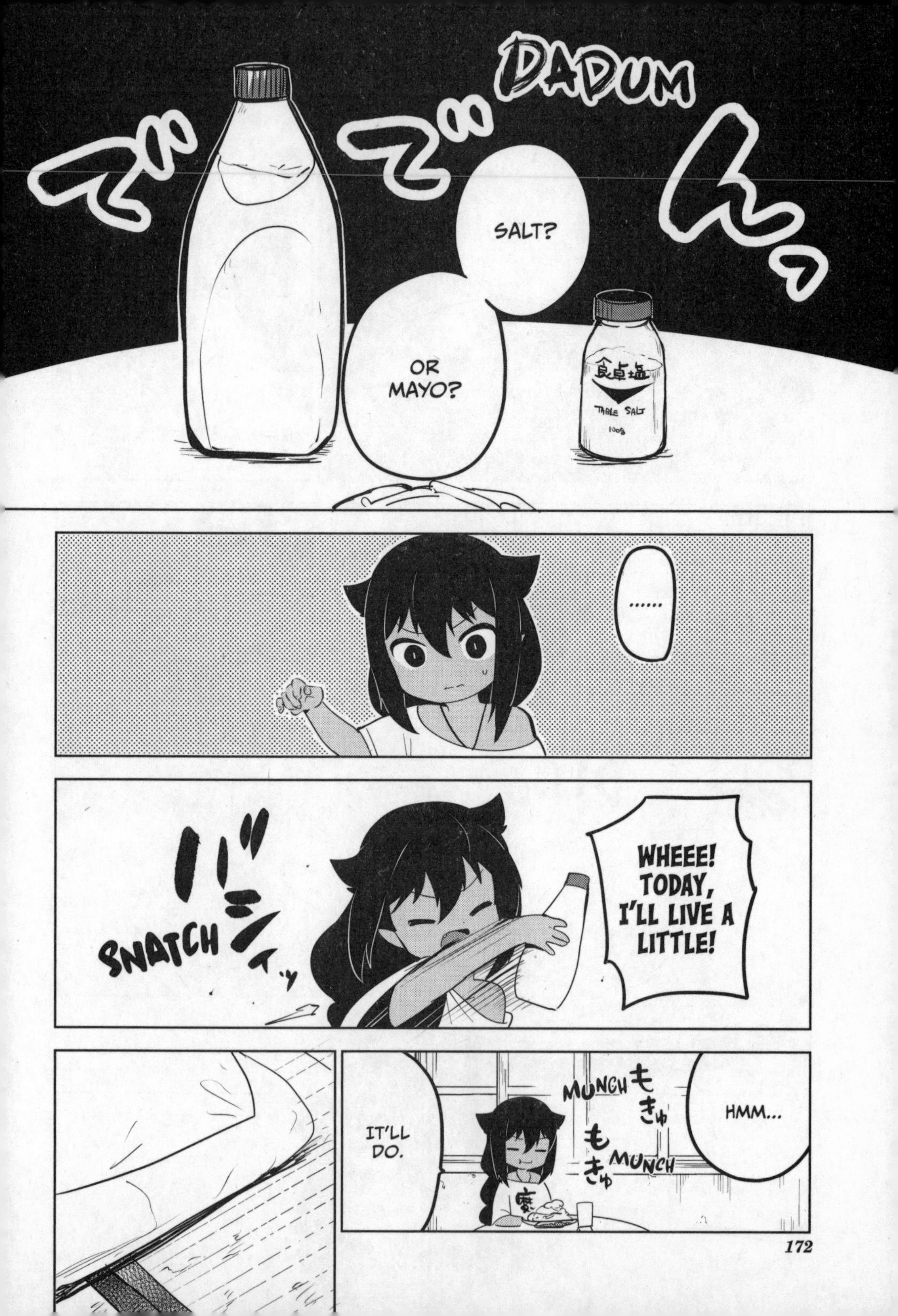
DADUM
SALT?
OR MAYO?
食卓塩
TABLE SALT
......
WHEEE! TODAY, I'LL LIVE A LITTLE!
SNATCH
HMM...
MUNCH
MUNCH
IT'LL DO.

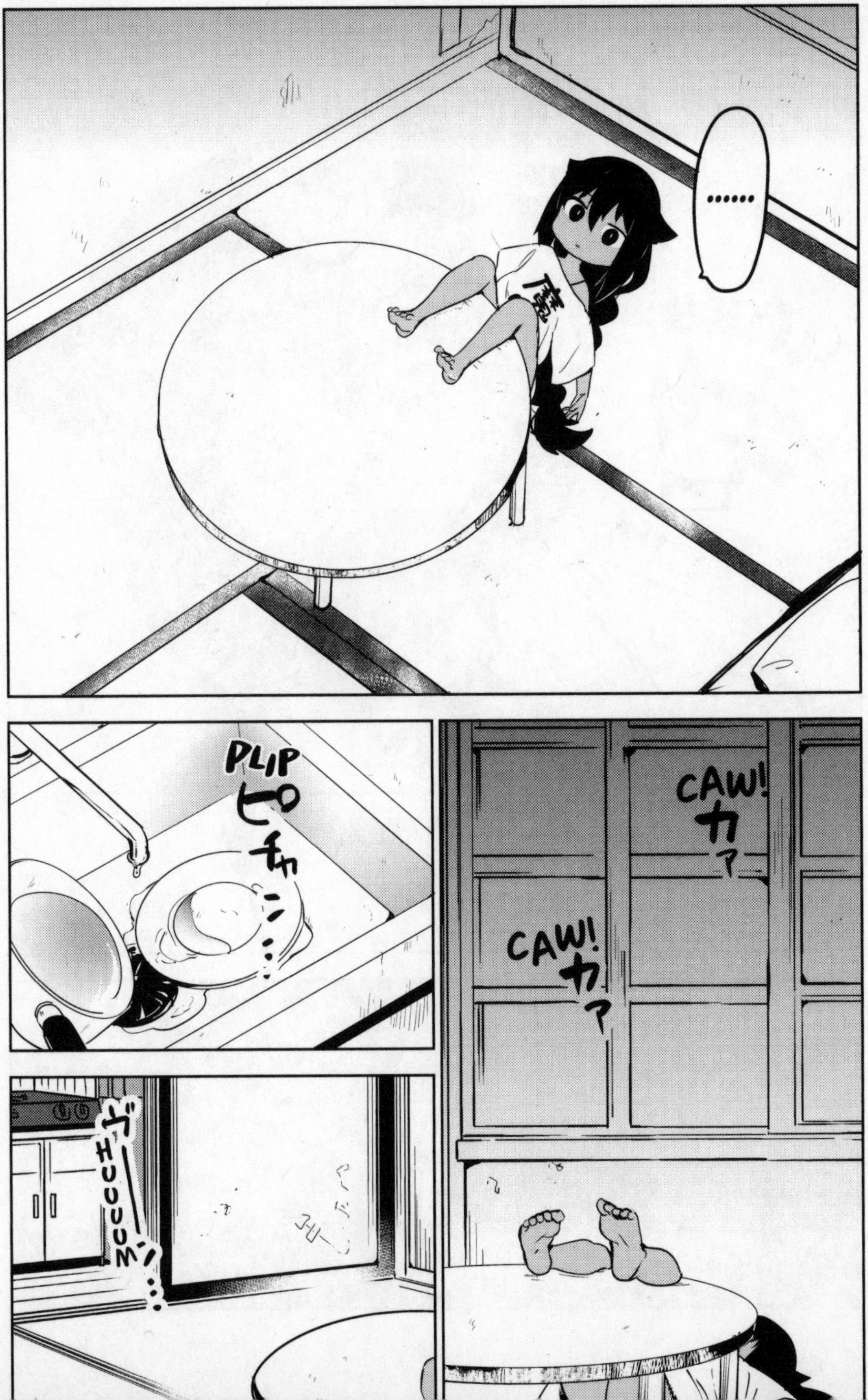
......
CAW!
カァ
CAW!
カァ
PLIP
ピチャン...
HUUUUM
ヴーーン...

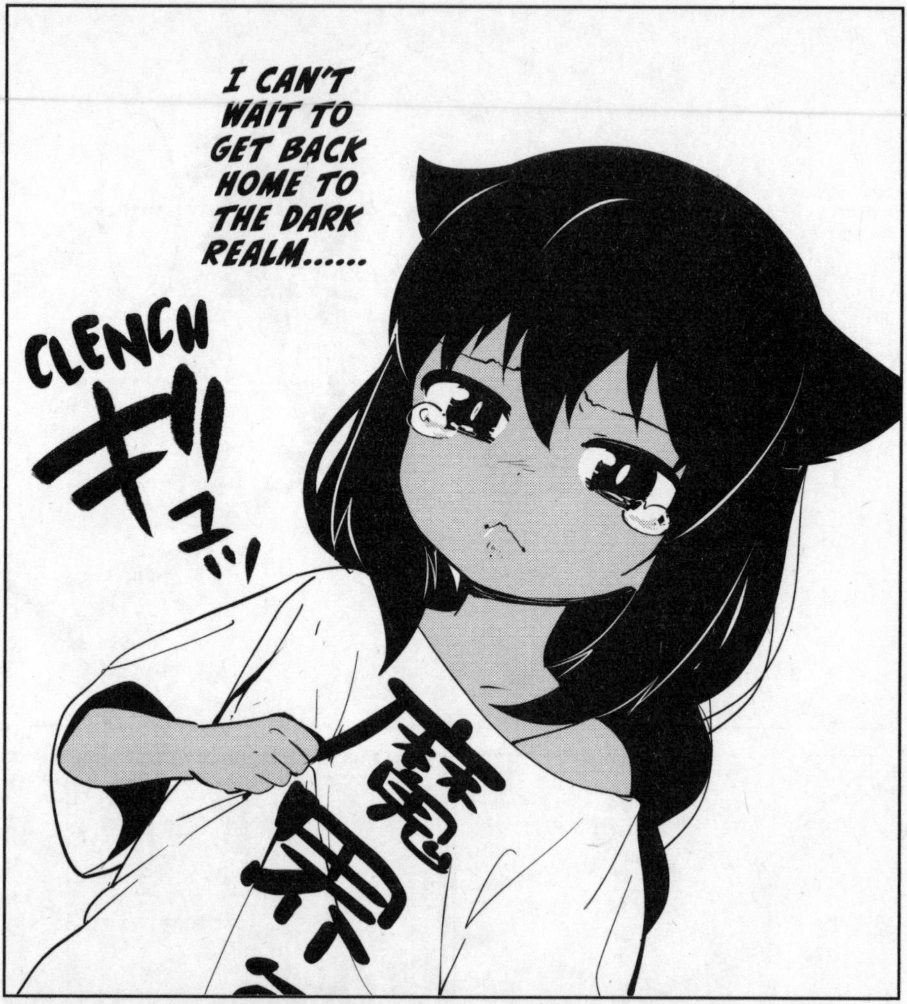
I CAN'T WAIT TO GET BACK HOME TO THE DARK REALM......
CLENCH
ギュッ
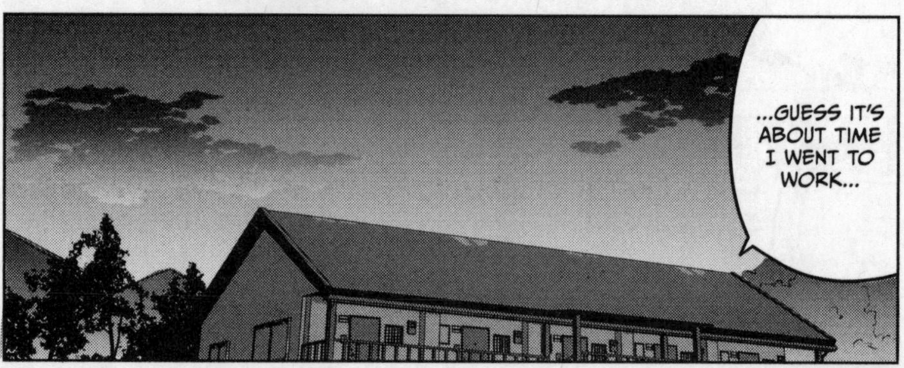
...GUESS IT'S ABOUT TIME I WENT TO WORK...

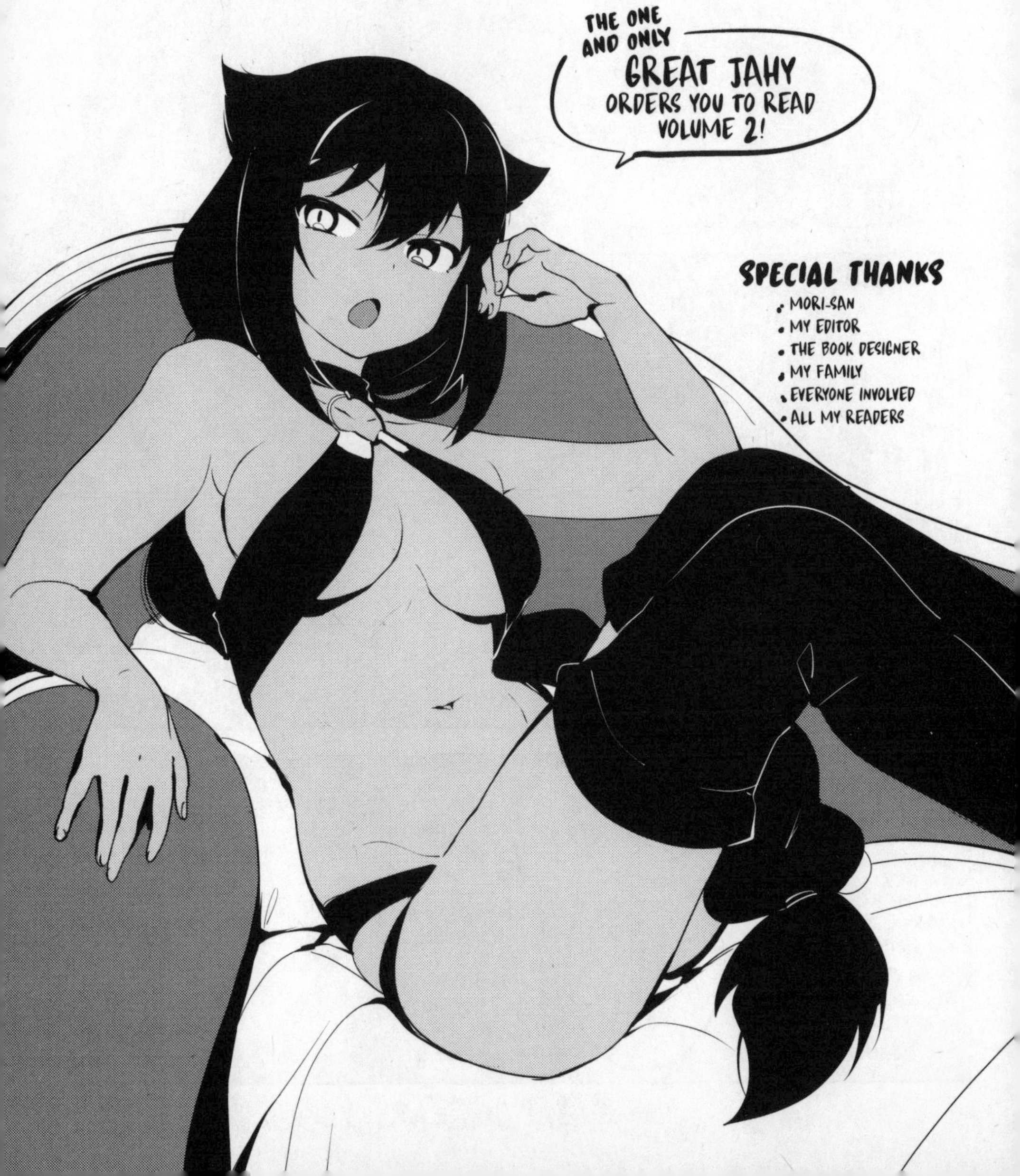
THE ONE AND ONLY GREAT JAHY ORDERS YOU TO READ VOLUME 2!
SPECIAL THANKS
• MORI-SAN
• MY EDITOR
• THE BOOK DESIGNER
• MY FAMILY
• EVERYONE INVOLVED
• ALL MY READERS

THE GREAT JAHY, SPACE PIRATE!!

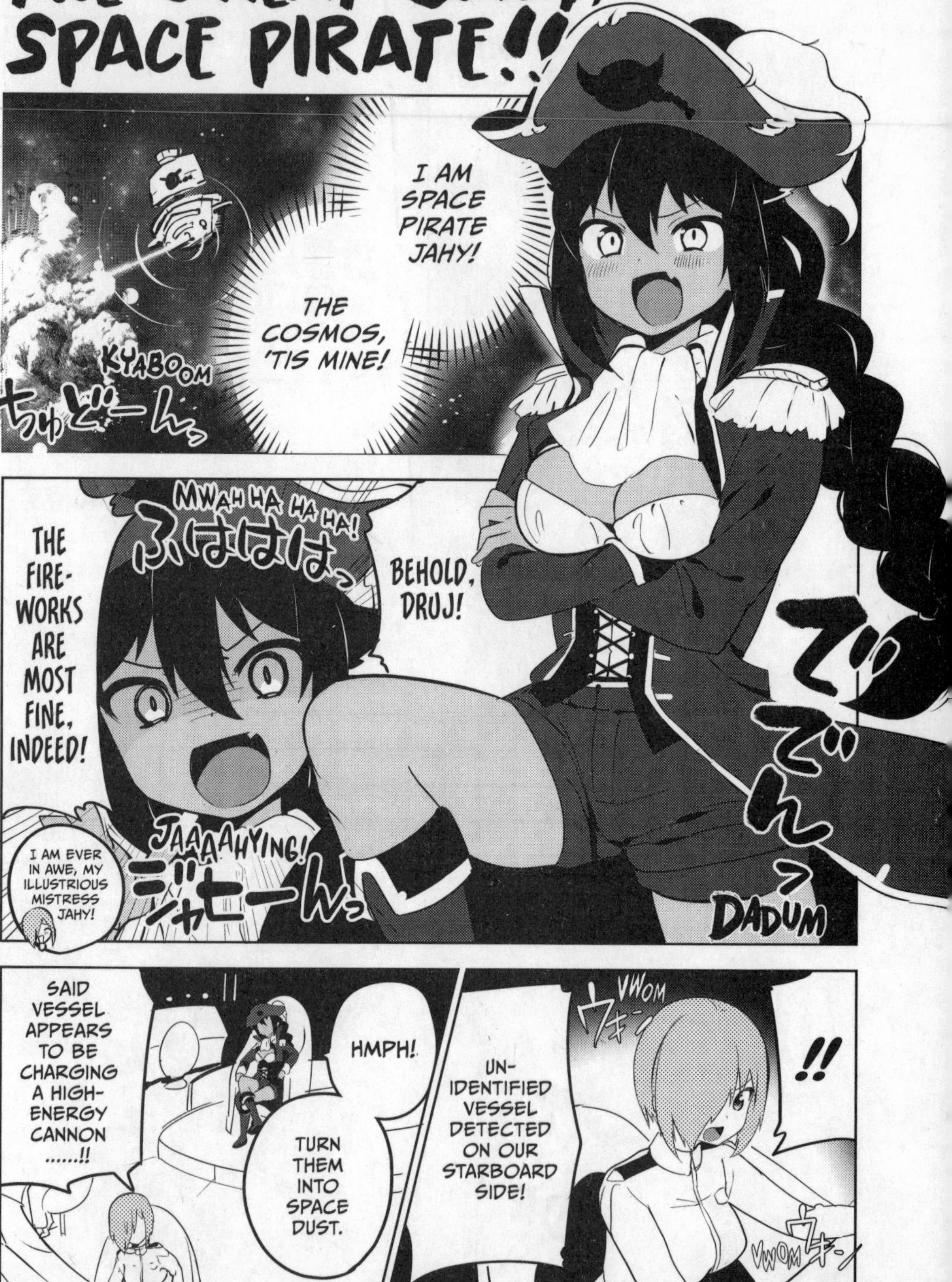
I AM SPACE PIRATE JAHY!
THE COSMOS, 'TIS MINE!
KYABOOM
MWAH HA HA HA!
BEHOLD, DRUJ!
THE FIRE-WORKS ARE MOST FINE, INDEED!
DADUM
JAAAAHYING!
I AM EVER IN AWE, MY ILLUSTRIOUS MISTRESS JAHY!
VWOM
!!
UN-IDENTIFIED VESSEL DETECTED ON OUR STARBOARD SIDE!
VWOM
HMPH!
TURN THEM INTO SPACE DUST.
......!!
SAID VESSEL APPEARS TO BE CHARGING A HIGH-ENERGY CANNON ......!!